WORDS
FROM HEAVEN®

By

A Friend of Medjugorje

Close-up view of the huge concrete cross on Mount Krizevac near Medjugorje erected in 1933 in honor of the 1900th anniversary of the death of Our Lord. This cross dominates the entire countryside.

WORDS FROM HEAVEN®

Messages of Our Lady from Medjugorje

A DOCUMENTED RECORD OF THE MESSAGES AND THEIR
MEANINGS GIVEN BY OUR LADY IN MEDJUGORJE TO THE
SIX VISIONARIES AND TWO INNER LOCUTIONISTS

Revised Eleventh Edition

by

A Friend of Medjugorje

*"...Little children, everyday read the messages I
gave you and transform them into life. I love you
and this is why I call you to the way of salvation
with God."*

-From Our Lady's Message
of December 25, 1989

Published with permission from S.J.P. by

CARITAS OF BIRMINGHAM
Sterrett, Alabama USA

The publisher realizes and accepts that the final authority regarding the Medjugorje Apparitions rests with the Holy See of Rome. We willingly submit to that judgement.

—The Publisher

Publishing History
First through Tenth printing – 79,500 copies
Eleventh printing June, 2009 – 2,500 copies

Published with permission from S.J.P. Lic. to Caritas of Birmingham

Copyright © 2009 S.J.P.
10 printings © 1991-2006 S.J.P.

Library of Congress Catalog Card No: 89-92808
ISBN: 1-878909-12-6

DTTUMAKCTJJJJABC February, 1990

Printed and bound in the United States of America.

For additional copies, contact your local bookstore or call Caritas of Birmingham at 205-672-2000 USA, ext. 315..

ABOUT THE AUTHOR

The author of this book is also the author of the Caritas of Birmingham Newsletter and other publications such as Look What Happened While You Were Sleeping®, How to Change Your Husband, I See Far, and "Words of the Harvesters." He wishes to be known only as "A Friend of Medjugorje." The author is not one looking in from the outside regarding Medjugorje, but one who is close to the events - many times, right in the middle of the events about which he has written.

Originally writing to only a few individuals in 1987, readership has grown to over 250,000 in the United States, with additional readers in over 130 foreign countries, who follow the spiritual insights and direction given through these writings. The author, when asked why he signs only as "A Friend of Medjugorje," stated:

I have never had an ambition or desire to write. I do so only because God has shown me, through prayer, that He desires this of me. So from the beginning, when I was writing to only a few people, I prayed to God and promised I would not sign anything; that the writings would have to carry themselves and not be built on a personality. I prayed that if it was God's desire for these writings to be inspired and known, then He could do it by His Will and grace and that my will be abandoned to it.

The Father has made these writings known and continues to spread them to the ends of the earth. These were Our Lord's last words before ascending: "Be a witness to the ends of the earth." These writings give testimony to that desire of Our Lord to be a witness with one's life. It is not important to be known. It is important to do God's Will.

For those who require "ownership" of these writings by the author in seeing his name printed on this work in order to give it more credibility, we state that we cannot reconcile the fact that these writings are producing hundreds of thousands of conversions and are requested worldwide from every corner of the earth. The author, therefore, will not take credit for a work that, by proof of the impact these writings have to lead hearts to conversion, have been Spirit-inspired with numbers increasing yearly, sweeping as a wave across the ocean. Indeed in this case, crossing every ocean of the earth. Our Lady gave this author a direct message for him through the visionary, Marija Lunetti, of Medjugorje, in which Our Lady said to him to witness not with words but through humility. It is for this reason that he wishes to remain simply, "A Friend of Medjugorje."

ACKNOWLEDGEMENT

God alone deserves the credit for the publication of this book. It is from Him that the messages are allowed to be given through Our Lady to all of mankind. He alone deserves the praise and honor.

Special thanks and gratitude to Richard and Gloria who, through their love and generosity, provided the grant to print the seventh edition of this book, which has perpetuated this eleventh edition. May God reward them one-hundred fold.

PUBLISHER'S PREFACE

The author's first estimate regarding the time it would take to publish the first edition of this book was two or three months. Four years and thousands of hours of research later, it was realized that the original estimate was greatly underestimated. So it is with Medjugorje. It's importance is constantly underestimated. Father Jozo has said that Medjugorje is always bigger than you think. Soon after starting WORDS FROM HEAVEN®, it was realized that it was not going to be an easy task. It was bigger than first thought.

This continuous work involves translating messages from Croatian and other languages into English, cross referencing with many other translations, changing, verifying, and researching. All this takes an enormous amount of time - necessary time to present to the reader the most pure, the most accurate messages of Our Lady. The author plans to continue to revise, to recheck, and to reexamine the original Croatian when possible to always obtain the purest translation of Our Lady's messages. Why? Our Lady said:

> **"....You need the spirit of truth to be able to convey the messages just the way they are, neither adding anything to them, nor taking anything whatsoever away from them, but just the way I said them."**
>
> (June 9, 1984)

Each message was painstakingly analyzed to make certain it was as close to the way Our Lady spoke it in Croatian. This is so important because Our Lady spoke about mysteries in Her messages. If the messages are not correct, or if they are changed, even a little, the reader may not discover what Our Lady is trying to convey. Sometimes, one Croatian word may have as many as five possible English translations. It is not enough that translators know Croatian and English. In order to obtain a pure translation, it is necessary that the translators know as much as possible about Medjugorje, Our Lady's plans, and what Our Lady means by a certain phrase. Only then can the precise word or words be translated. Sometimes this means going directly to the source, the visionaries.

With well over a thousand separate messages of the Virgin Mary in WORDS FROM HEAVEN®, we know there will be some mistakes in this book. Yet, with this eleventh edition, it is the largest and most accurate book to date containing the messages of the Virgin Mary of Medjugorje. It is used by those who are in the movement more than any other publication to research Our Lady's messages or to reference. It is hoped that all the effort and prayers put into this book will be a valuable tool in your conversion and help you to understand the greatness of Our Lady's messages.

—Saint James Publishing

MEDJUGORJE
The Story in Brief

THE VILLAGE SEES THE LIGHT is the title of a story which "Reader's Digest" published in February 1986. It was the first major news on a mass public scale that told of the Virgin Mary visiting the tiny village of Medjugorje, Bosnia-Hercegovina. At that time this village was populated by 400 families.

It was June 24, 1981, the Feast of John the Baptist, the proclaimer of the coming Messiah. In the evening the Virgin Mary appeared to two young people, Mirjana Dragicevic* and Ivanka Ivankovic.* The next day, four more young people, Marija Pavlovic,* Jakov Colo, Vicka Ivankovic,* and Ivan Dragicevic saw the Virgin Mary, bringing the total to six visionaries. These visionaries are not related to one another. Three of the six visionaries no longer see Our Lady on a daily basis. As of July, 2009, the Virgin is still appearing everyday to the remaining three visionaries; that's well over 12,820 apparitions. The supernatural event has survived all efforts of the Communists to put a stop to it, many scientific studies, and even the condemnation by the local bishop; yet, the apparitions have survived, giving strong evidence that this is from God because nothing and no one has been able to stop it. For twenty-eight years, the apparitions have proved themselves over and over. Now that credibility is so favorable around the world, the burden of proof that this is authentic has shifted from those who believe, to those who do not or who are opposed to it. Those against the apparitions are being crushed by the fruits of Medjugorje - millions and millions of conversions which are so powerful that they are changing and will continue to change the whole face of the earth.

---

* Names at the time of the apparitions, they are now married with last names **changed.**

TABLE OF CONTENTS

PART V

PART I

UNDERSTANDING
OUR LADY'S MESSAGES

Part I

UNDERSTANDING OUR LADY'S MESSAGES

It is very important to pray to the Holy Spirit before reading the following to understand it. This section says more than the words you'll read. The author purposely left out certain things, discerning that it would be better that you see them from the Holy Spirit rather than from words he had written. You'll only be able to fully grasp what is written and what is not written and also the spirit of love in which this was written by praying.

It is said that Our Lady's messages from Medjugorje are simple and repetitive. Many feel that Our Lady is only repeating messages which She has already said in past apparitions. While many people were very curious about the apparitions in the beginning, they quickly became bored with the messages because of the repetition and because they felt they were too general and not specific enough. Many have had these thoughts. This section will show how little is truly understood about what Our Lady is saying and, hopefully, present a whole new understanding of Our Lady's plans and Her messages.

At first glance, the messages of Our Lady do seem watery and repetitious; but, if this is true, why does Our Lady go to such lengths about Her messages and even want them read daily? Is it because there is so much to discover? How many times have we read the word, "little," in Her messages without giving it a

1

thought. Our Lady does not want us to approach Her messages with our intellects but with our hearts, as "little" children, so rather than appearing as dead words, they may come to life!

December 25, 1989

"...little children, read everyday the messages I gave you and transform them into life..."

We know we are Our Lady's children, but Her use of the word, "little," when addressing us who are not little, may seem strange until we see why. "Little" children are not clouded by adult thoughts, biases, busyness, philosophies, etc. They are open, pure, innocent, and impressionable. Any parent can tell a three-year-old child that his Guardian Angel is by his side, he can fly when he turns ten, or his dad is the strongest person in the world, and he will believe it. Most little children would never question their parents but simply believe them. Our Lady wishes us to approach and accept Her messages with the same innocence and faith. If we can go to Our Lady's messages, not just as children but as "little" children, She will be able to form us, lead us, and help us in the difficult task of changing the direction of our lives. Our Lady has said:

March 25, 1990

"...you must change the direction of your life..."

It is much easier for a little child to adjust to change than for an adult who is set in his ways, opinionated or rebellious. Changing your life is of the utmost importance because of the crisis the world faces. How important are Our Lady's messages? Our Lady's messages deliver such importance that She says not only must Her messages not be changed or added to in any way, but also the Spirit of Truth is needed just to convey them.

June 9, 1984

> **"Dear children, tomorrow night pray for the Spirit of Truth! Especially, you from the parish. Because you need the Spirit of Truth to be able to convey the messages <u>just the way they are, neither adding anything to them, nor taking anything whatsoever away from them</u>, but just the way I said them..."**

If we need the Spirit of Truth just to convey the messages, how much more do we need to understand them? Our Lady is very clear about Her messages and their importance. Once Our Lady said that She was about to cease giving messages because some did not accept Her. These people changed their hearts and Our Lady went on to give an utterly profound message, stating that She would speak to us in a way which has never happened since the dawn of man - the beginning of the world. Our Lady said:

April 4, 1985

> **"...Today is the day when I wished to stop giving the messages because some individuals did not accept me. The parish has been moved and <u>I wish to keep on giving you messages as it has never been in history from the beginning of the world</u>..."**

This message should easily get our attention when, contemplating the Scriptures, we realize just how personally God communicated with Adam and Eve. They had direct conversations with God! Through Eve, their fall caused them to lose many great gifts. Now we have the "Second Eve" coming and conveying messages for the whole of mankind from "<u>God</u>" in a way the world has never seen, even in the beginning, the time of Adam and Eve.

July 25, 1985

> **"...Today I am calling you to listen to my messages and then
> you will be able to live everything that <u>"God" tells me to
> convey to you</u>..."**

The gift we are receiving through Our Lady, God's words coming to us through Her, is so great that it cannot be overestimated.
Our Lady says:

October 25, 1988

> **"...pray that you may <u>comprehend</u> the <u>greatness</u> of this
> <u>message</u> which I am giving you..."**

Also regarding the greatness of Her messages which we are
receiving, Our Lady says:

March 25, 1990

> **"...<u>little</u> children, <u>understand</u> also the <u>greatness</u> of the gift
> which God is giving you through me..."**

The messages are unique in the way they are given. The visionaries are receiving such a grace that Our Lady tells Ivanka that
no one on earth has been given the gift they have been given.

May 7, 1985

> **"...No one in the world has had the grace which you, your
> brothers, and sisters** [the visionaries] **have received..."**

How should we understand Our Lady's messages? First of all,
to help us comprehend Our Lady's words we should think about
our many conversations. Much of what we say is useless chatter.
Listening to most conversations, much which is said amounts to
only a multiplication of words and many times leaves us empty.

Useless talk results in only pride, defense, gossip, complaints, or exaggerations. Our Lady said:

October 27, 1983

"...You will get nothing from chatter, but only from prayer..."

So what happens when Our Lady gives a message? When Marija first was told to write down a message from Our Lady, She did so; but afterwards she was depressed when turning it over to a priest. When she did, she started to cry, not just a few tears, but really in depth as if someone had died. When asked what was wrong, Marija explained: *"I have betrayed Our Lady. What I wrote on paper and what Our Lady said were not the same!"*

We must understand every word of Our Lady is of value. Marija has explained that when Our Lady gives a message, it is given to her audibly as well as to her heart. You might say it is infused into her. It is given with immense love, overpowering gentleness, and completeness in its truth. Our Lady is present three dimensionally in a glorified body, speaking to Marija and, on special occasions, even kissing her. Each word has meaning to the fullest. Once Marija writes it on paper, it betrays all the love, gentleness, power, and meaning in which it was given by Our Lady. What you read in a book when you read Our Lady's messages, after your initial conversion* or curiosity, <u>betrays the beauty in which the messages were given</u>. When Marija is given the messages, they are in the highest degree from Heaven; but when they are written down, they are reduced to ink on paper. At this point, many lose interest, become tired, and no longer want to listen to or live Our Lady's messages. Why? Because we are not conscious of the importance of the messages God sends us. We are not able to comprehend the great depth of graces available through these messages. If we did, we would pray with-

---

* Sometimes a profound grace is received by simply reading about Medjugorje or Our Lady's messages and many initial conversions have come about in this manner.

out stopping. Only through the Holy Spirit are we able to begin
to understand. Our Lady said on November 8, 1984:

> **"...you are not conscious of the messages which God is
> sending to you through me. He is giving you great graces,
> and you do not comprehend them. Pray to the Holy Spirit
> for enlightenment. If you only knew how great are the
> graces God is granting you, you would be praying without
> ceasing..."**

But if one does as Our Lady says and prays to understand the
greatness of the messages, prays to comprehend them, then rather than just paper and ink, the messages become filled with love,
filled with profound meaning, and a great source of grace to live
by. From the great heights from which Marija received them, to
the depths of paper and ink, then lifted back up through prayer,
we are able to taste the sweetness of Our Lady's love for us and
understand Her messages. They, like concrete foundations, are
solid enough to build our lives on for this time.

August 6, 1982

> **"...I will give you yet some <u>concrete</u> messages for our
> time..."**

Our Lady's words are not exaggerated. They are more significant than they appear. They understate what She is relaying.
The meaning goes way beyond the words. But the world does
not understand this. It is the opposite. It overstates, disguises,
debates, compromises, exaggerates. It is untruthful. It makes
evil appear good, denies or ignores the existence of sin, and
makes bad situations appear worse than they really are, in order
to lead more people to the acceptance of sin. Our Lady contra-
dicts the ways of the world. Her words do not exaggerate, and
we do not have to debate whether Our Lady is right or wrong.
There is a fullness and a completeness of truth. She does not
give us opinions but the very thoughts of God Himself.

After reading many of Our Lady's messages from Medjugorje, a nun once said: *"I've decided these messages are too superficial and not specific. The messages from the apparitions of Akita, Japan,* are very specific. I will devote my life to spreading those messages."* One needs to understand that Our Lady purposely gives Her messages without being specific. You might describe them as being loose. This is one of the "secret mysteries" which enable Our Lady's messages to continue to speak to you.

During the Middle East crisis,** Our Lady repeatedly called for prayer for peace. She said to Ivan several times on the mountain:

"...Pray for peace in this time..."

Week after week, month after month to both Ivan's prayer group and also to the world in the monthly messages, Our Lady asked us repeatedly to pray for peace. Although She never mentioned the Middle East situation, all the world knew what Our Lady was speaking about. So why wasn't Our Lady specific and mention the Middle East? What if ten years from now you are in a personal crisis? You are praying about your situation which has placed turmoil in your heart which desperately needs peace. When you read Our Lady's messages that say, "Pray for peace in this time," and you pray as Our Lady's messages say, peace can calm your heart. But what would it be like if Our Lady had been specific and said, "Pray for peace in the Middle East in this time?" These messages would be dated and tied only to this conflict. They would be historical messages with little use in the future except for helping to explain the past. The genius of Our

---

* Our Lady appeared in Akita, Japan, and gave a few messages which were specific. Medjugorje is where Our Lady has led us, and it's where She is leading the whole world from. The place these apparitions hold when compared to Medjugorje is explained in the booklet, *Medjugorje-The Fulfillment of All Marian Apparitions.* To order, write Caritas of Birmingham, 100 Our Lady Queen of Peace Dr., Sterrett, AL 35147 USA.

** Of course, there was unrest in many parts of the world including former Yugoslavia; however, it is understood that these peace messages during the time of the Iraqi crisis "primarily" concerned the Middle East situation but also applied to other places.

Lady's messages is that they are "<u>living</u>." They speak to us now, next week, and ten years from now. Each time these messages can say something different to us, addressing different situations. Our Lady's messages are given in a profound way purposely to give room for the Holy Spirit to say many things. That is why you can read these messages and receive them personally. Our Lady is speaking to you as an individual, yet these messages apply to every man on earth. These are not just messages. They are a guide for this age and future ages to live by. Are they on an equal with the Bible? Definitely NO! But they are something which the world has never received before. If the messages are not to be held as an equal with the Bible, how close to or how far from the Bible should they be held since Our Lady repeats many times that God is telling Her what to convey?

The Old Testament gives us some insights to consider regarding Our Lady's messages. In Exodus, God devotes many chapters for the "Theoktos," the Ark, which is to house the Ten Commandments. Chapter after chapter explains the size, the material, instructions to line the Ark with gold, etc. It is amazing to see how specific God's instructions are about the Ark of the Old Covenant. Even more surprising are the instructions on how sacred it is to be handled. There is great detail about who enters the tent, what kind of vestments are to be worn, even what kind of oil is to be used for the lamps. The penalty from God, not for touching the Ten Commandments, but for improperly handling the Ark itself, the "Theoktos," was death. God made it clear that the Ark, housing the Old Covenant, demanded this reverence. Several centuries later King David was moving the Ark, which had been placed on an ox cart by the priest. When the cart tilted, a soldier reached out to steady the Ark and he dropped dead.

If the Ark (vessel) of the Old Covenant was this important and deserved this much reverence, how much reverence does God want for the "Second Theoktos" which housed the New Covenant, Jesus Christ! Does this New Living Covenant and this Living Ark not have a greater degree of closeness to God than the old?

If the old Ark, made from the materials of the earth (gold, wood, etc.), was so sacred because of what it housed, how much more sacred is the vessel, the new Ark, the Virgin Mary, who housed Jesus for nine months in Her own body, Who, through the umbilical cord of life, nourishment flowed from Mary to Jesus? Whose body produced milk which nourished the Messiah's body - the Body and Blood of which we now partake of in the Eucharist? We can reason that Mary is nourishing us through the milk She nourished the Sacred Blood of Jesus with. Then, as a child, God had to be fed, bathed, clothed, and was totally dependant on His Mother, Mary, who sheltered Him with Her mantle, as the Ark sheltered the Ten Commandments. By contemplating this, do we realize in what context Our Lady's messages should be held? Of all the archangels, including Michael and Raphael, all the angels, all the prophets, including Abraham, Moses, and Elijah, and all the human race put together, no one has been as close to God as Mary. She is not a deity. Her place with God is above all angels and all mankind but below God. BETWEEN. So it is in this context that the messages of Medjugorje have to be understood. They are below the Bible, the inspired Word of God, but above all the books containing the greatest human wisdom and thought in all the world, throughout all the ages. Even the writings of scholars, philosophers and the saints together will not be on an equal basis with the messages of Our Lady from Medjugorje. This author predicts these **"words from Heaven"** will be scrutinized by the Church in somewhat the same way the early Church scrutinized the contents of the Bible in putting it together. Once we realize that we are in a Second Pentecost, we will be able to understand that this is not new revelation, but it is new revelation about Old Revelation. Never in 2,000 years have we had such a clear window explaining the Gospels. It's the reason Our Lady's said:

April 4, 1985

"...I wish to keep on giving you messages as it has never been in history from the beginning of the world..."

Just as Our Lady's role is not on an equal basis with any angel or man but above their roles and below God's, Her role is to lead us to God. So it is with Her messages. They are above all human books ever written but below the inspired Bible. Her "messages" parallel Her role, leading us to God. The Virgin Mary's messages will lead you to the Gospels, and you will understand the Gospels as never before. The messages are to be elevated to a supreme place above all philosophies, spiritual writings, books, etc.. This is why Our Lady says:

November 15, 1984

"...You are not conscious of every message which I am giving you. Now I just want to say – pray, pray, pray!..."

But why is it necessary for today's man to see the Gospels more clearly? Man today, as well as the last few decades, lives radically different than man did for the past several thousand years. Man, for thousands of years, lived, toiled, worked the soil, blacksmithed, and produced goods basically the same way. The threads of life were unchanged for thousands of years. The men who wrote the Bible relayed God's truths through the fabric of their daily lives and ways.

Our Lady's messages bring new light to the Scriptures, leading us to them, and to a better understanding of God's holy words. Her words are living just as God's words are living. Our Lady is speaking to us, to lead us to the living words of the Bible which are from a living God, instructing us, encouraging us, giving us hope. The Bible is not a dead tree manufactured into paper with ink pressed on it, but God's powerfully present voice, living and holy. And now Our Lady is coming daily giving living words, that are not on an equal level with God's words, but are given in order to lead us to those Heavenly words of the Bible. Her words will go down in history as a **preface** to understanding Holy Scriptures and to show us how to bring new life into the modern world which is presently dying. Why? Man, for six thousand years, has lived the same way. He basically plowed the fields the same way, lived in a village, supplying on a small scale to his local villagers the craft of his hands. In the course of this work, man has thought the same way from generation to generation, for centuries up until the present modern times. The Scriptures were written by minds which had a specific understanding, since the dawn of man, of man's ways and of his thinking. Scripture states:

"You shall not plow with an ox and an ass together."

"Man," before this modern age, clearly and precisely grasped the understanding of what is meant in the above passage in far greater detail than we today. Man, close to the soil, had the working hands-on knowledge. A mismatch such as an ox and an ass would result in two directions, a weaker and a stronger, crooked plowing, no harmony, disorder. From this example given in Scripture "man" could easily apply this to his life, spouse, children, village, politics, etc. His whole concept was different from those of us who work with modern technological advances in our daily lives. These technological advances have taken us from the field and work shops keeping our minds very busy, so busy, in fact, that we are left with no time to reflect in our intelligence about who we are and where we are going as a society. For thousands of years a blacksmith could apply this verse to his own work, knowing the stupidity of trying to work his heated metal with a wooden hammer, rather than a steel one. The heated metal and wooden hammer would be as an ox and ass together, which would be ridiculous. Then through the Holy Spirit, the blacksmith could easily discern the methods he was using with the relationships of his wife, friends, etc., were not working any more than an ox and an ass plowing together and that perhaps he must change his treatment of her or others. It is not to say that modern man cannot understand the Scriptures, but those who wrote it were not modern men. They were of another world than what exists today. Marija has said that Our Lady's messages are for today's man, to help him understand the Bible. As another example, how many modern men know and understand these words of Jesus?:

"It is easier for a camel to go through the eye of a needle than for a rich man to enter the kingdom of God."

For centuries, men knew an "eye of a needle" was an opening in the wall of a structure, such as a church, etc., built big enough for a man to go through, but small enough to keep out men on horseback. This "eye of the needle" as the entrance into a building was to safeguard against raids, invaders, etc. Perhaps it was possible that a camel could squeeze through on his knees, but only with great difficulty - and yet, perhaps this was not totally impossible. But modern man, reading this verse would deduce that any man who is rich is doomed, for it would be considered impossible for a camel to go through the eye of a sewing needle.

The world is totally and radically different from the world of only a century ago. Man (or perhaps we should say satan*) has never had technology that has the ability to actually enter into our own thought patterns and lead and direct our thinking. We are being given a preface to the Scriptures, an owner's manual (Our Lady's words) to the machine (the Bible) on how to use it, how to work it, how to understand it, how to make our lives better in this world through it. Man is so different from his past that probably few would be able to make it if we were to go back the way it was one hundred years ago and before. We no longer possess a clear understanding of how we can depend upon God to provide for us through the labor of our own hands.

The farmer and the blacksmith and many others had a busy

* satan does not deserve respect or honor when references are made to him. Most of you have probably noticed for years we have not capitalized his name because we refuse to give him this honor or recognition. Why should the application of grammar rules apply to him who has an insatiable desire to be exalted, even above God? We refrain in our references and writings from giving him the same stature afforded even a dog's name. We are not radical in that we don't tell others they must do the same. It's up to each individual to decide for themselves. For the harm he has done to man, whom he despises, we will not grant him that which is even reserved for man.

body and a free mind; a mind free to pray, to contemplate; a mind to understand his trials. The farmer had a greater ability to understand that God breaks man to form him just as he, the farmer, breaks up the soil, softening it to grow its fruits. The blacksmith could easily understand the purpose of God's purifying fire to mold and form man through tribulation, as he placed his metal in purifying fire to form a tool. However, with modern man, the opposite is true. His mind is occupied, and his body is free. Many actually get off from their jobs to go to work, working out in a gym. Yes, there are still jobs which are very physical, but even then many now are involved with technology, and the occupying of the mind limits its ability to contemplate. We cannot conceive praying four hours a day and would think it ridiculous, yet the farmer prayed all day. The blacksmith could contemplate God the whole day long, ten hours straight. His work could easily be prayer if he wanted. Modern man lives for his work. There is no room to let God in when we are staring into a computer, listening constantly to music, T.V., etc. We are simply not able to understand. And so the question must be posed: Is it possible for us to pray and live in today's world; today's work place?

April 24, 1984

"...Pray as much as you can, pray however you can, but pray more always. Each of you could pray even four hours a day. But I know that many do not understand because they think only of living for their work."*

Our Lady was speaking here to the village who is close to the soil, but in the last sentence, She says **"they"** (the world). To visit the peaceful hamlet of Medjugorje at the <u>time</u> this message was given, was like going back one hundred years. The people lived very simply. The outside world and the way "they" worked and lived was radically different. However, in time, after the

* This message is applied in the context of the moment it was given. The message, however, is not to be locked into this one meaning because it is living and is for us now, as well as many in the future to apply to their present situations.

apparitions began in Medjugorje, the world, through T.V., music, etc., began to be introduced in Medjugorje. It offered very harmful effects against their life and prayer. The above message was even a shock for a Franciscan priest in Medjugorje. They in the village were looking more towards today's world, the false promises conveyed through the introduction of T.V., music, etc., as the hope for the future and had already began to lose sight of St. Paul's words to pray unceasingly. Fr. Vlasic, the Franciscan, questioned Our Lady through the visionaries in regard to this specific message, *"If we tell the people to pray for four hours, they will turn away."* Our Lady answered:

"Even you do not understand. It is hardly a sixth of your day."

Our Lady first said, "They (society) don't understand" because their work clouds them, but She also says to Fr. Vlasic, **"Even you do not understand."** As the world encroaches upon Medjugorje, even the villagers, as they came into modern times, began to be clouded (refer back to the previously quoted message of April 24, 1984 to see more clearly the point being made)!

Our Lady's words are to change our modern society, not necessarily to vanquish technology, but to get rid of the anti-"Gods" and to master other technology rather than it master us. Our Lady's words are comparable to the gifts brought by the three kings and presented to Our Lady on behalf of Her young Son. Scripture tells us She treasured them. We too are to treasure, value, and hold in deep reverence and awe each word of Our Lady's.

Marija went to the United States to reside for three months. While in her host's home near Birmingham, Alabama in 1988, the first message Our Lady said was:

"May your life be prayer. May your work be offered as a prayer and may everything that you do bring you towards me..." (November 20, 1988)

This message was prophetic. It was about a future community, about their lives, their work, all before it actually came to be. The community was birthed shortly afterwards and continues to grow and is made up of many who have given up occupations, businesses, and careers in order to live and spread Our Lady's messages and offer their work, living and then spreading the messages, as prayer. For you it doesn't necessarily mean you are all to go out and change your occupation, but rather, through the messages let God lead you to what it is He wants you to do and where He wants you to go. It is interesting that for three months while Our Lady appeared, She gave many varied messages. Some were very strong, others beautiful. But in Her last apparition of January 26, 1989, Our Lady ended this chapter as She began it, with the very first words She spoke three months before:

"Dear children, I desire that your lives become prayer."

The focus of the Community of Caritas has always been Our Lady's words. Their whole life is built around them, and they are truly the guide to their every action of everyday life. Their work is performed with the thought of prayer, with the hope of it producing fruit. This is Our Lady's desire; that we not live for our work, but our work be filled with prayer and lessons of the Scriptures. Her messages, Her words, help show us how in today's society to do that, as this community has learned and gives witness to.

If these messages are as important as stated in this book, do we have a responsibility regarding them? Are we to be accountable to anyone for them? Many of us see Mary as a mother, letting many of our faults slide by but going to Jesus on our behalf and saying, "Forgive your child these offenses." This is so; however, we are receiving such enormous graces and gifts through Our Lady's apparitions that Our Lady Herself in justice says firmly:

February 6, 1986

> **"...I am giving messages first of all to the residents of the parish, and then to all the others. First of all you <u>must</u> accept the messages, and then the others. <u>You shall be answerable to 'me'</u> and to my Son, Jesus..."**

Finally, if Our Lady's messages are as important as shown, can we expect satan to be idle and not try to destroy or weaken them? Our Lady has said that She wants to save the world through the <u>Parish of Medjugorje</u>, "<u>here</u>" is the source of grace, and She has asked us to listen to Her messages "<u>here</u>," etc. The messages have been "imported" to Medjugorje from Heaven, and then they are to be "exported" from Medjugorje to the rest of the world. God has created a voice in and through Medjugorje through which Our Lady is to guide the whole world.

October 24, 1985

> **"...I wish to guide you..."**

The seriousness of what Our Lady's messages call us to is revealed. Our Lady said:

May 2, 1982

> **"I have come to call the world to conversion for the <u>last time.</u> Afterwards, I <u>will not appear</u> any more on this earth."**

Given the seriousness of this message, we must realize the messages are carrying a great grace, a gift directly from God of such proportions that we do not comprehend. Our Lady has given many messages similar to the following one:

April 25, 1990

> **"...I will pray for you and intercede for you before God that**

you understand the greatness of this gift which God is giving me that I can be with you..."

This gift is so great, so profound, that each one of us has a responsibility to respond according to our ability and what we've been given.

May 8, 1986

> **"...you are the ones responsible for the messages. The source of grace is <u>here</u>, but you, dear children, are the vessels which transport the gifts. Therefore, dear children, I am calling you to do your job with responsibility. Each one shall be responsible according to his own ability. Dear children, I am calling you to give the gifts to others with love, and not to keep them for yourselves..."**

satan wishes to lead many away from the real truth and toward half truths or falsehoods.

September 25, 1990

> **"...satan wishes to destroy my plans and hinder the desires which the Heavenly Father wants realized '<u>here</u>'** [in Medjugorje]**..."**

This is why Our Lady thanked those who remain firm to Her plan "here" and who do not betray Her presence.

January 25, 1991

> **"...Thank you that you will not betray my presence '<u>here</u>'** [Medjugorje]**..."**

Except for the birth, life, death and resurrection of Jesus Christ, and the death of the last apostle, the messages and apparitions of Medjugorje are the most important event in history in nearly 2,000 years for the following three reasons:

1. They are the most frequent apparitions ever.

2. Our Lady will give messages from Medjugorje as never in history since the beginning of the world.

3. They are the last apparitions on earth.

The plan of Medjugorje is beyond our total comprehension, <u>but through prayer</u>, we can receive glimpses of its magnitude. We finish with Our Lady's words about Her messages:

December 25, 1989

> **"...accept with seriousness and live the messages for your soul not to be sad when I will not be with you any more.... <u>little children, read everyday</u> the messages I gave you and transform them into life..."**

June 25, 1989

> **"...live the messages which I have been giving you... This is a time of graces and I desire that the grace of God be great for <u>every single</u> one of you..."**

October 27, 1983

> **"...If someone asks you about me, and about what I say, answer: 'It is no use to explain. It is in praying that we will understand better.'"**

April 25, 1987

> **"...pray in order that you may be able to comprehend all that I am giving here..."**

December 4, 1988

"I invite you to live the profoundness of the messages that I give."

September 12, 1983

"...When I give you this message, do not be content to just listen.... 'All' graces are at your disposal."

November 30, 1983

"You must warn the Bishop very soon, and the Pope, with respect to the <u>urgent</u> and the great importance of the message for all mankind..."

March 25, 1990

"...understand also the greatness of the gift which God is giving you through me..."

February 17, 1989

"...May each message be for you a new growth..."

January 28, 1987

"...Listen to me, my children! Meditate on my message in prayer."

✦

PART II

HOW TO USE
WORDS FROM
HEAVEN

PART II

HOW TO USE
WORDS FROM HEAVEN

Our Lady has told us countless times in Her messages that She wishes to <u>lead and guide</u> us. She said She wants to teach us and that it is to <u>Her voice</u> that She desires us to listen.

February 14, 1985

"...I want you, dear children, to listen to me and to live my messages..."

October 24, 1985

"...I wish to guide you..."

On December 25, 1989, Our Lady told us:

"...little children, read everyday the messages I gave you and transform them into life..."

There is much to discover within the messages of Our Lady of Medjugorje. Within these messages we can find the answers to all our questions, problems, and difficulties. Through these messages, man can discover once again how to make the Gospels come alive in his everyday life. The Community of Caritas of Birmingham discovered this, more or less, by accident. Our Lady said to read Her messages everyday and so they began to end their morning prayer each day with a message from Our

Lady. One community member would open up <u>Words From Heaven</u> and randomly choose a message to read aloud.

For Our Lady to speak, it sometimes is important for us to build into our lives openings for Her to do so. St. Francis' whole mission of poverty was confirmed, encouraged, and, to a large degree, launched through opening the Missal, after praying. Bernard had just confessed to St. Francis that he wanted to live like him and wanted to know what he must do. Bernard was the first to join him, but St. Francis felt of himself that he was too insignificant to make a decision like that, so he decided to go to Our Lord for help. Bernard and St. Francis went to church for Mass and then talked to the priest. The following account of this was taken from the book, <u>The Perfect Joy of St. Francis</u>, published by Image Books.

> *He (the priest) went with Francis to the altar, where the Missal was. Then Francis motioned to Bernard to approach and said to the priest: "Open the Holy Book three times in honor of the Blessed Trinity, and each time read a verse!" (in regard to Bernard joining Francis' life of poverty).*
>
> *The vicar did so. The **first time** he read: "If thou wilt be perfect, go, sell what thou hast, and give to the poor. And come, follow Me." The **second time**: "Take nothing for your journey, neither staff, nor wallet, nor bread, nor money." And the **third time** - with a sigh: "If anyone wishes to come after Me, let him deny himself, and take up his cross, and follow Me."*
>
> *The priest's tears were dropping onto the page, and he was trembling like a reed. Bernard showed his acceptance by kneeling down. And then Father Peter also fell on his knees, and holding out his hands toward Francis, he begged: "Me too - me too!" (The priest joined also).*

Many other saints, including St. Teresa the Little Flower, have found concrete guidance and direction from the Bible and other spiritual books in the same way.

In regard to the Caritas Community, they soon discovered using Words From Heaven in this manner surprised and moved them. Often times in morning prayer they have very specific things they are praying about. They began getting very specific answers to their problems and specific direction regarding certain paths to follow through the messages they opened up to each morning. Time and time again this would happen until all doubt that this was "coincidental" faded away and the community was astonished to find that Our Lady was truly fulfilling Her words to them "directly" through Her messages. She was indeed, leading and guiding them, teaching and directing them in the most amazing way. The following are just a few out of hundreds of examples they could share with you about their experience with the messages of Our Lady over the past twenty-two years.

The community had received several confirmations in prayer that it was God's Will for them to begin a certain project. But everything they did to get the project off the ground was blocked. Believing that this was due to satan's interference, they decided to offer a special sacrifice to God that He would break this hold satan had upon this project. They fasted nine days on bread and water. On the ninth day, the day the novena was to end, they opened up Words From Heaven for a message to finish the novena. They opened to:

December 18, 1989

> **"The prayers and sacrifices that you decide to offer in these days when I asked you were not done with love. I ask you to offer them with love as during the first days of the apparitions. What you have decided to do and to offer for my intentions during the novena was not enough. You have to choose to give more because you are able."**

This message had a very sobering affect on the community. Over the next few weeks they reflected on how they had not lived this novena from the heart, and they all realized that they truly didn't do it from the heart, nor with the love they should have. After a period of time, they again repeated the nine-day fast on bread and water, emphasizing doing it with real love and from the heart. At the end of the novena they opened to this message:

September 27, 1984

> **"Dear children, you have helped me along by your prayers to realize my plans. Keep on praying that my plans be completely realized. I request the families of the parish to pray the Family Rosary. Thank you for your response to my call."**

Shortly after this, they were able to easily proceed with their plans for the project, the success of which went beyond anything they could have imagined.

In one of their first experiences with the messages, Our Lady made it perfectly clear that She desired them to read Her messages each day to receive Her direction. It was Wednesday. The community had decided to begin a novena the following Tuesday for a specific need for their mission. The next morning they opened to:

December 15, 1989

> **"Prepare yourselves spiritually and physically for the Christmas Novena. In your prayers say one prayer especially for my intentions. Renounce [give up] something that you like the most."**

From this message it was felt that Our Lady was directing and advising them to add to the novena to give up something that

they liked the most. Friday morning they opened to this message.

June 2, 1984

> **"Dear children, tonight I wish to tell you during the days
> of this novena to pray for the outpouring of the Holy
> Spirit on your families and on your parish. Pray, and you
> shall not regret it. God will give you gifts by which you
> will glorify Him till the end of your life on this earth.
> Thank you for having responded to my call."**

Real excitement began to build in their hearts as these words
were read. On **Monday** morning they again opened up <u>Words
From Heaven.</u>

November 21, 1983

> **"<u>Tuesday</u>, that is <u>tomorrow</u>, the whole group will find peace
> in prayer. All its members will be invigorated in prayer, as it
> is the wish of Jesus. He entrusts something to each one, and
> wishes something from each one. It is necessary to make
> them come back to their promises, which were made at the
> beginning and to pray."**

Needless to say, their motivation to pray this novena had
increased one hundred fold, knowing they had established the
previous week that Tuesday would be the beginning of the
novena and for every day's message to lead up to that day so
clearly left them without words!!

There have been <u>many, many times</u> that the community has
discovered the path Our Lady desired them to take just through
this method. The danger, of course, is to go to the messages
every time you want to hear an answer from God and expect
it to be there without personal prayer, fasting, and sacrifices.
Sometimes God expects us to struggle to find our answers.

Sometimes He tests our faith by remaining silent for long periods of time. Our Lady has said that there are those who listen to Her messages out of curiosity and not with the desire to change their hearts. The attitude She desires from us is that we put Her words into action. The community members do not open <u>Words From Heaven</u> if they are not prepared to follow through with Her requests, whatever they may be. Prayer and fasting prepares their hearts to hear and follow Our Lady's words in their lives. Living this way, they have found great comfort in realizing how close Our Lady is to each one of them - when She has said so many times:

February 25, 1993

"...I am with you..."

She is always there whenever we need to hear Her voice.

A friend, who often visits the Caritas Community, adopted this method in her own prayer. She too was amazed at the intimacy She felt with Our Lady through Her messages. She wrote:

> *Our Lady shocked me last week. I was praying morning prayer outside, overwhelming myself with the trials that sometime surround me. I opened to the message:*

> **"Sing more joyfully. Why are you so pensive?"**

> *It just takes a few words from Her to set me straight. Especially after I learned from you the story about how Our Lady leaves quickly whenever the visionary Marija's child needs her (during her apparition time). I think - how quickly Mary must come to us when we need Her!*

One last example will show that the community goes to Our Lady not only for direction in their mission - but in their personal and family life as well. No matter seems to be too trivial for Our Lady when we search for answers out of love. The community mothers and children went out of town for a few days on a field trip. They fasted on Wednesday, but on Friday the question came up if Our Lady would mind them not fasting since they were on a field trip. No one wanted to take the liberty to say it would be alright, so they decided to go to the messages. They prayed, *"Mary, we ask if you would help us to know if you would like us to fast today?"* The mothers and children prayed the seven Our Father's, Hail Mary's, and Glory Be's, then opened up to pick a message. The message of November 26, 1983:

In answer to a question, Our Lady said:

"Prayer and fasting"

Their disappointment in not being able to eat was overshadowed by the delight they felt in having Our Lady answer them so directly. Not only did the message touch them, but also the explanation that preceded the message, as it placed them in an identical situation to hear Our Lady's words. It was a moment of real joy shared between the mothers and children with Our Lady.

We offer you this explanation for the purpose of encouraging you to turn to the messages of Our Lady of Medjugorje in your times of struggle, loneliness, distress, sorrow, and even in times of joy. However, don't even attempt this if you are not sincere or only curious. You cannot expect the Holy Spirit to be active out of curiosity and insincerity, rather with a childlike heart, full of faith and hope, will Our Lady be able to guide you. We hope and pray that you will discover an intimacy with Our Lady that you have never known before through these messages that you hold in your hands.

30

PART III

MEDJUGORJE
OUR LADY'S PLAN
TO
SAVE THE WORLD

PART III

MEDJUGORJE
OUR LADY'S PLAN
TO SAVE THE WORLD

Since 1981 Our Lady has appeared daily in Medjugorje. Everyday She prays. Everyday She speaks. What is the message She speaks? This is what we would like to discover now. From June 1981 to April 1984 the Blessed Virgin Mary talked to the visionaries and answered their questions. Those years were the years of the birth of the messages. From March 1, 1984 until the beginning of 1987, Our Lady gave a weekly message to the Parish of Medjugorje and to all people throughout the world who wanted to live Her messages. Since January 25, 1987, She has been giving a monthly message on the twenty-fifth of each month to the world. We are now in the year 2009, and we are still receiving these monthly messages.

Why is She appearing and giving messages for such a long period of time? Our Lady's answer is:

January 1, 1987

> **"...Dear children, you know that for your sake I have remained a long time so I might teach you how to make progress on the way of holiness..."**

Our Lady has remained in Medjugorje so long to teach us holiness; that is why we call Medjugorje "the School of Holiness." She cannot teach us holiness in a few weeks or years; it takes a long time because we are slow to respond. It is difficult for us

33

to be transformed. After each weekly or monthly message since 1984, Our Lady says:

"Thank you for having responded to my call."

The word, "POZIV," in Croatian means a "call." Our Lady is thankful because we answer Her call. Her call is Her message. In other words, **"Thank you for your readiness to live my messages."** First She thanks the visionaries, then the Parish, then every person who lives the messages. Her call is important. That is why She repeats Her thanks in each message. This is no accident. Our Lady is not just trying to be polite. It is more than that. This means: thank you for living my messages, because this call, these messages, are important. She appears to help us to live the messages:

October 30, 1986

"...Dear children, it is for your sake that I have stayed this long so I could help you to fulfill all the messages which I am giving you..."

"POZIV" in Croatian also means "invitation." The translation of this sentence would then be: **"Thank you for responding to my invitation."** Here again, Our Lady's invitation is Her message but it is also an invitation to come. The invitation to come is for the visionaries first. They come everyday to the apparition. Sometimes they have two apparitions a day. They are invited by the Blessed Mother on the hill at night and the visionaries respond to the invitation. **"Thank you for coming,"** says Our Lady, **"and thank you also for the pilgrims who come to Medjugorje, to the Church, and to the mountains."** This means it is important to come and this is why the Virgin Mary says, **"thank you,"** in each message. **"Thank you for coming to the spot of the apparitions."** Our Lady is happy to see people in Medjugorje. Usually when She sees a large crowd on Apparition Hill She says, **"I'm happy to see you in such large numbers."**

Why? Our Lady gives the answer on March 25, 1987:

"...today I am grateful to you for your presence in this place, where I am giving you SPECIAL GRACES..."

Come to Medjugorje to understand what special graces are! The Blessed Mother is grateful. **"Thank you,"** says She. See how She explains everything if we know how to look. It is very important for the Mother of God to see us come to Medjugorje. It is very important for Her to see us live Her messages. But what is this message, this invitation, this call?

CHAPTER 1

MEDJUGORJE: FIRST A CALL TO PRAYER

Prayer, as you may know, is the most frequent message of Our Lady in Medjugorje. It is rare not to have the word "prayer" in a message. Prayer is so important. But this world doesn't know that. Our Lady says:

October 2, 1986

> "...You, dear children, are not able to understand how great the value of prayer is as long as you yourselves do not say: now is the time for prayer, now nothing else is important to me, now not one person is important to me but God.' Dear children, consecrate yourselves to prayer with special love so that God will be able to render graces back to you..."

October 25, 1989 - and so many other times!

> "...dear children, pray, pray, pray..."

Medjugorje is: Pray! Pray! Pray! Prayer must be a daily offering to God:

May 30, 1985

> "...Let prayer, dear children, be your everyday food..."

Prayer is a powerful weapon:

> "...Through fasting and prayer, one can stop wars, one can suspend the laws of nature..." (July 21, 1982)

37

"...In prayer you shall perceive . . . the way out of every situation that has no exit..." (March 28, 1985)

Over and over Our Lady asks us to pray. She asks us to understand the value and nature of prayer. Prayer is the first step in our spiritual life and everything else depends upon that. Prayer has to become a way of life. We have to discover prayer. We have to be persistent in our prayers:

January 14, 1985

"...Be patient and persevere in prayer. Do not permit satan to take away your courage. He works very hard in the world. Be on your guard."

Yes! Prayer is a fight against the powers of darkness, against satan:

August 8, 1985

"...advance against satan by means of prayer.....put on the armor for battle and with the Rosary in your hand, defeat him!..."

The "armor for battle" is the strength of our prayers. Our Lady asked the prayer groups in Medjugorje to pray at least three hours a day. Why so many prayers?

September 13, 1984

"...You wonder why all these prayers? Look around you, dear children, and you will see how greatly sin has dominated the world. Pray, therefore, that Jesus conquers..."

What are the prayers we should pray? Our Lady asks for the three parts * (now four with the Luminous Mysteries) of the

* When Pope John Paul II announced the new Luminous Mysteries, Marija Lunetti, the Medjugorje visionary who receives the 25th message, said that Our Lady immediately accepted the new mysteries.

Rosary everyday, prayers to the Holy Spirit, prayers of consecration to the Sacred Heart of Jesus and to Her Immaculate Heart, and, of course, the highest form of prayer, the Holy Mass. Prayer can change the very structures of our mentality. A real profound prayer life is a life of constant transformation. This is the key to everything Our Lady does in Medjugorje. The quality of prayer is important. We have to see prayer like a real encounter with the Living God. We should pray with a living faith. Prayer should be a joy:

June 12, 1986

"...today I call you to begin to pray the Rosary with a living faith. That way I will be able to help you. You, dear children, wish to obtain graces, but you are not praying. I am not able to help you because you do not want to get started. Dear children, I am calling you to pray the Rosary and that your Rosary be an obligation which you shall fulfill with joy. That way you shall understand the reason I am with you this long. I desire to teach you to pray..."

The apparitions of Medjugorje, the meaning of Our Lady's presence: to teach us prayer. First, Medjugorje is a "school of prayer," then a "school of holiness." In this "school" Our Lady instructs us to **"pray with the heart."** (February 25, 1989 and so many other times):

May 29, 1986

"...Without love, dear children, you can do nothing..."

Love is the "motor" of everything. Without love we are not really alive. Therefore, we cannot pray without love. The heart is the symbol of love. Pray with the heart means: put love in the first place when you pray. To pray with the heart must be a decision: I decide to set aside everything, to concentrate, and to persevere in pure prayer. I decide to abandon myself to God

This is what we call prayer with the heart. Prayer must be something alive and active to be a joy. Praying with the heart also means "praying with joy." There is no real spiritual life without joy:

March 20, 1986

> **"...Today I call you to approach prayer actively.... Prayer will be your joy. If you make a start, it won't be boring to you because you will be praying out of joy..."**

But the thing is we have to start, to decide for ourselves to pray. Then God will lead us. Just get started. Put prayer in your life:

August 25, 1995

> **"...Let prayer be life for you..."**

This means let prayer be the activity which will bring real life in your lives, which will make you alive, really alive with the life of God Himself.

CHAPTER 2

MEDJUGORJE:
AN INVITATION TO EVERYONE

Our Lady started giving monthly messages in January 1987, and this first monthly message was a very important one. This message should be central in our understanding of Medjugorje. It expresses the reason for the apparitions which is **"the salvation of mankind,"** and tells us that **"each one of us is chosen by God in order...to save mankind."** Our Lady starts the message with a word we translate **"Behold."** At first it seems this word does not add anything to the actual meaning of the sentence. Seemingly the word is insignficant, but it is used to emphasize the great importance of the whole message. When a King, or in this case a Queen, prefaces a statement with "Behold," then the following words turn into a proclamation. The visionaries think that when Our Lady speaks of **"each one,"** She speaks in fact to every sincere man who hears this message and wants to live it. Father Jozo Zovko, the first parish priest of Medjugorje at the time of the first apparitions, thinks that this call to **"each one of us to save mankind"** concerns particularly and primarily each pilgrim who comes to Medjugorje. Each pilgrim is thus invited by God and chosen to have a **"great role in God's design for the salvation of mankind."** We already knew at the very beginning, that the desire of Our Lady through these apparitions was **"the conversion of the whole world."** (June 26, 1981) Now we hear that everyone is invited to participate in this plan of conversion. But first we have to change our lives. Here is this essential and crucial message in its entirety:

January 25, 1987

> **"Dear children, behold, also today I want to call you to start living a new life as of today. Dear children, I want you to comprehend that God has chosen EACH ONE OF YOU, in order to use you in a great plan for the salvation of mankind. You are not able to comprehend how great your role is in God's design. Therefore, dear children, pray so that in prayer you may be able to comprehend what God's plan is in your regard. I am with you in order that you may be able to bring it about in all its fullness. Thank you for having responded to my call."**

Here Our Lady says that She is with us, that She appears to fulfill the plan to save mankind through each one of us. But we cannot comprehend the magnitude of it all nor our role in this plan without prayer. Then in April of the same year, She confirms:

April 25, 1987

> **"...pray in order that you may be able to comprehend all that I am giving here....You know that without prayer you cannot comprehend all that God is planning through each one of you. Therefore, pray! I desire that through each one of you God's plan may be fulfilled..."**

The Mother of God starts something new. She does it with each one of us. She cannot do it without our prayers:

February 25, 1987

> **"...Therefore, dear children, pray, and in prayer you shall realize a new way of joy..."**

She is appearing each day for us. She is appearing to help to fulfill Her plan, God's plan, to save mankind. Our Lady said on October 30, 1986:

"...Dear children, it is for your sake that I have stayed this long, so I could help you to fulfill all the messages which I am giving you..."

Again and again, without our prayers nothing is possible!

October 23, 1986

"...Without your prayers, dear children, I cannot help you to fulfill the message which the Lord has given me to give to you..."

Sinful human nature blocks our intelligence so we are not able to understand the greatness of our role in God's plan. Only through prayer can this veil be removed so that we can see the reality and the truth - we are chosen personally by Our Lady. In June 1981, She gave four sentences to the visionaries, but those sentences were also said for us now, today:

"I invite you. I need you. I chose you. You are important."

Yes, we are important because Our Lady has said:

August 28, 1986

"...without you I am not able to help the world..."

Without us, without our prayers and conversion, She cannot help mankind.

44

CHAPTER 3

THE TREMENDOUS IMPORTANCE
OF THESE APPARITIONS

Even the people of Medjugorje don't realize the importance of what is going on in their parish:

May 9, 1985

> **"...no, you do not know how many graces God is giving you!..."**

The graces that God gives through the Queen of Peace in Medjugorje are tremendous:

June 2, 1984

> **"...God will give you gifts by which you will glorify Him till the end of your life on this earth..."**

During Ivanka's last daily apparition, the Queen of Peace told her:

May 7, 1985

> **"...No one in the world has had the grace which you, your brothers, and sisters have received..."**

The apparitions in Medjugorje are unique. They represent something that was never before done by God - daily apparitions for over twenty-eight years now. Our Lady also said that they were to be the last apparitions on earth. This statement caused some surprise, so the visionaries asked Our Lady questions about it many times and She confirmed:

May 2, 1982

"I have come to call the world to conversion for the last time. Afterwards, I will not appear any more on this earth."

However, this does not mean that there are no other apparitions going on now in the world while the apparitions in Medjugorje are happening. On the contrary, this is "a time of grace" where God is actively bringing men back to Him. But after the end of the Medjugorje apparitions, there won't be any more genuine apparitions on earth, **"only some false apparitions,"** says Our Lady.

We have many messages that tell us how Medjugorje is important to Our Lady. She wants Medjugorje to be an example for all parishes in the world, because this parish is special and has been chosen in a special way:

February 6, 1986

"...this parish, which I have chosen, is special and different from others. And I am giving great graces to all who pray with the heart..."

In 1987 Marija was asked this question by a French theologian: *"Why do I have to come to Medjugorje as Our Lady is everywhere where we pray to Her?"* Marija's answer was simple: *"In Medjugorje Our Lady gives SPECIAL GRACES."* Medjugorje is a special place, but the people of Medjugorje are a special people also:

November 15, 1984

"Dear children, you are a chosen people and God has given you great graces. You are not conscious of every message which I am giving you..."

Here Our Lady speaks to the people of Medjugorje. They are a "chosen people." They are called to be the instrument of a great plan. An important intention of the Mother of God is to make all of us realize the importance of Her plan because we are not conscious of it or the greatness of it all.

According to Vicka, *"What Our Lady does here has never been done before."* Our Lady explains on April 4, 1985 - Holy Thursday:

"...I wish to keep on giving you messages as it has never been in history from the beginning of the world..."

Our Lady accomplishes this project, which is so great and unique and the first of its kind, through a parish, a people She has chosen. This is very clear after studying the messages as a whole. Here is one example:

March 21, 1985

"...I love you and in a special way I have chosen this parish, one more dear to me than the others, in which I have gladly remained when the Almighty sent me..."

Although men remain men, with all their sins and shortcomings, these men and women of this little village of Herzegovina were chosen in a very special way. Many temptations, many of the seductions of the world attack them, but they are still the chosen ones. Sin and satan are powerful and even though the spiritual nature of the parish is in danger and may even die, the Blessed Mother continues to watch over Her chosen and dear children:

August 1, 1985

"...I wish to tell you that I have chosen this parish and that I am guarding it in my hands like a little flower that does not want to die..."

At least a small number will be saved to be the witnesses of God's peace in the world. After reading the following messages, it is obvious that Our Lady gave a special "privilege" to the parish of Medjugorje.

March 1, 1984

"...I have chosen this parish in a special way and I wish to lead it. I am guarding it in love and I want everyone to be mine..."

February 6, 1986

"...Dear children, I am giving messages first of all to the residents of the parish, and then to all the others..."

And this message given to Jelena (July 30, 1987):

"...Dear children, to be chosen by God is really something great, but it is also a responsibility for you to pray more, for you, the chosen ones, to encourage others, so you can be a light for people in darkness....Dear children, this is the reason for my presence among you for such a long time: to lead you on the path of Jesus. I want to save you and, THROUGH YOU, TO SAVE THE WHOLE WORLD..."

This message was addressed to the parish in general and in particular to the members of Jelena's prayer group. Our Lady wants to save the whole world through Medjugorje.

CHAPTER 4

THE WORLD IS IN DARKNESS

In this same message to Jelena which we just quoted, the Mother of God adds:

July 30, 1987

> **"...Children, darkness reigns over the whole world. People are attracted by many things and they forget about the more important....Many people now live without faith; some don't even want to hear about Jesus, but they still want peace and satisfaction! Children, here is the reason why I need your prayer: prayer is the only way to save the human race."**

This message sums up the spirit of Medjugorje. The entire basic message is here.

Our Lady also talks about **"...this unfaithful world walking in darkness..."** (June 5, 1986) The devil has a strong grip over modern society. Our Lady told Mirjana in 1982:

> **"...This century is under the power of the devil..."**

The situation of the world is bad:

> **"...A great struggle is about to unfold. A struggle between my Son and satan. Human souls are at stake."** (August 2, 1981)

> **"...satan exists! He seeks only to destroy..."** (February 14, 1982)

"...he (satan) **works very hard in the world..."** (January 14, 1985)

"...overcome all the troubles which satan is trying to inflict on the Catholic Church..." (June 25, 1985)

"...Dear children, do not allow satan to get control of your hearts, so you would be an image of satan and not of me..." (January 30, 1986)

"...satan is strong and is waiting to test each one of you..." (September 25, 1987)

Although there is a long list of messages about satan, Our Lady does not want to paint a picture of hopelessness in describing the power of the devil in our world. On the contrary, She wants to give us weapons against the powers of darkness. But we have to see the situation with lucidity: satan is powerful, he wants to seduce us. He is active in the world. According to Our Lady, satan is also very present in the parish of Medjugorje. The devil knows he can have a strong and decisive victory if he can stop or injure severely the plans of the Mother of God in Medjugorje itself. Here is one message among many which Our Lady gave to Mirjana on January 28, 1987. In this message, The Blessed Mother speaks to the parish of Medjugorje:

"...Whenever I come to you my Son comes with me, but so does satan. You permitted, without noticing, his influences on you and he drives you on..."

Actually satan by his work did destroy part of the plan of Our Lady in Medjugorje:

"...satan has taken part of the plan and wants to possess it..." (August 1, 1985)

But a month later, after a strong effort in prayer by the parish, Our Lady said:

September 5, 1985

"...today I thank you for all the prayers. Keep on praying
all the more so that satan will be far away from this place.
Dear children, satan's plan has failed. Pray for the fulfillment of what God plans in this parish..."

52

CHAPTER 5

THE PLAN OF OUR LADY
AGAINST SATAN

Prayer has defeated satan's plan. Prayer is the first weapon
against satan. Our Lady wants us to use five weapons (described
below) to overcome the power of satan in our lives and in the
world. This is Her "Peace Plan":

May 25, 1987

> **"...you are ready to commit sin, and to put yourselves in the
> hands of satan without reflecting..."**

This is the picture of modern society. The peace of the world
is in danger because faith is in danger. Our Lady said Spring
1982:

> **"...have you not observed that faith began to extinguish
> itself?..."**

This is the picture of modern world. The heart of man is not at
peace and many times it physically manifests itself in violence.
Therefore, Our Lady tells us that we must pray to have peace
in our hearts. When enough individuals do this, it is then that
peace will reign around us. Our Lady said:

September 6, 1984

> **"Dear children, without prayer there is no peace. Therefore,
> I say to you, dear children, pray at the foot of the Crucifix
> for peace..."**

We can change the world through prayer. It is very important for us to realize that.

THE FIRST WEAPON AGAINST SATAN: PRAYER

We talk about that all the time. This is the center of Our Lady's plan: Prayer! Again, this is the most frequent message in Medjugorje. Let us quote just a few more simple messages about prayer:

April 25, 1987

> **"...today also I am calling you to prayer. You know, dear children, that God grants special graces in prayer...I call you, dear children, to prayer with the heart..."**

To pray with the heart is to pray with abandonment, love, and trust and with concentration also. Prayer heals. Prayer heals human souls. Prayer heals history [history of sin]. Without prayer, we cannot have an experience of God:

February 25, 1989

> **"...without unceasing prayer, you cannot experience the beauty and greatness of the grace which God is offering you..."**

What are the prayers Our Lady recommends? The four mysteries of the Rosary everyday, the Adoration of the Holy Sacrament, prayers to the Holy Spirit (especially before Mass), prayers in front of the Crucifix, prayers of consecration to the Sacred Heart of Jesus and to the Immaculate Heart of Mary. Everybody should pray. Our Lady says:

August 25, 1989

"...Let prayer begin to rule in the whole world..."

In this way, through prayer, we will defeat satan's power, obtain peace and salvation for our souls:

February 25, 1988

"...You know that I love you and am coming here out of love, so I could show you the path of peace and salvation for your souls. I want you to obey me and not permit satan to seduce you. Dear children, satan is very strong and, therefore, I ask you to dedicate your prayers to me so that those who are under his influence may be saved. Give witness by your life, sacrifice your lives for the salvation of the world...Therefore, little children, do not be afraid. If you pray, satan cannot injure you even a little, because you are God's children and He is watching over you. Pray, and let the Rosary always be in your hands as a sign to satan that you belong to me..."

The power of satan is destroyed by prayer and he cannot harm us if we pray. That is why no Christian should be afraid of the future, unless he does not pray. And if he does not pray, is he a Christian? If we do not pray, we are naturally blind to many things; we cannot tell right from wrong. We lose our center; we lose our balance.

THE SECOND WEAPON AGAINST SATAN: FASTING

A message about fasting appeared on the third day of the apparitions when the Virgin said to Marija that to achieve peace, **"...it is necessary to believe, to pray, to fast, and to go to Confession."** (June 26, 1981)

In the Old Testament and in the New Testament, we see many examples of fasting. Jesus fasted. According to tradition, fasting is encouraged especially in times of great temptation or severe trials. Certain devils, *"can be cast out in no other way except by prayer and fasting,"* said Jesus. (Mark 9:29)

Fasting is an instrument to overcome the power of darkness present in the world now and it has a purification value. Our time is a time of darkness, that is why we should use fasting often. Our Lady recommends it twice a week:

August 14, 1984

"...Fast strictly on Wednesdays and Fridays..."

She requested us to accept this difficult message **"...with a firm will."** She asks us to **"...persevere in...fasting."** (June 25, 1982)

July 21, 1982

"...The best fast is on bread and water. Through fasting and prayer, one can stop wars, one can suspend the laws of nature. Charity cannot replace fasting...everyone, except the sick, must fast."

Again, fasting is a strong weapon against the devil:

November, 1981

"The devil tries to impose his power on you, but you must remain strong and persevere in your faith. You must pray and fast. I will always be close to you."

November 16, 1981

"The devil is trying to conquer us. Do not permit him. Keep the faith, fast, and pray. I will be with you at every step..."

Fasting is recommended in times of special trouble or for difficult situations:

"Pray for Father Jozo [who was in jail] **and fast tomorrow on bread and water..."** (October 19, 1981)

We have to **"...fast for the sick..."** to obtain their healing. (August 18, 1982)

July 25, 1982

"...For the cure of the sick, it is important to say the following prayers: the Creed, and seven times each, The Lord's Prayer, the Hail Mary, and the Glory Be, and to fast on bread and water..."

Our Lady also asked some special fasting for the Bishop of Mostar who does not believe in the apparitions:

July, 1983

"Fast two days a week for the intentions of the Bishop, who bears a heavy responsibility. If there is a need to, I will ask for a third day..."

Each visionary has or will receive 10 secrets. Some of those secrets concern chastisements or warnings to mankind because of its sins. In regard to one of the secrets that concerned a catastrophe, Our Lady told Mirjana:

November 6, 1982

"I have prayed; the punishment has been softened. Repeated prayers and fasting reduce punishments from God..."

We have to realize the power of fasting. Fasting means to make a sacrifice for God, to offer not only our prayers, but also to make our whole being, our body itself, participate in sacrifice. And we do that with love, for a special intention, and to purify ourselves and the world. This great task of purification needs sacrifices. We do not offer it because we must; we offer it because we love God and want to be courageous soldiers that also offer our bodies in the battle against evil.

THE THIRD WEAPON AGAINST SATAN: DAILY READING OF THE BIBLE

Usually Our Lady comes to the visionaries *"happy and joyful,"* as Ivan puts it after each apparition. But on some occasions Our Lady has appeared to be very sad. On other very rare occasions She has cried. One time She cried when She was talking about the Bible. Father Jozo says that, as a priest, he saw many mothers mourning their sons at funerals, but he never saw a mother so sad as the Mother of God when She talked about the Bible. Those tears are terrible tears. While crying, Our Lady said:

"You have forgotten the Bible."

The Bible is a book different from any other book on earth. Vatican II says that all the canonical books of the Bible were, *"...written under the inspiration of the Holy Spirit, they have God as their author."* (Dogmatic Constitution on Divine Revelation, Chapter 3.) This means that no other book can be compared to this book. That is why Our Lady asks us to separate THE BOOK from the other human books on the shelves. There is no writing even from a saint or inspired that can be compared to the Bible. That is why we are asked to place the Bible in a visible, separate place in our homes:

October 18, 1984

"Dear children, today I call you to read the Bible everyday in your homes and let it be in a visible place so as always to encourage you to read it and to pray..."

It is very rare to hear Our Lady say, **"you must."** She "desires," "calls," etc., but on one occasion She used a very strong Croatian verb that means **"must"**:

"...Every family must pray family prayer and read the Bible!..." (February 14, 1985)

THE FOURTH WEAPON AGAINST SATAN: CONFESSION

Our Lady asks for monthly confession. From the very first days of the apparitions, Our Lady spoke about Confession:

June 26, 1981

"...Make your peace with God and among yourselves. For that, it is necessary to believe, to pray, to fast, and to go to confession."

February 10, 1982

"Pray, pray! It is necessary to believe firmly, to go to Confession regularly, and likewise to receive Holy Communion. It is the only salvation."

The Mother of God stressed the force of repentance:

July 24, 1982

"Whoever has done very much evil during his life can go straight to Heaven if he confesses, is sorry for what he has done, and receives Communion at the end of his life."

The Western Church has disregarded Confession and its importance and concerning this Our Lady said:

August 6, 1982

"...Monthly Confession will be a remedy for the Church in the West. One must convey this message to the West..."

A pilgrim who comes to Medjugorje is always impressed by the number of people waiting for Confession and the number of priests hearing Confessions. Many priests have had extraordinary experiences during Confessions in Medjugorje. Our Lady said the following about Confessions during a certain feast day:

August 5, 1984

"The priests who will hear Confessions will have great joy on that day!"

But Confession should not be a habit that would actually *"make sinning easy."* Vicka says to every group of pilgrims, *"Confession is something that has to make a new human being out of you. Our Lady does not want you to think that Confession will free you from sin and allow you to continue the same life after that. No, confession is a call to transformation. You must become a new person!"* Our Lady explained the same idea to Jelena:

November 7, 1983

"Do not go to Confession through habit, to remain the same after it. No, it is not good. Confession should give an

impulse to your faith. It should stimulate you and bring you closer to Jesus. If Confession does not mean anything for you, really, you will be converted with great difficulty."

FIFTH WEAPON AGAINST SATAN: THE EUCHARIST

Our Lady also cried when She spoke about the Eucharist and the Mass. In 1985 She said:

"...You do not celebrate the Eucharist, as you should. If you would know what grace and what gifts you receive, you would prepare yourselves for it each day, for an hour at least..."

The evening Mass in Medjugorje is the most important moment of the day because Our Lady is present and She gives us Her Son in a special way. The Mass is more important than the daily apparition. Marija said that if she had to choose between the Eucharist and the apparition, she would choose the Eucharist. Our Lady said:

October 6, 1981

"The evening Mass must be kept permanently..."

She also asked that the prayer to the Holy Spirit always be said before Mass. Our Lady wants us to see the Holy Mass as "the highest form of prayer" and "the center of our lives," (according to Marija's words). Vicka also says that the Blessed Mother sees the Mass as "the most important and the most holy moment in our lives. We have to be prepared and pure to receive Jesus with a great respect. The Mass should be the center of our lives." Our Lady is crying because people do not have enough respect toward the Eucharist. The Mother of God is sad and cries especially because we do not realize the extreme beauty of the mystery of Mass. But She rejoices because:

"...There are many of you who have sensed the beauty of the Holy Mass...Jesus gives you His graces in the Mass..." (April 3, 1986)

Our Lady has come to give us the Living and Resurrected Jesus:

"...Let the Holy Mass be your life..." (April 25, 1988)

This means that the Sacrifice and Resurrection of Christ must become our life, together with the hope of His second coming. During Mass, we receive the Living Christ and in Him we receive the whole mystery of our salvation that must transform us, transfigure us. Mass is the perfect expression of the mystery of Christ in which we can fully participate in His life:

"Mass is the greatest prayer of God. You will never be able to understand its greatness. That is why you must be perfect and humble at Mass, and you should prepare yourselves for it." (1983)

Our Lady wants us to be full of joy and hope during Mass and She wants us to make an effort so that this moment will **"...be an experience of God..."** (May 16, 1985). Surrender to Jesus and to the Holy Spirit is a very important part of the messages, because, as we will see, it is the only way to holiness. To be open to the Holy Spirit in the Sacraments is the way we are going to be sanctified. In this way, Our Lady will obtain for us the grace so that we can become Her witnesses in the world to fulfill the plan of God and Her plan:

May 23, 1985

"...open your hearts to the Holy Spirit. Especially during these days the Holy Spirit is working through you. Open your hearts and surrender your lives to Jesus so that He works through your hearts..."

CHAPTER 6

"I AM THE QUEEN OF PEACE"

The first call and invitation of Our Lady is peace. She said on the third day of Her apparitions:

> **"Peace, peace, peace! Be reconciled! Only peace. Make your peace with God and among yourselves. For that, it is necessary to believe, to pray, to fast, and to go to Confession."**

Marija received this message on June 26, 1981, after she had the apparition with the other visionaries on top of Apparition Hill. While Marija went down the mountain, she was mysteriously pushed to the side of the trail by an unseen force. She saw the Virgin again. Our Lady was crying and there was a bare wooden cross behind Her. Later the Mother of God said that Her name for these Apparitions of Medjugorje was **"The Queen of Peace."** Then on Monday, August 24, 1981, many people in Medjugorje, including Father Jozo Zovko, saw a large inscription in the sky on top of Mount Krizevac. The word "MIR" appeared in large burning letters. "MIR" is Croatian for "peace." This is the central message of Medjugorje.

What is the meaning of the word "peace" in Christian tradition? In Hebrew, "shalom" indicates an idea of wholeness and unity. Jerusalem, for instance, means the "City of Peace," or more accurately, the "Seeing of Peace." This city is symbolically the place of unity between God and man. In Psalm 122, we have a song of peace for the *"City of Peace."* And in verse 3, we find the idea of wholeness and harmony: *"Jerusalem built as a city with compact unity."* Jerusalem is the place of peace not only because it is one, and united as a city, but also because this city is called to have complete unity with God, to be in harmony with God. From all this we can discover the real meaning of peace. Peace is harmony between God and man.

"Shalom" also includes the idea of happiness, joy, and prosperity. But real happiness, joy, and prosperity can come only through this peace, which comes from God and is a direct gift from the Holy Spirit:

> **"...When the Holy Spirit comes, peace will be established..."** (October, 1984)

Our Lady says:

> **"...I call you to peace. Live it in your heart and all around you so that all will know peace - peace which does not come from you but from God..."** (Christmas Day message, 1988)

Vicka says that Our Lady loves the feast of Christmas very much. She always appears on Christmas in golden vestments with Baby Jesus in Her arms, with immense joy. She gave one of Her main messages about peace on Christmas day:

> **"...Glorify the Nativity of Jesus through the peace that I give. It is for this peace that I have come as your Mother, Queen of Peace..."** (December 25, 1988)

Christmas time is a period of harmony between God and man because God becomes man! Christmas, Our Lady says, **"...is a great day! Rejoice with me!..."** (December 25, 1988). Here we find the joy aspect of peace, peace brought to every creature by the Incarnation which brings harmony in the world. At Christmas we feel and live this special spirit of harmony and beauty where the whole creation is as if touched by the love of God. The angels sang, *"Glory to God in the highest and on earth PEACE to those on whom His favor rests."* (Luke 2:14)

From this quote, we receive an even clearer bit of information about the nature of peace. Peace is a relationship between God and man. Peace is harmony between God in the highest who incarnates Himself to become man, and human beings who receive peace and blessing from above. Christmas has a lot to do with unity and harmony between Heaven and earth. Peace is a blessing from God. Our Lady wants us to extend Her own blessing to all to help the harmony to come to reality. On Christmas Day, 1988, She said:

"...I give you my Special Blessing. Bring it to all creation, so that all creation will know peace..." (December 25, 1988)

Before we start to speak about the path of holiness, we have to realize that a holy person or a saint is one who has achieved peace in his heart, which means one has achieved a high degree of harmony between himself and God. Peace - harmony - is a gift from God; only God can give it:

"...peace - peace which does not come from you but from God..." (December 25, 1988)

Christmas is the coming of the Prince of Peace as foretold in Isaiah 9:5: *"For a child is born to us, a son is given to us; upon his shoulder dominion rests. They name Him...Prince of Peace."* And the Queen of Peace says:

July 31, 1986

"...I call you always to bring harmony and peace..."

If we know a little bit about what the "Christmas spirit" is, we can begin to understand what the word "PEACE" means.

66

CHAPTER 7

THE ONLY SOLUTION
TO HEAL THE WORLD: HOLINESS

Our Lady says:

> **"...without you I am not able to help the world..."** (August 28, 1986)

> **"...I desire to lead you on the way of holiness..."** (October 9, 1986)

Her plan to save mankind is impossible without holiness. God always worked and saved through holiness. A period of history without saints is a period of history without God's glorious presence and God's work:

> **"...God has chosen each one of you, in order to use you in a great plan for the salvation of mankind..."** (January 25, 1987)

Our Lady's presence here is to fulfill this plan for the salvation of mankind:

> **"...I am with you in order that you may be able to bring it about** [the plan] **in all its fullness..."** (January 25, 1987)

Our Lady's presence here is also to teach us holiness, because, once again, without holiness there is no salvation of mankind:

> **"...Dear children, you know that for your sake I have remained a long time so I might teach you how to make progress on the way of holiness..."** (January 1, 1987)

In the same month, January, 1987, through those two messages (on the 1st and the 25th) Our Lady gave us two clues to explain the reason for those very long apparitions of Medjugorje: She came to save mankind and She came to call us to holiness. There is only one way to save mankind from the powers of darkness, from satan. We have to make a strong decision for God and against satan and we have to walk with Our Lady toward holiness. Our Lady's plan in Medjugorje is to save mankind through holiness. The goal of Our Lady's coming is just that: to lead us to holiness, to lead us to a better life with God on earth, and to lead us to Heaven. The message of May 25, 1987, sums up Her whole plan:

> **"...I call on each one of you to consciously decide for God and against satan. I am your Mother and, therefore, I want to lead you all to complete holiness. I want each one of you to be happy here on earth and to be with me in Heaven. That is, dear children, the purpose of my coming here and it's my desire..."**

Actually, holiness is to live on earth as if already in Heaven. In 1986 Our Lady said to Jelena:

> **"If you would abandon yourselves to me, you will not even feel the passage from this life to the next life. You will begin to live the life of Heaven on earth."**

> **"...Dear children, if you live the messages, you are living the seed of holiness..."** (October 10, 1985)

This means holiness will grow by itself in us.

Holiness is a danger, the "greatest" danger to satan's power. By his witnessing and his life itself, a saint directly attacks the core of satan's power in the world. The fight against darkness is a battle:

"...advance against satan by means of prayer....put on the armor for battle and with the Rosary in your hand, defeat him!..." (August 8, 1985)

"...By prayer you can completely disarm him [satan]**..."** (January 24, 1985)

Holiness comes from the Holy Spirit. Our Lady insists on the prayer to the Holy Spirit, especially before Mass. The prayer to the Holy Spirit is also said in Ivan's prayer group each time Ivan has his apparition. Just before the apparition, the *"Veni Creator Spiritus"* (Come O Spirit of Creation) is said in Croatian. We need the Holy Spirit to become new human beings:

"...Ask the Holy Spirit to renew your souls, to renew the entire world." (March 5, 1984)

Through the Holy Spirit we can become a new human being and live on the earth as if already in Heaven. The joy of the Resurrected Christ has to dwell in our hearts:

"Raise your hands, yearn for Jesus because in His Resurrection, He wants to fill you with graces. Be enthusiastic about the Resurrection. All of us in Heaven are happy, but we seek the joy of your hearts..." (April 21, 1984)

But to be enthusiastic about the Resurrection, we have to be immersed in the reality of the Cross. A real joy of the Resurrection may be born in our hearts only if a real love and knowledge of the fruitfulness of the cross is constantly present in us. If we spiritually participate in the sacrifice of Christ, we will be given the grace to see His victory already here on earth. Jesus must rise again in our hearts, and in our families:

"...May Jesus truly rise in your families..." (April 21, 1984)

We have to participate in Christ's Passion and in His Resurrection by the power of the Holy Spirit to become holy. In Holy Communion we receive Jesus Crucified and Resurrected. By the Holy Spirit we are transformed to become an image of Christ. That is why Holy Communion is life for us:

"...Let the Holy Mass be your life..." (April 25, 1988)

Jesus said: ***"I am the Resurrection and the life."*** (John 11:25) Through the grace of the Sacraments we receive the Holy Spirit to have light and to resemble Christ:

"...I wish that you all be the reflection of Jesus, which will enlighten this unfaithful world walking in darkness..." (June 5, 1986)

The highest call of Our Lady is for us to be the reflection of Jesus. By his own strength and work, nobody can be the reflection of Jesus. It can only happen if it is granted by God, through the Holy Spirit. The Holy Spirit is love and light:

"...The most important thing in the spiritual life is to ask for the gift of the Holy Spirit. When the Holy Spirit comes, peace will be established. When that occurs, everything changes around you..." (October, 1984)

"...Pray to the Holy Spirit for enlightenment..." (November 8, 1984)

The Death and Resurrection of Jesus opened a new era to mankind in which we could receive in a special way the grace to be a light to others. On Good Friday (April 20, 1984), Our Lady said to Jelena:

"You should be filled with joy! Today Jesus died for your salvation. He descends to Hell and opens the gates of Paradise. Let joy reign in your hearts!..."

By this joy and through this light that we receive as a gift at Baptism and with the Sacraments, we can be the witnesses of the light of Christ:

> **"...in your life you have all experienced light and darkness. God grants to every person to recognize good and evil. I am calling you to the light, which you should carry to all the people who are in darkness. People who are in darkness daily come into your homes. Dear children, give them the light!..."** (March 14, 1985)

This light can only come from the Holy Spirit. Our Lady says:

> **"...When you have the Holy Spirit, you have everything..."** (October 21, 1983)

The Holy Spirit makes us holy. The Holy Spirit can make us light to others. It is especially in the Sacraments of the Church and during the Holy Mass that we can receive the Holy Spirit:

> **"...I wish your Mass to be an experience of God. I wish especially to say to the young people: be open to the Holy Spirit because God wishes to draw you to Himself..."** (May 16, 1985)

CHAPTER 8

WHAT IS HOLINESS?

Again, holiness is a gift which comes only from God, through the Holy Spirit. We cannot achieve holiness by our own strength. Holiness is growth with God. Our Lady gave a definition of holiness:

> **"...today I am calling you to holiness. Without holiness you cannot live. Therefore, with love overcome every sin and with love overcome all the difficulties which are coming to you. Dear children, I beseech you to live love within your-selves..."** (July 10, 1986)

TO BE HOLY IS TO OVERCOME SIN BY LOVE. This is the definition of holiness. A saint does not overcome sin and difficulties through human means like the world would. A saint overcomes sin through love. The instrument we have to use always is love:

> **"...act with love. Let your only instrument always be love. By love turn everything into good which satan desires to destroy and possess. Only that way will you be completely mine and I shall be able to help you..."** (July 31, 1986)

Our Lady wishes us to be totally Hers. *"TOTUS TUUS"* (Totally Yours) is the motto that Pope John Paul II chose. The call of Mary is to abandon ourselves completely to Her and to God. This is one of the most frequent messages in Medjugorje - abandon yourselves to God. Holiness is total abandonment to the will of God! To renounce our own will and instead put the will of God in our lives is essential to holiness. Another thing is essential to holiness: to accept sacrifice. The spirit of sacrifice is an ingredient that God uses for purification and we badly need purification. Sacrifice, especially fasting, prepare our hearts to receive the gift of holiness:

> **"...prepare your hearts for these days when the Lord particularly desires to purify you from all the sins of your past... prepare your hearts in penance and fasting..."** (December 4, 1986)

If we choose holiness we should also be ready for change! We should be willing to change our lives:

> **"...I am calling you to pray with your whole heart and day by day to change your life...I am calling that by your prayers and sacrifices you begin to live in holiness...daily change your life in order to become holy..."** (November 13, 1986)

Medjugorje then is this "School of Holiness," where holiness is available and given to each pilgrim - if he wants! The only thing we have to do is to make a decision for holiness and abandon ourselves completely to God:

> **"...I am calling you to a complete surrender to God..."** (March 25, 1989 and many, many other messages)

> **"...put your life in God's hands..."** (January 25, 1988)

The "School of Holiness" is a school of love. This is very important. Our Lady does not think we can convert the world through anything else but love. Holiness is love in action. She does not think we can change the world through science or knowledge or intelligence or human strength. We can change hearts and change the world only through love in action and through love incarnate in human beings:

"...Without love, dear children, you can do nothing..." (May 29, 1986)

"...without love you will achieve nothing..." (December 13, 1984)

We will achieve neither holiness nor conversion without love because love is the motor of the whole process of inner transformation. The key to holiness is love:

"...decide for love..." (November 20, 1986)

"...love makes great things..." (April 12, 1987)

Holiness is the growth of love in our hearts:

"...I desire to call you to grow in love. A flower is not able to grow normally without water. So also you, dear children, are not able to grow without God's blessing..." (April 10, 1986)

A lot of people think that we should explain and convince the world to change its ways, that we should use intelligence, knowledge, politics, and science to make things go better. Our Lady says that we can accomplish much greater things if we use love as a tool. But the problem is that we have forgotten real love:

"...no, you don't know how to love..." (November 29, 1984)

This is why the Mother of God has come on the earth for twenty-eight years now, to teach us love. And if She teaches us love, She teaches us holiness at the same time.

The sin of the world in which we live is sometimes terrible. Our mission in this world is **"...with love overcome every sin..."** (July 10, 1986). Saints are those who **"...live love within yourselves..."** (July 10, 1986).

First of all, we should not fear becoming a saint. As Mother Teresa of Calcutta said: *"To be a saint is the duty of each Christian."* To be a saint is something that comes from God, not from us. We should be faithful in living the messages and then holiness will grow in us by itself as a gift coming from Heaven. This is what Our Lady meant when She said:

"...if you live the messages, you are living the seed of holiness..." (October 10, 1985)

First, live the messages; this is the first step toward holiness. Live the five main messages of Medjugorje, the five practical things you have to do in your life: Prayer, Fasting, Reading the Bible, Confession and Holy Mass. If you live these messages, you will put the seeds of holiness in your hearts. But only love can make them sprout and give fruit because:

"...without love you will achieve nothing..." (December 13, 1984)

"...love makes great things.." (April 12, 1987)

What is the most important thing in life? Jesus was asked this question in the form of, *"What is the most important commandment of all?"* Commandments of the Law were for the Jews the most important things in life. As you know, Jesus answered, **"Thou shalt love the Lord thy God with thy whole heart, and with thy whole soul, and with thy whole mind! This is the greatest and first commandment. And the second is like it. Thou shalt love thy neighbor as thyself! On these two commandments depend the whole Law and the Prophets."** (Matthew 22:34-40) Our Lady, who is just repeating the Gospel for our time, says, of course, the same thing:

"...today my call to you is that in your life you live love towards God and neighbor. Without love, dear children, you can do nothing..." (May 29, 1986)

Medjugorje is a constant message of love. Here are some examples which convey the message of love:

"...start loving from today with an ardent love, the love with which I love you..." (May 29, 1986)

"...By love you are able to do even that which you think is impossible..." (November 7, 1985)

"...today I call you to live the word this week: 'I love God.' Dear children, through love you will achieve everything and even what you think is impossible..." (February 28, 1985)

We will achieve holiness even if we think it's impossible!

"...I am calling you to the love of neighbor..." (November 7, 1985)

Our Lady also speaks of Her love towards us:

"...You know that I love you and that I burn out of love for you..." (November 20, 1986)

"...today again I want to show you how much I love you, but I am sorry that I am not able to help each one to understand my love..." (October 16, 1986)

We can neither imagine nor realize fully how great Our Lady's love is. Only in deep prayer and with Her blessing can we feel Her presence which is the presence of love. Many Medjugorje pilgrims have received this gift of approaching, at least a little, the immense mystery of Our Lady's great love. But She wants <u>our</u> love in return. Our Lady's path leads toward love; She speaks of the *"way of love"* (June 25, 1988); and She wants us to grow in love, which means to grow in holiness day by day:

"...so that God's love may be able to grow in you day by day..." (June 25, 1988)

We are called to perfect love.

> **"...Pray, because in prayer each one of you will be able to achieve complete love..."** (October 25, 1987)

Our love must be like Our Lady's love. We have to make a decision to love. We must be strong and decisive for love:

> **"...God does not want you lukewarm and undecided, but that you totally surrender to Him. You know that I love you and that I burn out of love for you. Therefore, dear children, you also decide for love so that you will burn out of love and daily experience God's love. Dear children, decide for love so that LOVE PREVAILS IN ALL OF YOU, but not human love, rather God's love..."** (November 20, 1986)

CHAPTER 9

THE FRUITS OF LOVE

We could say the *"fruits of conversion,"* or even the *"fruits of holiness."* The first fruits of our own conversion are joy and happiness that come from God:

> **"...I am calling you to great joy and peace which only God can give..."** (March 25, 1989)

God has been giving us many gifts in Medjugorje; this should fill us with joy:

> **"...rejoice in everything that you have received and give thanks to God because everything is God's gift to you..."** (April 25, 1989)

Through prayer, in our conversion, and with the love of God in our hearts, the world, the living reality around us, and all creation reveal their secrets. A life with God is a life of discovery in which we discover God Himself in His creation:

> **"...(You will) discover God in everything, even in the smallest flower..."** (You will discover a great joy. You will discover God)." (April 25, 1989)

The abundance of what God gives us if we abandon ourselves to Him is amazing. The joy of the love of God is something that can save the world, and Our Lady wants us to be the witnesses of that:

> **"...Be strong in God. I desire that through you the whole world may get to know the God of joy..."** (May 25, 1988)

The witnessing of Our Lady's messages is a mission by which we are called to save the world. We have to be witnesses of joy. Again and again, we know we are called to be witnesses to save the world:

"...God has chosen each one of you, in order to use you in a great plan for the salvation of mankind..." (January 25, 1987)

The whole meaning of the apparitions is contained here. How can we **"...bring harmony and peace..."** (July 31, 1986) to the world? We must unite our lives with God's life. We do that through Sacraments, especially Holy Communion which has to be "the center of our lives." In this way we live a new life with God. The whole purpose of creation is the love of God in our hearts and the beauty of the works of the Holy Spirit in our hearts. We answer to the beauty of God by our own spiritual beauty that we receive from Him. The fruit of God's love is spiritual beauty. Human souls desire the presence of the Holy Spirit. When we have the presence of God in us, we are beautiful in the eyes of God. Like flowers. The desire for God and for His light is very important in our spiritual life:

"...open your hearts to God like the spring flowers which crave for the sun..." (January 31, 1985)

Beauty is a fruit of love. Once Jelena asked Our Lady, *"Why are you so beautiful?"* Our Lady answered:

"I am beautiful because I love. If you want to be beautiful, love..." (March 25, 1985)

We should be a beautiful flower for Jesus and His Mother. Only through prayer can we attain spiritual beauty and complete love:

"...Pray, because in prayer each one of you will be able to achieve complete love..." (October 25, 1987)

Only through prayer can we be truly beautiful to God:

"...When you pray, you are much more beautiful, like flowers which, after the snow, show all their beauty and all their colors become indescribable..." (December 18, 1986)

With our lives united with God, we can truly discover the real life that God wants to unveil to us. The gift of life is in itself something marvelous. The intensity of life with God is a gift that comes from love. Life must be a joy, a discovery of joy. But that intense life which is a discovery of joy can only exist in God:

"See, little children, how nature is opening herself and is giving life and fruits. In the same way I am calling you to a life with God and a complete surrender to Him." (May 25, 1989)

A life with God is a discovery of the profoundness of the mystery of life:

"...Little children, I am with you and unceasingly I desire to lead you into the joy of life..." (May 25, 1989)

But real joy and the reality of life are only found in God, in union with Him:

"...I desire that each one of you discovers the joy and the love which is found only in God and which only God can give..." (May 25, 1989)

But this discovery can happen only with God, through prayer:

"...Pray that you may discover the greatness and the joy of life which God is giving you..." (May 25, 1989)

Life in abundance and joy are, like beauty, the very fruits of our love toward God and our neighbor. A great call of Our Lady is to rejoice in the life we have received from God:

"...today I invite you all to rejoice in the life which God gives you..." (August 25, 1988)

The mystery of life reveals itself to us in prayer and thanks to our love:

"...Little children, rejoice in God the Creator because He has created you so wonderfully..." (August 25, 1988)

If we can really discover <u>true life</u>, we will have an immense joy. And we will give this life and this joy to others in our mission of witnessing to the world. But we have to thank God always in return for everything we receive:

"...Pray that your life be a joyful thanksgiving, which flows out of your heart like a river of joy..." (August 25, 1988)

This river of joy will be the salvation of the world, because this joy is from God, through the Holy Spirit:

"...Joy will manifest in your hearts and thus you shall be joyful witnesses of that which I and My Son want from each one of you..." (February 25, 1987)

This world wants joy and satisfaction, but without Jesus and with sin:

"...some don't even want to hear about Jesus, but they still want peace and satisfaction!..." (July 30, 1987)

"...I want each one of you to be happy, but in sin nobody can be happy..." (February 25, 1987)

Our Lady wants our happiness, a lasting and eternal happiness, and that begins right here on this earth:

"...I want each one of you to be happy here on earth and to be with me in Heaven. That is, dear children, the purpose of my coming here and it's my desire..." (May 25, 1987)

The apparitions are to save us, to bring us to Heaven. Heaven can start right here on this earth if we live what Our Lady asks. From day to day we have to prepare ourselves to be closer and closer to God, ready to receive His gifts, to **"...become more beautiful..."** (October 24, 1985)

Usually, what we need first is to open our intelligence through prayer to understand all this. We are not aware of things of the spiritual life. We have to pray to the Holy Spirit to understand what is going on:

"...you are not conscious of the messages which God is sending to you through me. He is giving you great graces and you do not comprehend them. Pray to the Holy Spirit for enlightenment..." (November 8, 1984)

We are called to holiness in Medjugorje. Our Lady gives us Her great love. This is, once again, the meaning and the reason for the apparitions:

"...this long time that I am with you is a sign that I love you immeasurably, and what I desire of each individual is to become holy..." (October 9, 1986)

But satan wants to stop us on the way of holiness:

"...satan is strong....Pray, and that way he will neither be able to injure you nor block you on the way of holiness..." (September 25, 1987)

Let us pray that no one would be afraid of holiness; this is not something out of our reach. This is a gift that will be given to us if we humbly live the messages. All we have to think about is how to live the messages. Then the Holy Spirit will do the work in us; we are not going to be saints through our own willpower. Holiness is a gift from Heaven, just as the apparitions are a gift from Heaven.

CHAPTER 10

CONCLUSION

Each message added to the other during the years create a mosaic. If we casually read one message taken out of the context of all the rest of the messages, the message on its own may seem simplistic and dull. Similarly, a colored stone removed from a mosaic would seem to have no value by itself; but if we see the whole picture, we have a rich and beautiful picture. We have to see the whole picture:

"...by means of the messages I wish to make a very beautiful mosaic in your heart..." (November 25, 1989)

The whole pedagogy (way or technique of teaching) of Our Lady is to walk with us step by step, message by message, to reeducate us to be Christians. Today, a lot of people think it's not important to be a Christian. Other people want to live a traditional and superficial form of Christianity which is actually only a part of a certain social order with which you have to conform. This form of religion is something that makes Our Lady cry; therefore, again, She wants to show us through the messages the real face of Christianity. This is a long process because men went very far away from the truth, both in the Church and outside the Church. We have to accept being totally reeducated, little by little, by the Mother of God. The problem of mankind is not so much that people have bad intentions, we have plenty of good-hearted people around. The only thing is that they don't see the truth; they are in darkness, and many are just blind. They don't realize that they put themselves in the hands of satan because they do not know how to tell right from wrong. Many become the image of satan, as we realize when we watch

TV these days with all the horror shows, the "heavy metal-music," and the spectacle of crime and death constantly present in our living rooms through the news media. Even children's movies and shows are touched by some satanic influences. We can understand all that through the messages:

"...darkness reigns over the whole world..." (July 30, 1987)

"...this unfaithful world walking in darkness..." (June 5, 1986)

"...you are ready to commit sin, and to put yourselves in the hands of satan without reflecting..." (May 25, 1987)

"...do not allow satan to get control of your hearts, so you would be an image of satan and not of me..." (January 30, 1986)

If we want a general description of the beautiful mosaic of the messages, what would we have?

We know about five main messages:

PRAYER **"...prayer is the only way to save the human race."** (July 30, 1987)

FASTING **"...Repeated prayers and fasting reduce punishments from God..."** (November 6, 1982)

BIBLE READING **"You have forgotten the Bible,"** said Our Lady, crying.

CONFESSION **"...Monthly Confession will be a remedy for the Church in the West..."** (August 6, 1982)

THE EUCHARIST **"The Mass is the most important and the most holy moment in your lives."**

We also know that Our Lady wants each one of us to be a witness of Her apparitions to save mankind:

> **"...God has chosen each one of you, in order to use you in a great plan for the salvation of mankind..."** (January 25, 1987)

We know that we should seek holiness to fulfill this plan of salvation. Medjugorje is a call to holiness. Our Lady's main objective in Medjugorje is to lead us to holiness:

> **"...Dear children, you know that for your sake I have remained a long time so I might teach you how to make progress on the way of holiness..."** (January 1, 1987)

By living the messages, we are made holy, little by little:

> **"...if you live the messages, you are living the seed of holiness..."** (October 10, 1985)

Finally, we should know that we should do everything with love, and always place love in the first place:

> **"...without love you will achieve nothing..."** (December 13, 1984)

This is an approach to the whole picture, the **"...very beautiful mosaic..."** (November 25, 1989) of the messages of Our Lady, Queen of Peace, in Medjugorje.

PART IV

THE MESSAGES
AND
RESPONSES
OF
OUR LADY

CHAPTER 1

THE EARLY MESSAGES
OF OUR LADY
AND VARIOUS OTHER MESSAGES

(June 24, 1981 to March 18, 2009)

"I AM THE QUEEN OF PEACE." (The Transfiguration, August 6, 1981)

Since June, 1981, Our Lady's salutation to the visionaries is always, **"Praised be Jesus."** The visionaries' answer to this is, **"Forever Jesus and Mary."** Mary's parting words are always, **"Go in Peace,"** or **"Go in the Peace of God."** Sometimes Our Lady adds, **"My dear children,"** to the salutation or the parting words.

June 24, 1981

The first apparition takes place in the late afternoon. It is a silent and distant white silhouette on the summit of Podbrdo which later would be called Hill of Apparition or Apparition Mountain. Ivanka Ivankovic and Mirjana Dragicevic saw Our Lady when She first appeared, around 5:00 p.m. A little later, around 6:40 p.m., they returned, along with Vicka Ivankovic, Ivan Dragicevic, Ivan Ivankovic, and Milka Pavlovic, the little sister of Marija, and all saw Our Lady.

June 25, 1981

This is the first day the six visionaries, Ivanka Ivankovic, Mirjana Dragicevic, Vicka Ivankovic, Marija Pavlovic, Ivan Dragicevic, and Jakov Colo saw Our Lady, or the Gospa, on the hill. These six have become known as and remain "the visionaries." Our Lady said:

"Praised be Jesus!"

Ivanka asked about her mother who had died two months earlier.

"She is happy. She is with me." (Other version: **"She is your angel in Heaven."**)

The visionaries asked if Our Lady would return the next day. Our Lady responded with a nod of the head. Mirjana asked if Our Lady would give them a sign so that others would believe them. Mirjana believed she had received a sign when the Gospa smiled. Also, Mirjana noticed that her watch had changed time during the apparition. The time went backwards. [Endnote 2, see page 574]

"Good-bye, my angels. Go in the peace of God."

June 26, 1981

A crowd of nearly three thousand people were drawn to Apparition Mountain by the luminary signs coming from the hill. Holy water is sprinkled on Our Lady by Vicka. She asks Our Lady to stay if She is indeed the Virgin Mary. Our Lady smiles in response. Ivanka then asked why Our Lady is here and what does She want from the people. Our Lady responded:

"I have come because there are many true believers here. I wish to be with you to convert and to reconcile the whole world."

Ivanka asked if her mother has any message for her.

"Obey your grandmother and help her because she is old."

Mirjana wanted to know about her grandfather who had recently died.

"He is well."

The visionaries requested a sign for those who don't see Our Lady to prove that the apparition was really the Gospa.

"Blessed are those who have not seen and who believe."

Mirjana asked: *"Who are you?"*

"I am the Blessed Virgin Mary."

More questions from the visionaries: *"Why are you appearing to us? We are no better than others."*

"I do not necessarily choose the best."

"Will you come back?"

"Yes, to the same place as yesterday."

Marija reports that they asked Our Lady, *"Is there life on other planets?*

"That is not for you to know now."

While Marija goes down the mountain, she is mysteriously pushed to the side of the trail by an unseen force. She sees the Virgin again. Our Lady is crying and there is a bare wooden cross behind Her.

"Peace, Peace, Peace! Be reconciled! Only Peace. Make your peace with God and among yourselves. For that,

it is necessary to believe, to pray, to fast, and to go to Confession."

June 27, 1981

"Praised be Jesus!"

Jakov wanted to know what the Virgin expected of the Franciscans in Medjugorje.

"Have them persevere in the faith and protect the faith of the people."

Mirjana and Jakov were concerned because the people were treating them like liars. They asked Our Lady to leave a sign for the people.

"My angels, do not be afraid of injustices. They have always existed."

The visionaries asked: *"How must we pray?"*

"Continue to recite The Lord's Prayer, the Hail Mary, and the Glory Be seven times, but also add the Creed. Good-bye, my angels. Go in the peace of God."

Our Lady said to Ivan:

"Be in peace and take courage."

June 28, 1981

The visionaries want to know what the Gospa wishes.

"That people believe and persevere in the faith."

Vicka asked: *"What do you expect from the priests?"*

"That they remain strong in the faith and that they help you."

They asked Our Lady why She does not appear to everyone in the church.

"Blessed are they who believe without having seen."

They wanted to know if She would return.

"Yes, to the same place."

The visionaries ask if She prefers prayer or singing.

"Both, prayer and singing."

Vicka asked what Our Lady wished from the crowd gathered on the hill. According to the visionaries, Our Lady responded with a smile and a loving glance. At this point, the Gospa disappeared. The visionaries prayed, hoping She would return because She had not told them good-bye. It was during the song, *"You Are All Beautiful,"* that She returned.

Three times Vicka asked, *"Dear Gospa* (Croatian word for Our Lady), *what do you expect of these people?"*

"That those who do not see believe as those who see."

Once again the visionaries asked for a sign so that the people would not think of them as liars. They only received a smile from Our Lady as She told them good-bye and disappeared.

"Go in the peace of God."

June 29, 1981

The visionaries wanted to know if the Gospa was happy to see so many people present.

"More than happy."

They ask, *"How long will You stay?"*

"As long as you will want me to, my angels."

They questioned Our Lady about Her expectations about those who came despite the heat and the brambles.

"There is only one God, one faith. Let the people believe firmly and do not fear anything."

"What do you expect of us?" the visionaries inquired.

"That you have a solid faith and that you maintain confidence."

The visionaries wanted to know if they would be strong enough to endure persecutions because of the apparitions. Pressures and persecutions were severe.

"You will be able to, my angels. Do not fear. You will be able to endure everything. You must believe and have confidence in me."

At this point, Doctor Darinka Glamuzina, working for the Government, requests Vicka to ask a question for her: *"May I touch Our Lady?"*

"There have always been Judases who don't believe, but she can approach."

Vicka shows Doctor Glamuzina where to extend her hand and Doctor Glamuzina touches the Gospa. The doctor withdrew, humbled, with the fear of God.

The parents of a handicapped child ask the visionaries to intercede on behalf of the child. They ask the Virgin to cure the child so that people will believe them.

"Have them believe strongly in his cure. Go in the peace of God."

The child was cured later that same evening.

Between June 30, 1981 and December 31, 1981, the visionaries were being tracked down by the police. They had to find a discreet place to wait for the Virgin to appear.

June 30, 1981

Two social workers took the visionaries on a ride so they would miss the apparition on the hill. The apparition took place at Cerno, on the road between Ljbuski and Medjugorje. Mirjana asked Our Lady if She was angry because they were not on the hill. Our Lady responded:

"That doesn't matter."

Mirjana then asked if Our Lady would be angry if they did not return to the hill, but waited for the apparitions at the church. Somehow Our Lady seemed undecided (according to Mirjana), but then She agreed to appear in the church and added:

"Always at the same time. Go in the peace of God."

Mirjana, who had been reading an account of the apparitions at Lourdes, thought she understood that the Virgin would return for another three days, until Friday, as She had in Lourdes. However, this was only Mirjana's interpretation.

June, 1981

"I invite you. I need you. I chose you. You are important."

July 1, 1981

Again the visionaries ask the Gospa for a sign. Our Lady appeared to nod Her head.

"Good-bye, my dear angels."

July 21, 1981

Our Lady arrived:

"Praised be Jesus."

The visionaries asked again for a sign and the Gospa said yes. They asked how long She would continue to visit them.

"My sweet angels, even if I were to leave the sign, many people will not believe. Many people will only come here and bow down, but people must be converted and do penance."

The visionaries asked the Virgin about the sick and She said they would find the cure in strong faith. The Gospa then departed:

"Go in the peace of God."

July 22, 1981

"Praised be Jesus Christ. A good many people have been converted and among them some had not gone to Confession in 45 years, and now they are going to Confession. Go in the peace of God."

July 23, 1981

"Praised be Jesus Christ."

July 24, 1981

Again the visionaries asked questions concerning the sick.

"Without faith, nothing is possible. All those who will believe firmly will be cured."

July 25, 1981

After more questions about the sick, Our Lady answered:

"God, help us all!"

July 27, 1981

The visionaries ask the Virgin to bless some objects.

"In the name of the Father, and of the Son, and of the Holy Spirit."

Once again the visionaries asked about the sign.

"Wait, it will be soon."

Vicka asked to see Our Lady again this evening and She said:

"I will appear to you again at 11:15 p.m. Go in the peace of God."

As Our Lady was ascending back to Heaven, the visionaries saw the heart and the cross. Our Lady said:

"My angels, I send you my Son, Jesus, Who was tortured for His faith, and yet He endured everything. You also, my angels, will endure everything."

They see Jesus' head, brown eyes, beard, and long hair to prepare them for the suffering and persecution they were having to endure.

The visionaries are praised for their beautiful singing and praying.

"It is beautiful to listen to you. Continue in this manner. Don't be afraid for Jozo." [He was threatened by the police.]

July 29, 1981

The Virgin appeared in Vicka's room. They asked about a sick person.

"Praised be Jesus! She will be cured. She must believe firmly."

The visionaries asked to embrace Our Lady.

"Yes. Go in the peace of God."

July, 1981

"Carry out well your responsibilities and what the Church asks you to do."

Early August, 1981

The visionaries asked what Our Lady wanted of them later on in life.

"It would be good if you become priests and religious, but only if you, yourselves, would want it. It is up to you to decide."

August 2, 1981

From Marija's room, Our Lady asks her and 40 others:

"All of you together go to the meadow at Gumno. A great struggle is about to unfold. A struggle between my Son and satan. Human souls are at stake."

At the Gumno, Our Lady said:

"Everyone here may touch me."

When those in sin made Our Lady's dress become black where they touched her, the visionaries became upset and said, *"Go to Confession."* Marinko, Marija's neighbor, then repeated this, inviting all to go to Confession. Marija could see who those were in sin, but when the apparition ended, she mysteriously could not recall who they were, yet she knew clearly during the apparition.

August 6, 1981 (THE TRANSFIGURATION)

"I am the Queen of Peace."

August 7, 1981

Our Lady asked the young people to come to Cross Mountain at 2:00 a.m. and to pray that many people would do:

"That one do penance for sins.

August 8, 1981

"Do penance! Strengthen your faith through prayer and the sacraments."

August 17, 1981

"Do not be afraid. I wish that you would be filled with joy and that the joy could be seen on your face. I will protect Father Jozo." [The pastor, Fr. Jozo, was put in jail.]

August 22, 1981

"Father Jozo has nothing to fear. All troubles will pass."

August 23, 1981

"Praised be Jesus! I have been with Ivan until now. Pray, my angels, for these people. My children, I give you strength. I will always give it to you. When you need me, call me."

August 25, 1981

Some of the people present asked to touch the Virgin.

"It is not necessary to touch me. Many are those who do not feel anything when they touch me. On the matter of the sign, you do not have to become impatient for the day will come."

Our Lady also said and warned there was a spy among those gathered.

August 26, 1981

Because the visionaries see Our Lady, many have been seeking their advice. Our Lady responds:

"Praised be Jesus. Do not give advice to anyone. I know what you feel and that will pass, also."

August 27, 1981

On this day the visionaries again asked something regarding the sign.

"Very soon, I promise you. Be strong and courageous."

August 28, 1981

The visionaries have been waiting for the Virgin in Father Jozo's room. She does not come. This is the second time this has happened. The visionaries go to church to pray and Our Lady appears to them there.

"I was with Father Jozo. That is why I did not come. Do not trouble yourselves if I do not come. It suffices then to pray."

Today Ivan entered the seminary at Visoko. Our Lady told him:

"You are very tired. Rest, so that you can find strength. Go in the peace of God. Good-bye."

August 29, 1981

Jakov asks Our Lady several questions. *"Are you also appearing to Ivan in the seminary?"*

"Yes, just like for you."

"Is Ivan Ivankovic [who is in prison] *well?"*

**"He is well. He is enduring everything. All will pass.
Father Jozo sends you greetings."**

Ivan at the Seminary wants to know about the village.

"My angels perform their penance well."

Ivan asked Our Lady whether She was going to help him and his
friends in school.

"God's help manifests itself everywhere."

**"Go in the peace of God with the blessing of Jesus and
mine. Good-bye."**

Ivanka asks if a sign will be left soon.

"Again, a little patience."

August 30, 1981

Our Lady arrived and Vicka asks for confirmation about rumors
that Father Jozo's cell doors unlock themselves.

"Praised be Jesus! It is true, but no one believes it."

Ivanka asked about Mirjana.

**"Mirjana is sad because she is all alone. I will show her to
you."**

And the visionaries saw Mirjana crying.

Regarding young people who betray the Faith:

"Yes, there are many."

Regarding a woman who wants to leave her husband because he is cruel to her:

"Let her remain close to him and accept her suffering. Jesus, Himself, also suffered."

Regarding a sick young boy:

"He is suffering from a very grave illness. Let his parents firmly believe, do penance, then the little boy will be cured.'

Jakov asks about the sign.

"Again, a little patience."

Ivan wants to know how he will do in seminary.

"Be without fear. I am close to you everywhere and at all times."

Ivan asks if the people in his village are pious.

"Your village has become the most fervent parish in Hercegovina. A large number of people distinguish themselves by their piety and their faith."

End of August, 1981

The visionaries asked which is the best form of fasting.

"A fast on bread and water."

"I am the Queen of Peace."

September 1, 1981

The visionaries ask if there will be a Mass on Mt. Krizevac.

"Yes, my angels."

Jakov asks if a trap is being set around the church.

"There's nothing at all. Have the people pray and remain in church as long as possible."

Ivan prayed with Our Lady so that Jesus would help him in his vocation. Our Lady said:

"Go in the peace of God. Do not be afraid. I am close to you and I watch over you."

September 2, 1981

Vicka asked about a young person who hanged himself.

"satan took hold of him. This young man should not have done that. The devil tries to reign over the people. He takes everything into his hands, but the force of God is more powerful, and God will conquer."

Ivan wants to know how his friends and he will do in the seminary.

"You are, and you will always be my children. You have followed the path of Jesus. No one will stop you from propagating the faith in Jesus. One must believe strongly."

September 3, 1981

Jakov asked when the sign would be announced.

"Again, a little patience."

September 4, 1981

Ivanka and Marija are concerned that they will not have enough time to pray because they are only home on Saturdays and Sundays and far away at school during the week. (Marija stays in Mostar with relatives.)

"It is enough for you to pray. Come here on Saturdays and Sundays. I will appear to all of you."

Ivan asks when Our Lady will leave the sign.

"The sign will be given at the end of the apparitions."

Ivan inquires when that will be.

"You are impatient, my angels. Go in the peace of God."

September 5, 1981

"Praised be Jesus and Mary. Go in the peace of God, my angel. May the blessing of God accompany you. Amen. Good-bye*."

* Word by word: "Go with God" or "With God" as in the French "Adieu."

September 6, 1981

"Pray especially on Sunday, so that the great sign, the gift of God may come. Pray with fervor and a constancy so that God, may have mercy on His great children. Go in peace,

**my angel. May the blessing of God accompany you. Amen.
Good-bye."**

September 7, 1981

**"Be converted all of you who are still there. The sign will
come when you will be converted."**

September 8, 1981 (Feast of the Nativity of the Virgin)

**"I ask you only to pray with fervor. Prayer must become a
part of your daily life to permit the true faith to take root."**

Jakov wishes Our Lady a happy birthday.

**"For me it is a beautiful day. With respect to you, persevere
in the faith and in prayer. Do not be afraid. Remain in joy.
It is my desire. Let joy appear on your faces. I will continue
to protect Father Jozo."**

September 10, 1981

Ivan reports that after praying beautiful prayers with a feeling
from the heart filled with love and joy Our Lady says:

"Go in the peace of God, my angel. Amen. Good-bye."

September 13, 1981

The Virgin came near the image of Jesus after some seminary
students came from Confession.

**"This is your Father*, my angel. Go in the peace of God,
my angels."**

* Many known mystics referred, of course, to Jesus as our
Brother but in some rare occasions also as a Father. This is
theologically right, if unusual.

September 14, 1981

Our Lady told Vicka:

> **"Stay here so that Jakov will not be alone. Persevere, both of you, with patience. You will be rewarded."**

September 15, 1981

> **"If the people are not converted very soon, bad things will happen to them."**

September 16, 1981

> **"The militia will not stay here a long time. I will leave the sign. Be patient still. Don't pray for yourselves. You have been rewarded. Pray for others."**

September 17, 1981

Concerning someone ill.

> **"He will die very soon."**

To the visionaries:

> **"Persevere and you will be rewarded."**

September 20, 1981

To Vicka and Jakov:

> **"Do not be lax in your prayers. I ask both of you to fast for a week on bread and water."**

September 30, 1981

To Vicka and Jakov:

> **"Don't ask useless questions dictated by curiosity.   The most important thing is to pray, my angels."**

October 1, 1981

"Are all religions good?"

> **"Members of all faiths are equal before God.   God rules over each faith just like a sovereign over his kingdom.   In the world, all religions are not the same because all people have not complied with the Commandments of God.   They reject and disparage them."**

"Are all Churches the same?"

> **"In some, the strength of prayer to God is greater, in others, smaller.   That depends on the priests who motivate others to pray.   It depends also on the power which they have."**

"Why do You appear to us so often and to others who do not follow God's path?"(*) (*This must be about other apparitions in Hercegovina.)

> **"I appear to you often and in every place.   To others, I appear from time to time and briefly.   They do not yet follow the way of God completely.   They are not aware of the gift which He has made them.   That, no one deserves.   With time, they also will come to follow the right way."**

October 6, 1981

> **"The evening Mass must be kept permanently.   The Mass of the sick must be celebrated on a specific day, at a time which**

**is most convenient. Father Tomislav must begin with the
prayer group. It is very necessary. Have Father Tomislav
pray with fervor."**

October 7, 1981

In answer to the question whether there are other intermediaries, besides Jesus, between God and man:

**"There is only one mediator between God and man, and it
is Jesus Christ."**

In answer to Father Tomislav regarding founding a community
like that of Saint Francis of Assisi:

**"God has chosen Saint Francis as His elected one. It would
be good to imitate his life. In the meantime, we must realize
what God orders us to do."**

October 8, 1981

Our Lady has scolded Marija about missing Mass and staying
with her friends.

**"You would have done better to attend Mass rather than to
satisfy human curiosity."**

October 10, 1981

**"It is up to you to pray and to persevere. I have made
promises to you; also be without anxiety. Faith will not
know how to be alive without prayer. Pray more."**

October 11, 1981

The visionaries ask about an old man who disappeared.

"Tomo Lovic is dead."

October 12, 1981

Where is Paradise and the Kingdom of God?

"In Heaven."

Our Lady is asked if She is the Mother of God and if She went to Heaven before or after Her death.

"I am the Mother of God and the Queen of Peace. I went to Heaven before death."

When will the sign be left?

"I will not yet leave the sign. I shall continue to appear. Father Jozo sends you greetings. He is experiencing difficulties, but he will resist, because he knows why he is suffering."

October 17, 1981

On the sign:

"It is mine to realize the promise. With respect to the faithful, have them pray and believe firmly."

October 19, 1981

"Pray for Father Jozo and fast tomorrow on bread and water. Then you will fast for a whole week on bread and water. Pray, my angels. Now I will show you Father Jozo."

She shows them a vision of Father Jozo in prison and tells them not to fear for him because everything will work out fine.

On Marinko, the man who protected the visionaries:

"There are a few similar faithful. He's made a sufficient number of sacrifices for Jozo. He underwent many torments and sufferings."

To Marinko personally:

"Continue, and do not let anyone take the faith away from you."

October 20, 1981

Vicka asked Our Lady to intercede for Father Jozo during his trial and even to strike someone to stop the trial. Our Lady sings *"Jesus Christ, in Your Name"* [sung to the tune of *"The Battle Hymn of the Republic"*] with the visionaries. After the song was completed, Our Lady said:

"Go in the peace of God."

October 21, 1981

Because Vicka is concerned about Fr. Jozo's sentencing and knows that Our Lady is not motivated by vengeance, she begs Her to intercede that the people involved be reasonable and impartial.

"Jozo looks well and he greets you warmly. Do not fear for Jozo. He is a saint. I have already told you. Sentence will not be pronounced this evening. Do not be afraid, he will not be condemned to a severe punishment. Pray only, because Jozo asks from you prayer and perseverance. Do not be afraid because I am with you."

October 22, 1981

"Jozo has been sentenced. Let us go to church to pray."

The visionaries tell Our Lady they are saddened because of
Father Jozo.

"You should rejoice!"

They ask if the whiteness of the cross is a supernatural phenomenon.

"Yes, I confirm it."

Many saw the cross transform itself into a light and then into a
silhouette of Our Lady.

**"All of these signs are designed to strengthen your faith
until I leave you the visible and permanent sign."**

October 25, 1981

The visionaries asked Our Lady about the great light three girls
saw on their way home from Mass. Within the light, they saw
fifteen figures.

**"It was a supernatural phenomenon. I was among the
saints."**

October 26, 1981

**"Praised be Jesus. You are not to ask me any more ques-
tions on the subject of the sign. Do not be afraid, it will
surely appear. I carry out my promises. As far as you are
concerned, pray, persevere in prayer."**

October 28, 1981

The visionaries ask if the Gospa appeared at Krizevac the day before for thirty minutes.

"Yes, didn't you see me?"

Regarding the fire that hundreds of people saw that burned but did not consume anything:

"The fire, seen by the faithful, was of a supernatural character. It is one of the signs, a forerunner of the great sign."

October 29, 1981

"You, my angels, be on your guard. There is enough mendacious news which people are spreading. Of course, I will show you my mercy. Be a little patient. Pray!"

October 30, 1981

"Praised be Jesus!"

Jakov and Vicka questioned Our Lady about a sealed envelope which an official showed them wishing to trick them.

"Do not respond anything. It is a bad trick which they are playing on you. They have already given so much false news. Do not believe them. Continue to pray and to suffer! I will make the power of love appear."

The visionaries asked Our Lady when should Christmas Mass be celebrated.

"Have them celebrate it at midnight. Pray! Go in the peace of God!"

To Ivanka:

"Pray more. The others are praying and suffering more than you."

To the visionaries:

"Tell the young people not to allow themselves to be distracted from the true way. Let them remain faithful to their religion."

October 31, 1981

From Vicka's diary we learn that Mirjana has had daily apparitions in Sarajevo where she is a student at a professional school.

Our Lady counsels Mirjana as a wise mother would, telling her two times who to trust, who to distrust, and how to respond to those who rebuke her and attack God.

Our Lady knows and advised Mirjana to avoid a friend who wants to get her involved with drugs. Our Lady suggested that she answer questions when that would be helpful and to remain quiet when that would be more beneficial. Our Lady shared Her joy over the five visionaries being together and tells them that Father Jozo would not be in prison more than four years.

Regarding Danny Ljolje, Our Lady said:

"There is a lot of deception and erroneous information."

After showing the visionaries a part of paradise and telling them not to be afraid, Our Lady said:

"All those who are faithful to God will have that."

October, 1981

Concerning the conflict between the Franciscans and the Bishop of Mostar:

"It is going to find a solution. We must have patience and pray."

Regarding Poland:

"There will be great conflicts, but in the end, the just will take over."

Regarding Russia:

"The Russian people will be the people who will glorify God the most. Regarding the West: the West has made civilization progress, but without God, as if they were their own creators."

November 1, 1981

"Be persevering! Pray! Many people are beginning to convert."

November 2, 1981

The visionaries questioned the Gospa about Her reasons for showing them paradise some days earlier.

"I did it so that you could see the happiness which awaits those who love God."

Jesus then appears to them with injuries covering His body and wearing a crown of thorns.

"Do not be afraid. It is my Son. See how He has been

martyred. In spite of all, He was joyful and He endured all with patience."

Then Jesus says:

"Look at me. How I have been injured and martyred! In spite of all, I have gained the victory. You also, my angels, be persevering in your faith and pray so that you may overcome."

November 3, 1981

The song, *"Come, Come to Us Lord,"* was begun by Our Lady and the visionaries joined in with Her.

"I am often at Krizevac, at the foot of the cross, to pray there. Now I pray to my Son to forgive the world its sins. The world has begun to convert."

November 6, 1981

During this apparition, Our Lady disappears and the visionaries see a terrifying, horrendous vision of Hell. Then Our Lady reappears and says:

"Do not be afraid! I have shown you hell so that you may know the state of those who are there."

November 8, 1981

Our Lady appears kissing and lovingly embracing a picture of John Paul II.

"He is your father, the spiritual father of all. It is necessary to pray for him."

One account tells of Our Lady picking up the picture in the room.

The visionaries have a vision of Father Jozo in prison.

"Have you seen how our Father Jozo struggles for God?"

November 9, 1981

The militia passes by the room where Our Lady was about to appear.

"Do not be afraid of the militia. Do not provoke anybody. Be polite with everybody."

November 10, 1981

"Do not give in. Keep your faith. I will accompany you at every step."

November 13, 1981

"Praised be Jesus!"

Our Lady showed the visionaries a beautiful landscape with the Baby Jesus walking there. The visionaries were not able to recognize Him. Emphasizing the song She sang during the November 3, 1981 apparition.

"It is Jesus. On my arrival and when I depart, always sing the song, 'Come, Come to us O Lord.'"

November 15, 1981

This apparition was to take place in Fr. Jozo's room but Our Lady appeared later in the Church and said someone had placed (hidden) listening devices in the room. She relates:

"The world is on the point of receiving great favors from me and my Son. May the world keep a strong confidence."

November 16, 1981

"The devil is trying to conquer us. Do not permit him. Keep the faith, fast, and pray. I will be with you at every step."

Her words to Vicka and Jakov:

"Persevere with confidence in prayer and in faith."

November 22, 1981

The Gospa explains the cross, the heart, and the sun to the visionaries.

"These are the signs of salvation: The cross is a sign of mercy, just like the heart. The sun is the source of light, which enlightens us."

Again a shining silhouette takes the place of the cross on Krizevac. The visionaries asked the Blessed Virgin if it was She.

"Why do you ask me, my angels? Have you not seen me? The world must find salvation while there is time. Let it pray with fervor. May it have the spirit of faith."

November 23, 1981

Our Lady was indescribable and beautiful light radiated, flowed, shined, and sparkled around Her.

"The people have begun to convert. Keep a solid faith. I need your prayers."

November 26, 1981

The visionaries asked the Gospa questions about the sick.

"Have strong faith, pray, and fast and they will be cured. Be confident and rest in joy. Go in the peace of God. Be patient and pray for the cure. Good-bye, my dear angels."

November 28, 1981

All but Ivan were present. The visionary, Vicka, relates, *"We all felt a profound peace about and within us. Our Lady looked at us with a beautiful sweetness."*

"Ah, it is so beautiful to see all of you together! Go in the peace of God, my angels. Good-bye."

November 29, 1981

"It is necessary for the world to be saved while there is still time, for it to pray strongly, and for it to have the spirit of faith."

November, 1981

Vicka warns that this message is not just for the visionaries but for all.

"The devil tries to impose his power on you, but you must remain strong and persevere in your faith. You must pray and fast. I will always be close to you."

December 2, 1981

The visionaries asked about a young man who had suddenly had a memory loss and could no longer learn anything.

"It is necessary to hospitalize him."

The visionaries asked more questions.

"It is not necessary to ask questions on every subject."

December 3, 1981

"Pray and persevere through prayer."

December 6, 1981

**"Be strong and persevering. My dear angels, go in the
peace of God."**

December 7, 1981

Our Lady looked at the crowds of people.

**"The people are converting. It is true, but not yet all. Pray
and persist in prayers."**

After an apparition at Jakov's home, the letters "MIR
LJUDIMA" (Peace to the people) were on the wall in gold.

December 8, 1981 (Feast of the Immaculate Conception)

Our Lady answers the questions the visionaries have about their
futures.

**"It would be good if all of you become priests and religious,
but only if you desire it. You are free. It is up to you to
choose. If you are experiencing difficulties or if you need
something, come to me. If you do not have the strength to
fast on bread and water, you can give up a number of things.
It would be a good thing to give up television, because after**

seeing some programs, you are distracted and unable to pray. You can give up alcohol, cigarettes, and other pleasures. You yourselves know what you have to do."

Our Lady then profoundly kneels down, serious with Her hands extended. She prays to Jesus:

"My beloved Son, I beseech you to be willing to forgive the world its great sin through which it offends you."

December 9, 1981

While we were praying, Our Lady intervened:

"Oh, My Son Jesus, forgive these sins; there are so many of them!"

We stopped and became silent.

"Continue to pray, because prayer is the salvation of the people."

December 11, 1981

Vicka asked the Gospa to look after her parents in Germany.

"I promise to protect them. Everything will go well."

December 12, 1981

Our Lady told the visionaries She was happy because they would all be together during vacation.

"Very soon you will all be united. You will be able to have a beautiful time together."

December 16, 1981

"Kneel down, my children, and pray."

December 18, 1981

Our Lady sings *"Jesus Christ In Your Name"* and says:

"Come on, sing more joyfully. Why are you so pensive?"

She then began the song, *"The Queen of the Holy Rosary,"* before leaving.

December 21, 1981

"Be on your guard, my children. Prepare yourselves for difficult days. All kinds of people will come here."

December 24, 1981

"Celebrate the days which are coming. Rejoice with my Son! Love your neighbor. May harmony reign among you."

December 25, 1981 (CHRISTMAS)

The visionaries see Baby Jesus.

"Love one another, my children. You are brothers and sisters. Don't argue among yourselves. Give glory to God, glorify Him and sing, my angels."

December 30, 1981

Our Lady sings *"The Queen of the Holy Rosary."*

December 31, 1981

Ivan asked the Gospa how to help doubting priests understand the apparitions.

"It is necessary to tell them that from the very beginning I have been conveying the message of God to the world. It is a great pity not to believe in it. Faith is a vital element, but one cannot compel a person to believe. Faith is the foundation from which everything flows."

Ivan asks Our Lady if it is really She appearing at the foot of the cross.

"Yes, it is true. Almost everyday I am at the foot of the cross. My Son carried the cross. He has suffered on the cross, and by it, He saved the world. Everyday I pray to my Son to forgive the sins of the world."

1981

Vicka says that at the very beginning Our Lady told us:

"You may leave, but let little Jakov stay with me."

Vicka then adds that Our Lady thinks that Jakov is a precious boy.

January, 1982 - April 11, 1985

THE APPARITION CHAPEL

In January, the visionaries were moved to a side room to the right of the altar of St. James Church. This room was to become famous and considered by many as sacred ground. At one time, it was possible to participate in Mass in the "Chapel". It is no

longer available to have Mass in the "Chapel" now. Thousands
of apparitions took place in the "Chapel" and one could say Our
Lady dwelt there.

January 11, 1982

**"I invite you very specially to participate at Mass. Wait for
me at church, that is the agreeable place."**

January 14, 1982

Today, toward the end of the apparition, two of the visionaries
were reprimanded by Our Lady. The other visionaries could
not hear this correction for their behavior but Our Lady's
expression gave them an indication what it was about. Those
reprimanded later said that Our Lady was kind and respectful
to them.

January 18, 1982

Concerning a sick person with heart problems:

"There is little hope for her. I will pray for her."

January 20, 1982

The visionaries want to know if they should meet with children
from Izbicno who are also visionaries. They tell the Blessed
Virgin that the Izbicno children said She told them about this
meeting.

"It is not necessary for you to meet them."

The officials want to transfer Father Tomislav.

"If it is in God's design that he (Father Tomislav) **depart**

as has been the case with Father Jozo, have him abandon himself to the will of God. He must think very much and you must pray for him."

January 21, 1982

Again the visionaries asked about the sign.

"The sign will appear at the desired time."

Our Lady is also asked why apparitions occur at different places in Hercegovina.

"My children, don't you see that the faith begins to extinguish itself and that it is necessary to awaken the faith among men?"

The visionaries want to know what to do to stop quarrels among priests.

"Fast and pray!"

January 22, 1982

Concerning apparitions at Izbicno.

"They are coming from God."

Izbicno is 60 kilometers from Medjugorje. Eighteen people, mostly females, said they are having apparitions between 1982 and 1983.

February 2, 1982

Our Lady was asked when She would like the Feast of The Queen of Peace to be celebrated. She smiled and said:

"I would prefer that it take place June 25th. The faithful have come for the first time on that day, on the hill."

February 8, 1982

The visionaries asked about an emotionally sick person.

"He must pray. I will help him within the limitation of my power."

To some Slovenes who were praying during the apparition:

"Persevere in prayer."

February 9, 1982

"Pray for the sick. Believe firmly. I will come to help, according to that which is in my power. I will ask my Son, Jesus, to help them. The most important thing, in the meantime, is a strong faith. Numerous sick persons think that it is sufficient to come here in order to be quickly healed. Some of them do not even believe in God and even less in the apparitions, and then they ask for help from the Gospa!"

February 10, 1982

Jakov and Vicka ask Our Lady many questions and She answers them. They relate that Our Lady loves the Creed and prefers it to other prayers. They say they have never seen Her happier than during this prayer. Our Lady's message:

"Pray, pray! It is necessary to believe firmly, to go to Confession regularly, and likewise to receive Holy Communion. It is the only salvation."

February 11, 1982

"Pray my angels, persevere! Do not let the enemy take possession of you in anything. Be courageous. Go in the peace of God, my angels. Good-bye."

February 12, 1982

"Be more calm, more poised. Do not take sides with other children. Be agreeable, well mannered, pious!"

The visionaries relate that Our Lady prays with Her hands folded and when She speaks, She spreads them, Her palms turned upwards.

February 13, 1982

For seminarians attending the apparition:

"Through prayer, one obtains everything."

February 14, 1982

The visionaries are happy because four of them are together.

"Be together like brothers and sisters. Do not argue. satan exists! He seeks only to destroy. With regard to you, pray and persevere in prayer. No one will be able to do anything against you."

February 16, 1982

Vicka relates she has never seen Our Lady sad. Her countenance is always smiling, joyful, and serene. It attracts us and inspires us to be the same way.

"satan only says what he wants. He interferes in everything. You, my angels, be ready to endure everything. Here, many things will take place. Do not allow yourselves to be surprised by him."

February 19, 1982

Vicka's diary states that the visionaries ask Our Lady if they could pray the Hail Mary and She says yes. Our Lady smiled as they prayed but did not pray with them. Vicka writes that seeing Our Lady, Her beauty, is indescribable and she would do whatever She asks.

"Listen attentively at Holy Mass. Be well mannered. Do not chat during Holy Mass."

February 21, 1982

"Be together, do not argue, and do not be disorderly. My angels, I will make you attentive. I will guide you on a sure way."

February 23, 1982

The visionaries ask if someone is alive.

"Do not ask me any more questions! I know what there is in each sick person or what there is within my power to help him. I will pray to my Son to put out His mercy on each one."

February 25, 1982

"Be persevering and courageous. Do not fear anything. Pray and do not pay attention to others."

Concerning Father Jozo:

"Do not fear for him."

February 28, 1982

"Thank Tomislav very much for he is guiding you very well. Go in the peace of God, my angels!"

March 1, 1982

"All of you, be happy and may my blessing accompany you at each step."

In response to the Yugoslavian authorities' demand that the prayer meetings for the young people end:

"It is better to temporarily suspend prayer meetings and those of meditation because of the authorities. Take them up later, when it will be possible."

March 2, 1982

Smiling at two large pictures of the Pope brought by a woman from Osijek, Our Lady said:

"He is your father, my angels."

Our Lady began The Lord's Prayer, and on leaving said:

"Open the door well, follow the Mass well! Go in the peace of God, my angels! If you suffer for a just cause, blessings will be still more abundant for you."

March 4, 1982

Regarding a woman who had no children:

**"Let her believe firmly. God, who comes to help every-
one, will likewise help her. Be patient, my angels, do not
be afraid of anything. I am at your side and guard you. If
you have any problems, whatever it be, call me. I will come
immediately and help you in advising you on best resolving
the difficulty. Go in peace, my angels. Good-bye."**

March 7, 1982

Regarding Ivan at the Seminary at Visoko:

**"He prays well; he is obedient. He follows my instruc-
tions."**

March 8, 1982

Regarding a sixteen-year-old boy who had disappeared for a
week:

**"He left because of many troubles. He himself created
some of the problems."**

March 9, 1982

Regarding a young man from Hadromilje who disappeared
from his home:

**"He has serious problems. It is necessary to pray for him
very much, my angels. The people are beginning to be converted. Prayer has been taken up again in the homes where
people had no longer prayed."**

Beginning of April, 1982

Mirjana asked the Blessed Virgin when She would like to be
honored.

"I wish a feast for the Queen of Peace on the 25th of June, the anniversary of the first apparition."

April 11, 1982 (EASTER SUNDAY)

Concerning the formation of prayer groups:

"It is necessary, but not only here. Communities of prayer are necessary in all parishes."

April 21, 1982

To a question asked by Father Tomislav Vlasic, Our Lady answers:

"Be patient! Everything is developing according to God's plan. His promises will be realized. May one continue to pray, to do penance, and to be converted."

April 22, 1982

Concerning the luminous signs at the cross on Krizevac:

"They are signs of God and not of natural phenomena. 'S' and 'T' are signs of salvation."

"S" stands for salvation. "T" stands for the cross.

April 24, 1982

Concerning what needs to be done in order to have more cures:

"Pray! Pray and believe firmly. Say the prayers which have already been requested. (The Lord's Prayer, the Hail Mary, and the Glory Be seven times each, and the Creed.) **Do more penance."**

May 2, 1982

**"I have come to call the world to conversion for the last time.
Afterwards, I will not appear any more on this earth."**

May 6, 1982

Concerning putting the date and description of the sign in a
sealed envelope and putting it in the archives:

**"No! I have entrusted that only to you. You will unveil
it when I will tell you. Many persons will not believe you,
I know, and you will suffer very much for it. But you will
endure everything and you will finally be the happiest."**

May 13, 1982

Concerning the assassination attempt on the life of John Paul
II:

**"His enemies have wanted to kill him, but I protected
him."**

Spring, 1982

The Pastor at Izbicno has the visionaries ask questions concerning all of the signs in Hercegovina and Our Lady's appearing in
so many places:

**"It is God who gives them. My children, have you not
observed that faith began to extinguish itself? There are
many who do not come to church except through habit. It
is necessary to awaken the faith. It is a gift from God. If it
is necessary, I will appear in each home."**

To the visionaries regarding seeing the seers from Izbicno:

"Did I not tell you not to come together with those children? I am your Mother, you must obey me."

To Jakov, crying because he saw Vicka ill:

"The cross is necessary because of the sins of the world."

June 23, 1982

Responses from Our Lady regarding questions asked by Father Tomislav Vlasic. Vicka asked the Gospa the questions for Father Tomislav. He reported the answers in the parish Chronicle.

1. The most important thing is that you, the visionaries, remain united. Let peace be among you. Pay very close attention to that. Obey and do what the priests and your parents tell you. Go often to Holy Mass and receive Communion. Be very attentive these days. Some dishonest people will come to you, in numbers, in order to tempt you. Be careful of your statements. These days I am expecting of you a very special discipline. Do not move around anywhere, or often, and do not separate from one another.

2. A number of those who have been very enthusiastic will cool off. But you, persist and be proud of each of my words. Have the people pray very much. Have them pray more for salvation and only for salvation, because it is in prayer. And let the people be converted so long as it is possible. There are many sins, vexations, curse words, lies, and other bad things. Let them be converted, go to Confession, and receive Holy Communion.

3. Let them not print books on the apparitions before the anniversary has passed, because that could have some undesirable consequences.

4. You have asked me to keep good and faithful priests in this parish who will continue the work. Do not be afraid of anything.

This grace must be given to you. From priests, I do not demand anything other than prayer with perseverance and preaching. May they be patient and wait for the promise of God.

Concerning the number of natures of the Holy Spirit:

5. He has only one nature, the Divine nature.

Concerning these apparitions being the last ones on earth:

6. These apparitions are the last in the world.

June 24, 1982 or June 25, 1982 (date not certain)

> **"Thank the people in my name for the prayers, the sacrifices, and the** (acts of) **penance. Have them persevere in prayer, fasting, and conversion and have them wait with patience for the realization of my promise. Everything is unfolding according to God's plan."**

July 12, 1982

Concerning a third world war:

> **"The third world war will not take place."**

July 21, 1982

Concerning Purgatory:

> **"There are many souls in Purgatory. There are also persons who have been consecrated to God - some priests, some religious. Pray for their intentions, at least The Lord's Prayer, the Hail Mary, and the Glory Be seven times each, and the Creed. I recommend it to you. There is a large number of souls who have been in Purgatory for a long time because no one prays for them."**

Concerning fasting:

> **"The best fast is on bread and water. Through fasting and prayer, one can stop wars, one can suspend the laws of nature. Charity cannot replace fasting. Those who are not able to fast can sometime replace it with prayer, charity, and a Confession; but everyone, except the sick, must fast."**

July 24, 1982

> **"You go to Heaven in full conscience: that which you have now. At the moment of death, you are conscious of the separation of the body and soul. It is false to teach people that you are reborn many times and that you pass to different bodies. One is born only once. The body, drawn from the earth, decomposes after death. It never comes back to life again. Man receives a transfigured body."**

Regarding a question asked about being bad all one's life and asking forgiveness:

> **"Whoever has done very much evil during his life can go straight to Heaven if he confesses, is sorry for what he has done, and receives Communion at the end of his life."**

July 25, 1982

Concerning hell:

> **"Today many persons go to hell. God allows His children to suffer in hell due to the fact that they have committed grave, unpardonable sins. Those who are in hell no longer have a chance to know a better lot."**

Other answers from Our Lady state that people who commit grave sins live in hell while here on earth and continue this hell in eternity. They actually go to hell because they chose it in life and at the moment of death.

Concerning cures:

> **"For the cure of the sick, it is important to say the following prayers: the Creed, and seven times each, The Lord's Prayer, the Hail Mary, and the Glory Be, and to fast on bread and water. It is good to impose one's hands on the sick and to pray. It is good to anoint the sick with Holy Oil. All priests do not have the gift of healing. In order to receive this gift, the priest must pray with perseverance and believe firmly."**

August 6, 1982 (THE TRANSFIGURATION)

Concerning Confession:

> **"One must invite people to go to Confession each month, especially the first Saturday. Here, I have not spoken about it yet. I have invited people to frequent Confession. I will give you yet some concrete messages for our time. Be patient because the time has not yet come. Do what I have told you. They are numerous who do not observe it. Monthly Confession will be a remedy for the Church in the West. One must convey this message to the West."**

That night, after the apparition, two luminary signs in the form of rays of light were displayed on the Cross at Krizevac and on the Church. Ivan and a group of young people had been praying on the hill of Bijakovici. Before the sign appeared, Our Lady said:

> **"Now I am going to give you a sign in order to strengthen your faith."**

Many members of the prayer group saw this sign.

August 10, 1982

Our Lady told the visionaries that priests could give out written information about certain things.

August 11, 1982

The visionaries were scolded by Our Lady for their conduct during the evening Mass. No special message was given.

August 15, 1982

Vicka and Ivanka were given a new secret during the seven-minute apparition. The others could not hear the voice of Our Lady, but they understood that a secret had been given.

August 16, 1982

Our Lady corrected the speed and quality of the prayers of those in church as well as the visionaries.

During the apparition, Mirjana reports that she sees Heavenly Beings, such as Jesus, Mary, and angels, in three dimensions, as one sees another, and earthly people in two dimensions (as in a picture or photograph). She saw Father Jozo or Ivan Ivankovic, who have been imprisoned because of their faith, as if in a motion picture and two-dimensional.

August 18, 1982

Concerning the sick, Mirjana reports:

"Have them believe and pray; I cannot help him who does not pray and does not sacrifice. The sick, just like those who are in good health, must pray and fast for the sick. The more you believe firmly, the more you pray and fast for the same intention, the greater is the grace and the mercy of God."

Concerning a planned marriage between a Catholic and an
Orthodox:

**"In my eyes and in the sight of God, everything is equal.
But for you, it is not the same thing because you are divided.
If it is possible, it is better if she were not to marry this man
because she will suffer and her children also. She will be
able to live and follow only with difficulty, the way of her
faith."**

August 29, 1982

Concerning reports that the apparitions have divided the priests
in Hercegovina:

**"I have not desired your division. On the contrary, I desire
that you be united. Do not ignore the fact that I am the
Queen of Peace. If you desire practical advise: I am the
Mother who has come from the people; I cannot do anything without the help of God. I, too, must pray like you.
It is because of that, that I can only say to you: Pray, fast,
do penance, and help the weak. I am sorry if my preceding
answer was not agreeable to you. Perhaps you do not want
to understand it."**

August 31, 1982

**"I do not dispose all graces. I receive from God what I
obtain through prayer. God has placed His complete trust
in me. I particularly protect those who have been consecrated to me. The great sign has been granted. It will appear
independently of the conversion of the people."**

September 4, 1982

**"Jesus prefers that you address yourselves directly to Him
rather than through an intermediary. In the meantime, if**

you wish to give yourselves completely to God and if you wish that I be your protector, then confide to me all your intentions, your fasts, and your sacrifices so that I can dispose of them according to the will of God."

September 26, 1982

Concerning a religious from Rome:

"Have her strengthen the faith of those who have been entrusted to her."

Concerning Father Robert Faricy and Fr. Forrest:

"They are on the good path. Have them persist."

Concerning the Pope:

"Have him consider himself the father of all mankind and not only of Christians. Have him spread untiringly and with courage the message of peace and love among all mankind."

October 1, 1982

"I am happy because you have begun to prepare the monthly observance of the Sacrament of Reconciliation. That will be good for the whole world. Persevere in prayer. It is the true way which leads you toward my Son."

November 4, 1982

Concerning the vision of Andja, from Mostar, of 13 people coming from the East and on another occasion, six persons:

"It is about a true vision. They were some souls of her close family from Purgatory. It is necessary to pray for them."

November 6, 1982

Concerning the eighth secret, Mirjana is frightened and prays to
Our Lady for mercy on mankind:

**"I have prayed; the punishment has been softened. Repeated
prayers and fasting reduce punishments from God, but it is
not possible to avoid entirely the chastisement. Go on the
streets of the city, count those who glorify God and those
who offend Him. God can no longer endure that."**

November 8, 1982

Concerning the necessity of writing to the Bishop and priests
about asking the faithful to intensify their prayers or waiting for
other events:

"It is better to wait than to precipitate that."

November 15, 1982

Jakov asked Our Lady concerning Vicka's illness and the advis-
ability of her being admitted to a hospital in Zagreb. He asked
because Vicka would not ask, desiring to be left to the will of
God.

"It is necessary to send Vicka to Zagreb."

December 18, 1982

Concerning responding to the Bishop of Mostar about his article
concerning events in Medjugorje:

"Yes, respond!"

December 20, 1982

Concerning the same article, the visionaries wanted to know the necessity of giving objective information to the faithful in Hercegovina.

"No!"

Should the visionaries only pray with Our Lady and the pilgrims ask their questions only to the priests?

"Yes, it is better that the children pray with me and that the pilgrims ask the priests and look for solutions with them. Meanwhile, I will continue to answer the questions which they ask me."

Before December 26, 1982

This is information which Mirjana gave to Father Tomislav Vlasic on November 5, 1983. He conveyed this information to the Pope on December 16, 1983. Father Vlasic's letter was published in Is the Virgin Mary Appearing at Medjugorje? (Paris, 1984), with this introduction:

"During the apparition of December 25, 1982, according to Mirjana, the Madonna confided to her the tenth and last secret, and revealed to her, the dates in which the different secrets will be realized. The Blessed Virgin revealed to Mirjana some aspects of the future, up to this point, in greater detail than to the other seers. For this reason, I am reporting here what Mirjana told me in a conversation of November 5, 1983. I summarized the essentials of her account, without literal quotation. Mirjana told me:

'Before the visible sign is given to mankind, there will be three warnings to the world. The warnings will be in the form of events on earth. Mirjana will be a witness to them. Ten days before one of the admonitions, Mirjana will

*notify a priest of her choice. The witness of Mirjana will
be a confirmation of the apparitions and a stimulus for the
conversion of the world.*

*'After the admonitions, the visible sign will appear on the
site of the apparitions in Medjugorje for all the people to
see. The sign will be given as a testimony to the apparitions
and in order to call people back to faith.*

*'The ninth and tenth secrets are serious. They concern
chastisement for the sins of the world. Punishment is
inevitable, for we cannot expect the whole world to be
converted. The punishment can be diminished by prayer
and penance, but it cannot be eliminated. Mirjana says
that one of the evils that threatened the world, the one
contained in the seventh secret, has been averted thanks to
prayer and fasting. That is why the Blessed Virgin continues to encourage prayer and fasting:*

**"'You have forgotten that through prayer and fasting you
can avert wars and suspend the laws of nature."**

*'After the first admonition, the others will follow in a rather
short time. Thus, people will have some time for conversion.*

*'That interval will be a period of grace and conversion.
After the visible sign appears, those who are still alive will
have little time for conversion. For that reason, the Blessed
Virgin invites us to urgent conversion and reconciliation.
The invitation to prayer and penance is meant to avert evil
and war, but most of all to save souls.'*

*"According to Mirjana, the events predicted by the Blessed Virgin
are near. By virtue of this experience, Mirjana proclaims to the
world: "Convert as quickly as possible. Open your hearts to
God."*

"In addition to this basic message, Mirjana related an apparition she had in 1982 which we believe sheds some light on some aspects of Church history. She spoke of an apparition in which satan appeared to her. satan asked Mirjana to renounce the Madonna and follow him. That way she could be happy in love and in life. He said that following the Virgin, on the contrary, would only lead to suffering. Mirjana rejected him, and immediately the Virgin gave her the following message, in substance:"

"Excuse me for this, but you must realize that satan exists. One day he appeared before the throne of God and asked permission to submit the Church to a period of trial. God gave him permission to try the Church for one century. This century is under the power of the devil, but when the secrets confided to you come to pass, his power will be destroyed. Even now he is beginning to lose his power and has become aggressive. He is destroying marriages, creating division among priests and is responsible for obsessions and murder. You must protect yourselves against these things through fasting and prayer, especially community prayer. Carry blessed objects with you. Put them in your house, and restore the use of holy water."

December 24, 1982

For Mirjana:

"On Christmas I will appear to you for the last time."

After this apparition, it was apparent to the few people present that Mirjana was very sad. After a time, her mother asked her what the matter was. This caused Mirjana to leave the room, crying. After composing herself, she returned to the room and stated that this was her next to the last apparition. On Christmas Day Our Lady would come to her again as a gift but would not be giving her daily apparitions anymore. Mirjana was given the tenth secret, a particularly grave one.

On her birthday, March 18, for the rest of her life, Our Lady promised to appear to her.

December 25, 1982 (CHRISTMAS)

Our Lady's apparition to Mirjana lasted 45 minutes. Mirjana states that she will always remember these words of Our Lady:

> **"Now you will have to turn to God in the faith like any other person. I will appear to you on the day of your birthday and when you will experience difficulties in life. Mirjana, I have chosen you; I have confided in you everything that is essential. I have also shown you many terrible things. You must now bear it all with courage. Think of Me and think of the tears I must shed for that. You must remain courageous. You have quickly grasped the messages. You must also understand now that I have to go away. Be courageous."**

Mirjana has said that Our Lady prepared her for this meeting for a month. In a motherly manner, Our Lady had explained that Her task was accomplished and Mirjana had received sufficient information. While Mirjana felt that her conversations with Our Lady were so necessary for her soul, Our Lady promised that as long as she remained close to God, She would help her and be beside her always, assisting her in her most difficult times. But now she must return to the normal state of each Christian.

This was Mirjana's saddest Christmas ever. This last meeting left her feeling as if she had lost the most beautiful thing in her life. Our Lady knew her pain and was there to cheer her up and to pray with her. Mirjana was asked to sing and praise God. Mirjana prayed the Hail Holy Queen, the prayer she always said when she was alone with Our Lady.

As Our Lady had warned, the first month after this last apparition was most difficult. Mirjana experienced depression, avoided people, and shut herself in her room where she had waited for Our Lady. She cried and called out to Our Lady and did feel Her presence. She waited for her birthday.

Many who know Mirjana claim that since the apparitions stopped, she has become much more mature in her inner life as well as in her character. Our Lady has been the best of educators.

December 27, 1982

Concerning placing the new statue of Our Lady, Queen of Peace, in the church:

"Yes, you may!"

This statue was sculpted by Vipotnik and painted by Luka Stojaknac and Florijan Mickovic. Luka is Orthodox and working on this statue has been a blessing for him.

December 31, 1982

Concerning the new year:

"Pray as much as possible and fast! You must persevere in prayer and fasting. I wish that the new year will be spent in prayer and penance. Persevere in prayer and in sacrifice and I will protect you and will hear your prayers."

1982-1983

Marija went before Our Lady on behalf of a seminarian and asked the question: *"Was it okay to read the book the Poem of the Man-God?"* Marija relayed that Our Lady affirmed it was okay by answering:

"Yes. It makes for good reading."

This was asked because the book was once on the Church's index of forbidden books. The index was done away with, and the Church's canon laws changed, allowing the publication of private revelations. Many began to read these volumes, while others began condemning anyone who read them because of their past history of being on the index. Through this confusion, Our Lady's wisdom was sought in giving an answer as to whether it was okay to read - hence the resulting message above.

Still, afterwards, some refused to accept Our Lady's messages and continued to condemn the books as well as anyone who read them. The controversy grew until a letter was written to Cardinal Ratzinger on July 21, 1992, asking for the Church to speak as to whether or not the faithful could read the books and still remain in the grace of the Church. Cardinal Ratzinger wrote back eleven months later. On May 11, 1993, the Community of Caritas of Birmingham received a letter through their Bishop, Raymond J. Boland, in which Cardinal Ratzinger asked him to inform the founder, who originally wrote the Vatican, of Caritas of Birmingham, of their conclusion. It relayed that Ratzinger had contacted the Italian Bishops conference. The conclusion was that future publications must state that they could not be declared as supernatural, rather they were the literary forms used by the author to describe Christ's life and that this admonition should be known by those who read these volumes.

This conclusion cleared the way for the books to be read by the faithful and was a clear victory in harmony with Our Lady's message that they could be read. The Community of Caritas of Birmingham uses them, recommends them strongly, and contends that Our Lady's answer confirms and encourages their reading because they offer good spiritual direction with many spiritual lessons.

January 1, 1983 (HOLY MARY, MOTHER OF GOD)

Concerning Our Lady's appearances to Mirjana:

"After Christmas, I am no longer appearing to her for the present."

January 5, 1983

Ivan, Jakov, Marija, and Vicka relate the following information to Father Tomislav: Marija has received seven secrets; Vicka has received eight; Jakov, Ivanka, and Ivan have received nine; and Mirjana has received ten. As to how long the apparitions will last or why Our Lady no longer appears to Mirjana after Christmas, we do not know. Our Lady constantly invites us to prayer, fasting, and conversion and She confirms Her promises.

Ivan's explanation of why Mirjana has ceased having regular apparitions is that she did not pray enough. He further adds that Our Lady probably did it so Mirjana would learn to pray in faith. (On the contrary, others have interpreted the cessation of the apparitions as a sign of achievement and maturity.)

Regarding the time of the sign, its month and year, Ivan says: *"It is forecasted."*

January 7, 1983

The visionaries are invited to record Our Lady's testimony as She begins to tell them Her life; but, until they receive Her authorization, they will not be able to make this information public. Jakov will receive information until April; Ivanka, until May 22; and Marija, until July 17. When in Medjugorje, Marija receives an abridged account as most of the week she is attending a school for hairdressers in Mostar. For Vicka, this transmission lasted until April 10, 1985 and filled three notebooks.

January 10, 1983

Mirjana shared with Fr. Tomislav Vlasic that during the year and a half that she had been receiving apparitions, she had

experienced the maternal love and intimacy of Our Lady and
questioned Her why God could so "mercilessly" send sinners to
hell forever.

**"Men who go to hell no longer want to receive any benefit
from God. They do not repent nor do they cease to revolt
and to blaspheme. They make up their mind to live in hell
and do not contemplate leaving it."**

Regarding Purgatory:

**"In Purgatory there are different levels; the lowest is close
to hell and the highest gradually draws near to Heaven. It
is not on All Souls Day, but at Christmas, that the greatest
number of souls leave Purgatory. There are in Purgatory,
souls who pray ardently to God, but for whom no relative
or friend prays on earth. God makes them benefit from
the prayers of other people. It happens that God permits
them to manifest themselves in different ways, close to their
relatives on earth, in order to remind men of the existence
of Purgatory and to solicit their prayers to come close to
God who is just, but good. The majority of people go to
Purgatory. Many go to hell. A small number go directly
to Heaven."**

January 12, 1983

There was present a U.S. television crew that was filming the
events in Medjugorje. Fr. John Bertolucci was the narrator.
The name of the television program was *"The Glory of God."*
Concerned about the police and the oppression still going on at
that time, they were worried about getting the film out of the
country. They were delighted and at the same time assured
because Our Lady cleverly used their title in Her answer.

**"There will be some difficulties, but it will be for the glory
of God."**

April 21, 1983

To the visionaries and especially Jakov concerning behavior during Mass and around others:

"You must behave well; be pious and set a good example for the faithful."

April 24, 1983

Message for an Italian doctor:

"I bless him just as [I bless] those who work with him at the hospital in Milan, for everything they are doing. Have them continue, and pray. I bless the sick of this hospital, just as the sick for whom you have prayed this evening, and those for whom you will pray."

June 1, 1983

"Dear children! I hoped that the world would begin to be converted on its own. Do now everything you can so that the world can be converted."

June 2, 1983

"Read what has been written about Jesus. Meditate on it and convey it to others."

June 3, 1983

Concerning Father Tomislav Vlasic's attempt to form a prayer group, has it begun well?

"Yes, it is good. Have him continue."

What should be done so that the authorities will not send away
the priests of the parish who work with faith and love?

**"Pray and fast for this intention. I will tell you when the
moment comes what you must do."**

Should Father Tomislav ask the parish to fast and pray in hopes
that the Church will recognize the supernatural events taking
place in Medjugorje?

**"Yes, it is a good way. Have the parish pray for this gift.
Have them pray also for the gift of the Holy Spirit so that all
those who come here will feel the presence of God."**

June 12, 1983

Concerning whether the priests should start new work around
the church or ask permission from the authorities:

**"Do not begin the work until receiving permission from the
authorities. Otherwise, someone will inform the latter and
the works would be forbidden. Go, and kindly request the
authorization. It will be given to you."**

June 14, 1983

Concerning what the priests should preach during the novena
before the anniversary of the first apparitions:

**"Have them do what they think is best. It would be good to
remind the faithful of the events which have been happening here in relation to my coming. Have them remind the
faithful of the reasons for my coming here."**

Spring, 1983

> "Hasten your conversion. Do not await the sign which has been announced for those who do not believe; it will be too late. You who believe, be converted and deepen your faith."

June 24, 1983

> "The sign will come, you must not worry about it. The only thing that I would want to tell you is to be converted. Make that known to all my children as quickly as possible. No pain, no suffering is too great for me in order to save you. I will pray to my Son not to punish the world; but I plead with you, be converted.

> "You cannot imagine what is going to happen nor what the Eternal Father will send to earth. That is why you must be converted! Renounce everything. Do penance. Express my thanks to all my children who have prayed and fasted. I carry all this to my Divine Son in order to obtain an alleviation of His justice against the sins of mankind.

> "I thank the people who have prayed and fasted. Persevere and help me to convert the world."

June 26, 1983

> "Love your enemies. Pray for them and bless them."

July 1, 1983

This apparition took place at 11:00 p.m. on Cross Mountain.

> "I thank all those who have responded to my call. I bless all of you. I bless each of you. In these days, I ask you to pray for my intentions."

Beginning of July, 1983

Regarding the problem with Bishop Zanic and the parish and apparitions:

> **"Fast two days a week for the intentions of the Bishop, who bears a heavy responsibility. If there is a need to, I will ask for a third day. Pray each day for the Bishop."**

July 26, 1983 - To Marija:

> **"Dear children, today I would like to invite you to constant prayer and penance. Particularly, have the young people of this parish become more active in their prayer."**

August 6, 1983

Jakov questions Our Lady concerning orders from the Bishop to have Father Pervan, the parish priest, stop the visionaries from saying the Rosary and The Lord's Prayer, the Hail Mary, and the Glory Be the customary seven times at the beginning of prayer:

> **"If it is so, then do not go against it so as not to provoke any quarrels. If it is possible, talk about it tomorrow among yourselves. All of you come to an agreement beforehand."**

August 12, 1983

This apparition lasted longer than usual, approximately 38 minutes.

> **"Pray more for your spiritual life. Do your utmost in this sense. Pray for your Bishop."**

August 23, 1983

Concerning Canadian Fr. Tardiff, who has an important healing ministry, Canadian Fr. Pierre Rancourt, and Dr. Madre, Deacon in the Lion of Juda Community - now known as the Community of the Beatitudes:

"I myself invited here each one of you, for I need you to spread my messages in the entire world."

August 25, 1983

Concerning the arrest and expulsion of Father Tardif, Father Raucourt, and Dr. Phillippe Madre by the Yugoslavian authorities:

"Do not worry for them. Everything is in God's plan."

August 29, 1983

Concerning a group of young people before they leave for their pilgrimage to Siroki Brijeg at a youth festival:

"I wish that you pray throughout your trip, and that you glorify God. There, you will be able to meet other young people. Convey the messages which I have given you. Do not hesitate to speak to them about it. Some begin to pray and to fast just as they have been told, but they get tired very quickly, and thus loose the graces which they have acquired."

September 5, 1983

Concerning Jakov's mother who died:

"Your mother is with me in Heaven."

September 12, 1983

"Pray. When I give you this message, do not be content to just listen to it. Increase your prayer and see how it makes you happy. All graces are at your disposal. All you have to do is to gain them. In order to do that, I tell you - Pray!"

September 26, 1983

To Jakov:

"My Son suffers very much because the world is not converting. May the world be converted and make peace."

October 15, 1983

"My Son suffers very much because men do not want to be reconciled. They have not listened to me. Be converted, be reconciled."

It is not certain whether this message and the September 26, 1983 message may have been duplicated by accident, or may have been given twice.

October 21, 1983

"The important thing is to pray to the Holy Spirit so that He may descend on you. When you have the Holy Spirit, you have everything. People make a mistake when they turn only to the saints to request something."

Advent, 1983

"Begin by calling on the Holy Spirit each day. The most important thing is to pray to the Holy Spirit. When the Holy Spirit descends on earth, then everything becomes clear and everything is transformed."

November 26, 1983

In answer to a question, Our Lady said:

"Prayer and fasting."

November 30, 1983

To Marija, given for a priest:

"You must warn the Bishop very soon, and the Pope, with respect to the urgent and the great importance of the message for all mankind. I have already said many times that the peace of the world is in a state of crisis. Become brothers among yourselves; increase prayer and fasting in order to be saved."

December 26, 1983

To Ivan regarding a question asked by Father Laurentin:

"Our Lady prays for that. May he who undertakes it, do it in prayer. It is there that he will find his inspiration."

1983

"I know that many will not believe you, and that many who have an impassioned faith will cool off. You remain firm, and motivate people to instant prayer, penance and conversion. At the end, you will be happier."

To the Visionaries:

"When you will suffer difficulties, and need something, come to me."

Regarding cures:

> **"I cannot cure. God alone cures. Pray! I will pray with you. Believe firmly. Fast, do penance. I will help you as long as it is in my power to do it. God comes to help everyone. I am not God. I need your sacrifices and your prayers to help me."**

Regarding Faith:

> **"Faith cannot be alive without prayer."**

Regarding the Mass:

> **"The Mass is the greatest prayer of God. You will never be able to understand its greatness. That is why you must be perfect and humble at Mass, and you should prepare yourselves for it."**

To a Priest who asks if it is preferable to pray to Our Lady or to Jesus:

> **"I beseech you, pray to Jesus! I am His Mother, and I intercede for you with Him. But all prayers go to Jesus. I will help, I will pray, but everything does not depend solely on me, but also on your strength, and the strength of those who pray."**

Regarding souls in Purgatory:

> **"These persons wait for your prayers and your sacrifices."**

On other topics:

> **"The most beautiful prayer is the Creed."**

> **"The most important thing is to believe."**

"All prayers are good, if they are said with faith."

"My Son wants to win all souls to Him, but the devil strives to obtain something. The devil makes a great effort to infiltrate among you, at all costs."

January, 1984

Advice to the pilgrims from Our Lady:

"When you are in the room of the apparitions or at the church, you should not preoccupy yourselves with taking pictures. Rather, you should use the time to pray to Jesus, especially in those moments of particular grace during the apparitions."

Lent, 1984

"Do not be afraid for yourselves, you are already saved. Pray rather for those who are in sin and who do not believe."

ON MARCH 1, 1984, OUR LADY STARTED GIVING WEEKLY MESSAGES TO MARIJA PAVLOVIC FOR THE PARISH AND FOR THE WORLD. SEE CHAPTER 2 FOR THESE MESSAGES.

March 1, 1984

"Thursday (day of the Eucharist), may each one find his way to fast; he who smokes, may abstain from smoking; he who drinks alcohol, have him not drink. Have each one give up something which is dear to him. May these recommendations be conveyed to the parish."

March 14, 1984

"Pray and fast so that the kingdom of God may come among you. Let my Son set you aglow with His fire."

March 19, 1984

"Dear children, sympathize with me! Pray, pray, pray!"

March 25, 1984 (ANNUNCIATION)

"Rejoice with me and with my angels because a part of my plan has already been realized. Many have been converted, but many do not want to be converted. Pray."

This was the 1,000th apparition at Medjugorje, and after these above words, the Blessed Virgin sadly looked at the visionaries and cried.

March 28, 1984

"Many persons come here out of curiosity and not as pilgrims."

March 30, 1984

"I wish that your hearts would be united to mine, like my heart is united to that of my Son."

April 5, 1984

"If you would be strong in the faith, satan would not be able to do anything against you. Begin to walk the path of my messages. Be converted, be converted, be converted."

April 8, 1984

"I ask you to pray for the conversion of everyone. For that, I need your prayers."

April 22, 1984 (EASTER SUNDAY)

"We all rejoice in Heaven. Rejoice with us!"

April 23, 1984

To the priests of Medjugorje:

"There is no need to give more information to the people, they already know what they are supposed to do."

April 24, 1984

Our Lady appeared very sad. With tears She said:

"So many people, after they have begun to pray, to be converted, to fast, and to do penance here, quickly forget when they return to their homes and to their bad habits."

To the priests of Medjugorje:

"The information suffices. People already know enough. Tell them this place is a place of prayer. Pray as much as you can, pray however you can, but pray more always. Each of you could pray even four hours a day. But I know that many do not understand because they think only of living for their work."

Father Vlasic questions Our Lady concerning telling the people to pray four hours a day and having them turn away. Our Lady then said:

"**Even you do not understand. It is hardly a sixth of your day.**"

June 13, 1984

"**Dear children, I invite you to pray more, you and the entire parish, until the day of the anniversary. Let your prayer become a sign of offering to God. Dear children, I know that you are all tired. You do not know how to offer yourselves to me. Offer yourselves completely to me these days.**"

June 24, 1984 (THIRD ANNIVERSARY)

"**My children, I thank you for each sacrifice that you have made during these days. Be converted, forgive each other, fast, pray, pray, pray!**"

June 25, 1984

"**Thank you for all your sacrifices.**"

June 26, 1984

"**When I say, 'pray, pray, pray,' I do not only want to say to increase the number of hours of prayer, but also to reinforce the desire for prayer, and to be in contact with God. Place yourself permanently in a state of spirit bathed in prayer.**"

July 16, 1984

"**I pray for the priests and the parishioners, that no one may be troubled. I know the changes which will take place soon** [in the parish clergy]. **At the time of the changes, I will be there. Also, do not be afraid; there will be in the future signs concerning sinners, unbelievers, alcoholics, and young people. They will accept me again.**"

July 20, 1984

Our Lady appears on Apparition Mountain in the late evening.

"Open your hearts to me, come close. Say in a loud voice your intentions and your prayers."

Our Lady was very attentive to the prayers of the visionaries. While praying for Bishop Zanic of Mostar, Her eyes filled up with tears and She says:

"You are my little flowers. Continue to pray; my task is lighter because of it."

She then blessed the visionaries and the people with a Crucifix and ascended back to Heaven crying.

August 5, 1984 (OUR LADY'S TWO THOUSANDTH BIRTHDAY)

For three days before the celebration of the second millennium of Mary's birthday, there was fasting and continuous prayer. Confessions were heard by seventy priests without respite; great numbers of people were converted.

"Never in my life have I cried with sorrow, as I have cried this evening with joy. Thank you!"

In anticipation of this day, Our Lady said:

"The priests who will hear Confessions will have great joy on that day."

The visionaries say Our Lady was "very joyful" during these three days of fasting and continuous prayer and Our Lady repeated:

**"I am very happy! Continue, continue. Continue to pray
and to fast. Continue and make me happy each day."**

Later, the priests involved related that never in their lives had
they felt such joy in their hearts.

August 6, 1984

"Continue and make me happy each day."

August 11, 1984 (SATURDAY)

**"Dear children, pray, because satan wishes to complicate
my plans still further. Pray with the heart and surrender
yourselves to Jesus in prayer."**

August 25, 1984

To Mirjana:

**"Wait for me September 13th; I will speak to you about the
future."**

August 31, 1984

**"I love the cross which you have providentially erected on
Mount Krizevac in a very special way. Go there more often
and pray."**

October 8, 1984

Because Jakov was sick, Our Lady appeared to him at his
home.

**"Dear children, all the prayers which you recite in the eve-
ning in your homes, dedicate them to the conversion of sin-**

ners because the world is immersed in a great moral decay.
Recite the Rosary each evening."

October 13, 1984

Concerning the Marian Movement of Priests:

"A message to you and to all those who love me: Dear children, pray unceasingly and ask the Holy Spirit to inspire you
always. In everything that you ask, in everything that you
do, look only for the will of God. Live according to your
convictions and respect others."

October 20, 1984

"When you pray you must feel more. Prayer is a conversation with God. To pray means to listen to God. Prayer
is useful for you because after prayer everything is clear.
Prayer makes one know happiness. Prayer can teach you
how to cry. Prayer can teach you how to blossom. Prayer
is not a joke. Prayer is a dialogue with God."

October 24, 1984

This apparition took place at 10:00 p.m. on Cross Mountain.

"My dear children, I am so happy to see you pray. Pray
with me so that God's plan may be realized thanks to your
prayers and to mine. Pray more, and more intensely."

October, 1984

"I would like to guide you spiritually, but I would not know
how to help you if you are not open. It suffices for you to
think, for example, where you were with your thoughts yesterday during Mass. When you go to Mass, your trip from

**home to church should be a time of preparation for Mass.
You should also receive Holy Communion with an open
and pure heart, with purity of heart, and with openness. Do
not leave the church without an appropriate act of thanksgiving. I can help you only if you are accessible to my sug-
gestions; I cannot help you if you are not open. The most
important thing in the spiritual life is to ask for the gift of
the Holy Spirit. When the Holy Spirit comes, peace will be
established. When that occurs, everything changes around
you. Things will change."**

October, 1984

While living in the Holy Land, Father Philip Pavich, O.F.M.,
requested Our Lady's pleasure about his moving to Medjugorje
to help English-speaking pilgrims. Through Ivan, Our Lady
gave this response:

**"If he has the will, let him come to help us to spread God's
message."**

Father Philip arrived in May, 1987, to begin ministry in
Medjugorje.

December 17, 1984

Concerning Monsignor Franic, Archbishop of Split.

"You will have to suffer more."

December 25, 1984

Although Our Lady did not give a message, She appeared carrying the Christ Child in Her arms.

1984

In response to a question about Oriental meditations such as Zen and Transcendental:

"Why do you call them 'meditations,' when it deals with human works? The true meditation is a meeting with Jesus. When you discover joy, interior peace, you must know there is only one God, and only one Mediator, Jesus Christ." * [See endnote, page 574.]

Regarding prayer:

"Your days will not be the same according to whether you pray, or you do not pray." * [See endnote, page 574.]

1984-1985

Mirjana reports:

"Tell the faithful that I need their prayers, and prayers from all the people. It is necessary to pray as much as possible and do penance because very few people have been converted up until now. There are many Christians who live like pagans. There are always so few true believers."

A Priest asked what they should do.

"Carry out your responsibility, and do what the Church asks you to do."

Jakov received a reproach from Our Lady because of his behavior toward his friends at school.

"You must love them all."

He responded that he did but that they are so annoying to him.
Our Lady said:

"Then accept it as a sacrifice, and offer it."

Marija shares Our Lady's message with a group of seminarians
from Zagreb and Djakovo who attended an apparition:

"Tell them, that with prayer, one obtains everything."

Mirjana asks Our Lady why She received a young nun with open
arms but kept Her hands joined before the others.

**"I will take with me very soon, all those to whom I extended
my arms."**

To a nun regarding her brother who had died in an accident:

**"I understand the question. He died in the state of grace.
He needs Masses and prayers."**

Mirjana reported this message to a close friend, a religious:

**"The hour has come when the demon is authorized to act
with all his force and power. The present hour, is the hour
of satan.**

**"Many pretend to see Jesus and me, and to understand our
words, but they are, in fact, lying. It is a very grave sin, and
it is necessary to pray very much for them.**

**"I am anxious for people to know what is happening in
Medjugorje. Speak about it, so that all will be converted."**

Our Lady is questioned regarding her insistence in saying, **"It
presses me to...,"** by Mirjana:

"When you will be in Heaven, you will understand why I am so pressed."

To the visionaries regarding the apparitions and their purpose:

"Is it, after all, that I bore you? Everything passes exactly according to God's plan. Have patience, persevere in prayer and in penance. Everything happens in its own time."

Responding to the confusion of a Catholic Priest over the cure of an Orthodox child:

"Tell this priest, tell everyone, that it is you who are divided on earth. The Muslims and the Orthodox, for the same reason as Catholics, are equal before my Son and me. You are all my children. Certainly, all religions are not equal, but all men are equal before God, as St. Paul says. It does not suffice to belong to the Catholic Church to be saved, but it is necessary to respect the Commandments of God in following one's conscience."

"Those who are not Catholics, are no less creatures made in the image of God, and destined to rejoin someday, the House of the Father. Salvation is available to everyone, without exception. Only those who refuse God deliberately are condemned. To him who has been given little, little will be asked for. To whomever has been given much (to Catholics)**, very much will be required. It is God alone, in His infinite justice, Who determines the degree of responsibility and pronounces judgment."**

January 2, 1985

This apparition of Our Lady, surrounded by angels, took place at 11:30 p.m. on Cross Mountain.

"I am very happy to have been able to come here for three

years, thanks to the prayers of believers. Continue to pray thusly. A part of my plan has been realized. God blesses in a special way all those who are here. You can return happily to your homes. You do not immediately understand the reasons. Offer your prayers of thanksgiving for next week."

January 9, 1985

"I thank the faithful for having come to church in very bad and cold weather."

January 14, 1985

To Vicka:

"My dear children, satan is strong. He wishes with all his strength to destroy my plans. Pray only, and do not stop doing it. I will also pray to my Son so that all the plans that I have begun will be realized. Be patient and persevere in prayer. Do not permit satan to take away your courage. He works very hard in the world. Be on your guard."

February 3, 1985

"I wish for Father Slavko to stay here, to guide the life, and to assemble all the news so that when I leave, there will be a complete image of everything that has happened here. I am also praying now for Slavko and for all those who work in this parish."

February 17, 1985

"Pray, dear children, so that God's plan may be accomplished, and all the works of satan be changed in favor of the glory of God."

February 25, 1985

To Marija:

"For next week I invite you to say these words: 'I love God
in everything.' With love, one obtains everything. You can
receive many things, even the most impossible. The Lord
wishes all the parishes to surrender to Him, and I too, in
Him, desire it. Each evening, make your examination of
conscience, but only to give thanks in acknowledgment for
everything that His love offers us at Medjugorje."

End of February, 1985 or Early March, 1985

Our Lady was asked what should be done about all the discus-
sions and publications regarding Medjugorje and She responded:

"See! Now I am there, in each family, in each home. I am
everywhere because I love. Do the same. The world lives
from love."* [See endnote, page 574.]

After singing a song three times, Our Lady said:

"Excuse me for making you repeat, but I wish you to sing
with the heart. You must really do everything with the
heart."* [See endnote, page 574.]

Regarding the beginning of prayer: (The following two messages may be two versions of the same message)

"One has to be already prepared. If there are some sins,
one must pull them out, otherwise, one will not be able to
enter into prayer. If one has concerns, he should submit
them to God."* [See endnote, page 574.]

"You must not preoccupy yourselves during prayer. During prayer, you must not be preoccupied with your sins. Sins must remain behind."* [See endnote, page 574.]

February, 1985 - March, 1985

"Dear children! You have always prayed that I not abandon you. Now I ask of you, in turn, not to abandon me. Especially during these days, satan wants to disperse you. For that, pray very much these days. Dear children, I came again to thank you. You have not yet understood what that means, to give joy to my heart. It is a very great thing. I ask you only to persevere in prayer. As long as you pray, I will have words for you. Good-bye, I thank you dear children. My love for you is unlimited; be happy with me, because I am happy with you."

March 9, 1985

"You can receive a grace immediately, or in a month, or in ten years. I do not need The Lord's Prayer said a hundred or two hundred times. It is better to pray only one, but with a desire to encounter God. You should do everything out of love. Accept all annoyances, all difficulties, everything, with love. Dedicate yourselves to love."

March 13, 1985

This message was given to Vicka as a warning that she not make the same mistake as Ivan. Ivan had been persuaded to write down information concerning the sign and seal it in an envelope which was not to have been opened; however, it was and caused a stir.

"Pray, pray, pray! It is only with prayer that you will be able to avoid Ivan's error. He should not have written; and

after that, he had to clearly acknowledge it so as not to plant any doubts."

March 18, 1985

To Mirjana:

"The Rosary is not an ornament for the home, as one often times limits himself to using it. Tell everyone to pray it.

"Right now many are greatly seeking money, not only in the parish, but in the whole world. Woe to those who seek to take everything from those who come, and blessed are those from whom they take everything.

"May the priests help you because I have entrusted to you a heavy burden, and I suffer from your difficulties. Ivan did not make a big mistake. I have sufficiently reprimanded him for the error. It is not necessary to scold him anymore."

March 24, 1985

"Today I wish to call you all to Confession, even if you have confessed a few days ago. I wish that you all experience my feast day within yourselves. But you cannot experience it unless you abandon yourselves completely to God. Therefore, I am inviting you all to reconciliation with God!"

March 25, 1985 (THE ANNUNCIATION)

"Through my joy and the joy of this people, I say to all of you this evening, 'I love you and I wish you well.'"

April 5, 1985 (Good Friday)

To Ivanka:

**"You, the members of this parish, have a large and heavy
cross to bear; but do not be afraid to carry it. My Son is
here to help you."**

April 11, 1985 - September 1987

The Closing of the Chapel

In a letter dated March 25, Bishop Zanic ordered that the
church and all contiguous rooms were forbidden to be used for
the apparitions. They now begin taking place in a bedroom in
the rectory.

April 15, 1985

**"You must begin to work in your hearts as you work in the
field. Work and change your hearts so that the new spirit of
God can dwell there."**

May 7, 1985

For at least an hour, Our Lady and two angels appeared to
Ivanka at her home. More beautiful than ever, She asked
Ivanka what she wished and approved of her request to see
her mother. The mother of Ivanka soon appeared. Smiling,
she embraced Ivanka, told her how proud she was of her, and
embraced her again before she disappeared. During this apparition Our Lady said:

**"My dear child, today is our last meeting, do not be sad. I
will return to see you at each anniversary of the first apparition [June 25], beginning next year. Dear child, do not think**

that you have done anything bad, and that this would be the reason why I'm not returning near to you. No, it is not that. With all your heart you have accepted the plans which my Son and I formulated, and you have accomplished everything. No one in the world has had the grace which you, your brothers, and sisters have received. Be happy because I am your Mother and I love you from the bottom of my heart. Ivanka, thank you for the response to the call of my Son. Thank you for persevering and remaining always with Him as long as He will ask you. Dear child, tell all your friends that my Son and I are always with them when they call on us. What I have told you during these years on the secrets, do not speak to anyone about them. Go in the peace of God."

June 25, 1985 (Fourth Anniversary Of The First Apparition)

Marija asks Our Lady what She wants from the priests.

"I urge you to ask everyone to pray the Rosary. With the Rosary you will overcome all the troubles which satan is trying to inflict on the Catholic Church. Let all priests pray the Rosary. Give time to the Rosary."

July 1, 1985

Our Lady appeared on Apparition Mountain

"I thank all those who have responded to my call. I bless all of you, I bless each of you. These days, I ask you to pray for my intentions. Go in the peace of God."

August 5, 1985 (Birthday of Our Lady - Special Blessing)

The Church celebrates September 8 as Our Lady's birthday but She told the visionaries that August 5 is the actual date. Our

Lady appeared dressed in golden splendor and was indescribable. She gives a special gift on Her birthday. This is the first
time that She gives the SPECIAL BLESSING and She gives
it several times later, generally on Feast Days. However, this
blessing was not completely understood until August 15, 1988
when Marija spoke of it to a Caritas group in Medjugorje.
(For an explanation of "THE SPECIAL BLESSING," see the
November 29, 1988 message on pages 427-428 in the American
Message Section.

Our Lady said to Ivan:

**"Praised be Jesus Christ. My children, I'm happy to be with
you this evening and to see you so numerous. I bless you
with a Special Blessing. Make progress in holiness through
the messages, I will help you. Give your utmost and we will
go together, sensitive to the sweetness of life, light, and joy.
Go in the peace of God, my children, my little children."**

August 14, 1985

To Ivan:

**"Observe the complete fasts, Wednesdays and Fridays.
Pray at least an entire Rosary: Joyous, Sorrowful and
Glorious Mysteries."**

September 10, 1985

Regarding temptations from the devil:

**"With respect to sin, it suffices to give it serious consider-
ation, and soon, move ahead and correct the sin."*** [See
endnote, page 574.]

"Your humility must be proud [high minded]. **Your pride
should be humble."*** [Jelena - See endnote, page 574.]

"If you have received a gift from God, you must be proud but do not say that it is yours. Say, rather, that it is God's."* [See endnote, page 574.]

September, 1985

To Marija:

"I have given you my love, so that you may give it to others."

October 8, 1985

"Those who say, 'I do not believe in God,' how difficult it will be for them when they will approach the Throne of God and hear the voice: 'Enter into Hell.'"* [See endnote, page 574.]

October 21, 1985

A few weeks before Father Slavko's first visit to Ireland, he asked the visionaries to ask Our Lady for a message for Ireland. When Our Lady was first asked, She just smiled. Father Slavko again asked the question a couple days before his trip and Our Lady responded through Ivan:

"That they may be the messengers of my messages: prayer, conversion, peace, and repentance, and that they may never forget that their Mother loves them and prays for them."

October 25, 1985

To Mirjana concerning unbelievers:

"They are my children. I suffer because of them. They do not know what awaits them. You must pray more for them."

Our Lady showed Mirjana the first secret - the earth was desolate:

"It is the upheaval of a region of the world. In the world there are so many sins. What can I do, if you do not help me. Remember that I love you. God does not have a hard heart. Look around you and see what men do, then you will no longer say that God has a hard heart. How many people come to church, to the house of God, with respect, a strong faith, and love God? Very few! Here you have a time of grace and conversion. It is necessary to use it well."

Mirjana chose Father Petar Ljubicic to reveal the secrets to the world. Ten days before the first secret is to be revealed, Father Petar will be given a parchment containing the ten secrets. This parchment was given to Mirjana by Our Lady. Anyone can see this parchment but it cannot be read by those viewing it. When Father Petar receives the parchment, he will only be able to read the first secret. During the ten days, Father Petar is to spend the first seven days in fasting and prayer. Three days before the event takes place, he is to announce it to the world. At the proper time, he will be able to see and read the second secret, and then the third, etc., according to the schedule of Heaven.

"Pray very much for Father Petar, to whom I send a Special Blessing. I am a Mother, that is why I come. You must not fear for I am here."

November 16, 1985

After an hour of prayers of petition, Our Lady says:

"Have you forgotten that you are in my hands?"* [See endnote, page 574.]

December 4, 1985

Marija questions Our Lady regarding discernment sought by Gianni Sgreva, an Italian Passionist who was inspired to found a "Community of Consecrated," on the message of Medjugorje:

"I prefer to answer him personally."

This community opened on May 18, 1987. (See message given on June 7, 1986.)

1985

"Let the faithful meditate each day on the life of Jesus, while praying the Rosary."

"Every prayer, which comes from the heart, is agreeable to God."

"You do not celebrate the Eucharist, as you should. If you would know what grace, and what gifts you receive, you would prepare yourselves for it each day, for an hour at least. You should go to Confession once a month. You should consecrate three days to reconciliation, each month: the first Friday of the month, followed by Saturday, and Sunday."

In Medjugorje the following has been established: an hour of adoration before the Most Blessed Sacrament on each Thursday; an hour of devotion before the Crucifix with prayers for sinners on each Friday; and two late evening (10:00 - 11:00 p.m. during Summer months; 9:00 – 10:00 p.m. during the Winter months) Adoration Services on Wednesday and Saturday nights.

Undated

A sculptor was asked to do a statue of the Blessed Mother and he said, *"Only if Our Lady wants it."* When the visionaries asked Our Lady about this, She said:

"Do one of Jesus instead, but be inspired by the words, 'COME TO ME ALL WHO ARE WEARY.'"

January 6, 1986

To Vicka:

"If you agree to it, I will not appear to you anymore for 50 days."

Vicka agreed to this.

March 18, 1986

Father Milan Mikulich called Mirjana Dragicevic and asked her to pray for Danica Radic who was suffering from liver disease for seven years. During Mirjana's birthday apparition Our Lady said:

"Danica will be alright. She will need human help."

In October, 1988, Danica received a successful liver transplant and as of March, 1990, she is doing extremely well and is working.

March 24, 1986

To the Prayer Group:

"Dear children, receive all that the Lord offers you. Do not have your hands paralyzed and do not repeat, 'Jesus, give me.' But open your hands, and take everything that the Lord offers you."

March 25, 1986 (ANNUNCIATION)

"Today, before God, I say my 'Fiat' for all of you. I repeat it: I say my 'Fiat' for all of you.

"Dear children, pray, so that in the whole world may come the Kingdom of Love. How mankind would be happy if love reigned!"* [See endnote, page 574.]

April 17, 1986

To the prayer group which questioned Our Lady's advice regarding watching television and reading newspapers as too difficult:

"If you look at the programs, if you look at the newspapers, your heads are filled with news, then there is no longer any place for me in your hearts.

"Pray. Fast. Let God act!

"Pray for the gift of love, for the gift of faith, for the gift of prayer, for the gift of fasting."* [See endnote, page 574.]

The Week Preceding May 3, 1986

To the prayer group:

"I give you the best that I can give anyone. I give myself and my Son."* [See endnote, page 574.]

May 3, 1986

For Marija's prayer group:

"Dear children, seek to make your hearts happy through

the means of prayer. **Dear children, be the joy for all mankind, be the hope of mankind. You will only be able to
obtain it through the means of prayer. Pray, pray!"*** [See
endnote, page 574.]

Toward May 12, 1986

To the prayer group:

**"You will be happy if you do not judge yourselves accord-
ing to your faults, but if you understand that in your faults
even graces are offered to you."*** [See endnote, page 574.]

June 6, 1986

**"Love. If you do not love, you are not able to transmit the
testimony. You are not able to witness, either for me, or for
Jesus."*** [See endnote, page 574.]

June 7, 1986

Through Marija concerning Father Pere Gianni Sgreva, who
wanted to organize a new community based on the messages of
Medjugorje:

**"Yes, one must pray. What you are doing pleases me. For
the time being, keep a very active prayer life, and God will
then light up the other plans."**

June 20, 1986

**"Pray before the Crucifix. Special graces come from the
Crucifix. Consecrate yourselves to the Cross. Do not blaspheme either Jesus or the Crucifix."*** [See endnote, page
574.]

June 24, 1986 (SPECIAL BLESSING)

There were 30,000 to 50,000 people present. This is the third
time Our Lady gives the SPECIAL BLESSING in which those
receiving it may bless others in Our Lady's name.

To Marija and Ivan with the Prayer Group on Cross Mountain:

**"You are on a Tabor. You receive blessings, strength, and
love. Carry them into your families and into your homes.
To each one of you, I grant a Special Blessing. Continue in
joy, prayer, and reconciliation."**

To the Prayer Group:

**"I beseech you, withdraw in silence. Your obligation is not
so much to do, but to adore God, to stay with Him."**

June 26, 1986

**"You will have as many graces as you want. That depends
on you. You will have love when you want it, as long as you
want it. That depends on you."*** [See endnote, page 574.]

July 10, 1986

To the prayer group after an evaluation:

**"I thank you for that. You have done well, but do not for-
get (. . .); basically, God's Will is decisive."*** [See endnote,
page 574.]

August 4, 1986

"I wish only that for you the Rosary become your life."*
[See endnote, page 574.]

August 5, 1986

"Read each Thursday the Gospel of Matthew, where it is said: 'No one can serve two masters....You cannot serve God and money.'" * [See endnote, page 574.]

September 12, 1986

"Many have begun to pray for healing here at Medjugorje, but, when they have returned to their homes, they abandon prayer, forget, and also lose many graces." * [See endnote, page 574.]

October 6, 1986

Permission was given by Fr. Pervan for an individual from Birmingham, Alabama, to ask Marija to present a question to Our Lady. The individual explained why he would like this asked of Our Lady as well as other information concerning the Birmingham area so that Marija would have a clear understanding of why this was desired. After discussing several things about the region, Marija requested to keep the question and stated that if Our Lady gave an answer, (many times She gives no answer), she would write it down and return it following the apparition that night.

The question: *"Dear Blessed Mother, if it is God's Will, we humbly ask that the conversion taking place in Medjugorje be allowed to take place in the Parish of Blessed Sacrament in Alabama and that it 'divinely' be spread throughout the whole region. We surrender this Parish to you and ask if there is anything you request."* Marija and Jakov went to the kitchen and Marija wrote down Our Lady's answer which starts off with, *"Gospa says"*: (Gospa means Blessed Mother.)

"Pray and by your life witness. Not with words but rather through prayer will you attain what your desire is.

Therefore, pray more and live in humility."

Below is a photo of Our Lady's response, written in Marija's handwriting in Croatian.

Our Lady's answer was prophetic and not completely understood until November 18, 1988 when Marija came to Birmingham, Alabama, and Our Lady prayed, blessed, and converted tens of thousands of people who traveled there from as far away as South America, the Caribbean, and even Russia. (See American Messages, starting on page 421.)

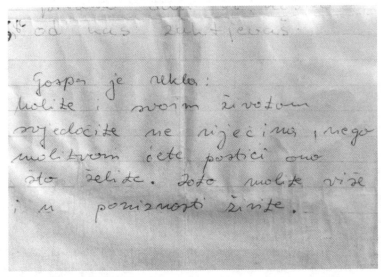

December 29, 1986

An answer for Father Tomislav Vlasic about his writing to address lies and injustices:

"Do not waste your time. Pray and love. You cannot even imagine how powerful God is."* [See endnote, page 574.]

1986

The following is an answer from Our Lady regarding Church
authority and the Church's approval of the apparitions in
Medjugorje.

"One must follow the authority of the Church with certain-
ty. Yet, before She expresses an opinion, it is necessary to
advance spiritually, because She will not be able to express a
judgment in a vacuum, but in a confirmation which presup-
poses growth of the child. First comes birth, followed by
Baptism, then Confirmation. The Church comes to confirm
him, who is born of God. We must walk and advance in the
spiritual life, affected by these messages."

Undated

To Vicka:

"Do you want to offer yourself, also, for the salvation of the
world? I need your sacrifices."* [See endnote, page 574.]

January 28, 1987

To Mirjana, at Sarajevo:

"My dear children! I come to you in order to lead you to
purity of soul and then to God. How have you listened to
me? At the beginning without believing and with fear and
defiance toward these young people whom I have chosen,
then afterwards, most of you listened to me in your heart
and began to carry out my maternal requests. But that did
not last for long. Whenever I come to you my Son comes
with me, but so does satan. You permitted, without notic-
ing, his influences on you and he drives you on. Sometimes
you understand that something you have done is not agree-
able to God, but quickly you no longer pay attention to it.

"Do not let that happen, my children. Wipe from my face the tears that I cry in seeing what you do. Wake up to yourselves. Take time to meet with God in the church. Come to visit in your Father's house. Take the time to meet among yourselves for family prayer and implore the grace of God. Remember your deceased. Give them joy with the celebration of the Holy Mass. Do not look with scorn on those who beg you for a piece of bread. Do not turn them away from your full tables. Help them and God will also help you. Perhaps it is in this way that God will hear you, and the blessing that He wants to give you in thanks will be realized.

"You have forgotten all this my children. satan has influenced you also in this. Do not let that happen! Pray with me! Do not deceive yourselves into thinking, 'I am good, but my brother next door is no good.' You would be wrong. I, your Mother, love you and it is for that reason that I am warning you about this. Concerning the secrets, my children, these are not known by the people. But when they will learn of them, it will be too late. Return to prayer! There is nothing more important! I would dearly wish that the Lord would permit me to enlighten you a little more on these secrets, but the grace which is offered to you is already great enough.

"Think how much you have offended Him. What are you offering to Him of yourself? When was the last time you renounced something for the Lord? I no longer wish to reprimand you in this way, but I want to invite you once more to prayer, fasting, and penance. If you wish to obtain a grace from God by fasting, then let no one know that you are fasting. If you wish to receive a grace from God by a gift to the poor, let no one know except you and the Lord that you have given this gift. Listen to me, my children! Meditate on my message in prayer."

March 21, 1987

To Vicka in Zagreb:

**"I bless you with the benediction of a Mother. Pray every
day and confide yourselves to my Son, Jesus. In this way
you will understand what God asks of each of you."**

March 22, 1987

Vicka related the apparition of March 22: *"Right away She
held Her hands over us and said an interior prayer that I did not
understand. She came surrounded by five little angels. Then She
confided a few things to me and left."*

June 24, 1987 (SPECIAL BLESSING)

On June 24, 1987, at 11:30 p.m., Our Lady asked everyone to
come to the mountain (of the Cross) for a special apparition.
Close to 50,000 people were there while a military helicopter
hovered overhead. It flew away three or four minutes prior to
the apparition at 11:25 p.m., presumedly to refuel. It came back
five to ten minutes after the apparition ended. Several times the
lights from the helicopter flooded the crowd. The apparition
lasted about ten minutes. A recount from Marija of the apparition follows. . . .

Anniversary Apparition: *"Tonight when Our Lady came She
was happy and She immediately prayed over all of us for a certain
amount of time. We asked Her for a blessing. Then She spoke to
us and gave a message which sounds like this"*:

**"Dear children, I want to lead you to the path of conver-
sion and I wish that you convert the world, that your life be
conversion for others."**

*"Then Our Lady said She does not want us to be unfaithful and
She desires each of us to surrender ourselves fully to Her will and
the will of God. Our Lady said from today She is granting us
special graces, and She's giving us, especially, a gift of conversion so that all of us can take the blessing with us to our homes
and truly encourage others to conversion. God gave us the gift
tonight through Our Lady. Then Our Lady prayed over all of us
for some time. We prayed with Her for the needs of each one of
us who were here tonight. Our Lady said,* **"Go in God's Peace,"**
and then She left."

1987

In response to being questioned whether She wanted to create a new order or a new structure or a particular "Medjugorje
Community," Our Lady said:

**"Children of mine, you don't know what you ask. You
don't know what is waiting for you. You cannot comprehend the plans of God! I ask of you that you accomplish
what I show you."**

1987

**"Love your Serbian Orthodox and Muslim brothers, and
the atheists who persecute you."**

**"All your prayers touch me very much, especially your daily
Rosary."**

March 18, 1988 - Mirjana's Annual Apparition

Mirjana had an apparition on her birthday which lasted only
four or five minutes. Our Lady asked her:

"Pray for unbelievers."

June 25, 1988 - Ivanka's Annual Apparition

During Ivanka's anniversary apparition, she said to the crowd who had gathered at her home, *"Our Lady wishes for all present to kneel down."* After Our Lady ascended back to Heaven, Ivanka went outside and announced to the crowd that when Our Lady asked everyone to kneel down, She gave them a SPECIAL BLESSING and said:

"The people here will be witnesses of the love of God."

She then told the group that Our Lady spoke of the third and fourth secrets.

Undated

For several years the visionary, Vicka, had been suffering from an inoperable brain cyst which caused her terrible headaches. During the course of her illness, Our Lady continued to appear to her and once, on her way to the hospital in Zagreb, Our Lady offered her two choices, saying:

"I will give you health with no apparitions or I will give you your cross with apparitions."

Because she had been suffering so tremendously she chose health but later regretted it. After forty days of not having apparitions, Our Lady appeared to her and gave her the offer once again. She joyfully took her cross back. (Vicka was miraculously healed in 1988 and as of this writing, remains so.)

Approximately the First Quarter of 1989

In a recent message to Vicka Ivankovic, when the visionary was visiting Bologna, Italy, Our Lady again asked for prayers for young people:

"Dear children, I again ask you to pray for all the young people of the world because they find themselves in a difficult situation. You can help them with your love and prayers of the heart."

January 26, 1989

Jakov says, *"Our Lady is very sad because of the sinners in this world. She is also very sad because we don't live Her messages. Our Lady asks for prayer especially in the families for these two intentions."*

March 18, 1989 - Mirjana's Annual Apparition

This is Mirjana's birthday apparition. Our Lady appeared sad, very sad. This is rare. Our Lady then said:

"One more time I beseech all of you to pray, to help by your prayers the unbelievers, those who do not have the grace to experience God in their hearts with a living faith. I do not want to threaten again! My wish is just to warn you all as a Mother. I beg you for people who do not know about the secrets.... I want to tell you how I suffer for all because I am the Mother of all."

April, 1989

This date is approximate. In April, Mirjana made this statement: *"I'd like to relay to the young people a petition from Our Lady."* The petition is:

"If they can't believe in God, they should spend at least five minutes a day in silent meditation. During that time, they should think about the God they say doesn't exist."

June 25, 1989 - Ivanka's Annual Apparition

This is Ivanka's annual apparition which lasted approximately eight minutes in all. In 1988, Our Lady spoke to her about the third and fourth secrets and in 1989, as if continuing that discussion, She spoke about the fifth secret. After the apparition, Ivanka immediately wrote down an important message which Our Lady had given her. The following is the message:

"Pray because you are in great temptation and danger because the world and material goods lead you into slavery. satan is active in this plan. I want to help each of you in prayer. I am interceding to my Son for you."

June 25, 1990 - Ivanka's Annual Apparition

Ivanka ceased seeing Our Lady on a regular basis after her May 7, 1985 apparition; however, Our Lady promised to visit her each June 25th [the anniversary of the beginning of the apparitions in Medjugorje] for the rest of her life.

Ivanka had just given birth to her second child ten days before so no one except close family was allowed to be present during the apparition. The following is the account of the June 25, 1990 apparition.

With her family, Ivanka prayed the Rosary. Upon finishing it and just prior to 6:40 p.m., Ivanka prayed The Lord's Prayer, the Hail Mary, and the Glory Be three times each. Our Lady then appeared to her and Ivanka saw Her in three dimensions, just as anyone would see someone before them - except Our Lady was floating on a cloud and was radiant.

She came without angels and with Her hands stretched out. Our Lady was very joyful and happy. She blessed all who had recommended their prayers to Her.

In 1988, Our Lady spoke to Ivanka about the third and fourth secrets. During that period of the apparition on June 25, 1988, Ivanka's face became very serious and grave. That apparition lasted 15 minutes. Ivanka's 1989 apparition lasted eight minutes. During some of that time, as if continuing where She left off, Our Lady spoke to Ivanka about the first part of the fifth secret. Again this year, Our Lady continued, this time speaking about the last half of the fifth secret. During this time, Our Lady was not happy and it was reflected in Ivanka's face.

Remarkably during this apparition, Ivanka again saw her mother who had died a couple of months before the apparitions began in 1981. Ivanka said Her mother just smiled at her. Possibly because Ivanka had just given birth, Our Lady said:

"I thank you for giving your life to allow other life."

The apparition lasted approximately nine minutes. Our Lady ended by saying,

"Go with God, my dear children."

December, 1990

To Vicka:

"When I started to speak to you and to call you to peace, you thought everything was calm and there was no need to pray in a special way for peace. The absence of peace was in the hearts, now the absence of peace has come into the world."

The above message was shared by Vicka in Paris, France, in February, 1991. On October 30, 1991, Vicka explained that Our Lady did, indeed, say this during the Gulf War and explained the message and what Our Lady meant the following way:

"When war comes, it is because there is war already in your hearts. Then this war which is in your hearts comes out (eventually manifests itself physically) and real war starts. Instead of war in your hearts, if you make peace in your hearts, then on the outside, THE WAR WILL STOP."

Vicka goes on and adds that these words from Our Lady were for every war going on, not only the Gulf War.

January 11, 1991

Marija was sick and Our Lady appeared to her in her room.

"I need your prayers and sacrifices for peace."

Ivan was with thirty priests who were on retreat in Medjugorje. During his 5:40 p.m. apparition, Our Lady was happy to see all the priests, blessed all of them, and asked the priests to pray for peace.

March 18, 1991 - Mirjana's Annual Apparition

The following is Mirjana's description of her annual birthday apparition:

"Five days before my birthday, while in prayer, I found out that Our Lady would appear to me at 7:30 p.m. On that evening, many people gathered and we prayed. Exactly at 7:30 p.m. She appeared, this time not as sad as last year. You could say Her mood was normal. This time no light preceded Her as it did during the time of Her daily apparitions. She stayed for seven minutes. Upon leaving, the Heavens opened and I saw three angels waiting for Her. Only in August 1981 had I seen the angels waiting for Her like this after She had been with us.

"On this occasion She did not speak to me about the secrets. During the apparition I prayed three "Our Fathers" with Her, one for non-believers, one for all those who needed it, and one for all the sick who were present. She then blessed all of us and all the holy objects that had been brought to Her. I also had a lot of questions to ask, given to me by others. For all those who asked something, She gave but one answer":

"Pray all three mysteries of the Rosary daily for non-believers and attend Mass specially for them once a month. God knows what their own needs are which they must bring to Him."

The following is the message from Our Lady given to Mirjana in Bijakovici during her annual apparition:

"Dear children! I am glad that you have gathered in such a large number. I would desire that you gather often in communal prayer to my Son.

"Most of all I would desire that you dedicate prayers for my children who do not know my love and the love of my Son. Help them to come to know it! Help me as a Mother of all of you!

"My children, how many times I have already invited you here in Medjugorje to prayer and I will invite you again because I desire you to open your hearts to my Son, to allow Him to come in and fill you with peace and love. Allow Him, let Him enter!

"Help Him by your prayers in order that you might be able to spread peace and love to others, because that is now most necessary for you in this time of battle with satan.

"I have often spoken to you: pray, pray, because only by

**means of prayer will you drive off satan and all the evil that
goes along with him.**

**"I promise you, my children, that I will pray for you, but
I seek from you more vigorous prayers and I seek you to
spread peace and love which I am asking you in Medjugorje
already nearly ten years.**

"Help me, and I will pray my Son for you."

Date Unknown

"You have forgotten the Bible."

This message was possibly given to Father Jozo.   He has
described never seeing a mother so sad as the Mother of God
when She talked about the Bible.

June 25, 1991 - Ivanka's Annual Apparition

Our Lady appeared to Ivanka for approximately eight minutes.
Many crowded in her living room. Ivanka's facial expressions
ranged from intensely serious to supremely joyful. Ivanka
recommended all present to Our Lady. She said Our Lady
spoke to her about the first half of the sixth secret.

It has been realized that during Ivanka's last four annual apparitions Our Lady has spoken about the secrets in progression. In
1988, Our Lady spoke about the third and fourth secrets. In
1989, She spoke about the first half of the fifth secret. In 1990,
as if continuing where She left off the previous year, Our Lady
spoke about the last half of the fifth secret. In 1991, Our Lady
spoke to her about the first half of the sixth secret. Everything
Our Lady does and says is done for a reason. The discussion of
these secrets in this progression is in itself a message to us.

Ivanka stated that Our Lady said:

"I pray that you pray more strongly* for peace and that you become more rooted in faith."

* The Croatian word which was used means "unbreakable." The closest grammatically correct English translation is "more strongly." The English translation, "more strongly," is weaker than the word which Our Lady used meaning "unbreakable."

November 1991

"When you are sick, when you suffer from something, don't say, 'Oh, why has this happened to me and not to somebody else.' No, say instead: 'Lord, I thank you for the gift you are giving me.' For sufferings are really great gifts from God. They are sources of great graces for you and for others. When you are sick, many of you only pray and repeat, 'Heal me, heal me.' No, dear children, this is not correct because your hearts are not open; you shut your hearts through your sickness. You cannot be open to the will of God nor to the graces He wants to give you. Pray this way: 'Lord, Thy will be done in me.' Then only can God communicate His graces to you, according to your real needs that He knows better than you. It can be healing, new strength, new joy, new peace - only open your hearts."

February 14, 1992

"Do not forget I am with you."

March 18, 1992 - Mirjana's Annual Apparition

Every year since 1983, Mirjana has had an apparition on her birthday. A considerably large group gathered together in prayer. They began praying at 1:30 p.m. The apparition took

place at 1:50 p.m. and lasted for eight minutes. Together with
Our Lady she prayed for the sick, for those who do not know
God's love, i.e. for unbelievers, and for those present. This time
also Mirjana wept, but from happiness. Our Lady gave a message, which is:

**"Dear children, I need your prayers now more than ever
before. I beseech you to take the Rosary in your hands now
more than ever before. Grasp it strongly and pray with all
your heart in these difficult times. Thank you for having
gathered in such a number and for having responded to my
call."**

June 25, 1992

On this anniversary of Our Lady's apparitions in Medjugorje,
Vicka made a special presentation to Our Lady of the first
completed coloring books from "Children of America, Save
Medjugorje." Four children from Caritas of Birmingham had
colored their pages, offering up their prayers and sacrifices
to Our Lady for peace. Their coloring books were carried to
Medjugorje for the Anniversary by the Caritas crew who accompanied the most recent PRM flight to Medjugorje and the surrounding areas. Two refugees from a near-by village also had
drawings to present to our Lady. The following was conveyed:

*"On the 25th during the course of the apparition, Vicka gave
Her the first drawings from the children as a gift for the
Anniversary. The Virgin showed Her great joy and blessed
the coloring books as well as the children who did them.
Vicka is waiting impatiently for the others."*

June 25, 1992 - Ivanka's Annual Apparition

Our Lady held Ivanka's hands during her annual apparition this
year. Our Lady had a sad expression on Her face and said:

"I ask you to conquer satan. The arms to conquer him are fasting and prayers. Pray for peace, because satan wants to destroy the little peace you have."

August 2, 1992

Ivan's daily apparition was in the Adoration Chapel for all the young people of the youth festival. Our Lady gave this message:

"Dear children, today I call you to decide for God during these days. You, young people, put God at the first place in your life; thus you will have with Him a way that is sure. I invite you to pray for my intentions of peace."

March 18, 1993 - Mirjana's Annual Apparition

Mirjana's annual birthday message from Our Lady:

"Dear children, my desire is that you give me your hands that I may, as a Mother, lead you on the right path to bring you to the Father. Open your hearts. Allow me to enter. Pray, because in prayer I am with you. Pray and allow me to lead you. I will lead you to peace and happiness."

March 18, 1994 - Mirjana's Annual Apparition

Our Lady's annual birthday message to Mirjana:

"Dear children! Today my heart is filled with happiness. I would like for you to find yourselves in prayer every day, as today, this great day of prayer. Only thus, can you proceed towards true happiness and true fulfillment of body and soul. As Mother, I want to help you in this. Allow me to do so. I am telling you again to open your hearts to me and allow me to lead you. My way leads to God. I invite you

that we may proceed together because you see for your-selves, that with our prayers, all evils are destroyed. Let us pray and hope."

March 18, 1995 - Mirjana's Annual Apparition

"Dear children! As a Mother, for many years already, I am teaching you faith and love for God. Neither have you shown gratitude to the dear Father nor have you given Him glory. You have become 'empty' and your heart has become 'hard' and without love for the sufferings of your neighbors. I am teaching you love and I am showing you that the dear Father has loved you, but you have not loved Him. He sacrificed His Son for your salvation, my children. For as long as you do not love, you will not come to know the love of your Father. You will not come to know Him because God is Love. Love, and have no fear, my children, because in love there is no fear. If your hearts are open to the Father and if they are full of love towards Him, why then fear what is to come. Those who do not love are afraid because they expect punishment and because they know how empty and hard they are. I am leading you, children, towards love, towards the dear Father. I am leading you into Eternal Life. Eternal Life is my Son. Accept Him and you will have accepted Love."

Our Lady appeared to Mirjana at 3:15 p.m. for ten minutes. Mirjana's face, though it was serious, was radiating with great love and intensity. Tears flowed from her eyes. She prayed three "Our Fathers" and three "Glory Be" with Our Lady. Mirjana said after the apparition Our Lady's three intentions: First, for the unbelievers (those who do not know yet the love of God), then for the souls in Purgatory; then for those who were present. Our Lady blessed all present and also all religious articles. When Our Lady left, Mirjana felt great sorrow.

After the apparition, Fr. Slavko received the following words from Mirjana: *"I asked Our Lady three questions and I received three answers. Our Lady was not completely happy as She had been sometimes for my birthdays. She spoke to me about the secrets, but I cannot say anything about that. I cried because it is very difficult for me when She leaves. When I am with Her, everything is in 'its fullness'.*

"When She leaves, in that same moment, I am here on earth, and I continue without Her as if I were abandoned. But I know I am not abandoned. But She went, and She left me! This is really difficult...really difficult! When She leaves, it is so difficult that if this happened often, I don't know how I would 'cope'...I understood this message as a message of Love and Consolation. We have nothing to fear if we have love. I invite all of you to Live Love."

May 31, 1995

On the Feast of the Visitation, the founder of the Community and Mission of Caritas of Birmingham was with Marija in Italy at her home. There were only the two of them present for the apparition on this day. The apparition lasted longer than normal. At the end of the apparition, Marija immediately left to go into the kitchen but said to him to remain in prayer and to recite the "Magnificat". It was a privilege to pray the "Magnificat" in closing the apparition on the feast day in which Our Lady Herself recited it before Elizabeth. He knew something happened during the apparition because of its length and realized when Marija sat down immediately with pen and paper that Our Lady had given a specific message. Though for years he had been around the apparitions and many times received messages, never had he experienced Our Lady giving an individual a message without being prompted by a question first, and then, too, of the many who asked, rarely an answer was given. Marija then relayed that the message was for he, his family, and the community. This message he understood, by a special grace during the apparition, was a clear mandate; that Our Lady had brought this mission and community to a special point by trials and the purifying fire of tribulations in order to now be used by Her in a special way.

Our Lady said to literally "get souls" close to Her heart and bring them to God. She wants of him and the community to be Her extended hands, Her tools which She desires to use just as any craftsman uses his tools. Our Lady said:

"Little children, I desire that through your lives you are witnesses, that you are my extended hands, my instruments. Get as many hearts as you can close to my heart and lead them to God, to a way of salvation."

Marija was very surprised by this. She knew immediately by Our Lady's intimacy in saying "Little Children" that it was also for the community at Caritas and its mission. Marija was questioned by the one who was present at this apparition about "to a way". Marija said specifically Our Lady meant "to 'a' way of salvation". This was important to him because of the spirituality at Caritas and what it is he believes Our Lady has shown by way of this path of salvation, namely of turning away from certain ways and things the world offers. By Our Lady's words, he understood clearly Her desire to lead others along this way, and that She was strongly endorsing and blessing this path. After She spoke this message, Our Lady gave a blessing before returning to Heaven. He understood that he and the community were not to frown on or look with indifference on other paths of salvation, but to be strong in gathering hearts and showing them what Our Lady has taught them at Caritas and how She has guided their mission and the community. It had been eight and one-half years since Our Lady had given the very first message to this same individual on October 6, 1986. The advice and encouragement She gave to him then, is now extended through this most recent message, to the community of Caritas who is following in this "witness", this "way of salvation". (See Early Messages, pages 184-185).

June 25, 1995 - Ivanka's Annual Apparition

Our Lady appeared to Ivanka and gave the following message:

"satan wants to destroy the family. The family is in crisis. Pray."

March 18, 1996 - Mirjana's Annual Apparition

"Dear children! On this message, which I give you today through my servant, I desire for you to reflect a long time. My children, great is the love of God. Do not close your eyes, do not close your ears while I repeat to you: Great is His love! Hear my call and my supplication which I direct to you. Consecrate your heart and make in it the home of the Lord. May He dwell in it forever. My eyes and my heart will be here, even when I will no longer appear. Act in everything as I ask you and lead you to the Lord. Do not reject from yourself the name of God, that you may not be rejected. Accept my messages that you may be accepted. Decide, my children, it is the time of decision. Be of just and innocent heart, that I may lead you to your Father, for this, that I am here, is His great love. Thank you for being here!"

The apparition lasted six minutes. Afterwards, Mirjana wrote the following: *"We prayed two Our Father's and two Glory Be's for those present and for those who have not yet come to know the love of God. We also spoke of other things, but I cannot speak of them. There was no talk of the secrets. Our Lady blessed all those present and all religious articles. At the beginning of the apparition, Our Lady was joyful and gentle. After that, She was sad for awhile and in the end was again joyful. I, Mirjana, who saw and felt Our Lady's love, call you to truly reflect on and to live this message!"*

June 25, 1996 - Ivanka's Annual Apparition

The apparition took place in Ivanka's family home and lasted seven minutes. After the apparition, Ivanka said that this had been one of the most beautiful apparitions that she had had up tot he present. She also shared the following:

> *"Our Lady thanks us for our prayer and for our love and desires that prayer and love become interwoven into every day. In conclusion, She invited us to pray for those who were under diabolic possession."*

August 26, 1996

Our Lady gave the following message to Vicka in response to a novena that was being prayed by the Community of Caritas for the visionaries, villagers, and village of Medjugorje that Vicka presented to Our Lady. Our Lady's words:

"Whatever you are doing with the heart, it is all precious to Me."

March 18, 1997 - Mirjana's Annual Apparition

Our Lady appeared to Mirjana at approximately 1:50 p.m. The apparition lasted six minutes. Mirjana displayed an array of emotions from smiling to serious. For the most part, she was very serious. Her emotions fully displayed who it was that was before her. The tent where the apparition took place is behind St. James Church. It was filled to capacity, with some of the hundreds of people spilling outside the tent. Mirjana was before an altar which had a small statue of Our Lady on it. She prayed a mystery of the Rosary and then began the Seven-Seven-Seven prayers. Our Lady appeared during these prayers. Our Lady gave a message that was like the 25th message in that it began with **"Dear children"** and ended with **"Thank you for having**

responded to my call." The following is the translation from Croatian:

> **"Dear children! As a mother I ask that you do not go on the path that you have been on, that is the path without love towards neighbor and towards my Son. On this path, you will find only hardness and emptiness of heart, and not peace which you all long for. Truthful peace will have only that one, who in his neighbor sees and loves my Son. In the heart of the one where only my Son reigns, that one knows what peace and security is. Thank you for having responded to my call."**

Mirjana said that Our Lady was saddened only when She was giving the message, otherwise, it was like normal. She blessed everyone present and all religious articles. Our Lady prayed with Mirjana an Our Father and Glory Be for unbelievers. Our Lady said nothing of the secrets.

As you may know, Mirjana's March 18th apparition is on her birthday, but it is not the reason why Our Lady appears to her on that day. Our Lady has never given Mirjana a salutation of "Happy Birthday". Her annual March 18th apparition is because of the date and has nothing to do with Mirjana's birthday. So March 18th is a significant day, and we will know why in the future.

June 25, 1997 - Ivanka's Annual Apparition

Our Lady stayed with Ivanka for 6 minutes. After the apparition Ivanka said, *"Our Lady talked to me about the fifth secret and spoke the following message"*:

> **"Dear children, pray with the heart to know how to forgive and to be forgiven. I thank you for your prayers and for the love you give me."**

October 31, 1997

Our Lady appeared to Marija in the Community of Caritas' Mission House in Medjugorje. The only ones present were five members from the community and one of Marija's close friends. It was the longest apparition Our Lady had given in over a month that Marija had been in Medjugorje. The Rosary prayed in preparation of the apparition was filled with such a peace that those present felt as though they could physically hold the peace in their hands. Surprisingly Our Lady gave a message for the Community of Caritas. Our Lady gave the following message to the community through Marija:

"I want you to be Jesus' joy."

March 18, 1998 - Mirjana's Annual Apparition

The apparition lasted between four and five minutes. Our Lady spoke to her about the secrets, blessed all those present, and gave the following message:

"Dear children! I call you to be my light, in order to enlighten all those who still live in darkness, to fill their hearts with Peace, my Son. Thank you for having responded to my call!"

June 25, 1998 - Ivanka's Annual Apparition

Ivanka had her apparition in her home. It lasted six minutes. Ivanka related the following after her apparition:

"Our Lady was joyful. I asked Her to bless everyone, which She did. Our Lady talked to me about all the secrets. She invited us to pray for the families of this time and especially to pray for the sick. She called us to open our hearts and to thank Her Son for the grace He has given us. At the end, Our Lady thanked us for our prayers and love."

September 12, 1998 - Jakov's last regular apparition

While on his journey in America, Jakov reported the following
text from Miami.

*"On Friday, September 11th, during the regular apparition,
Our Lady told me to prepare myself specially by prayer for
tomorrow's apparition because She will confide the 10th
secret to me. On Saturday, September 12th, Our Lady came
at 11:15 a.m. (local time). When She came She greeted me
as always with* **'Praised be Jesus.'** *While She was confiding
the 10th secret to me, She was sad. Then with a gentle smile,
She said to me"*:

**"Dear child! I am your mother and I love you unconditionally. From today I will not be appearing to you every day,
but only on Christmas, the birthday of my Son. Do not be
sad, because as a mother I will always be with you and like
every true mother I will never leave you. And continue further to follow the way of my Son, the way of peace and love
and try to persevere in the mission that I have confided to
you. Be an example of that man who has known God and
God's love. Let people always see in you an example of
how God acts on people and how God acts through them.
I bless you with my Motherly blessing and I thank you for
having responded to my call."**

The apparition ended at 11:45 a.m.

December 25, 1998 - Jakov's Annual Apparition

After the apparition, which began at 11:50 a.m. and lasted 12
minutes, Jakov wrote:

"Our Lady came joyful. She greeted me as always with
'Praised be Jesus!' *She spoke to me about the secrets and
afterwards, gave me this message"*:

**"Dear children! Today, on the birthday of my Son, my
heart is filled with immeasurable joy, love, and peace. As
your mother, I desire for each of you to feel that same joy,
peace, and love in the heart. That is why, do not be afraid
to open your heart and to completely surrender yourself
to Jesus, because only in this way, can He enter into your
heart and fill it with love, peace, and joy. I bless you with
my Motherly blessing."**

Jakov prayed with his family. He prepared himself for the apparition with Confession and Holy Mass. After the apparition, he
cried for a while.

March 18, 1999 - Mirjana's Annual Apparition

**"Dear children! I want you to surrender your hearts to me
so that I may take you on the way which leads to the light
and to eternal life. I do not want your hearts to wander in
today's darkness. I will help you. I will be with you on this
way of discovery of the love and the mercy of God. As a
mother, I ask you to permit me to do this. Thank you for
having responded to my call."**

The apparition lasted for 6 minutes from 10:14 a.m. to 10:20 a.m.
Our Lady spoke about the secrets. She blessed everyone.

June 25, 1999 - Ivanka's Annual Apparition

Ivanka had the apparition, which lasted 7-8 minutes, in her own
family home. Present for the apparition were only Ivanka's
family, husband and three children. After the apparition,
Ivanka said that during the apparition she prayed for the parish
and families, and she recommended all in her prayer. Our Lady
gave the following message:

**"Dear children, thank my Son for all the graces that He has
given you. Pray for peace, pray for peace, pray for peace."**

December 25, 1999 - Jakov's Annual Apparition

At the last daily apparition of September 12, 1998, Our Lady told Jakov Colo that he will have an apparition once a year and that it would be on Christmas day, December 25th. Thus, it was also this year. The apparition began at 3:00 p.m. and lasted 10 minutes. Our Lady came joyful and in a golden dress with the baby Jesus in Her arms. She spoke about the secrets and blessed everyone. She gave the following message:

> **"Dear children! Today on the birthday of my Son, when my heart is filled with immeasurable joy and love, I invite you to a complete openness and to a complete abandonment to God. Throw all darkness out of your heart and allow God's light and God's love to enter into your heart and to dwell there forever. Be carriers of God's light and love to all mankind, so that all in you and through you may feel and experience true light and love which only God can give you. I bless you with my Motherly blessing."**

January 1, 2000

Marija received Our Lady in the apparition in the chapel of the Oasis of Peace on January 1st, the Feast of the Mother of God. Marija said that though Our Lady gave no message, She appeared radiant and looked attentively at each person present, blessing them individually. The apparition was longer than usual.

January 2, 2000

Marija visited a near-by orphanage in Citluk. The orphanage cares for more than 90 children and is managed by Sr. Josipa. The children, knowing Our Lady would be with them during the apparition on this day, prepared special songs to sing to Our Lady, which they did, while Marija was in ecstasy. After the apparition, Marija was happy to tell the children that Our Lady had listened to them, smiling tenderly while they sang. Our Lady looked at each of the children attentively and blessed them. Our Lady stayed a long time and gave the following message:

"I am the Queen of Peace, and I am also your Mother. Don't forget that I am your Mother and I love you."

March 18, 2000 - Mirjana's Annual Apparition

The following is an account of Mirjana's annual apparition on March 18, 2000. The apparition started at 9:55 a.m. and lasted about five minutes. Our Lady prayed over everyone and blessed everyone. Mirjana especially recommended the sick. This time Our Lady did not say anything about the secrets.

"Dear children! Do not seek peace and happiness in vain, in the wrong places and in the wrong things. Do not permit your hearts to become hard by loving vanity. Invoke the name of my Son. Receive Him in your heart. Only in the name of my Son will you experience true happiness and true peace in your heart. Only in this way will you come to know the love of God and spread it further. I am calling you to be my apostles."

June 25, 2000 – Ivanka's Annual Apparition

"Dear children, I introduced myself as the Queen of Peace. I call you again to peace, fasting, and prayer. Renew the family prayer. Receive my blessing."

Ivanka said that Our Lady was extremely happy and that She spoke about the sixth secret. The apparition lasted seven minutes. Ivanka was radiantly happy. Even her children were in tears because of the happiness that was on their mother's face.

They were embracing and kissing each other immediately after
the apparition.

December 25, 2000 - Jakov's Annual Apparition

Jakov's apparition lasted 10 minutes. Our Lady came joyful and
Baby Jesus in Her arms. She blessed everyone. She gave the
following message:

> **"Dear children! Today when Jesus is born and by His birth
> brings immeasurable joy, love and peace, I call you, in a spe-
> cial way, to say your 'yes' to Jesus. Open your hearts so that
> Jesus enters into them, comes to dwell in them and starts to
> work through you. Only in this way will you be able to com-
> prehend the true beauty of God's love, joy and peace. Dear
> children, rejoice in the birth of Jesus and pray for all those
> hearts that have not opened to Jesus so that Jesus may enter
> into each of their hearts and may start working through time
> - so that every person would be an example of a true person
> through whom God works."**

January 1, 2001

On January 1st, the first day of the New Year, during Marija's
regular apparition at 5:45 p.m., Our Lady made a special request
of Marija. She asked Marija to go up to Apparition Hill that
night for an apparition at 10:30 p.m. It has been a long time,
even years since Our Lady has asked Marija to go up one of
the mountains. Even more special, Our Lady asked this of
Marija on the very first day of the new millennium in the New
Year 2001. This signifies a certain importance. A call to the
mountain on the first day of the new millennium, the second
apparition in the same day, to give an important message – a
message Our Lady signified She wanted heard by setting it up
out of the context of the normal apparition time, asking Marija
to come to a second apparition. Our Lady appeared to Marija

at 10:30 p.m. Marija said that Our Lady came with five angels.
During this special apparition Our Lady gave the following very
important message:

**"My dear children, now that when satan is unchained, I
desire you to be consecrated to My Heart and the Heart of
My Son Jesus. I bless you with my Motherly blessing."**

March 18, 2001 - Mirjana's Annual Apparition

The following is Our Lady's annual apparition to Mirjana
Soldo on March 18, 2001. Our Lady appeared at 9:43 a.m. The
apparition lasted 3 minutes and 55 seconds. Our Lady blessed
everyone and gave a message. She was clear and resolute in the
words She gave.

**"Dear children! Today I call you to love and mercy. Give
love to each other as your Father gives it to you. Be merciful** (Our Lady paused at this point and then added) **with the
heart. Do good works, not permitting them to wait for you
too long. Every mercy that comes from the heart brings you
closer to my Son."**

Mirjana said that when Our Lady paused, She did that to
emphasis the words She would speak next, **"with the heart."** A
few of our community members were right in front of Mirjana,
less than twenty feet, and could see clearly her face throughout
the apparition. They relayed that Mirjana's emotions ranged
from looking very serious, wincing her eyes, tears falling down
her cheeks, leaning forward two to three times during the apparition to a clear look of joy or somewhat satisfied, which did not
happen until the very end of the apparition. Our Lady seemed
to be speaking a lot to Mirjana because Mirjana nodded several
times during the apparition. Mirjana seemed very intense. At
different times during the apparition, she seemed to have a difficult time catching her breath.

June 25, 2001 - Ivanka's Annual Apparition

At her last daily apparition on May 7, 1985, Our Lady told Ivanka that She would have an apparition once a year on the anniversary of the apparitions. It was that way also this year. Ivanka had the apparition in the presence of her family. She says that Our Lady was joyful and that She spoke to her about the future of the Church. Our Lady gave the following message:

"Dear angels! Thank you for your prayers, because through them my plan is being realized. This is why, angels, pray, pray, pray, so that my plan may be realized. Receive my Motherly blessing."

December 25, 2001 - Jakov's Annual Apparition

At the last daily apparition to Jakov Colo on September 12, 1998, Our Lady told him that from now on, he would have one apparition a year, every December 25th, on Christmas Day. This is also how it was this year. The apparition began at 3:30 p.m. and lasted five minutes. Our Lady gave the following message:

"Dear children, today when Jesus is born anew for you, in a special way, I want to call you to conversion. Pray, pray, pray for the conversion of your heart, so that Jesus may be born in you all and may dwell in you and come to reign over your entire being. Thank you for having responded to my call."

March 18, 2002 - Mirjana's Annual Apparition

The following is Mirjana's annual apparition with Our Lady on March 18, 2002:

"Dear children! As a mother I implore you, open your heart and offer it to me, and fear nothing. I will be with you and will teach you how to put Jesus in the first place. I will teach you to love Him and to belong to Him completely. Comprehend, dear children, that without my Son there is no salvation. You should become aware that He is your beginning and your end. Only with this awareness can you be happy and merit eternal life. As your mother I desire this for you. Thank you for having responded to my call."

June 25, 2002 - Ivanka's Annual Apparition

The following is Ivanka's Annual Apparition with Our Lady on June 25, 2002:

"The apparition lasted about six minutes. Our Lady told me details about Her life on this earth. Then Our Lady told me:"

"Do not get tired of prayer! Pray for peace, peace, peace!"

December 25, 2002 - Jakov's Annual Apparition

At the last daily apparition to Jakov Colo on September 12, 1998, Our Lady told him that henceforth he would have one apparition a year, every December 25th, on Christmas Day. This is also how it was this year. The apparition began at 5:20 p.m. and lasted 7 minutes. Our Lady gave the following message:

"Dear children! Today, on the day of love and peace, with Jesus in my arms, I call you to pray for peace. Little children, without God and prayer you cannot have peace. Therefore, little children, open your heart so that the King of Peace may be born in your heart. Only in this way you

**can witness and carry God's peace to this peaceless world. I
am with you and bless you with my Motherly blessing.**

March 18, 2003 - Mirjana's Annual Apparition

Our Lady's annual apparition to Mirjana lasted approximately
seven minutes. Mirjana stated that she was in "awe" of Our
Lady, both in what Our Lady said and did. Mirjana stated that
she has seen the Mother of God display every kind of emotion
throughout the years, but never had she seen how Our Lady
appeared to her on this March 18th. Mirjana said that Our
Lady was "stern" throughout the apparition. This attitude She
displayed awed Mirjana. The following is Our Lady's message
to Mirjana:

**"Dear children! Particularly at this holy time of penance
and prayer, I call you to make a choice. God gave you free
will to choose life or death. Listen to my messages with the
heart that you may become cognizant of what you are to do
and how you will find the way to life. My children, without
God you can do nothing; do not forget this even for a single
moment. For, what are you and what will you be on earth,
when you will return to it again. Do not anger God, but follow me to life. Thank you for being here."**

June 25, 2003 - Ivanka's Annual Apparition

The apparition lasted 10 minutes. Ivanka had the apparition at
home in the presence of her family, her husband, and their three
children. Our Lady gave the following message:

**"Dear children! Do not be afraid, I am always with you.
Open your heart for love and peace to enter into it. Pray
for peace, peace, peace."**

Our Lady came joyful and spoke to Ivanka more extensively
about Her life.

December 25, 2003 - Jakov's Annual Apparition

The apparition began at 3:15 p.m. and lasted 8 minutes. Our Lady gave the following message:

> **"Dear children! Today, when in a special way, Jesus desires to give you His peace, I call you to pray for peace in your hearts. Children, without peace in your hearts you cannot feel the love and joy of the birth of Jesus. Therefore, little children, today in a special way, open your hearts and begin to pray. Only through prayer and complete surrender, will your heart be filled with the love and peace of Jesus. I bless you with my Motherly blessing."**

March 18, 2004 - Mirjana's Annual Apparition

This year several thousand pilgrims gathered to pray the Rosary in preparation for Mirjana's apparition. The apparition lasted from 1:58 p.m. to 2:03 p.m. Our Lady gave the following message:

> **"Dear children! Also today, watching you with a heart full of love, I desire to tell you that what you persistently seek, what you long for, my little children, is before you. It is sufficient that, in a cleaned heart, you place my Son in the first place, and then you will be able to see. Listen to me and permit me to lead you to this in a motherly way."**

June 25, 2004 - Ivanka's Annual Apparition

Ivanka had her apparition at home with her family present. Our Lady gave the following message:

> **"Dear children! Pray for those families who have not come to know the love of my Son. Receive my Motherly blessing."**

Our Lady came very joyful and spoke to Ivanka more about Her personal life while on earth.

December 25, 2004 - Jakov's Annual Apparition

Jakov's apparition began at 2:30 p.m. and lasted 7 minutes. Our Lady gave the following message:

> "Dear children! Today, on a day of grace, with little Jesus in my arms, in a special way I call you to open your hearts and to start to pray. Little children, ask Jesus to be born in each of your hearts and to begin to rule in your lives. Pray to Him for the grace to be able to recognize Him always in every person. Little children, ask Jesus for love, because only with God's love can you love God and all people. I carry you all in my heart and give you my Motherly blessing."

March 18, 2005 - Mirjana's Annual Apparition

> "Dear children, I come to you as the Mother who, above all, loves Her children. My children, I desire to teach you to love also. I pray for this. I pray that you will recognize my Son in each of your neighbors. The way to my Son, who is true peace and love, passes through the love for all neighbors. My children, pray and fast for your heart to be open for this my intention."

Several thousand pilgrims gathered to pray with Mirjana. The apparition lasted from 2:09 p.m. to 2:14 p.m.

April 2, 2005

The following is a description of Ivan Dragicevic daily apparition on April 2, 2005:

> *"At Ivan's apparition tonight, Ivan was recommending inten-*

*tions to Our Lady when Pope John Paul II appeared on Her
right. He was smiling, young, and very happy. All in white
with a long gold cape. Our Lady turned, smiling, to look
at the Pope and he was looking at Our Lady, smiling. Our
Lady then said to Ivan":*

"This is my son; he is with me."

June 25, 2005 - Ivanka's Annual Apparition

The visionary Ivanka had her regular annual apparition on June
25, 2005. The apparition lasted 10 minutes. Ivanka had the
apparition at home in the presence of her family, her husband,
and her three children. Our Lady gave the following message:

**"Dear children, love each other with the love of my Son.
Peace, peace, peace."**

Our Lady was joyful and spoke to Ivanka about the 6th secret.

December 25, 2005 - Jakov's Annual Apparition

The following is Jakov Colo's annual apparition of Our Lady
on Christmas Day, December 25, 2005. The apparition began at
2:45 p.m. and lasted 7 minutes.

**"Dear children! Today, with Jesus in my arms, in a special
way I call you to conversion. Children, through all this time
which God permitted me to be with you, I continuously
called you to conversion. Many of your hearts remained
closed. Little children, Jesus is peace, love, and joy; therefore now decide for Jesus. Start to pray. Pray to Him for the
gift of conversion. Little children, only with Jesus can you
have peace, joy, and a heart filled with love. Little children,
I love you. I am your mother and give you my Motherly
blessing."**

January 1, 2006

To Marija:

"Dear children, do not forget that I am your Mother and that I love you with a tender love."

March 18, 2006 - Mirjana's Annual Apparition

The following is Mirjana's annual apparition with Our Lady Queen of Peace on March 18, 2006. Several thousand pilgrims were present for the apparition. The apparition lasted from 1:59 p.m. to 2:04 p.m. The following is Our Lady's message:

"Dear children! In this Lenten time, I call you to interior renunciation. The way to this leads you through love, fasting, prayer, and good works. Only with total interior renunciation will you recognize God's love and the signs of the time in which you live. You will be witnesses of these signs and will begin to speak about them. I desire to bring you to this. Thank you for having responded to me."

June 25, 2006 - Ivanka's Annual Apparition

The visionary Ivanka Elez had her regular annual apparition on June 25, 2006. According to the visionaries, Vicka, Marija and Ivan continue to have daily apparitions, and Mirjana, Ivanka and Jakov have an annual apparition.

At Her last daily apparition on May 7, 1985, Our Lady confided to Ivanka the 10th secret and told her that she would have an apparition once a year on the anniversary of the apparitions. It was that way also this year. The apparition lasted 7 minutes. Ivanka had the apparition at home in the presence of her family, her husband and her three children.

Our Lady gave the following message:

"Dear children, thank you for having responded to my call. Pray, pray, pray."

Our Lady was joyful and spoke about the seventh secret.

December 25, 2006 - Jakov's Annual Apparition

The following is Jakov Colo's annual apparition of Our Lady on December 25, 2006:

"Today is a great day of joy and peace. Rejoice with me. Little children, in a special way, I call you to holiness in your families. I desire, little children, that each of your families be holy and that God's joy and peace, which God sends you today in a special way, may come to rule and dwell in your families. Little children, open your hearts today on this day of grace, decide for God and put Him in the first place in your family. I am your Mother. I love you and give you my Motherly blessing."

March 18, 2007 - Mirjana's Annual Apparition

The following is Our Lady Queen of Peace of Medjugorje's annual apparition to Mirjana Soldo on March 18, 2007.

The apparition lasted from 2:07 p.m. to 2:12 p.m. Our Lady gave the following message:

"Dear children! I come to you as a Mother with gifts. I come with love and mercy. Dear children, mine is a big heart. In it, I desire all of your hearts, purified by fasting and prayer. I desire that, through love, our hearts may triumph together. I desire that through that triumph you may see the real Truth, the real Way and the real Life. I desire that you may see my Son. Thank you."

June 25, 2007 - Ivanka's Annual Apparition

Today's apparition to Ivanka lasted 17 minutes. Ivanka's husband and their three children were present for the apparition. Following is the description of the apparition from Ivanka:

"Our Lady remained with me for 17 minutes. She was joyful and spoke to me about Her life. Our Lady said":

"Dear children, receive my Motherly blessing."

December 25, 2007 - Jakov's Annual Apparition

The following is Jakov Colo's annual apparition from Our Lady on December 25, 2007.

The apparition began at 2:29 p.m. and lasted 6 minutes. The following is Our Lady's message:

"Dear children! Today, in a special way I call you to become open to God and for each of your hearts today to become a place of Jesus' birth. Little children, through all this time that God permits me to be with you, I desire to lead you to the joy of your life. Little children, the only true joy of your life is God. Therefore, dear children, do not seek joy in things of this earth but open your hearts and accept God. Little children, everything passes, only God remains in your heart. Thank you for having responded to my call."

March 18, 2008 - Mirjana's Annual Apparition

Our Lady appeared to Mirjana on March 18, 2008 for her annual apparition. Our Lady appeared to Mirjana at 2:01 p.m. The apparition lasted 7 minutes. Mirjana relayed the following:

"I have never seen Our Lady address us in this manner. She extended Her hands towards us and with Her hands extended in this way, She said":

"Dear children, today I extend my hands towards you. Do not be afraid to accept them. They desire to give you love and peace and to help you in salvation. Therefore, my children, receive them. Fill my heart with joy and I will lead you towards holiness. The way on which I lead you is difficult and full of temptations and falls. I will be with you and my hands will hold you. Be persevering so that, at the end of the way, we can all together, in joy and love, hold the hands of my Son. Come with me; fear not. Thank you."

June 25, 2008 - Ivanka's Annual Apparition

Ivanka was the second Medjugorje visionary to receive all 10 secrets and to stop seeing Our Lady on a regular basis. Her last daily apparition was May 7, 1985. Our Lady promised Ivanka that She would appear to her once a year for the rest of her life on June 25th, the anniversary of the apparitions.

Our Lady appeared to Ivanka at home with her family present on June 25, 2008. The apparition lasted six minutes. After the apparition, Ivanka stated:

"Our Lady spoke to me about the ninth secret. She gave us Her Motherly blessing."

December 25, 2008 - Jakov's Annual Apparition

When Jakov received his last daily apparition on September 12, 1998, Our Lady told him that he would have one apparition a year for the rest of his life on Christmas Day, December 25th. So Our Lady appeared to Jakov Christmas morning. The apparition began at 9:49 a.m. and lasted 6 minutes. Our Lady gave the following message:

"Dear children! Today, in a special way, I call you to pray for peace. Without God you cannot have peace or live in

peace. **Therefore, little children, today on this day of grace
open your hearts to the King of Peace, for Him to be born in
you and to grant you His peace - and you be carriers of peace
in this peaceless world. Thank you for having responded to
my call."**

March 18, 2009 - Mirjana's Annual Apparition

Our Lady appeared to Mirjana on March 18, 2009 for her annual
apparition. The apparition took place at the Blue Cross. Our
Lady appeared to Mirjana at 1:53 p.m. The apparition lasted
about four and a half minutes, ending at 1:58 p.m. Our Lady gave
the following message:

**"Dear children! Today I call you to look into your hearts
sincerely and for a long time. What will you see in them?
Where is my Son in them and where is the desire to follow
me to Him? My children, may this time of renunciation be
a time when you ask yourself: 'What does my God desire
of me personally? What am I to do?' Pray, fast, and have a
heart full of mercy. Do not forget your shepherds. Pray that
they may not get lost, that they may remain in my Son so as
to be good shepherds to their flock."**

"Our Lady looked at all those present and said":

**"Again I say to you, if you knew how much I love you, you
would cry with happiness. Thank you."**

<u>Early Messages And</u>
<u>Various Other Messages</u>

CHAPTER 2

THE WEEKLY MESSAGES OF OUR LADY THROUGH MARIJA

(March 1, 1984 to January 8, 1987)

"PLEASE DO NOT LET MY HEART WEEP TEARS OF BLOOD." (May 24, 1984)

These messages were given for the parish and to all in the world who want to live them. The weekly and monthly messages for the parish are always given to Marija.

March 1, 1984

"Dear children, I have chosen this parish in a special way and I wish to lead it. I am guarding it in love and I want everyone to be mine. Thank you for having responded tonight. I wish you always to be with my Son and me in ever greater numbers. I shall speak a special message to you every Thursday."

March 8, 1984

"Thank you for having responded to my call. Dear children, you in the parish, be converted. This is my other wish. That way all those who shall come here shall be able to convert."

March 15, 1984

This day, like every Thursday evening, the faithful were worshipping the Most Holy Sacrament, but this evening it was noticed that many people remained in the church for adoration, although they had worked hard in the fields.

"Tonight also, dear children, I am grateful to you in a special way for being here. Unceasingly adore the Most Blessed Sacrament of the Altar. I am always present when the faithful are adoring. Special graces are then being received."

March 22, 1984

"Dear children, in a special way this evening, I am calling you during Lent to honor the wounds of my Son, which He received from the sins of this parish. Unite yourselves with my prayers for the parish so that His sufferings may be bearable. Thank you for having responded to my call. Try to come in ever greater numbers."

March 29, 1984

"Dear children, in a special way this evening, I am calling you to perseverance in trials. Consider how the Almighty is still suffering today on account of your sins. So when sufferings come, offer them up as a sacrifice to God. Thank you for having responded to my call."

April 5, 1984

"Dear children, this evening I pray that you especially venerate the Heart of my Son, Jesus. Make reparation for the wound inflicted on the Heart of my Son. That Heart is offended by all kinds of sin. Thank you for coming this evening."

April 12, 1984

"Dear children, today I beseech you to stop slandering and to pray for the unity of the parish, because my Son and I have a special plan for this parish. Thank you for having responded to my call."

April 19, 1984 (HOLY THURSDAY)

"Dear children, sympathize with me! Pray, pray, pray!"

April 26, 1984

Although this was Thursday, Our Lady gave no message, therefore, Marija concluded that perhaps Our Lady would give the Thursday messages only during Lent.

April 30, 1984 (MONDAY)

Today is Monday and Marija asked Our Lady, *"Dear Madonna, why didn't you give me a message for the parish on Thursday?"* Our Lady replied to Marija:

"I don't wish to force anyone to do that which he neither feels nor desires, even though I had special messages for the parish by which I wanted to awaken the faith of every believer. But only a really small number has accepted my Thursday messages. In the beginning there were quite a few. But it's become a routine affair for them. And now recently some are asking for the message out of curiosity, and not out of faith and devotion to my Son and me."

May 3, 1984

No message was given.

May 10, 1984

Many of the faithful felt shaken by the last message of Our Lady. Some had the feeling that Our Lady would not give any more messages to the parish, but this evening She said:

"I am speaking to you and I wish to speak further. You, just listen to my instructions!"

May 17, 1984

"Dear children, today I am very happy because there are many who want to consecrate themselves to me. Thank you. You have not made a mistake. My Son, Jesus Christ, wishes to bestow on you special graces through me. My Son is happy because of your dedication. Thank you for having responded to my call."

May 24, 1984

"Dear children, I have told you already that I have chosen you in a special way, just the way you are. I, the Mother, love you all. And in any moment that is difficult for you, do not be afraid! Because I love you even when you are far from my Son and me. Please, do not let my heart weep with tears of blood because of the souls who are being lost in sin. Therefore, dear children, pray, pray, pray! Thank you for having responded to my call."

May 31, 1984 (ASCENSION THURSDAY)

There were many people present from abroad. Our Lady did not give a message for the parish. She told Marija that She would give a message on Saturday to be announced at the Sunday parish Mass.

June 2, 1984 (SATURDAY)

Today is Saturday, one of the days during which the Novena
to the Holy Spirit (prior to Pentecost) is being conducted. The
message to Marija is:

> **"Dear children, tonight I wish to tell you during the days of
> this novena to pray for the outpouring of the Holy Spirit on
> your families and on your parish. Pray, and you shall not
> regret it. God will give you gifts by which you will glorify
> Him till the end of your life on this earth. Thank you for
> having responded to my call."**

June 7, 1984

No message was given today. Our Lady promised to give it on
Saturday.

June 9, 1984 (SATURDAY)

Today is Saturday, the Vigil of Pentecost, and once again Our
Lady did not give a Thursday message for the parish; however,
She promised to give the message this evening. The message
is:

> **"Dear children, tomorrow night pray for the Spirit of Truth!
> Especially, you from the parish. Because you need the
> Spirit of Truth to be able to convey the messages just the
> way they are, neither adding anything to them, nor taking
> anything whatsoever away from them, but just the way I
> said them. Pray for the Holy Spirit to inspire you with the
> spirit of prayer, so you will pray more. I, your Mother,
> tell you that you are praying little. Thank you for having
> responded to my call."**

June 14, 1984

No special message was given.

June 21, 1984

> **"Pray, pray, pray! Thank you for having responded to my call."**

June 28, 1984

No special message was given.

July 5, 1984

> **"Dear children, today I wish to tell you, always pray before your work and end your work with prayer. If you do that, God will bless you and your work. These days you have been praying too little and working a lot; therefore, pray. In prayer, you will find rest. Thank you for your response to my call."**

July 12, 1984

> **"Dear children, these days satan wants to frustrate my plans. Pray that his plan not be realized. I will pray to my Son, Jesus, to give you the grace to experience the victory of Jesus in the temptations of satan. Thank you for having responded to my call."**

July 19, 1984

> **"Dear children, these days you have been experiencing how satan is working. I am always with you, and do not be afraid of temptations because God is always watching over us. Also I have given myself to you and I sympathize with you even in the smallest temptation. Thank you for having responded to my call."**

July 26, 1984

> **"Dear children, today also I would like to call you to persistent prayer and penance. Especially, let the young people of this parish be more active in their prayers. Thank you for having responded to my call."**

August 9, 1984

> **"Dear children, satan continues to hinder my plans. Pray, pray, pray! In prayer, abandon yourselves to God. Pray with the heart. Thank you for your response to my call."**

August 14, 1984 (TUESDAY)

This apparition was unexpected. Ivan was praying at home. After that he started to get ready to go to church for the evening services. By surprise Our Lady appeared to him and told him to relate to the people.

> **"I would like the people to pray along with me these days. Pray all the more. Pray as much as possible! Fast strictly on Wednesdays and Fridays, and every day pray at least one Rosary: the Joyful, Sorrowful, and Glorious Mysteries."**

Our Lady asked that we accept this message with a firm will. She especially requested this of the parishioners and believers from the surrounding places.

August 16, 1984

> **"Dear children, I beseech you, especially those from this parish, to live my messages and convey them to others, to whomever you meet. Thank you for having responded to my call."**

August 23, 1984

"Pray, pray, pray!"

Marija said that She also invited the people, and especially the young people, to keep order during the Mass.

August 30, 1984

This message was regarding the cross, erected on Mount Krizevac in 1933 for the 1950th anniversary of the Death and Resurrection of Jesus:

> **"Dear children, the cross was also in God's plan when you built it. These days especially, go on the mountain and pray before the cross. I need your prayers. Thank you for having responded to my call."**

September 6, 1984

> **"Dear children, without prayer there is no peace. Therefore, I say to you, dear children, pray at the foot of the Crucifix for peace. Thank you for having responded to my call."**

September 13, 1984

> **"Dear children, I still need your prayers. You wonder why all these prayers? Look around you, dear children, and you will see how greatly sin has dominated the world. Pray, therefore, that Jesus conquers. Thank you for having responded to my call."**

September 20, 1984

> **"Dear children, today I call on you to begin fasting with the heart. There are many people who are fasting, but only because everyone is fasting. It has become a custom which**

no one wants to stop. I ask the parish to fast out of gratitude
because God has allowed me to stay this long in this parish.
**Dear children, fast and pray with the heart. Thank you for
having responded to my call."**

September 27, 1984

**"Dear children, you have helped me along by your prayers
to realize my plans. Keep on praying that my plans be
completely realized. I request the families of the parish to
pray the Family Rosary. Thank you for your response to
my call."**

October 4, 1984

**"Dear children, today I want to tell you that again and
again you make me happy by your prayer, but there are
enough of those in this very parish who do not pray and my
heart is saddened. Therefore, pray that I can bring all your
sacrifices and prayers to the Lord. Thank you for having
responded to my call."**

October 11, 1984

In this message, Our Lady refers to a testing. This testing was a
long rain during the middle of the reaping season which caused
a great deal of damage to the crops.

**"Dear children, thank you for dedicating all your hard work
to God even now when He is testing you through the grapes
you are picking. Be assured, dear children, that He loves
you and, therefore, He tests you. You just always offer up
all your burdens to God and do not be anxious. Thank you
for having responded to my call."**

October 18, 1984

"Dear children, today I call on you to read the Bible every day in your homes and let it be in a visible place so as always to encourage you to read it and to pray. Thank you for having responded to my call."

October 25, 1984

"Dear children, pray during this month. God allows me every day to help you with graces to defend yourselves against evil. This is my month. I want to give it to you. You just pray and God will give you the graces you are seeking. I will help along with it. Thank you for having responded to my call."

November 1, 1984

"Dear children, today I call you to the renewal of prayer in your homes. The work in the fields is over. Now devote yourselves to prayer. Let prayer take the first place in your families. Thank you for having responded to my call."

November 8, 1984

"Dear children, you are not conscious of the messages which God is sending to you through me. He is giving you great graces and you do not comprehend them. Pray to the Holy Spirit for enlightenment. If you only knew how great are the graces God is granting you, you would be praying without ceasing. Thank you for having responded to my call."

November 15, 1984

"Dear children, you are a chosen people and God has given you great graces. You are not conscious of every message

which I am giving you. Now I just want to say - pray, pray, pray! I don't know what else to tell you because I love you and I want you to comprehend my love and God's love through prayer. Thank you for having responded to my call."

November 22, 1984

"Dear children, these days live all the main messages [conversion, Confession, prayer, fasting and Holy Mass] **and keep rooting them into your hearts till Thursday. Thank you for having responded to my call."**

November 29, 1984

"Dear children, no, you don't know how to love and you don't know how to listen with love to the words I am saying to you. Be conscious, my beloved, that I am your Mother and I have come on earth to teach you how to listen out of love, to pray out of love and not compelled by the fact that you are carrying a cross. By means of the cross, God is glorified through every person. Thank you for having responded to my call."

December 6, 1984

"Dear children, these days I am calling you to family prayer. In God's Name, many times I have been giving you messages, but you have not listened to me. This Christmas will be unforgettable for you only if you accept the messages which I am giving you. Dear children, don't allow that day of joy to become my most sorrowful day. Thank you for having responded to my call."

December 13, 1984

"Dear children, you know that the season of joy is getting

closer, but without love you will achieve nothing. So first of all, begin to love your own family, everyone in the parish, and then you'll be able to love and accept all who are coming over here. Now let these seven days be a week when you need to learn to love. Thank you for having responded to my call."

December 20, 1984

"Dear children, today I am asking you to do something concrete for Jesus Christ. As a sign of dedication to Jesus, I want each family of the parish to bring a single flower before that happy day. I want every member of the family to have a single flower by the crib so Jesus can come and see your dedication to Him! Thank you for having responded to my call."

December 27, 1984

"Dear children, this Christmas satan wanted in a special way to spoil God's plans. You, dear children, have discerned satan even on Christmas Day itself. But God is winning in all your hearts. So let your hearts keep on being happy. Thank you for having responded to my call."

January 3, 1985

"Dear children, these days the Lord has bestowed upon you great graces. Let this week be one of thanksgiving for all the graces God has granted you. Thank you for having responded to my call."

January 10, 1985

"Dear children, today I want to thank you for all your sacrifices but special thanks to those who have become dear to my heart and come here gladly. There are enough parishioners who are not listening to the messages, but because of those who are in a special way close to my heart, because of them I am giving messages for the parish. And I will go on giving them because I love you and I want you to spread my messages with your heart. Thank you for having responded to my call."

January 17, 1985

"Dear children, these days satan is working underhandedly against this parish, and you, dear children, have fallen asleep in prayer and only some are going to Mass. Withstand the days of temptation! Thank you for having responded to my call."

January 24, 1985

"Dear children, these days you have experienced God's sweetness through the renewals which have been in this parish. satan wants to work still more fiercely to take away your joy from each one of you. By prayer you can completely disarm him and ensure your happiness. Thank you for having responded to my call."

January 31, 1985

"Dear children, today I wish to tell you to open your hearts to God like the spring flowers which crave for the sun. I am your Mother and I always want you to be closer to the Father and that He will always give abundant gifts to your hearts. Thank you for having responded to my call."

February 7, 1985

"Dear children, these days satan is manifesting himself in a special way in this parish. Pray, dear children, that God's plan is brought into effect and that every work of satan ends up for the glory of God. I have stayed with you this long so

I might help you along in your trials. Thank you for having responded to my call."

February 14, 1985

"Dear children, today is the day when I give you a message for the parish, but the whole parish is not accepting the messages and is not living them. I am saddened and I want you, dear children, to listen to me and to live my messages. Every family must pray family prayer and read the Bible! Thank you for having responded to my call."

February 21, 1985

"Dear children, from day to day I have been inviting you to renewal and prayer in the parish, but you are not accepting it. Today I am calling you for the last time! Now it's Lent and you as a parish can turn to my message during Lent out of love. If you don't do that, I don't wish to keep on giving messages. God is permitting me that. Thank you for having responded to my call."

February 28, 1985

"Dear children, today I call you to live the word this week: 'I love God!' Dear children, through love you will achieve everything and even what you think is impossible. God wants this parish to belong completely to Him. And that's what I want too. Thank you for having responded to my call."

March 7, 1985

"Dear children, today I call you to renew prayer in your families. Dear children, encourage the very young to prayer and the children to go to Holy Mass. Thank you for having responded to my call."

March 14, 1985

"Dear children, in your life you have all experienced light and darkness. God grants to every person to recognize good and evil. I am calling you to the light, which you should carry to all the people who are in darkness. People who are in darkness daily come into your homes. Dear children, give them the light! Thank you for having responded to my call."

March 21, 1985

"Dear children, I wish to keep on giving messages and, therefore, today I call you to live and accept my messages! Dear children, I love you and in a special way I have chosen this parish, one more dear to me than the others, in which I have gladly remained when the Almighty sent me. Therefore, I call on you - accept me, dear children, that it might go well with you. Listen to my messages. Thank you for having responded to my call."

March 28, 1985

"Dear children, today I wish to call you to pray, pray, pray! In prayer you shall perceive the greatest joy and the way out of every situation that has no exit. Thank you for starting up prayer. Each individual is dear to my heart. And I thank all who have urged prayer in their families. Thank you for having responded to my call."

April 4, 1985 (HOLY THURSDAY)

"Dear children, I thank you for having started to think more about God's glory in your hearts. Today is the day when I wished to stop giving the messages because some individuals did not accept me. The parish has been moved and I wish to keep on giving you messages as it has never been in history from the beginning of the world. **Thank you for having responded to my call."**

April 11, 1985

"Dear children, today I wish to say to everyone in the parish to pray in a special way to the Holy Spirit for enlightenment. From today God wants to test the parish in a special way in order that He might strengthen it in faith. Thank you for having responded to my call."

April 18, 1985

"Dear children, today I thank you for every opening of your hearts. Joy overtakes me for every heart that is opened to God especially from the parish. Rejoice with me! Pray all the prayers for the opening of sinful hearts. I desire that. God desires that through me. Thank you for having responded to my call."

April 25, 1985

"Dear children, today I want to tell you to begin to work in your hearts as you are working in the fields. Work and change your hearts so that a new spirit from God can take its place in your hearts. Thank you for having responded to my call."

May 2, 1985

"Dear children, today I call you to prayer with the heart, and not just from habit. Some are coming but do not wish to move ahead in prayer. Therefore, I wish to warn you like a Mother. Pray that prayer prevails in your hearts in every moment. Thank you for having responded to my call."

May 9, 1985

"Dear children, no, you do not know how many graces God is giving you. You do not want to move ahead during these days when the Holy Spirit is working in a special way. Your hearts are turned toward the things of earth and they preoccupy you. Turn your hearts toward prayer and seek the Holy Spirit to be poured out on you. Thank you for having responded to my call."

May 16, 1985

"Dear children, I am calling you to a more active prayer and attendance at Holy Mass. I wish your Mass to be an experience of God. I wish especially to say to the young people: be open to the Holy Spirit because God wishes to draw you to Himself in these days when satan is at work. Thank you for having responded to my call."

May 23, 1985

"Dear children, these days I call you especially to open your hearts to the Holy Spirit. Especially during these days the Holy Spirit is working through you. Open your hearts and surrender your lives to Jesus so that He works through your hearts and strengthens you in faith. Thank you for having responded to my call."

May 30, 1985

"Dear children, I call you again to prayer with the heart. Let prayer, dear children, be your everyday food in a special way when your work in the fields is so wearing you out that you cannot pray with the heart. Pray, and then you shall overcome even every weariness. Prayer will be your joy and your rest. Thank you for having responded to my call."

June 6, 1985

"Dear children, during these days people from all nations will be coming into the parish. And now I am calling you to love: love first of all your own household members, and then you will be able to accept and love all who are coming. Thank you for having responded to my call."

June 13, 1985

"Dear children, until the anniversary day I am calling you, the parish, to pray more and to let your prayer be a sign of surrender to God. Dear children, I know that you are all tired, but you don't know how to surrender yourselves to me. During these days surrender yourselves completely to me! Thank you for having responded to my call."

June 20, 1985

"Dear children, for this Feast Day I wish to tell you to open your hearts to the Master of all hearts. Give me all your feelings and all your problems! I wish to comfort you in all your trials. I wish to fill you with peace, joy, and love of God. Thank you for having responded to my call."

June 28, 1985 (FRIDAY)

"Dear children, today I am giving you a message through which I desire to call you to humility. These days you have felt great joy because of all the people who have come and to whom you could tell your experiences with love. Now I invite you to continue in humility and with an open heart, speak to all those who are coming. Thank you for having responded to my message."

July 4, 1985

"Dear children, I thank you for every sacrifice you have offered. And now I urge you to offer every sacrifice with love. I wish you, the helpless ones, to begin helping with confidence and the Lord will keep on giving to you in confidence. Thank you for having responded to my call."

July 11, 1985

"Dear children, I love the parish and with my mantle I protect it from every work of satan. Pray that satan retreats from the parish and from every individual who comes into the parish. In that way you shall be able to hear every call of God and answer it with your life. Thank you for having responded to my call."

July 18, 1985

"Dear children, today I call you to place more blessed objects in your homes and call everyone to put some blessed object on yourself. Bless all the objects and thus satan will attack you less because you will have armor against him. Thank you for having responded to my call."

July 25, 1985

"Dear children, I desire to lead you, but you do not want to listen to the messages. Today I am calling you to listen to my messages and then you will be able to live everything that God tells me to convey to you. Open yourselves to God and God will work through you and keep on giving you everything you need. Thank you for having responded to my call."

August 1, 1985

"Dear children, I wish to tell you that I have chosen this
parish and that I am guarding it in my hands like a little
flower that does not want to die. I call you to surrender to
me so that I can keep on presenting you to God, fresh and
without sin. satan has taken part of the plan and wants to
possess it. Pray that he does not succeed in that, because
I wish you for myself so I can keep on giving you to God.
Thank you for having responded to my call."

August 8, 1985

"Dear children, today I call you especially now to advance
against satan by means of prayer. satan wants to work still
more now that you know he is at work. Dear children, put
on the armor for battle and with the Rosary in your hand,
defeat him! Thank you for having responded to my call."

August 15, 1985 (THE ASSUMPTION)

"Dear children, today I am blessing you and I wish to tell
you that I love you and that I urge you to live my messages.
Today I am blessing you with the solemn blessing that the
Almighty grants me. Thank you for having responded to
my call."

August 22, 1985

"Dear children, today I wish to tell you that God wants to
send you trials which you can overcome by prayer. God is
testing you through daily chores. Now pray to peacefully
withstand every trial. From everything through which God
tests you, come out more open to God and approach Him
with love. Thank you for having responded to my call."

August 29, 1985

This message has a spiritual meaning.

> **"Dear children, I am calling you to prayer, especially since satan wishes to take advantage of the yield of your vineyards. Pray that satan does not succeed in his plan. Thank you for your response to my call."**

September 5, 1985

> **"Dear children, today I thank you for all the prayers. Keep on praying all the more so that satan will be far away from this place. Dear children, satan's plan has failed. Pray for the fulfillment of what God plans in this parish. I especially thank the young people for the sacrifices they have offered up. Thank you for having responded to my call."**

September 12, 1985

This message was given to Marija before the celebration of the Feast of the Holy Cross which was the day of the largest pilgrimage of the year at Krizevac:

> **"Dear children, I want to tell you that the cross should be central these days. Pray especially before the Crucifix from which great graces are coming. Now in your homes make a special consecration to the Crucifix. Promise that you will neither offend Jesus nor abuse the Crucifix. Thank you for having responded to my call."**

September 19, 1985

No message was given by Our Lady.

September 20, 1985 (FRIDAY)

"Dear children, today I invite you to live in humility all the messages which I am giving you. Do not become arrogant living the messages and saying, 'I am living the messages.' If you shall bear and live the messages in your heart, everyone will feel it so that words, which serve those who do not obey, will not be necessary. For you, dear children, it is necessary to live and witness by your lives. Thank you for having responded to my call."

September 26, 1985

"Dear children, I thank you for all the prayers. Thank you for all the sacrifices. I wish to tell you, dear children, to renew the messages which I am giving you. Especially live the fast, because by fasting you will achieve and cause me the joy of the whole plan, which God is planning here in Medjugorje, being fulfilled. Thank you for having responded to my call."

October 3, 1985

"Dear children, I wish to tell you to thank God for all the graces which God has given you. For all the fruits thank the Lord and glorify Him! Dear children, learn to give thanks in little things and then you will be able to give thanks also for the big things. Thank you for having responded to my call."

October 10, 1985

"Dear children, I wish also today to call you to live the messages in the parish. Especially I wish to call the youth of the parish, who are dear to me. Dear children, if you live the messages, you are living the seed of holiness. I, as the Mother, wish to call you all to holiness so that you can

bestow it on others. You are a mirror to others! Thank you for having responded to my call."

October 17, 1985

"Dear children, everything has its own time. Today I call you to start working on your hearts. Now that all the work in the fields is over, you are finding time for cleaning even the most neglected areas, but you leave your heart aside. Work more and clean with love every part of your heart. Thank you for having responded to my call."

October 24, 1985

"Dear children, from day to day I wish to clothe you in holiness, goodness, obedience, and God's love, so that from day to day you become more beautiful and more prepared for your Master. Dear children, listen to and live my messages. I wish to guide you. Thank you for having responded to my call."

October 31, 1985

"Dear children, today I wish to call you to work in the Church. I love all the same and I desire from each one to work as much as possible. I know, dear children, that you can, but you do not wish to because you feel small and humble in these things. You need to be courageous and with little flowers do your share for the Church and for Jesus so that everyone can be satisfied. Thank you for having responded to my call."

November 7, 1985

"Dear children, I am calling you to the love of neighbor and love toward the one from whom evil comes to you. In that way you will be able to discern the intentions of hearts.

Pray and love, dear children! By love you are able to do even that which you think is impossible. Thank you for having responded to my call."

November 14, 1985

"Dear children, I, your Mother, love you and wish to urge you to prayer. I am tireless, dear children, and I am calling you even then, when you are far away from my heart. I am a Mother, and even though I feel pain for each one who goes astray, I forgive easily and am happy for every child who returns to me. Thank you for having responded to my call."

November 21, 1985

"Dear children, I want to tell you that this season is especially for you from the parish. When it was summer, you saw that you had a lot of work. Now you don't have work in the fields, work on your own self personally! Come to Mass because this is the season given to you. Dear children, there are enough of those who come regularly despite bad weather, because they love me and want to show their love in a special way. What I want from you is to show me your love by coming to Mass, and the Lord will reward you abundantly. Thank you for having responded to my call."

November 28, 1985

"Dear children, I want to thank everyone for all you have done for me, especially the youth. I beseech you, dear children, come to prayer with awareness. In prayer you shall come to know the greatness of God. Thank you for having responded to my call."

December 5, 1985

"Dear children, I am calling you to prepare yourselves for Christmas by means of penance, prayer, and works of charity. Dear children, do not look toward material things, because then you will not be able to experience Christmas. Thank you for having responded to my call."

December 12, 1985

"Dear children, for Christmas my invitation is that together we glorify Jesus. I present Him to you in a special way on that day and my invitation to you is that on that day we glorify Jesus and His Nativity. Dear children, on that day pray still more and think more about Jesus. Thank you for having responded to my call."

December 19, 1985

"Dear children, today I wish to call you to love of neighbor. The more you will to love your neighbor, the more you shall experience Jesus especially on Christmas Day. God will bestow great gifts on you if you surrender yourselves to Him. I wish in a special way on Christmas Day to give mothers my own Special Motherly blessing and Jesus will bless the rest with His own blessing. Thank you for having responded to my call."

December 25, 1985 (CHRISTMAS - SPECIAL BLESSING)

Our Lady gives a Special Motherly blessing to mothers and Jesus blesses the rest. [See the weekly message of December 19, 1985.]

December 26, 1985

"Dear children, I wish to thank all who have listened to my

messages and who on Christmas Day have lived what I said. Undefiled by sin from now on, I wish to lead you further in love. Abandon your hearts to me! Thank you for having responded to my call."

January 2, 1986

"Dear children, I invite you to decide completely for God. I beseech you, dear children, to surrender yourselves completely and you shall be able to live everything I am telling you. It shall not be difficult for you to surrender yourselves completely to God. Thank you for having responded to my call."

January 9, 1986

"Dear children, I invite you by your prayers to help Jesus along in the fulfillment of all of the plans which He is forming here. And offer your sacrifices to Jesus in order that everything is fulfilled the way He has planned it and that satan can accomplish nothing. Thank you for having responded to my call."

January 16, 1986

"Dear children, today also I am calling you to prayer. Your prayers are necessary to me so that God may be glorified through all of you. Dear children, I pray you obey and live the Mother's invitation, because only out of love am I calling you in order that I might help you. Thank you for having responded to my call."

January 23, 1986

"Dear children, again I call you to prayer with the heart. If you pray with the heart, dear children, the ice of your brothers' hearts will melt and every barrier shall disappear.

Conversion will be easy for all who desire to accept it. You must pray for this gift which by prayer you must obtain for your neighbor. Thank you for having responded to my call."

January 30, 1986

"Dear children, today I call you to pray that God's plans for us may be realized and also everything that God desires through you! Help others to be converted, especially those who are coming to Medjugorje. Dear children, do not allow satan to get control of your hearts, so you would be an image of satan and not of me. I call you to pray for how you might be witnesses of my presence. Without you, God cannot bring to reality that which He desires. God has given a free will to everyone, and it's in your control. Thank you for having responded to my call."

February 6, 1986

"Dear children, this parish, which I have chosen, is special and different from others. And I am giving great graces to all who pray with the heart. Dear children, I am giving messages first of all to the residents of the parish, and then to all the others. First of all you must accept the messages, and then the others. You shall be answerable to me and to my Son, Jesus. Thank you for having responded to my call."

February 13, 1986

"Dear children, this Lent is a special incentive for you to change. Start from this moment. Turn off the television and renounce various things that are of no value. Dear children, I am calling you individually to conversion. This season is for you. Thank you for having responded to my call."

February 20, 1986

"Dear children, the second message of these Lenten days is that you renew prayer before the Crucifix. Dear children, I am giving you special graces and Jesus is giving you special gifts from the Cross. Take them and live! Reflect on Jesus' Passion and in your life be united with Jesus! Thank you for having responded to my call."

February 27, 1986

"Dear children, in humility live the messages which I am giving you. Thank you for having responded to my call."

March 6, 1986

"Dear children, today I call you to open yourselves more to God, so that He can work through you. The more you open yourselves, the more you receive the fruits. I wish to call you again to prayer. Thank you for having responded to my call."

March 13, 1986

"Dear children, today I call you to live this Lent by means of your little sacrifices. Thank you for every sacrifice you have brought me. Dear children, live that way continuously, and with your love help me to present the sacrifice. God will reward you for that. Thank you for having responded to my call."

March 20, 1986

"Dear children, Today I call you to approach prayer actively. You wish to live everything I am telling you, but you are not succeeding because you are not praying. Dear children, I beseech you to open yourselves and begin to pray. Prayer will be your joy. If you make a start, it won't be boring to you because you will be praying out of joy. Thank you for having responded to my call."

March 27, 1986

"Dear children, I wish to thank you for all the sacrifices and I invite you to the greatest sacrifice, the sacrifice of love. Without love, you are not able to accept either me or my Son. Without love, you cannot give an account of your experiences to others. Therefore, dear children, I call you to begin to live love within yourselves. Thank you for having responded to my call."

April 3, 1986

"Dear children, I wish to call you to a living of the Holy Mass. There are many of you who have sensed the beauty of the Holy Mass, but there are also those who come unwillingly. I have chosen you, dear children, but Jesus gives you His graces in the Mass. Therefore, consciously live the Holy Mass and let your coming to it be a joyful one. Come to it with love and make the Mass your own. Thank you for having responded to my call."

April 10, 1986

"Dear children, I desire to call you to grow in love. A flower is not able to grow normally without water. So also you, dear children, are not able to grow without God's blessing. From day to day you need to seek His blessing so you will grow normally and perform all your actions in union with God. Thank you for having responded to my call."

April 17, 1986

"Dear children, you are absorbed with material things, but

in the material you lose everything that God wishes to give you. I call you, dear children, to pray for the gifts of the Holy Spirit which are necessary for you now in order to be able to give witness to my presence here and to all that I am giving you. Dear children, surrender to me so I can lead you completely. Don't be absorbed with material things. Thank you for having responded to my call."

April 24, 1986

"Dear children, today my invitation is that you pray. Dear children, you are forgetting that you are all important. The elderly are especially important in the family. Urge them to pray. Let all the young people be an example to others by their lives and let them witness to Jesus. Dear children, I beseech you, begin to change through prayer and you will know what you need to do. Thank you for having responded to my call."

May 1, 1986

"Dear children, I beseech you to start changing your life in the family. Let the family be a harmonious flower that I wish to give to Jesus. Dear children, let every family be active in prayer for I wish that the fruits in the family be seen one day. Only that way shall I give all, like petals, as a gift to Jesus in fulfillment of God's plan. Thank you for having responded to my call."

May 8, 1986

"Dear children, you are the ones responsible for the messages. The source of grace is here, but you, dear children, are the vessels which transport the gifts. Therefore, dear children, I am calling you to do your job with responsibility. Each one shall be responsible according to his own ability. Dear children, I am calling you to give the gifts to others with love, and not to keep them for yourselves. Thank you for having responded to my call."

May 15, 1986

"Dear children, today I call you to give me your heart so I can change it to be like mine. You are wondering, dear children, why you cannot respond to that which I am seeking from you. You are not able to because you have not given me your heart so I can change it. You are talking but you are not doing. I call on you to do everything that I am telling you. That way I will be with you. Thank you for having responded to my call."

May 22, 1986

"Dear children, today I wish to give you my own love. You do not know, dear children, how great my love is, and you do not know how to accept it. In various ways I wish to show it to you, but you, dear children, do not recognize it. You do not understand my words with your heart and neither are you able to comprehend my love. Dear children, accept me in your life so you will be able to accept all I am saying to you and to which I am calling you. Thank you for having responded to my call."

May 29, 1986

"Dear children, today my call to you is that in your life you live love towards God and neighbor. Without love, dear children, you can do nothing. Therefore, dear children, I am calling you to live in mutual love. Only in that way will you be able to love and accept both me and all those around you who are coming into your parish. Everyone will sense my love through you. Therefore, I beseech you, dear children, to start loving from today with an ardent love, the love with which I love you. Thank you for having responded to my call."

June 5, 1986

"**Dear children, today I am calling on you to decide whether or not you wish to live the messages which I am giving you. I wish you to be active in living and spreading the messages. Especially, dear children, I wish that you all be the reflection of Jesus, which will enlighten this unfaithful world walking in darkness. I wish all of you to be the light for everyone and that you give witness in the light. Dear children, you are not called to the darkness, but you are called to the light. Therefore, live the light with your own life. Thank you for having responded to my call.**"

June 12, 1986

"**Dear children, today I call you to begin to pray the Rosary with a living faith. That way I will be able to help you. You, dear children, wish to obtain graces, but you are not praying. I am not able to help you because you do not want to get started. Dear children, I am calling you to pray the Rosary and that your Rosary be an obligation which you shall fulfill with joy. That way you shall understand the reason I am with you this long. I desire to teach you to pray. Thank you for having responded to my call.**"

June 19, 1986

"**Dear children, during these days my Lord is allowing me to be able to intercede for more graces for you. Therefore, I wish to urge you once more to pray, dear children! Pray without ceasing! That way I will give you the joy which the Lord gives to me. With these graces, dear children, I want your sufferings to be a joy. I am your Mother and I desire to help you. Thank you for having responded to my call.**"

June 26, 1986

"Dear children, God is allowing me along with Himself to bring about this oasis of peace. I wish to call on you to protect it and that the oasis always be unspoiled. There are those who by their carelessness are destroying the peace and the prayer. I am inviting you to give witness and by your life to help to preserve the peace. Thank you for having responded to my call."

July 3, 1986

"Dear children, today I am calling you all to prayer. Without prayer, dear children, you are not able to experience either God or me or the graces which I am giving you. Therefore, my call to you is that the beginning and end of your day always be prayer. Dear children, I wish to lead you daily more and more in prayer, but you are not able to grow because you do not desire it. My call, dear children, is that for you prayer be in the first place. Thank you for having responded to my call."

July 10, 1986

"Dear children, today I am calling you to holiness. Without holiness you cannot live. Therefore, with love overcome every sin and with love overcome all the difficulties which are coming to you. Dear children, I beseech you to live love within yourselves. Thank you for having responded to my call."

July 17, 1986

"Dear children, today I am calling you to reflect upon why I am with you this long. I am the Mediatrix between you and God. Therefore, dear children, I desire to call you to live always out of love all that which God desires of you.

For that reason, dear children, in your own humility live all the messages which I am giving you. Thank you for having responded to my call."

July 24, 1986

"Dear children, I rejoice because of all of you who are on the way of holiness and I beseech you, by your own testimony help those who do not know how to live in holiness. Therefore, dear children, let your family be a place where holiness is born. Help everyone to live in holiness, but especially your own family. Thank you for having responded to my call."

July 31, 1986

"Dear children, hatred gives birth to dissensions and does not regard anyone or anything. I call you always to bring harmony and peace. Especially, dear children, in the place where you live, act with love. Let your only instrument always be love. By love turn everything into good which satan desires to destroy and possess. Only that way will you be completely mine and I shall be able to help you. Thank you for having responded to my call."

August 7, 1986

"Dear children, you know that I promised you an oasis of peace, but you don't know that beside an oasis stands the desert, where satan is lurking and wants to tempt each one of you. Dear children, only by prayer are you able to overcome every influence of satan in your place. I am with you, but I cannot take away your freedom. Thank you for having responded to my call."

August 14, 1986

"Dear children, my call to you is that your prayer be the joy of an encounter with the Lord. I am not able to guide you as long as you yourselves do not experience joy in prayer! From day to day I desire to lead you more and more in prayer, but I do not wish to force you. Thank you for having responded to my call."

August 21, 1986

"Dear children, I thank you for the love which you are showing me. You know, dear children, that I love you immeasurably, and daily I pray the Lord to help you to understand the love which I am showing you. Therefore, you, dear children, pray, pray, pray!"

August 28, 1986

"Dear children, my call is that in everything you would be an image for others, especially in prayer and witnessing. Dear children, without you I am not able to help the world. I desire that you cooperate with me in everything, even in the smallest things. Therefore, dear children, help me by letting your prayer be from the heart and all of you surrendering completely to me. That way I shall be able to teach and lead you on this way which I have begun with you. Thank you for having responded to my call."

September 4, 1986

"Dear children, today again I am calling you to prayer and fasting. You know, dear children, that with your help I am able to accomplish everything and force satan not to be seducing you to evil and to remove himself from this place. Dear children, satan is lurking for each individual. Especially in everyday affairs, he wants to spread confusion among each one of you. Therefore, dear children, my call to you is that your day would be only prayer and complete surrender to God. Thank you for having responded to my call."

September 11, 1986

"Dear children, for these days while you are joyfully celebrating the cross, I desire that your cross also would be a joy for you. Especially, dear children, pray that you may be able to accept sickness and suffering with love the way Jesus accepted them. Only that way shall I be able with joy to give out to you the graces and healings which Jesus is permitting me. Thank you for having responded to my call."

September 18, 1986

"Dear children, today again I thank you for all that you have accomplished for me in these days. Especially, dear children, I thank you in the name of Jesus for the sacrifices which you offered during this past week. Dear children, you are forgetting that I desire sacrifices from you so I can help you and to drive satan away from you. Therefore, I am calling you again to offer sacrifices with a special reverence toward God. Thank you for having responded to my call."

September 25, 1986

"Dear children, by your own peace I am calling you to help others to see and begin to seek peace. You, dear children, are at peace and not able to comprehend non-peace. Therefore, I am calling you, so that by your prayer and your life you help to destroy everything that's evil in people and uncover the deception that satan makes use of. You pray that the truth prevails in all hearts. Thank you for having responded to my call."

October 2, 1986

"Dear children, today again I am calling you to pray. You, dear children, are not able to understand how great the value of prayer is as long as you yourselves do not say: 'now is the time for prayer, now nothing else is important to me, now not one person is important to me but God.' Dear children, consecrate yourselves to prayer with special love so that God will be able to render graces back to you. Thank you for having responded to my call."

October 9, 1986

"Dear children, you know that I desire to lead you on the way of holiness, but I do not want to compel you to be saints by force. I desire that each of you by your own little self-denials help yourself and me so I can lead you from day to day to holiness. Therefore, dear children, I do not desire to force you to observe the messages. But rather this long time that I am with you is a sign that I love you immeasurably, and what I desire of each individual is to become holy. Thank you for having responded to my call."

October 16, 1986

"Dear children, today again I want to show you how much I love you, but I am sorry that I am not able to help each one to understand my love. Therefore, dear children, I am calling you to prayer and complete surrender to God, because satan wants to sift you through everyday affairs and in your life he wants to snatch the first place. Therefore, dear children, pray without ceasing! Thank you for having responded to my call."

October 23, 1986

"Dear children, today again I call you to pray. Especially,

dear children, do I call you to pray for peace. **Without your prayers, dear children, I cannot help you to fulfill the message which the Lord has given me to give to you. Therefore, dear children, pray, so that in prayer you realize what God is giving you. Thank you for having responded to my call."**

October 30, 1986

"Dear children, today again I desire to call you to take seriously and carry out the messages which I am giving you. Dear children, it is for your sake that I have stayed this long so I could help you to fulfill all the messages which I am giving you. Therefore, dear children, out of love for me carry out all the messages which I am giving you. Thank you for having responded to my call."

November 6, 1986

"Dear children, today I wish to call you to pray daily for the souls in purgatory. For every soul prayer and grace is necessary to reach God and the love of God. By doing this, dear children, you obtain new intercessors who will help you in life to realize that all the earthly things are not important for you, that only Heaven is that for which it is necessary to strive. Therefore, dear children, pray without ceasing that you may be able to help yourselves and the others to whom your prayers will bring joy. Thank you for having responded to my call."

November 13, 1986

"Dear children, today again I am calling you to pray with your whole heart and day by day to change your life. Especially, dear children, I am calling that by your prayers and sacrifices you begin to live in holiness, because I desire that each one of you who has been to this fountain of grace will come to Paradise with the special gift which you shall

give me, and that is holiness. Therefore, dear children, pray
and daily change your life in order to become holy. I shall
always be close to you. Thank you for having responded to
my call."

November 20, 1986

"Dear children, today also I am calling you to live and follow with a special love all the messages which I am giving
you. Dear children, God does not want you lukewarm and
undecided, but that you totally surrender to Him. You
know that I love you and that I burn out of love for you.
Therefore, dear children, you also decide for love so that
you will burn out of love and daily experience God's love.
Dear children, decide for love so that love prevails in all of
you, but not human love, rather God's love. Thank you for
having responded to my call."

November 27, 1986

"Dear children, again today I call you to consecrate your life
to me with love, so I am able to guide you with love. I love
you, dear children, with a special love and I desire to bring
you all to Heaven unto God. I want you to realize that this
life lasts briefly compared to the one in Heaven. Therefore,
dear children, decide again for God. Only that way will I be
able to show how much you are dear to me and how much I
desire all to be saved and to be with me in Heaven. Thank
you for having responded to my call."

December 4, 1986

"Dear children, today I call you to prepare your hearts for
these days when the Lord particularly desires to purify you
from all the sins of your past. You, dear children, are not
able by yourselves, therefore, I am here to help you. You
pray, dear children! Only that way shall you be able to rec-

ognize all the evil that is in you and surrender it to the Lord so the Lord may completely purify your hearts. Therefore, dear children, pray without ceasing and prepare your hearts in penance and fasting. Thank you for having responded to my call."

December 11, 1986

"Dear children, I am calling you to pray especially at this time in order to experience the joy of meeting with the newborn Jesus. Dear children, I desire that you experience these days just as I experienced them. With joy I wish to guide you and show you the joy into which I desire to bring each one of you. Therefore, dear children, pray and surrender completely to me. Thank you for having responded to my call."

December 18, 1986

"Dear children, once again I desire to call you to prayer. When you pray, you are much more beautiful, like flowers which, after the snow, show all their beauty and all their colors become indescribable. So also you, dear children, after prayer show more before God all that is beautiful to please Him. Therefore, dear children, pray and open your inner self to the Lord so that He makes of you a harmonious and beautiful flower for Paradise. Thank you for having responded to my call."

December 25, 1986 (CHRISTMAS DAY)

"Dear children, today also I give thanks to the Lord for all that He is doing for me, especially for this gift that I am able to be with you also today. Dear children, these are the days in which the Father grants special graces to all who open their hearts. I bless you and I desire that you too, dear children, become alive to the graces and place everything at God's disposal so that He may be glorified through you. My heart carefully follows your steps. Thank you for having responded to my call."

January 1, 1987

"Dear children, today I wish to call on all of you that in the New Year you live the messages which I am giving you. Dear children, you know that for your sake I have remained a long time so I might teach you how to make progress on the way of holiness. Therefore, dear children, pray without ceasing and live the messages which I am giving you for I am doing it with great love toward God and toward you. Thank you for having responded to my call."

January 8, 1987

"Dear children, I desire to thank you for every response to the messages. Especially, dear children, thank you for all the sacrifices and prayers which you have presented to me. Dear children, I desire to keep on giving you still further messages, only not every Thursday, dear children, but on the 25th of each month. The time has come when what my Lord desired has been fulfilled. Now I will give you fewer messages but I am still with you. Therefore, dear children, I beseech you, listen to my messages and live them, so I can guide you. Dear children, thank you for having responded to my call."

CHAPTER 3

THE MONTHLY MESSAGES OF OUR LADY THROUGH MARIJA

(January 25, 1987 to April 25, 2009)

"I GIVE YOU MY SPECIAL BLESSING." (December 25, 1988)

January 8, 1987, Our Lady said She would continue Her messages, but instead of weekly, monthly, on the twenty-fifth of each month.

January 25, 1987

"Dear children, behold, also today I want to call you to start living a new life as of today. Dear children, I want you to comprehend that God has chosen each one of you, in order to use you in a great plan for the salvation of mankind. You are not able to comprehend how great your role is in God's design. Therefore, dear children, pray so that in prayer you may be able to comprehend what God's plan is in your regard. I am with you in order that you may be able to bring it about in all its fullness. Thank you for having responded to my call."

February 25, 1987

"Dear children, today I want to wrap you all in my mantle and lead you all along the way of conversion. Dear children, I beseech you, surrender to the Lord your entire past,

all the evil that has accumulated in your hearts. I want each one of you to be happy, but in sin nobody can be happy. Therefore, dear children, pray, and in prayer you shall realize a new way of joy. Joy will manifest in your hearts and thus you shall be joyful witnesses of that which I and My Son want from each one of you. I am blessing you. Thank you for having responded to my call."

March 25, 1987 (SPECIAL BLESSING)

"Dear children, today I am grateful to you for your presence in this place, where I am giving you special graces. I call each one of you to begin to live as of today that life which God wishes of you and to begin to perform good works of love and mercy. I do not want you, dear children, to live the message and be committing sin which is displeasing to me. Therefore, dear children, I want each of you to live a new life without the murder* of all that God produces in you and is giving you. I give you my Special Blessing and I am remaining with you on your way of conversion. Thank you for having responded to my call."

* "Murder" rather than "destroy" was chosen for the translation of the Croatian word, "ubijanje," because Our Lady used a very strong word meaning to kill something living. An automobile as well as a human being can be destroyed. The purest translation is "murder."

April 25, 1987

"Dear children, today also I am calling you to prayer. You know, dear children, that God grants special graces in prayer. Therefore, seek and pray in order that you may be able to comprehend all that I am giving here. I call you, dear children, to prayer with the heart. You know that without prayer you cannot comprehend all that God is planning through each one of you. Therefore, pray! I desire that through each one of you God's plan may be fulfilled, that all which God has planted in your heart may keep on growing. So pray that God's blessing may protect each one of you from all the evil that is threatening you. I bless you, dear children. Thank you for having responded to my call."

May 25, 1987

"Dear children, I am calling everyone of you to start living in God's love. Dear children, you are ready to commit sin, and to put yourselves in the hands of satan without reflecting. I call on each one of you to consciously decide for God and against satan. I am your Mother and, therefore, I want to lead you all to complete holiness. I want each one of you to be happy here on earth and to be with me in Heaven. That is, dear children, the purpose of my coming here and it's my desire. Thank you for having responded to my call."

June 25, 1987 (SPECIAL BLESSING)

"Dear children, today I thank you and I want to invite you all to God's peace. I want each one of you to experience in your heart that peace which God gives. I want to bless you all today. I am blessing you with God's Blessing and I beseech you, dear children, to follow and to live my way. I love you, dear children, and so not even counting the number of times, I go on calling you and I thank you for all that you are doing for my intentions. I beg you, help me to present you to God and to save you. Thank you for having responded to my call."

July 25, 1987

"Dear children, I beseech you to take up the way of holiness beginning today. I love you and, therefore, I want you to be

holy. I do not want satan to block you on that way. Dear
children, pray and accept all that God is offering you on a
way which is bitter. But at the same time, God will reveal
every sweetness to whomever begins to go on that way, and
He will gladly answer every call of God. Do not attribute
importance to petty things. Long for Heaven. Thank you
for having responded to my call."

August 25, 1987

"Dear children, today also I am calling you all in order that
each one of you decides to live my messages. God has permitted me also in this year, which the Church has dedicated
to me, to be able to speak to you and to be able to spur you
on to holiness. Dear children, seek from God the graces
which He is giving you through me. I am ready to intercede
with God for all that you seek so that your holiness may be
complete. Therefore, dear children, do not forget to seek,
because God has permitted me to obtain graces for you.
Thank you for having responded to my call."

September 25, 1987

"Dear children, today also I want to call you all to prayer.
Let prayer be your life. Dear children, dedicate your time
only to Jesus and He will give you everything that you are
seeking. He will reveal Himself to you in fullness. Dear
children, satan is strong and is waiting to test each one of
you. Pray, and that way he will neither be able to injure
you nor block you on the way of holiness. Dear children,
through prayer grow all the more toward God from day to
day. Thank you for having responded to my call."

October 25, 1987

"My dear children, today I want to call all of you to decide
for Paradise. The way is difficult for those who have not

decided for God. Dear children, decide and believe that God is offering Himself to you in His fullness. You are invited and you need to answer the call of the Father, who is calling you through me. Pray, because in prayer each one of you will be able to achieve complete love. I am blessing you and I desire to help you so that each one of you might be under my Motherly mantle. Thank you for having responded to my call."

November 25, 1987

"Dear children, today also I call each one of you to decide to surrender again everything completely to me. Only that way will I be able to present each of you to God. Dear children, you know that I love you immeasurably and that I desire each of you for myself, but God has given to all a freedom which I lovingly respect and humbly submit to. I desire, dear children, that you help so that everything God has planned in this parish shall be realized. If you do not pray, you shall not be able to recognize my love and the plans which God has for this parish and for each individual. Pray that satan does not entice you with his pride and deceptive strength. I am with you and I want you to believe me, that I love you. Thank you for having responded to my call."

December 25, 1987

"Dear children, rejoice with me! My heart is rejoicing because of Jesus and today I want to give Him to you. Dear children, I want each one of you to open your heart to Jesus and I will give Him to you with love. Dear children, I want Him to change you, to teach you, and to protect you. Today I am praying in a special way for each one of you and I am presenting you to God so He will manifest Himself in you. I am calling you to sincere prayer with the heart so that every prayer of yours may be an encounter with God. In your work and in your everyday life, put God in the first place. I call you today with great seriousness to obey me and to do as I am calling you. Thank you for having responded to my call."

January 25, 1988

"Dear children, today again I am calling you to complete conversion, which is difficult for those who have not chosen God. I am calling you, dear children, to convert fully to God. God can give you everything that you seek from Him. But you seek God only when sicknesses, problems, and difficulties come to you and you think that God is far from you and is not listening and does not hear your prayers. No, dear children, that is not the truth! When you are far from God, you cannot receive graces because you do not seek them with a firm faith. Day by day, I am praying for you and I want to draw you ever closer to God; but I cannot if you don't want it. Therefore, dear children, put your life in God's hands. I bless you all. Thank you for having responded to my call."

February 25, 1988

"Dear children, today again I am calling you to prayer and complete surrender to God. You know that I love you and am coming here out of love, so I could show you the path of peace and salvation for your souls. I want you to obey me and not permit satan to seduce you. Dear children, satan is very strong and, therefore, I ask you to dedicate your prayers to me so that those who are under his influence may be saved. Give witness by your life, sacrifice your lives for the salvation of the world. I am with you and I am grateful to you, but in Heaven you shall receive the Father's reward which He has promised you. Therefore, little children, do not be afraid. If you pray, satan cannot injure you even a little, because you are God's children and He is watching over you. **Pray, and let the Rosary always be in your hands as a sign to satan that you belong to me. Thank you for having responded to my call."**

March 25, 1988

"**Dear children, today also I am calling you to a complete surrender to God. You, dear children, are not conscious of how God loves you with such a great love. Because of it He permits me to be with you so I can instruct you and help you to find the way of peace. That way, however, you cannot discover if you do not pray. Therefore, dear children, forsake everything and consecrate your time to God and then God will bestow gifts upon you and bless you. Little children, do not forget that your life is fleeting like the spring flower which today is wondrously beautiful, but tomorrow has vanished. Therefore, pray in such a way that your prayer, your surrender to God may become like a road sign. That way, your witness will not only have value for yourselves, but for all of eternity. Thank you for having responded to my call."**

April 25, 1988

"**Dear children, God wants to make you holy. Therefore, through me He is calling you to complete surrender. Let the Holy Mass be your life. Understand that the Church is God's palace, the place in which I gather you and want to show you the way to God. Come and pray! Neither look to others nor slander them, but rather let your life be a testimony on the way of holiness. Churches deserve respect and are set apart as holy because God, Who became Man, dwells in them day and night. Therefore, little children, believe and pray that the Father increases your faith, and then ask for whatever you need. I am with you and I rejoice because of your conversion and I am protecting you with my Motherly mantle. Thank you for having responded to my call."**

May 25, 1988

"Dear children, I am calling you to a complete surrender to God. Pray, little children, that satan does not sway you like branches in the wind. Be strong in God. I desire that through you the whole world may get to know the God of joy. Neither be anxious nor worried. God will help you and show you the way. I want you to love all men with my love, both the good and the bad. Only that way will love conquer the world. Little children, you are mine. I love you and I want you to surrender to me so I can lead you to God. Pray without ceasing so that satan cannot take advantage of you. Pray so that you realize that you are mine. I bless you with the blessing of joy. Thank you for having responded to my call."

June 25, 1988

"Dear children, today I am calling you to the love which is loyal and pleasing to God. Little children, love bears everything bitter and difficult for the sake of Jesus Who is love. Therefore, dear children, pray God to come to your aid, not, however, according to your desires but according to His love. Surrender yourselves to God so that He may heal you, console you, and forgive everything inside you which is a hindrance on the way of love. In this way, God can mold your life and you will grow in love. Dear children, glorify God with the canticle of love so that God's love may be able to grow in you day by day to its fullness. Thank you for having responded to my call."

July 25, 1988

"Dear children, today I am calling you to a complete surrender to God. Everything you do and everything you possess give over to God so that He can take control in your life as King of all that you possess. That way, through me,

God can lead you into the depths of the spiritual life. Little children, do not be afraid because I am with you even when you think there is no way out and that satan is in control. I am bringing peace to you. I am your Mother and the Queen of Peace. I am blessing you with the blessing of joy so that for you God may be everything in life. Thank you for having responded to my call."

August 25, 1988

"Dear children, today I invite you all to rejoice in the life which God gives you. Little children, rejoice in God the Creator because He has created you so wonderfully. Pray that your life be a joyful thanksgiving, which flows out of your heart like a river of joy. Little children, give thanks unceasingly for all that you possess, for each little gift which God has given you, so that a joyful blessing always comes down from God upon your life. Thank you for having responded to my call."

September 25, 1988

"Dear children, today I am calling all of you without exception to the way of holiness in your life. God gave you the gift of holiness. Pray that you may more and more comprehend it and in that way, you will be able by your life to bear witness for God. Dear children, I am blessing you and I intercede for you to God so that your way and your witness may be a complete one and a joy for God. Thank you for having responded to my call."

October 25, 1988

"Dear children, my call that you live the messages which I am giving you is a daily one, especially, little children, because I want to draw you closer to the Heart of Jesus. Therefore, little children, I am calling you today to the prayer of Consecration to Jesus, my dear Son, so that each of your hearts may be His. And then I am calling you to Consecration to my Immaculate Heart. I want you to consecrate yourselves as individuals, families, and parishes so that all belongs to God through my hands. Therefore, dear little children, pray that you may comprehend the greatness of this message which I am giving you. I do not want anything for myself, rather, all for the salvation of your souls. satan is strong and, therefore, you, little children, by constant prayer press tightly to my Motherly heart. Thank you for having responded to my call."

The next three Monthly Messages were given while Marija was in America. See Part IV, Chapter 5 - American Messages.

November 25, 1988

"Dear children, I call you to prayer for you to have an encounter with God in prayer. God gives Himself to you, but He wants you to answer in your own freedom to His invitation. That is why, little children, during the day find yourselves a special time when you can pray in peace and humility and have this meeting with God, the Creator. I am with you and I intercede for you in front of God. Watch in vigil so that every encounter in prayer be the joy of your contact with God. Thank you for having responded to my call."

December 25, 1988 (SPECIAL BLESSING)

"Dear children, I call you to peace. Live it in your heart and all around you so that all will know peace - peace which does not come from you but from God. Little children, today is a great day! Rejoice with me! Glorify the Nativity of Jesus through the peace that I give. It is for this peace that I have come as your Mother, Queen of Peace. Today I give you my Special Blessing. Bring it to all creation, so that all creation will know peace. Thank you for having responded to my call."

January 25, 1989

"Dear children, today I am calling you to the way of holiness. Pray that you may comprehend the beauty and the greatness of this way, where God reveals Himself to you in a special way. Pray that you may be open to everything that God does through you so that in your life you may be enabled to give thanks to God and to rejoice over everything that He does through each individual. I give you my blessing. Thank you for having responded to my call."

February 25, 1989

"Dear children, today I am calling you to prayer of the heart. Throughout this season of grace, I desire each of you to be united with Jesus; but without unceasing prayer, you cannot experience the beauty and greatness of the grace which God is offering you. Therefore, little children, at all times fill your heart with even the smallest prayers. I am with you and unceasingly I keep watch over every heart which is given to me. Thank you for having responded to my call."

March 25, 1989

"Dear children, I am calling you to a complete surrender to God. I am calling you to great joy and peace which only God can give. I am with you and I intercede for you everyday before God. I call you, little children, to listen to me and to live the messages which I am giving you. For years you have been invited to holiness, but you are still far away. I am blessing you. Thank you for your response to my call."

April 25, 1989

"Dear children, I am calling you to a complete surrender to God. Let everything that you possess be in the hands of God. Only in that way shall you have joy in your heart. Little children, rejoice in everything that you have and give thanks to God because everything is God's gift to you. That way in your life you should be able to give thanks for everything and discover God in everything, even in the smallest flower. Thank you for your response to my call."

May 25, 1989

"Dear children, I am calling you to openness to God. You see, little children, how nature is opening herself and is giving life and fruits. In the same way I am calling you to a life with God and a complete surrender to Him. Little children, I am with you and unceasingly I desire to lead you into the joy of life. I desire that each one of you discovers the joy and the love which is found only in God and which only God can give. God wants nothing else from you but your surrender. Therefore, little children, decide seriously for God because everything passes away. God alone does not pass away. Pray that you may discover the greatness and the joy of life which God is giving you. Thank you for having responded to my call."

June 25, 1989

"Dear children, today I call you to live the messages which I have been giving you during the past eight years. This is a time of graces and I desire that the grace of God be great for every single one of you. I am blessing you and I love you with a special love. Thank you for having responded to my call."

July 25, 1989

"**Dear children, today I am calling you to renew your heart. Open yourself to God and surrender to Him all your difficulties and crosses so God may turn everything into joy. Little children, you cannot open yourselves to God if you do not pray; therefore, from today decide to consecrate a time and a day only for an encounter with God in silence. In that way you will be able, with God, to witness my presence here. Little children, I do not wish to force you; rather, freely give God your time, like children of God. Thank you for having responded to my call.**"

August 25, 1989

"**Dear children, today I call you to prayer. By means of prayer, little children, you will obtain joy and peace. Through prayer you are richer in the mercy of God. Therefore, little children, let prayer be the light for each one of you. Especially, I call you to pray so that all those who are far from God may be converted. Then our hearts shall be richer because God will rule in the hearts of all men. Therefore, little children, pray, pray, pray. Let prayer begin to rule in the whole world. Thank you for your response to my call!**"

September 25, 1989

"**Dear children, today I invite you to give thanks to God for all the gifts you have discovered in the course of your life and even for the least gift you have received. I give thanks with you and want all of you to experience the joy of these gifts, and I want God to be everything for each one of you. And then, little children, you can grow continuously on the way of holiness. Thank you for responding to my call.**"

October 25, 1989

"Dear children, today also I am inviting you to prayer. I am
always inviting you, but you are still far away. Therefore,
from today, decide seriously to dedicate time to God. I am
with you and I wish to teach you to pray with the heart. In
prayer with the heart, you shall encounter God. Therefore,
dear children, pray, pray, pray. Thank you for having
responded to my call."

November 25, 1989

"Dear children, I have been inviting you for years by these
messages which I am giving you. Little children, by means
of the messages I wish to make a very beautiful mosaic in
your heart so I may be able to present each one of you to
God like the original image. Therefore, little children, I
desire that your decisions be free before God, because He
has given you freedom. Therefore, pray so that, free from
any influence of satan, you may decide only for God. I am
praying for you before God and I am seeking your surrender to God. Thank you for responding to my call."

December 25, 1989 (SPECIAL BLESSING)

"Dear children, today I bless you in a special way with my
Motherly blessing and I intercede for you to God for Him to
give you the gift of the conversion of the heart. For years I
have been calling you to encourage you to a profound spiritual life in simplicity, but you are so cold! Therefore, little
children, accept with seriousness and live the messages for
your soul not to be sad when I will not be with you anymore
and when I will not guide you anymore like an insecure
child in his first steps. Therefore, little children, read everyday the messages I gave you and transform them into life.
I love you and this is why I call you to the way of salvation
with God. Thank you for having responded to my call."

January 25, 1990

"Dear children, today I invite you to decide for God once again and to choose Him before everything and above everything, so that He may work miracles in your life and that day by day your life may become joy with Him. Therefore, little children, pray and do not permit satan to work in your life through misunderstandings, not understanding and not accepting one another. Pray that you may be able to comprehend the greatness and the beauty of the gift of life. Thank you for having responded to my call."

February 25, 1990

"Dear children! I invite you to surrender to God. In this season I especially want you to renounce all the things to which you are attached but are hurting your spiritual life. Therefore, little children, decide completely for God, and do not allow satan to come into your life through those things that hurt both you and your spiritual life. Little children, God is offering Himself to you in fullness, and you can discover and recognize Him only in prayer. Therefore, make a decision for prayer! Thank you for having responded to my call."

March 25, 1990

"Dear children, I am with you even if you are not conscious of it. I want to protect you from everything that satan offers you and through which he wants to destroy you. As I bore Jesus in my womb, so also, dear children, do I wish to bear you unto holiness. God wants to save you and sends you messages through men, nature, and so many things which can only help you to understand that you must change the direction of your life. Therefore, little children, understand also the greatness of the gift which God is giving you through me, so that I may protect you with my mantle and

**lead you to the joy of life. Thank you for having responded
to my call."**

April 25, 1990

**"Dear children, today I invite you to accept with seriousness
and to live the messages which I am giving you. I am with
you and I desire, dear children, that each one of you be ever
closer to my heart. Therefore, little children, pray and seek
the will of God in your everyday life. I desire that each one
of you discover the way of holiness and grow in it until eternity. I will pray for you and intercede for you before God
that you understand the greatness of this gift which God
is giving me that I can be with you. Thank you for having
responded to my call."**

May 25, 1990

**"Dear children, I invite you to decide with seriousness to
live this novena** [in preparation for Pentecost]**. I am with
you and I desire to help you to grow in renunciation and
mortification that you may be able to understand the beauty
of the life of people, who go on giving themselves to me in
a special way. Dear children, God blesses you day after day
and desires a change of your life. Therefore, pray that you
may have the strength to change your life. Thank you for
having responded to my call."**

June 25, 1990 (SPECIAL BLESSING)

**"Dear children, today I desire to thank you for all your
sacrifices and for all your prayers. I am blessing you with
My Special Motherly blessing. I invite you all to decide for
God and from day to day to discover His will in prayer. I
desire, dear children, to call all of you to a full conversion
so that joy will be in your hearts. I am happy that you are
here today in such great numbers. Thank you for having
responded to my call."**

July 25, 1990

"Dear children, today I invite you to peace. I have come here as the Queen of Peace and I desire to enrich you with my Motherly peace. Dear children, I love you and I desire to bring all of you to the peace which God gives and which enriches every heart. I invite you to become carriers and witnesses of my peace to this unpeaceful world. Let peace rule in the whole world, which is without peace and longs for peace. I bless you with my Motherly blessing. Thank you for having responded to my call."

August 25, 1990

"Today I desire to invite you to take with seriousness and put into practice the messages which I am giving you. You know, little children, that I am with you, that I desire to lead you along the same path to Heaven which is beautiful for those who discover it in prayer. Therefore, little children, do not forget that these messages which I am giving you have to be put into your everyday life in order that you might be able to say: 'There, I have taken the messages and tried to live them.' Dear children, I am protecting you before the Heavenly Father by my own prayers. Thank you for having responded to my call."

September 25, 1990

"Dear children, I invite you to prayer with the heart, in order that your prayer may be a conversation with God. I desire each one of you to dedicate more time to God. satan is strong and wants to destroy and deceive you in many ways. Therefore, my dear children, pray every day that your lives would be a goodness for yourselves and for all those you meet. I am with you and I am protecting you even though satan wishes to destroy my plans and hinder the desires which the Heavenly Father wants realized here. Thank you for having responded to my call."

October 25, 1990

"Dear children, today I call you to pray in a special way and to offer up sacrifices and good deeds for peace in the world. satan is strong and, with all his strength, tries to destroy the peace which comes from God. Therefore, dear children, pray in a special way with me for peace. I am with you and I desire to help you with my prayers and I desire to guide you on the path of peace. I bless you with my Motherly blessing. Do not forget to live the messages of peace. Thank you for responding to my call."

November 25, 1990

"Dear children, today I invite you to do works of mercy with love and out of love for me and for your and my brothers and sisters. All that you do for others, do it with great joy and humility towards God. I am with you and day after day I offer your sacrifices and prayers to God for the salvation of the world. Thank you for having responded to my call!"

December 25, 1990

"Dear children, today I invite you in a special way to pray for peace. Dear children, without peace you cannot experience the birth of the little Jesus neither today nor in your daily lives. Therefore, pray the Lord of peace that He may protect you with His mantle and that He may help you to comprehend the greatness and the importance of peace in your hearts. In this way, you shall be able to spread peace from your hearts throughout the whole world. I am with you and I intercede for you before God. Pray because satan wants to destroy my plans of peace. Be reconciled with one another and by means of your lives help peace to reign on the whole earth. Thank you for having responded to my call."

January 25, 1991

"Dear children, today, like never before, I invite you to prayer. Your prayer should be a prayer for peace. satan is strong and wishes not only to destroy human life but also nature and the planet on which you live. Therefore, dear children, pray that you can protect yourselves through prayer with the blessing of God's peace. God sent me to you so that I can help you. If you wish to, grasp for the Rosary. Already, the Rosary alone can do miracles in the world and in your lives. I bless you and I stay among you as long as it is God's Will. Thank you that you will not betray my presence here and I thank you because your response is serving God and peace. Thank you for having responded to my call!"

February 25, 1991

"Dear children, today I invite you to decide for God because distance from God is the fruit of the lack of peace in your hearts. God is peace itself. Therefore, approach Him through your personal prayer and then live peace in your hearts, and in this way peace will flow from your hearts like a river into the whole world. Do not speak about peace, but make peace. I am blessing each of you and each good decision of yours. Thank you for having responded to my call."

March 25, 1991

"Again today I invite you to live the passion of Jesus in prayer, and in union with Him. Decide to give more time to God who gave you these days of grace. Therefore, dear children, pray and renew in a special way the love for Jesus in your hearts. I am with you and I accompany you with my blessing and my prayers. Thank you for having responded to my call."

April 25, 1991

"Dear children, today I invite you all so that your prayer be prayer with the heart. Let each of you find time for prayer, so that in your prayer you discover God. I do not desire you to talk about prayer, but to pray. Let your every day be filled with prayer of gratitude to God for life and for all that you have. I do not desire your life to pass by in words, but that you glorify God with deeds. I am with you and I am grateful to God for every moment spent with you. Thank you for having responded to my call!"

May 25, 1991

"Dear children, today I invite all of you who have heard my message of peace to realize it with seriousness and with love in your life. There are many who think that they are doing a lot by talking about the messages but do not live them. Dear children, I invite you to life and to change all the negative in you, so that it all turns into the positive and life. Dear children, I am with you and I desire to help each of you to live and, by living, to witness the good news. I am here, dear children, to help you and to lead you to Heaven, and in Heaven is the joy through which you can already live Heaven now. Thank you for having responded to my call!"

June 25, 1991 (TENTH ANNIVERSARY)

This Tenth Anniversary message has a lot more to it than appears here. It should be read with prayer.

"Dear children, today on this great day which you have given to me, I desire to bless all of you and to say: These days while I am with you are days of grace. I desire to teach you and to help you walk on the path of holiness. There are many people who do not desire to understand my messages

and to accept with seriousness what I am saying. But you I therefore call and ask that by your lives and your daily living you witness my presence. If you pray, God will help you discover the true reason for my coming. Therefore, little children, pray and read the Sacred Scriptures so that through my coming you discover the message in Sacred Scripture for you. Thank you for responding to my call."

July 25, 1991

"Dear children, today I invite you to pray for peace. At this time, peace is threatened in a special way and I am seeking from you to renew fasting and prayer in your families. Dear children, I desire you to grasp the seriousness of the situation and that much of what will happen depends on your prayers, and you are praying a little bit! Dear children, I am with you and I am inviting you to begin to pray and fast seriously as in the first days of my coming. Thank you for having responded to my call."

August 25, 1991

"Dear children, today also I invite you to prayer, now as never before when my plan has begun to be realized. satan is strong and wants to sweep away plans of peace and joy and make you think that my Son is not strong in His decisions. Therefore, I call all of you, dear children, to pray and fast still more firmly. I invite you to renunciation for nine days so that with your help everything I wanted to realize through the secrets I began in Fatima may be fulfilled. I call you dear children to understand now the importance of my coming and the seriousness of the situation. I desire to save all souls and to present them to God. Therefore, we pray that all I have started may be completely realized in its fullness. Thank you for having responded to my call."

September 25, 1991

"Dear children! Today in a special way I invite you all to prayer and renunciation. For now as never before satan wants to show the world his shameful face by which he wants to seduce as many people as possible onto the way of death and sin. Therefore, dear children, help my Immaculate Heart to triumph in the sinful world. I beseech all of you to offer prayers and sacrifices for my intentions so I can present them to God for what is most necessary. Forget your desires, dear children, and pray for what God desires and not for what you desire. Thank you for having responded to my call!"

October 25, 1991

"Dear children, pray, pray, pray."

Marija was insistently asked if Our Lady had added anything to the message like, **"Thank you for having responded to my call."** Marija said *"NO, Our Lady didn't add a single word to that message."* This makes this message a gravely serious one.

November 25, 1991

"Dear children, this time also I am inviting you to prayer. Pray that you might be able to comprehend what God desires to tell you through my presence and through the messages I am giving you. I desire to draw you ever closer to Jesus and to His wounded heart that you might be able to comprehend the immeasurable love which gave itself for each one of you. Therefore, dear children, pray that from your heart would flow a fountain of love to every person both to the one who hates you and to the one who despises you. That way you will be able through Jesus' love to overcome all the misery in this world of sorrows, which is without hope for those who do not know Jesus. I am with you

and I love you with the immeasurable love of Jesus. Thank
you for all your sacrifices and prayers. Pray so I might be
able to help you still more. Your prayers are necessary to
me. Thank you for having responded to my call."

December 25, 1991

"Dear children, today in a special way I bring the little Jesus
to you, that He may bless you with His blessing of peace and
love. Dear children, do not forget that this is a grace which
many people neither understand nor accept. Therefore,
you who have said that you are mine and seek my help, give
all of yourself. First of all, give your love and an example
in your families. You say that Christmas is a family feast,
therefore, dear children, put God in the first place in your
families so that He may give you peace and may protect
you not only from war, but also during peace, protect you
from every satanic attack. When God is with you, you have
everything. But when you do not want Him, then you are
miserable and lost, and you do not know on whose side you
are. Therefore, dear children, decide for God and then you
will get everything. Thank you for having responded to my
call."

January 25, 1992

"Dear children, today, I am inviting you to a renewal of
prayer in your families so that way every family will become
a joy to my Son, Jesus. Therefore, dear children, pray
and seek more time for Jesus and then you will be able to
understand and accept everything, even the most difficult
sicknesses and crosses. I am with you and I desire to take
you into my heart and protect you, but you have not yet
decided. Therefore, dear children, I am seeking for you to
pray, so through prayer you would allow me to help you.
Pray, my dear little children, so prayer becomes your daily
bread. Thank you for having responded to my call."

February 25, 1992

"**Dear children, today I invite you to draw still closer to God through prayer. Only that way will I be able to help you and to protect you from every attack of satan. I am with you and I intercede for you with God, that He protect you. But I need your prayers and your 'yes.' You get lost easily in material and human things, and forget that God is your greatest friend. Therefore, my dear little children, draw close to God so He may protect you and guard you from every evil. Thank you for having responded to my call!**"

March 25, 1992

"**Dear children, today as never before I invite you to live my messages and to put them into practice in your life. I have come to you to help you and therefore I invite you to change your life because you have taken a path of misery, a path of ruin. When I told you, 'Convert, pray, fast, be reconciled,' you took these messages superficially. You started to live them and then you stopped, because it was difficult for you. No, dear children, when something is good, you have to persevere in the good, and not think, 'God does not see me, He is not listening, He is not helping.' And so you have gone away from God and from me because of your miserable interest. I wanted to create of you an oasis of peace, love and goodness. God wanted you with your love and with His help to do miracles and thus give an example. Therefore, here is what I say to you, 'satan is playing with you and with your souls and I cannot help you because you are far from my heart. Therefore, pray, live my messages and then you will see the miracles of God's love in your every day life. Thank you for having responded to my call.'**"

April 25, 1992

"**Dear children, today also I invite you to prayer. Only by** prayer and fasting can war be stopped. Therefore, my dear little children, pray and by your life give witness that you are mine and that you belong to me, because satan wishes in these turbulent days to seduce as many souls as possible. Therefore, I invite you to decide for God and He will protect you and show you what you should do and which path to take. I invite all those who have said 'yes' to me to renew their consecration to my Son, Jesus, and to His heart and to me so we can take you more intensely as instruments of peace in this unpeaceful world. Medjugorje is a sign to all of you and a call to pray and live the days of grace that God is giving you. Therefore, dear children, accept the call to prayer with seriousness. I am with you and your suffering is also mine. Thank you for having responded to my call."

May 25, 1992

"Dear children, today also I invite you to prayer so that through prayer you come yet closer to God. I am with you and wish to lead you on the path to salvation which Jesus gives. From day to day I am closer and closer to you, although you are not conscious of it and do not want to admit that you are connected to me in prayer only a little bit. When temptations and problems arise you say: 'Oh God, Oh Mother, where are you?' And I only wait for you to give me your 'yes' so that I pass it on to Jesus and that He may bestow you with graces. Therefore, once again accept my call and begin anew to pray, until prayer becomes a joy for you. And then you will discover that God is Almighty in your everyday life. I am with you and I wait for you. Thank you for having responded to my call."

June 25, 1992

"Dear children, today I am happy despite there still being some sadness in my heart for all those who began to take this path and then abandoned it. My presence here is there-

fore to lead you on a new path, the path of salvation. Thus
I call you day after day to conversion, but if you do not pray
you cannot say you are converting. I pray for you and intercede before God for peace: first for peace in your hearts,
then around you, so that God may be your peace. Thank
you for having responded to my call."

July 25, 1992

"Dear children, today again I invite all of you to prayer,
a joyful prayer, so that in these sad days, none of you
feels sadness in prayer, but a joyful meeting with God his
Creator. Pray, little children, so that you can be closer to
me, and feel through prayer what I desire from you. I am
with you, and everyday I bless you with my Motherly blessing, so that the Lord may bestow you with the abundance
of His grace for your daily life. Thank God for the gift of
my being with you, because I am telling you: this is a great
grace. Thank you for having responded to my call."

August 25, 1992

"Dear children, today I wish to tell you that I love you. I
love you with my Motherly love and I call upon you to open
yourselves completely to me, so that through each of you I
may be enabled to convert and save the world, where there
is much sin and many things that are evil. Therefore, my
dear little children, open yourselves completely to me so
that I may be able to lead you more and more to the marvelous love of God, the Creator, who reveals Himself to you
day by day. I am at your side and I wish to reveal to you
and show you the God who loves you. Thank you for having responded to my call."

September 25, 1992

"Dear children, today also I wish to tell you: I am with you also in these restless days in which satan wishes to destroy everything which I and my Son, Jesus, are building up. In a special way he [satan] wishes to destroy your souls. He wishes to guide you as far away as possible from Christian life as well as from the Commandments, to which the Church is calling you so you may live them. satan wishes to destroy everything which is holy in you and around you. Therefore, little children, pray, pray, pray, in order to be able to comprehend all which God is giving you through my comings. Thank you for having responded to my call!"

October 25, 1992

"Dear children, I invite you to prayer, now when satan is strong and wishes to make as many souls as possible his own. Pray, dear children, and have more trust in me, because I am here in order to help you and to guide you on a new path towards a new life. Therefore, dear little children, listen and live what I tell you, because it is important for you, when I shall not be with you any longer, that you remember my words and all that I told. I call you to begin to change your life from the beginning and that you decide for conversion not with words but with life. Thank you for having responded to my call."

November 25, 1992

"Dear children, today like never before I invite you to pray. May your life in its entirety become prayer, but without love prayer becomes impossible. Therefore, I call you to love first God, the Creator of your lives; then you will be able to recognize and love God in every man as He loves you. Dear children, the fact of my being with you is a grace! Therefore, accept and live my messages for your own good. I love you and therefore I am with you to teach you and guide you to a new life of conversion and renunciation. Only in this way will you be able to discover God and all that is now foreign

to you. Therefore, pray, little children! Thank you for having responded to my call!"

December 25, 1992

"Dear children, today I wish to place you all under my mantle to protect you from every satanic attack. Today is the
day of Peace, but throughout the whole world there is much
lack of peace. Therefore, I call you to build up a new world
of Peace together with me, by means of prayer. Without
you, I cannot do that, and, therefore, I call all of you, with
my Motherly love, and God will do the rest. Therefore,
open yourselves to God's plans and purposes for you to be
able to cooperate with Him for peace and for good. And
do not forget that your life does not belong to you, but is a
gift with which you must bring joy to others and lead them
to Eternal Life. May the tenderness of little Jesus always
accompany you. Thank you for having responded to my
call."

January 25, 1993

"Dear children, today I call you to accept and live my messages with seriousness. These days are the days when you
need to decide for God, for peace, and for the good. May
every hatred and jealousy disappear from your life and your
thoughts, and may there only dwell love for God and for
your neighbor. Thus, only thus, shall you be able to discern
the signs of this time. I am with you, and I guide you into
a new time, a time which God gives you as grace, so that
you may get to know Him more. Thank you for having
responded to my call!"

February 25, 1993

"Dear children, today I bless you with my Motherly blessing and invite you all to conversion. I wish that each of you

decides himself for a change of life and that each of you works more in the Church, not through words and thoughts but through example, so that your life may be a joyful testimony for Jesus. You cannot say that you are converted, because your life must become a daily conversion. In order to understand what you have to do, little children, pray and God will give you what you concretely have to do, and where you have to change. I am with you and place you all under my mantle. Thank you for having responded to my call."

March 25, 1993

"Dear children, today like never, I call you to pray for peace; for peace in your hearts, peace in your families, and peace in the whole world, because satan wants war, wants lack of peace, wants to destroy all which is good. Therefore, dear children, pray, pray, pray. Thank you for having responded to my call."

April 25, 1993

"Dear children, today I invite you all to awaken your hearts to love. Go into nature and look how nature is awakening and it will be a help for you to open your hearts to the love of God the Creator. I desire you to awaken love in your families so that where there is unrest and hatred, love will reign and when there is love in your hearts, then there is also prayer. And, dear children, do not forget that I am with you and I am helping you with my prayer that God may give you the strength to love. I bless and love you with my Motherly love. Thank you for having responded to my call."

May 25, 1993

"Dear children, today, I invite you to open yourselves to God by means of prayer so the Holy Spirit may begin to work miracles in you and through you. I am with you and I intercede before God for each one of you because, dear children, each one of you is important in my plan of salvation. I invite you to be carriers of good and peace. God can give you peace only if you convert and pray. Therefore, dear little children, pray, pray, pray and do that which the Holy Spirit inspires you. Thank you for having responded to my call."

June 25, 1993

"Dear children, today I also rejoice at your presence here. I bless you with my Motherly blessing and intercede for each one of you before God. I call you anew to live my messages and to put them into life and practice. I am with you and bless all of you day by day. Dear children, these times are particular and therefore I am with you to love and protect you, to protect your hearts from satan and to bring you all closer to the Heart of My Son Jesus. Thank you for having responded to My call!"

July 25, 1993

"Dear children, I thank you for your prayers and for the love you show toward me. I invite you to decide to pray for my intentions. Dear children, offer novenas, making sacrifices wherein you feel the most bound. I want your life to be bound to me. I am your Mother, little children, and I do not want satan to deceive you, for he wants to lead you the wrong way. But he cannot if you don't permit him. Therefore, little children, renew prayer in your hearts and then you will understand my call and my live desire to help you. Thank you for having responded to my call."

August 25, 1993

"Dear children, I want you to understand that I am your Mother, that I want to help you and call you to prayer. Only by prayer can you understand and accept my messages and practice them in your life. Read Sacred Scripture, live it, and pray to understand the signs of the time. This is a special time. Therefore, I am with you to draw you close to my heart and the Heart of my Son, Jesus. Dear little children, I want you to be children of the light and not of the darkness. Therefore, live what I am telling you. Thank you for having responded to my call."

September 25, 1993

"Dear children, I am your Mother and I invite you to come closer to God through prayer, because only He is your peace, your Saviour. Therefore, little children, do not seek comfort in material things; rather, seek God. I am praying for you and I intercede before God for each individual. I am looking for your prayers, that you accept me and accept my messages as in the first days of the apparitions. And only then, when you open your hearts and pray, will miracles happen. Thank you for having responded to my call."

October 25, 1993

"Dear children, these years I have been calling you to pray, to live what I am telling you, but you are living my messages a little. You talk but do not live, that is why, dear little children, this war is lasting so long. I invite you to open yourselves to God and to live with God in your hearts, living the good and giving witness to my messages. I love you and wish to protect you from every evil, but you do not desire it. Dear children, I cannot help you if you do not live God's Commandments, if you do not live the Mass, if you do not abandon sin. I invite you to become Apostles of love and goodness. In this world without peace, give witness to God and God's love and God will bless you and give you what you seek of Him. Thank you for having responded to my call."

November 25, 1993

"Dear children, I invite you now in this time, like never before, to prepare for the coming of Jesus. Let little Jesus reign in your hearts and only then, when Jesus is your friend, will you be happy. It will not be difficult for you either to pray or offer sacrifices or to witness Jesus' greatness in your life, because He will give you strength and joy in this time. I am close to you by my intercession and prayer and I love and bless all of you. Thank you for having responded to my call."

December 25, 1993

"Dear children, today I rejoice with the little Jesus and I desire that Jesus' joy may enter into every heart. Little children, with the message I give you a blessing with my Son Jesus, so that in every heart peace may reign. I love you, little children, and I invite all of you to come closer to me by means of prayer. You talk and talk but do not pray. Therefore, little children, decide for prayer. Only in this way will you be happy and God will give you what you seek from Him. Thank you for having responded to my call."

January 25, 1994

"Dear children, you are all my little children. I love you. But, little children, you must not forget that without prayer you cannot be close to me. In this time, satan wants to create disorder in your hearts and in your families. Little children, do not give in. You must not permit him to lead you and your life. I love you and intercede for you before God. Little children, pray! Thank you for having responded to my call."

February 25, 1994

"**Dear children, today I thank you for your prayers. You all have helped me so that this war may finish as soon as possible. I am close to you and I pray for each one of you and I beg you, Pray, Pray, Pray. Only through prayer we can defeat evil and protect all that which satan wants to destroy in your life. I am your Mother and I love you all the same, and I intercede for you before God. Thank you for having responded to my call!**"

March 25, 1994

"**Dear children, today I rejoice with you and I invite you to open yourselves to me, and become an instrument in my hands, for the salvation of the world. I desire, little children, that all of you who have felt the fragrance of holiness, through these messages which I am giving you, to carry it in this world, hungry for God and God's love. I thank you all for having responded in such a number and I bless you all with my Motherly blessing. Thank you for having responded to my call!**"

April 25, 1994

"**Dear children, today, I invite all of you to decide to pray for my intention. Little children, I invite all of you to help me realize my plan through this parish. Now, in a special way, little children, I invite you to decide to go the way of holiness. Only then will you be close to me. I love you and want to lead you all with me to Paradise. But, if you do not pray and if you are not humble and obedient to the messages I am giving you, I cannot help you. Thank you for having responded to my call.**"

May 25, 1994

"Dear children, I invite you all to have more trust in me and to live my messages more deeply. I am with you and I intercede before God for you, but also I wait for your hearts to open up to my messages. Rejoice because God loves you and gives you the possibility to convert every day and to believe more in God, the Creator. Thank you for having responded to my call."

June 25, 1994

"Dear children, today I rejoice in my heart in seeing you all present here. I bless you and I call you all to decide to live my messages which I give you here. I desire, little children, to guide you all to Jesus because He is your salvation. Therefore, little children, the more you pray the more you will be mine and of my Son Jesus. I bless you all with my Motherly blessing and I thank you for having responded to my call."

July 25, 1994

"Dear children, today, I invite you to decide to give time patiently for prayer. Little children, you cannot say you are mine and that you have experienced conversion through my messages if you are not ready to give time to God every day. I am close to you and I bless you all. Little children, do not forget that if you do not pray, you are not close to me, nor are you close to the Holy Spirit who leads you along the path to holiness. Thank you for having responded to my call."

August 25, 1994

"Dear children, today I am united with you in prayer in a special way, praying for the gift of the presence of my beloved Son in your home country. Pray, little children, for the health of my most beloved son, who suffers and whom I have chosen for these times. I pray and intercede before my Son, Jesus, so that the dream that your fathers had may be fulfilled. Pray, little children, in a special way because satan is strong and wants to destroy hope in your heart. I bless you. Thank you for having responded to my call."

September 25, 1994

"Dear children, I rejoice with you and I invite you to prayer. Little children, pray for my intention. Your prayers are necessary to me, through which I desire to bring you closer to God. He is your salvation. God sends me to help you and to guide you towards Paradise, which is your goal. Therefore, little children, pray, pray, pray. Thank you for having responded to my call."

October 25, 1994

"Dear children, I am with you and I rejoice today because the Most High has granted me to be with you and to teach you and to guide you on the path of perfection. Little children, I wish you to be a beautiful bouquet of flowers which I wish to present to God for the day of All Saints. I invite you to open yourselves and to live, taking the saints as an example. Mother Church has chosen them, that they may be an impulse for your daily life. Thank you for having responded to my call."

November 25, 1994

"Dear children! Today I call you to prayer. I am with you and I love you all. I am your Mother and I wish that your hearts be similar to my heart. Little children, without prayer you cannot live and say that you are mine. Prayer is joy. Prayer is what the human heart desires. Therefore,

get closer, little children, to my Immaculate Heart and you will discover God. Thank you for having responded to my call."

December 25, 1994

"Dear children! Today I am joyful with you and I pray with you for peace; peace in your hearts, peace in your families, peace in your desires, and peace in the whole world. May the King of Peace bless you today and give you peace. I bless you and I carry each of you in my heart. Thank you for having responded to my call."

January 25, 1995

"Dear children, I invite you to open the door of your heart to Jesus as the flower opens itself to the sun. Jesus desires to fill your hearts with peace and joy. You cannot, little children, realize peace if you are not at peace with Jesus. Therefore, I invite you to Confession so Jesus may be your truth and peace. So, little children, pray to have strength to realize what I am telling you. I am with you and I love you. Thank you for having responded to my call."

February 25, 1995

"Dear children! Today I invite you to become missionaries of my messages, which I am giving here through this place that is dear to me. God has allowed me to stay this long with you, and therefore, little children, I invite you to live with love the messages I give and to transmit them to the whole world, so that a river of love flows to people who are full of hatred and without peace. I invite you, little children, to become peace where there is no peace and light where there is darkness, so that each heart accepts the light and the way of salvation. Thank you for having responded to my call."

March 25, 1995

"Dear children! Today I invite you to live peace in your hearts and families. There is no peace, little children, where there is no prayer, and there is no love where there is no faith. Therefore, little children, I invite you all to decide again today for conversion. I am close to you and I invite you all, little children, into my embrace to help you, but you do not want it, and so satan is tempting you, and in the smallest things your faith disappears. This is why, little children, pray and through prayer you will have blessing and peace. Thank you for having responded to my call."

April 25, 1995

"Dear children! Today I call you to love. Little children, without love you cannot live, neither with God nor with brother. Therefore, I call all of you to open your hearts to the love of God that is so great and open to each one of you. God, out of love for man, has sent me among you to show you the path of salvation, the path of love. If you do not first love God, then you will neither be able to love neighbor nor the one you hate. Therefore, little children, pray and through prayer you will discover love. Thank you for having responded to my call."

May 25, 1995

"Dear children! I invite you, little children, to help me, through your prayers, so that as many hearts as possible come close to my Immaculate Heart. satan is strong and with all his forces wants to bring the most people possible closer to himself and to sin. That is why he is on the prowl to snatch more every moment. I beg you, little children, pray and help me to help you. I am your Mother and I love you and that is why I wish to help you. Thank you for having responded to my call."

June 25, 1995

"Dear children! Today I am happy to see you in such great numbers, that you have responded and have come to live my messages. I invite you, little children, to be my joyful carriers of peace in this troubled world. Pray for peace so that as soon as possible a time of peace, which my heart waits impatiently for, may reign. I am near to you, little children, and I intercede for every one of you before the Most High. I bless you with my Motherly blessing. Thank you for having responded to my call."

July 25, 1995

"Dear children! I invite you to prayer because only in prayer can you understand my coming here. The Holy Spirit will enlighten you to understand that you must convert. Little children, I wish to make of you a most beautiful bouquet prepared for eternity, but you do not accept the way of conversion, the way of salvation that I am offering you through these apparitions. Little children, pray, convert your hearts, and come closer to me. May good overcome evil. I love you and bless you. Thank you for having responded to my call."

August 25, 1995

"Dear children! Today I invite you to prayer. Let prayer be life for you. A family cannot say that it is in peace if it does not pray. Therefore, let your morning begin with morning prayer, and the evening end with thanksgiving. Little children, I am with you, and I love you and I bless you and I wish for everyone of you to be in my embrace. You cannot be in my embrace if you are not ready to pray every day. Thank you for having responded to my call."

September 25, 1995

"Dear children! Today, I invite you to fall in love with the Most Holy Sacrament of the Altar. Adore Him, little children, in your parishes and in this way you will be united with the entire world. Jesus will become your friend and you will not talk of Him like someone whom you barely know. Unity with Him will be a joy for you and you will become witnesses to the love of Jesus that He has for every creature. Little children, when you adore Jesus you are also close to me. Thank you for having responded to my call."

October 25, 1995

"Dear children! Today I invite you to go into nature because there you will meet God the Creator. Today I invite you, little children, to thank God for all that He gives you. In thanking Him you will discover the Most High and all the goods that surround you. Little children, God is great and His love for every creature is great. Therefore, pray to be able to understand the love and goodness of God. In the goodness and the love of God the Creator, I am also with you as a gift. Thank you for having responded to my call."

November 25, 1995

"Dear children! Today, I invite you that each of you begin anew to love - first of all, God, who saved and redeemed each of you, and then brothers and sisters near you*. Without love, little children, you cannot grow in holiness and cannot do good deeds. Therefore, little children, pray, without ceasing pray, so that God reveals His love to you. I have invited all of you to unite with me and to love**. Today, I am with you and I invite you to discover love in your hearts and in the families. For God to live in your hearts, you must love. Thank you for having responded to my call."

* See next page for * and ** explanation.

* In Croatian, the literal translation says, "brothers and sisters in nearness."

** In Croatian, the literal translation says, "with me and loving."

December 25, 1995

"**Dear children! Today, I also rejoice with you and I bring you little Jesus, so that He may bless you. I invite you, dear children, so that your life may be united with Him. Jesus is the King of Peace and only He can give you the peace that you seek. I am with you and I present you to Jesus in a special way, now in this new time in which one should decide for Him. This time is the time of grace. Thank you for having responded to my call.**"

January 25, 1996

"**Dear children! Today I invite you to decide for peace. Pray that God give you the true peace. Live peace in your hearts and you will understand, dear children, that peace is the gift of God. Dear children, without love you cannot live peace. The fruit of peace is love and the fruit of love is forgiveness. I am with you and I invite all of you, little children, that before all else forgive in the family and then you will be able to forgive others. Thank you for having responded to my call.**"

February 25, 1996

"**Dear children! Today I invite you to conversion. This is the most important message that I have given you here. Little children, I wish that each of you become a carrier of my messages. I invite you, little children, to live the messages that I have given you over these years. This time is a time of grace. Especially now, when the Church also is** inviting you to prayer and conversion. I also, little children, invite you to live my messages that I have given you during the time since I appear here. Thank you for having responded to my call."

March 25, 1996

"Dear children! I invite you to decide again to love God above all else. In this time, when due to the spirit of consumerism, one forgets what it means to love and to cherish true values, I invite you again, little children, to put God in the first place in your life. Do not let satan attract you through material things but, little children, decide for God who is freedom and love. Choose life and not death of the soul, little children, and in this time when you meditate upon the suffering and death of Jesus, I invite you to decide for life which blossomed through the Resurrection, and that your life may be renewed today through conversion that shall lead you to eternal life. Thank you for having responded to my call."

April 25, 1996

"Dear children! Today I invite you again to put prayer in the first place in your families. Little children, when God is in the first place, then you will, in all that you do, seek the will of God. In this way your daily conversion will become easier. Little children, seek with humility that which is not in order in your hearts. Conversion will become a daily duty that you will do with joy. Little children, I am with you, I bless you all and I invite you to become my witnesses by prayer and personal conversion. Thank you for having responded to my call."

May 25, 1996

"Dear children! Today I wish to thank you for all your

prayers and sacrifices that you, during this month which is dedicated to me, have offered to me. Little children, I also wish that you all become active during this time that is through me connected to Heaven in a special way. Pray in order to understand that you all, through your life and your example, ought to collaborate in the work of salvation. Little children, I wish that all people convert and see me and my Son, Jesus, in you. I will intercede for you and help you to become the light. In helping the other, your soul will also find salvation. Thank you for having responded to my call."

June 25, 1996

"Dear children! Today I thank you for all the sacrifices you have offered me these days. Little children, I invite you to open yourselves to me and to decide for conversion. Your hearts, little children, are still not completely open to me and therefore, I invite you again to open to prayer so that in prayer the Holy Spirit will help you, that your hearts become flesh and not of stone. Little children, thank you for having responded to my call and for having decided to walk with me toward holiness."

July 25, 1996

"Dear children! Today I invite you to decide every day for God. Little children, you speak much about God, but you witness little with your life. Therefore, little children, decide for conversion, that your life may be true before God, so that in the truth of your life you witness the beauty God gave you. Little children, I invite you again to decide for prayer because through prayer, you will be able to live the conversion. Each one of you shall become in the simplicity, similar to a child which is open to the love of the Father. Thank you for having responded to my call."

August 25, 1996

"**Dear children! Listen, because I wish to speak to you and to invite you to have more faith and trust in God, who loves you immeasurably. Little children, you do not know how to live in the grace of God, that is why I call you anew, to carry the Word of God in your heart and in thoughts. Little children, place the Sacred Scripture in a visible place in your family, and read and live it. Teach your children, because if you are not an example to them, children depart into godlessness. Reflect and pray and then God will be born in your heart and your heart will be joyous. Thank you for having responded to my call.**"

September 25, 1996

"**Dear children! Today, I invite you to offer your crosses and suffering for my intentions. Little children, I am your Mother and I wish to help you by seeking for you the grace from God. Little children, offer your sufferings as a gift to God so they become a most beautiful flower of joy. That is why, little children, pray so that you may understand that suffering can become joy and the cross the way of joy. Thank you for having responded to my call.**"

October 25, 1996

"**Dear children! Today I invite you to open yourselves to God the Creator, so that He changes you. Little children, you are dear to me. I love you all and I call you to be closer to me and that your love towards my Immaculate Heart be more fervent. I wish to renew you and lead you with my Heart to the Heart of Jesus, which still today suffers for you and calls you to conversion and renewal. Through you, I wish to renew the world. Comprehend, little children, that you are today the salt of the earth and the light of the world. Little children, I invite you and I love you and in a special**

way implore: Convert! Thank you for having responded
to my call."

November 25, 1996

"Dear children! Today, again, I invite you to pray, so that
through prayer, fasting, and small sacrifices you may prepare yourselves for the coming of Jesus. May this time, little
children, be a time of grace for you. Use every moment and
do good, for only in this way will you feel the birth of Jesus
in your hearts. If with your life you give an example and
become a sign of God's love, joy will prevail in the hearts of
men. Thank you for having responded to my call."

December 25, 1996

"Dear children! Today I am with you in a special way, holding little Jesus in my lap and I invite you, little children, to
open yourselves to His call. He calls you to joy. Little children, joyfully live the messages of the Gospel, which I am
repeating in the time since I am with you. Little children,
I am your Mother and I desire to reveal to you the God of
love and the God of peace. I do not desire for your life to be
in sadness but that it be realized in joy for eternity, according to the Gospel. Only in this way will your life have meaning. Thank you for having responded to my call."

January 25, 1997

"Dear children! I invite you to reflect about your future.
You are creating a new world without God, only with your
own strength and that is why you are unsatisfied and without joy in the heart. This time is my time and that is why,
little children, I invite you again to pray. When you find
unity with God, you will feel hunger for the Word of God
and your heart, little children, will overflow with joy. You
will witness God's love wherever you are. I bless you and I

repeat to you that I am with you to help you. Thank you for having responded to my call."

February 25, 1997

"Dear children! Today I invite you in a special way to open yourselves to God the Creator and to become active. I invite you, little children, to see at this time who needs your spiritual or material help. By your example, little children, you will be the extended hands of God, which mankind is seeking. Only in this way will you understand, that you are called to witness and to become joyful carriers of God's Word and of His love. Thank you for having responded to my call."

March 25, 1997

"Dear children! Today, in a special way, I invite you to take the cross in the hands and to meditate on the wounds of Jesus. Ask of Jesus to heal your wounds, which you, dear children, during your life sustained because of your sins or the sins of your parents. Only in this way, dear children, you will understand that the world is in need of healing of faith in God the Creator. By Jesus' passion and death on the cross, you will understand that only through prayer you, too, can become true apostles of faith; when, in simplicity and prayer, you live faith which is a gift. Thank you for having responded to my call."

April 25, 1997

"Dear children! Today I call you to have your life be connected with God the Creator, because only in this way will your life have meaning and you will comprehend that God is love. God sends me to you out of love, that I may help you to comprehend that without Him there is no future or joy and, above all, there is no eternal salvation. Little chil-

dren, I call you to leave sin and to accept prayer at all times, that you may in prayer come to know the meaning of your life. God gives Himself to him who seeks Him. Thank you for having responded to my call."

May 25, 1997

"Dear children! Today I invite you to glorify God for the Name of God to be holy in your hearts and in your life. Little children, when you are in the holiness of God, He is with you and gives you peace and joy which come only from God through prayer. That is why, little children, renew prayer in your families and your heart will glorify the Holy Name of God and Heaven will reign in your heart. I am close to you and I intercede for you before God. Thank you for having responded to my call."

June 25, 1997

"Dear children! Today I am with you in a special way and I bring you my Motherly blessing of peace. I pray for you and I intercede for you before God, so that you may comprehend that each of you is a carrier of peace. You cannot have peace if your heart is not at peace with God. That is why, little children, pray, pray, pray, because prayer is the foundation of your peace. Open your heart and give time to God so that He will be your friend. When true friendship with God is realized, no storm can destroy it. Thank you for having responded to my call."

July 25, 1997

"Dear children! Today I invite you to respond to my call to prayer. I desire, dear children, that during this time you find a corner for personal prayer. I desire to lead you towards prayer with the heart. Only in this way will you comprehend that your life is empty without prayer. You will discover the meaning of your life when you discover God in prayer. That is why, little children, open the door of your heart and you will comprehend that prayer is joy without which you cannot live. Thank you for having responded to my call."

August 25, 1997

"Dear children! God gives me this time as a gift to you, so that I may instruct and lead you on the path of salvation. Dear children, now you do not comprehend this grace, but soon a time will come when you will lament for these messages. That is why, little children, live all of the words which I have given you through this time of grace and renew prayer, until prayer becomes a joy for you. Especially, I call all those who have consecrated themselves to my Immaculate Heart to become an example to others. I call all priests and religious brothers and sisters to pray the Rosary and to teach others to pray. The Rosary, little children, is especially dear to me. Through the Rosary open your heart to me and I am able to help you. Thank you for having responded to my call."

September 25, 1997

"Dear children! Today I call you to comprehend that without love you cannot comprehend that God needs to be in the first place in your life. That is why, little children, I call you all to love, not with a human love, but with God's love. In this way, your life will be more beautiful and without an interest. You will comprehend that God gives Himself to you in the simplest way out of love. Little children, so that you may comprehend my words which I give out of love, pray, pray, pray and you will be able to accept others with love and to forgive all who have done evil to you. Thank you for having responded to my call."

October 25, 1997

"Dear children! Also today I am with you and I call all of you to renew yourselves by living my messages. Little children, may prayer be life for you and may you be an example to others. Little children, I desire for you to become carriers of peace and of God's joy to today's world without peace. That is why, little children, pray, pray, pray! I am with you and I bless you with my motherly peace. Thank you for having responded to my call."

November 25, 1997

"Dear children! Today I invite you to comprehend your Christian vocation. Little children, I led and am leading you through this time of grace, that you may become conscious of your Christian vocation. Holy martyrs died witnessing: I am a Christian and love God over everything. Little children, today also I invite you to rejoice and be joyful Christians, responsible and conscious that God called you in a special way to be joyfully extended hands toward those who do not believe, and that through the example of your life, they may receive faith and love for God. Therefore, pray, pray, pray that your heart may open and be sensitive for the Word of God. Thank you for having responded to my call."

December 25, 1997

"Dear children! Also today I rejoice with you and I call you to the good. I desire that each of you reflect and carry peace in your heart and say: I want to put God in the first place in my life. In this way, little children, each of you will become holy. Little children, tell everyone, I want the good for you and He will respond with the good and, little children, good will come to dwell in the heart of each man. Little children, tonight I bring to you the good of my Son who gave His life

to save you. That is why, little children, rejoice and extend your hands to Jesus who is only good. Thank you for having responded to my call."

January 25, 1998

"Dear children! Today again I call all of you to prayer. Only with prayer, dear children, will your heart change, become better, and be more sensitive to the Word of God. Little children, do not permit satan to pull you apart and to do with you what he wants. I call you to be responsible and determined and to consecrate each day to God in prayer. May Holy Mass, little children, not be a habit for you, but life. By living Holy Mass each day, you will feel the need for holiness and you will grow in holiness. I am close to you and intercede before God for each of you, so that He may give you strength to change your heart. Thank you for having responded to my call."

February 25, 1998

"Dear children! Also today I am with you and I, again, call all of you to come closer to me through your prayers. In a special way, I call you to renunciation in this time of grace. Little children, meditate on and live, through your little sacrifices, the passion and death of Jesus for each of you. Only if you come closer to Jesus will you comprehend the immeasurable love He has for each of you. Through prayer and your renunciation you will become more open to the gift of faith and love towards the Church and the people who are around you. I love you and bless you. Thank you for having responded to my call."

March 25, 1998

"Dear children! Also today I call you to fasting and renunciation. Little children, renounce that which hinders you from being closer to Jesus. In a special way I call you: Pray, because only through prayer will you be able to overcome your will and discover the will of God even in the smallest things. By your daily life, little children, you will become an example and witness that you live for Jesus or against Him and His will. Little children, I desire that you become apostles of love. By loving, little children, it will be recognized that you are mine. Thank you for having responded to my call."

April 25, 1998

"Dear children! Today I call you, through prayer, to open yourselves to God as a flower opens itself to the rays of the morning sun. Little children, do not be afraid. I am with you and I intercede before God for each of you so that your heart receives the gift of conversion. Only in this way, little children, will you comprehend the importance of grace in these times and God will become nearer to you. Thank you for having responded to my call."

May 25, 1998

"Dear children! Today I call you, through prayer and sacrifice, to prepare yourselves for the coming of the Holy Spirit. Little children, this is a time of grace and so, again, I call you to decide for God the Creator. Allow Him to transform and change you. May your heart be prepared to listen to, and live, everything which the Holy Spirit has in His plan for each of you. Little children, allow the Holy Spirit to lead you on the way of truth and salvation towards eternal life. Thank you for having responded to my call."

June 25, 1998

"Dear children! Today I desire to thank you for living my messages. I bless you all with my Motherly blessing and I bring you all before my Son Jesus. Thank you for having responded to my call."

July 25, 1998

"Dear children! Today, little children, I invite you, through prayer, to be with Jesus, so that through a personal experience of prayer you may be able to discover the beauty of God's creatures. You cannot speak or witness about prayer, if you do not pray. That is why, little children, in the silence of the heart, remain with Jesus, so that He may change and transform you with His love. This, little children, is a time of grace for you. Make good use of it for your personal conversion, because when you have God, you have everything. Thank you for having responded to my call."

August 25, 1998

"Dear children! Today I invite you to come still closer to me through prayer. Little children, I am your mother, I love you and I desire that each of you be saved and thus be with me in Heaven. That is why, little children, pray, pray, pray until your life becomes prayer. Thank you for having responded to my call."

September 25, 1998

"Dear children! Today, I call you to become my witnesses by living the faith of your fathers. Little children, you seek signs and messages and do not see that, with every morning sunrise, God calls you to convert and to return to the way of truth and salvation. You speak much, little children, but you work little on your conversion. That is why, convert and start to live my messages, not with your words but with your life. In this way, little children, you will have the strength to decide for the true conversion of the heart. Thank you for having responded to my call."

October 25, 1998

"**Dear children! Today I call you to come closer to my Immaculate Heart. I call you to renew in your families the fervor of the first days when I called you to fasting, prayer, and conversion. Little children, you accepted my messages with open hearts, although you did not know what prayer was. Today, I call you to open yourselves completely to me so that I may transform you and lead you to the heart of my Son Jesus, so that He can fill you with His love. Only in this way, little children, will you find true peace - the peace that only God gives you. Thank you for having responded to my call.**"

November 25, 1998

"**Dear children! Today I call you to prepare yourselves for the coming of Jesus. In a special way, prepare your hearts. May Holy Confession be the first act of conversion for you and then, dear children, decide for holiness. May your conversion and decision for holiness begin today and not tomorrow. Little children, I call you all to the way of salvation and I desire to show you the way to Heaven. That is why, dear children, be mine and decide with me for holiness. Little children, accept prayer with seriousness and pray, pray, pray. Thank you for having responded to my call.**"

December 25, 1998

"**Dear children! In this Christmas joy I desire to bless you with my blessing. In a special way, little children, I give you the blessing of little Jesus. May He fill you with His peace. Today, little children, you do not have peace and yet you yearn for it. That is why, with my Son Jesus, on this day I call you to pray, pray, pray, because without prayer you do not have joy or peace or a future. Yearn for peace and seek it, for God is true peace. Thank you for having responded to my call.**"

January 25, 1999

"**Dear children! I again invite you to prayer. You have no excuse to work more because nature still lies in deep sleep. Open yourselves in prayer. Renew prayer in your families. Put Holy Scripture in a visible place in your families, read it, reflect on it, and learn how God loves His people. His love shows itself also in present times because He sends me to call you upon the path of salvation. Thank you for having responded to my call."**

February 25, 1999

"**Dear children! Also today I am with you in a special way contemplating and living the passion of Jesus in my heart. Little children, open your hearts and give me everything that is in them: joys, sorrows, and each, even the smallest, pain, that I may offer them to Jesus; so that with His immeasurable love, He may burn and transform your sorrows into the joy of His Resurrection. That is why, I now call you in a special way, little children, for your hearts to open to prayer, so that through prayer you may become friends of Jesus. Thank you for having responded to my call."**

March 25, 1999

"**Dear children! I call you to prayer with the heart. In a special way, little children, I call you to pray for conversion of sinners, for those who pierce my heart and the heart of my Son Jesus with the sword of hatred and daily blasphemies. Let us pray, little children, for all those who do not desire to come to know the love of God, even though they are in the Church. Let us pray that they convert, so that the Church may resurrect in love. Only with love and prayer, little children, can you live this time which is given to you for conversion. Place God in the first place, then the risen Jesus will become your friend. Thank you for having responded to my call."**

April 25, 1999

> "Dear children! Also today I call you to prayer. Little children, be joyful carriers of peace and love in this peaceless world. By fasting and prayer, witness that you are mine and that you live my messages. Pray and seek! I am praying and interceding for you before God that you convert; that your life and behavior always be Christian. Thank you for having responded to my call."

May 25, 1999

> "Dear children! Also today I call you to convert and to more firmly believe in God. Children, you seek peace and pray in different ways, but you have not yet given your hearts to God for Him to fill them with His love. So, I am with you to teach you and to bring you closer to the love of God. If you love God above all else, it will be easy for you to pray and to open your hearts to him. Thank you for having responded to my call."

June 25, 1999

> "Dear children! Today I thank you for living and witnessing my messages with your life. Little children, be strong and pray so that prayer may give you strength and joy. Only in this way will each of you be mine and I will lead you on the way of salvation. Little children, pray and with your life witness my presence here. May each day be a joyful witness for you of God's love. Thank you for having responded to my call."

July 25, 1999

> "Dear children! Also today I rejoice with you and I call you all to prayer with the heart. I call all of you, little children, to give thanks to God here with me for the graces which He

gives to you through me. I desire for you to comprehend that I want to realize here, not only a place of prayer but also a meeting of hearts. I desire for my, Jesus' and your heart to become one heart of love and peace. That is why, little children, pray and rejoice over everything that God does here, despite that satan provokes quarrels and unrest. I am with you and I lead you all on the way of love. Thank you for having responded to my call."

August 25, 1999

"Dear children! Also today I call you to give glory to God the Creator in the colors of nature. He speaks to you also through the smallest flower about His beauty and the depth of love with which He has created you. Little children, may prayer flow from your hearts like fresh water from a spring. May the wheat fields speak to you about the mercy of God towards every creature. That is why, renew prayer of thanksgiving for everything He gives you. Thank you for having responded to my call."

September 25, 1999

"Dear children! Today again I call you to become carriers of my peace. In a special way, now when it is being said that God is far away, He has truly never been nearer to you. I call you to renew prayer in your families by reading the Sacred Scripture and to experience joy in meeting with God who infinitely loves His creatures. Thank you for having responded to my call."

October 25, 1999

"Dear children! Do not forget: this is a time of grace; that is why, pray, pray, pray! Thank you for having responded to my call."

November 25, 1999

"Dear children! Also today I call you to prayer. In this time of grace, may the cross be a sign-post of love and unity for you through which true peace comes. That is why, little children, pray especially at this time that little Jesus, the Creator of peace, may be born in your hearts. Only through prayer will you become my apostles of peace in this world without peace. That is why, pray until prayer becomes a joy for you. Thank you for having responded to my call."

December 25, 1999

"Dear children! This is the time of grace. Little children, today in a special way with little Jesus, whom I hold in my embrace, I am giving you the possibility to decide for peace. Through your 'yes' for peace and your decision for God, a new possibility for peace is opened. Only in this way, little children, this century will be for you a time of peace and well-being. Therefore, put little newborn Jesus in the first place in your life and He will lead you on the way of salvation. Thank you for having responded to my call."

January 25, 2000

"Dear children! I call you, little children, to pray without ceasing. If you pray, you are closer to God and He will lead you on the way of peace and salvation. That is why I call you today to give peace to others. Only in God is there true peace. Open your hearts and become those who give a gift of peace and others will discover peace in you and through you and in this way you will witness God's peace and love which He gives you. Thank you for having responded to my call."

February 25, 2000

"Dear children! Wake up from the sleep of unbelief and sin, because this is a time of grace which God gives you. Use this time and seek the grace of healing of your heart, from God, so that you may see God and man with the heart. Pray in a special way for those who have not come to know God's love, and witness with your life so that they also can come to know God and His immeasurable love. Thank you for having responded to my call."

March 25, 2000

"Dear children! Pray and make good use of this time because this is a time of grace. I am with you and I intercede for each one of you before God, for your heart to open to God and to God's love. Little children, pray without ceasing, until prayer becomes a joy for you. Thank you for having responded to my call."

April 25, 2000

"Dear children! Also today I call you to conversion. You are concerned too much about material things and little about spiritual ones. Open your hearts and start again to work more on your personal conversion. Decide everyday to dedicate time to God and to prayer until prayer becomes a joyful meeting with God for you. Only in this way will your life have meaning and with joy you will contemplate eternal life. Thank you for having responded to my call."

May 25, 2000

"Dear children! I rejoice with you and in this time of grace I call you to spiritual renewal. Pray, little children, that the Holy Spirit may come to dwell in you in fullness, so that you may be able to witness in joy to all those who are far from faith. Especially, little children, pray for the gifts of the Holy Spirit so that in the spirit of love, every day and in each situation, you may be closer to your fellow man; and that in wisdom and love you may overcome every difficulty. I am with you and I intercede for each of you before Jesus. Thank you for having responded to my call."

June 25, 2000

"Dear children! Today I call you to prayer. The one who prays is not afraid of the future. Little children, do not forget I am with you and I love you all. Thank you for having responded to my call."

July 25, 2000

"Dear children! Do not forget that you are here on earth on the way to eternity and that your home is in Heaven. That is why, little children, be open to God's love and leave egoism and sin. May your joy be only in discovering God in daily prayer. That is why, make good use of this time and pray, pray, pray, and God is near to you in prayer and through prayer. Thank you for having responded to my call."

August 25, 2000

"Dear children! I desire to share my joy with you. In my Immaculate Heart I feel that there are many of those who have drawn closer to me and are, in a special way, carrying the victory of my Immaculate Heart in their hearts by praying and converting. I desire to thank you and to inspire you to work even more for God and His kingdom with love and the power of the Holy Spirit. I am with you and I bless you with my Motherly blessing. Thank you for having responded to my call."

September 25, 2000

"Dear children! Today I call you to open yourselves to prayer. May prayer become joy for you. Renew prayer in your families and form prayer groups. In this way, you will experience joy in prayer and togetherness. All those who pray and are members of prayer groups are open to God's Will in their hearts and joyfully witness God's love. I am with you, I carry all of you in my heart and I bless you with my Motherly blessing. Thank you for having responded to my call."

October 25, 2000

"Dear children! Today I desire to open my Motherly Heart to you and to call you all to pray for my intentions. I desire to renew prayer with you and to call you to fast which I desire to offer to my Son Jesus for the coming of a new time - a time of spring. In this Jubilee year many hearts have opened to me and the Church is being renewed in the Spirit. I rejoice with you and I thank God for this gift; and you little children, I call to pray, pray, pray - until prayer becomes a joy for you. Thank you for having responded to my call."

November 25, 2000

"Dear children! Today when Heaven is near to you in a special way, I call you to prayer so that through prayer you place God in the first place. Little children, today I am near you and I bless each of you with my Motherly blessing so that you have the strength and love for all the people you meet in your earthly life and that you can give God's love. I rejoice with you and I desire to tell you that your brother Slavko has been born into Heaven and intercedes for you. Thank you for having responded to my call."

December 25, 2000

"**Dear children! Today when God granted to me that I can be with you, with little Jesus in my arms, I rejoice with you and I give thanks to God for everything He has done in this Jubilee year. I thank God especially for all the vocations of those who said 'yes' to God completely. I bless you all with my blessing and the blessing of the newborn Jesus. I pray for all of you for joy to be born in your hearts so that in joy you too carry the joy I have today. In this Child I bring to you the Savior of your hearts and the One who calls you to the holiness of life. Thank you for having responded to my call.**"

January 25, 2001

"**Dear children! Today I call you to renew prayer and fasting with even greater enthusiasm until prayer becomes a joy for you. Little children, the one who prays is not afraid of the future and the one who fasts is not afraid of evil. Once again, I repeat to you: only through prayer and fasting also wars can be stopped - wars of your unbelief and fear for the future. I am with you and am teaching you little children: your peace and hope are in God. That is why draw closer to God and put Him in the first place in your life. Thank you for having responded to my call.**"

February 25, 2001

"**Dear children! This is a time of grace. That is why pray, pray, pray until you comprehend God's love for each of you. Thank you for having responded to my call.**"

March 25, 2001

"**Dear children! Also today I call you to open yourselves to prayer. Little children, you live in a time in which God** gives great graces but you do not know how to make good use of them. You are concerned about everything else, but the least for the soul and spiritual life. Awaken from the tired sleep of your soul and say yes to God with all your strength. Decide for conversion and holiness. I am with you, little children, and I call you to perfection of your soul and of everything you do. Thank you for having responded to my call."

April 25, 2001

"Dear children! Also today, I call you to prayer. Little children, prayer works miracles. When you are tired and sick and you do not know the meaning of your life, take the Rosary and pray; pray until prayer becomes for you a joyful meeting with your Savior. I am with you, little children, and I intercede and pray for you. Thank you for having responded to my call."

May 25, 2001

"Dear children! At this time of grace, I call you to prayer. Little children, you work much but without God's blessing. Bless and seek the wisdom of the Holy Spirit to lead you at this time so that you may comprehend and live in the grace of this time. Convert, little children, and kneel in the silence of your hearts. Put God in the center of your being so that, in that way, you can witness in joy the beauty that God continually gives in your life. Thank you for having responded to my call."

June 25, 2001

Marija and her husband Paolo built a chapel next to their home in Medjugorje. When in Medjugorje, this is where Marija has her daily apparitions. They completed the chapel right before the twentieth anniversary (June 25th). Paolo and Marija did a novena so that Our Lady would name their new chapel. Although this apparition did not take place in the chapel, Marija told Our Lady, *"We give this chapel for you. What name do you desire it to be given?"* When asked, Our Lady smiled and lovingly held up Her first two fingers, signifying the number two, and then pointed to Her heart and traced a heart with Her finger. Marija was flooded with emotion, tears, and joy and understood in her heart that Our Lady named it **The Chapel of The Two Hearts.** As Marija was relaying this afterwards, she could barely speak. It was very obvious that Paolo and Marija were both very moved that Our Lady would name, without a word spoken, their chapel in this simple profound way. The following is Our Lady's monthly message which was given the same day that Our Lady named Paolo and Marija's chapel.

> **"Dear children! I am with you and I bless you all with my Motherly blessing. Especially today when God gives you abundant graces, pray and seek God through me. God gives you great graces, that is why, little children, make good use of this time of grace and come closer to my heart so that I can lead you to my Son Jesus. Thank you for having responded to my call."**

July 25, 2001

> **"Dear children! In this time of grace, I call you to come even closer to God through your personal prayer. Make good use of the time of rest and give your soul and your eyes rest in God. Find peace in nature and you will discover God the Creator Whom you will be able to give thanks to for all creatures; then you will find joy in your heart. Thank you for having responded to my call."**

August 25, 2001

> **"Dear children! Today I call all of you to decide for holiness. May for you, little children, always in your thoughts**

and in each situation holiness be in the first place, in work
and in speech. In this way, you will also put it into practice;
little by little, step by step, prayer and a decision for holiness will enter into your family. Be real with yourselves and
do not bind yourselves to material things but to God. And
do not forget, little children, that your life is as passing as a
flower. Thank you for having responded to my call."

September 25, 2001

"Dear children! Also today I call you to prayer, especially
today when satan wants war and hatred. I call you anew,
little children: pray and fast that God may give you peace.
Witness peace to every heart and be carriers of peace in this
world without peace. I am with you and intercede before
God for each of you. And you do not be afraid because the
one who prays is not afraid of evil and has no hatred in the
heart. Thank you for having responded to my call."

October 25, 2001

"Dear children! Also today I call you to pray from your
whole heart and to love each other. Little children, you are
chosen to witness peace and joy. If there is no peace, pray
and you will receive it. Through you and your prayer, little
children, peace will begin to flow through the world. That is
why, little children, pray, pray, pray, because prayer works
miracles in the hearts of mankind and in the world. I am
with you and I thank God for each of you who has accepted
and lives prayer with seriousness. Thank you for having
responded to my call."

November 25, 2001

"Dear children! In this time of grace, I call you anew to
prayer. Little children, pray and prepare your hearts for the
coming of the King of Peace, that with His blessing He may

give peace to the whole world. Peacelessness has begun to reign in hearts and hatred reigns in the world. That is why, you who live my messages be the light and extended hands to this faithless world that all may come to know the God of Love. Do not forget, little children, I am with you and bless you all. Thank you for having responded to my call."

December 25, 2001

"Dear children! I call you today and encourage you to prayer for peace. Especially today I call you, carrying the newborn Jesus in my arms for you, to unite with Him through prayer and to become a sign to this peaceless world. Encourage each other, little children, to prayer and love. May your faith be an encouragement to others to believe and to love more. I bless you all and call you to be closer to my heart and to the heart of little Jesus. Thank you for having responded to my call."

January 25, 2002

"Dear children! At this time while you are still looking back to the past year I call you, little children, to look deeply into your heart and to decide to be closer to God and to prayer. Little children, you are still attached to earthly things and little to spiritual life. May my call today also be an encouragement to you to decide for God and for daily conversion. You cannot be converted, little children, if you do not abandon sins and do not decide for love towards God and neighbor. Thank you for having responded to my call."

February 25, 2002

"Dear children! In this time of grace, I call you to become friends of Jesus. Pray for peace in your hearts and work for your personal conversion. Little children, only in this way will you be able to become witnesses of peace and of the love of Jesus in the world. Open yourselves to prayer so that prayer becomes a need for you. Be converted, little children, and work so that as many souls as possible may come to know Jesus and His love. I am close to you and I bless you all. Thank you for having responded to my call."

March 25, 2002

"Dear children! Today I call you to unite with Jesus in prayer. Open your heart to Him and give Him everything that is in it: joy, sorrows, and illnesses. May this be a time of grace for you. Pray, little children, and may every moment belong to Jesus. I am with you and I intercede for you. Thank you for having responded to my call."

April 25, 2002

"Dear children! Rejoice with me in this time of spring when all nature is awakening and your hearts long for change. Open yourselves, little children, and pray. Do not forget that I am with you and I desire to take you all to my Son and He may give you the gift of sincere love towards God and everything that is from Him. Open yourselves to prayer and seek a conversion of your hearts from God; everything else He sees and provides. Thank you for having responded to my call."

May 25, 2002

"Dear children! Today I call you to put prayers in the first place in your life. Pray and may prayer, little children, be a joy for you. I am with you and intercede for all of you, and you, little children, be joyful carriers of my messages. May your life with me be joy. Thank you for having responded to my call."

June 25, 2002

"**Dear children! Today I pray for you and with you that the Holy Spirit may help you and increase your faith, so that you may accept even more the messages that I am giving you here in this holy place. Little children, comprehend that this is a time of grace for each of you; and with me, little children, you are secure. I desire to lead you all on the way of holiness. Live my messages and put into life every word that I am giving you. May they be precious to you because they come from Heaven. Thank you for having responded to my call.**"

July 25, 2002

"**Dear children! Today I rejoice with your patron saint and call you to be open to God's Will, so that in you and through you, faith may grow in the people you meet in your everyday life. Little children, pray until prayer becomes joy for you. Ask your holy protectors to help you grow in love towards God. Thank you for having responded to my call.**"

August 25, 2002

"**Dear children! Also today I am with you in prayer so that God gives you an even stronger faith. Little children, your faith is small and you are not even aware how much, despite this, you are not ready to seek the gift of faith from God. That is why I am with you, little children, to help you comprehend my messages and put them into life. Pray, pray, pray and only in faith and through prayer your soul will find peace and the world will find joy to be with God. Thank you for having responded to my call.**"

September 25, 2002

"**Dear children! Also in this peaceless time, I call you to** prayer. Little children, pray for peace so that in the world every person would feel love towards peace. Only when the soul finds peace in God, it feels content and love will begin to flow in the world. And in a special way, little children, you are called to live and witness peace - peace in your hearts and families - and, through you, peace will also begin to flow in the world. Thank you for having responded to my call."

October 25, 2002

"Dear children! Also today I call you to prayer. Little children, believe that by simple prayer miracles can be worked. Through your prayer you open your heart to God and He works miracles in your life. By looking at the fruits, your heart fills with joy and gratitude to God for everything He does in your life and, through you, also to others. Pray and believe little children, God gives you graces and you do not see them. Pray and you will see them. May your day be filled with prayer and thanksgiving for everything that God gives you. Thank you for having responded to my call."

November 25, 2002

"Dear children! I call you also today to conversion. Open your heart to God, little children, through Holy Confession and prepare your soul so that little Jesus can be born anew in your heart. Permit Him to transform you and lead you on the way of peace and joy. Little children, decide for prayer. Especially now, in this time of grace, may your heart yearn for prayer. I am close to you and intercede before God for all of you. Thank you for having responded to my call."

December 25, 2002

"Dear children! This is a time of great graces, but also a time of great trials for all those who desire to follow the way of peace. Because of that, little children, again I call you to pray, pray, pray, not with words but with the heart. Live my messages and be converted. Be conscious of this gift that God has permitted me to be with you, especially today when in my arms I have little Jesus - the King of Peace. I desire to give you peace, and that you carry it in your hearts and give it to others until God's peace begins to rule the world. Thank you for having responded to my call."

January 25, 2003

"Dear children! With this message I call you anew to pray for peace. Particularly now when peace is in crisis, you be those who pray and bear witness to peace. Little children, be peace in this peaceless world. Thank you for having responded to my call."

February 25, 2003

"Dear children! Also today I call you to pray and fast for peace. As I have already said and now repeat to you, little children, only with prayer and fasting can wars also be stopped. Peace is a precious gift from God. Seek, pray, and you will receive it. Speak about peace and carry peace in your hearts. Nurture it like a flower which is in need of water, tenderness, and light. Be those who carry peace to others. I am with you and intercede for all of you. Thank you for having responded to my call."

March 25, 2003

"Dear children! Also today I call you to pray for peace. Pray with the heart, little children, and do not lose hope because God loves His creatures. He desires to save you, one by one, through my coming here. I call you to the way of holiness. Pray, and in prayer you are open to God's Will; in this way, in everything you do, you realize God's plan in you and through you. Thank you for having responded to my call."

April 25, 2003

"Dear children! I call you also today to open yourselves to prayer. In the foregone time of Lent, you have realized how small you are and how small your faith is. Little children, decide also today for God, that in you and through you He may change the hearts of people, and also your hearts. Be joyful carriers of the risen Jesus in this peaceless world, which yearns for God and for everything that is from God. I am with you, little children, and I love you with a special love. Thank you for having responded to my call."

May 25, 2003

"Dear children! Also today I call you to prayer. Renew your personal prayer and in a special way pray to the Holy Spirit to help you pray with the heart. I intercede for all of you, little children, and call all of you to conversion. If you convert, all those around you will also be renewed and prayer will be a joy for them. Thank you for having responded to my call."

June 25, 2003

"Dear children! Also today, I call you with great joy to live my messages. I am with you and I thank you for putting into life what I am saying to you. I call you to renew my messages even more, with new enthusiasm and joy. May prayer be your daily practice. Thank you for having responded to my call."

July 25, 2003

"Dear children! Also today I call you to prayer. Little

children, pray until prayer becomes a joy for you. Only in this way each of you will discover peace in the heart and your soul will be content. You will feel the need to witness to others the love that you feel in your heart and life. I am with you and intercede before God for all of you. Thank you for having responded to my call."

August 25, 2003

"Dear children! Also today I call you to give thanks to God in your heart for all the graces which He gives you, also through the signs and colors that are in nature. God wants to draw you closer to Himself and moves you to give Him glory and thanks. Therefore, little children, I call you anew to pray, pray, pray and do not forget that I am with you. I intercede before God for each of you until your joy in Him is complete. Thank you for having responded to my call."

September 25, 2003

"Dear children! Also today I call you to come closer to my heart. Only in this way, will you comprehend the gift of my presence here among you. I desire, little children, to lead you to the heart of my Son Jesus, but you resist and do not desire to open your hearts to prayer. Again, little children, I call you not to be deaf but to comprehend my call, which is salvation for you. Thank you for having responded to my call."

October 25, 2003

"Dear children! I call you anew to consecrate yourselves to my heart and the heart of my Son Jesus. I desire, little children, to lead you all on the way of conversion and holiness. Only in this way, through you, we can lead all the more souls on the way of salvation. Do not delay, little children, but say with all your heart: 'I want to help Jesus and Mary that all the more brothers and sisters may come to know the way of holiness.' In this way, you will feel the contentment of being friends of Jesus. Thank you for having responded to my call."

November 25, 2003

"Dear children! I call you that this time be for you an even greater incentive to prayer in this time. Little children, pray that Jesus be born in all hearts, especially in those that do not know Him. Be love, joy, and peace in this peaceless world. I am with you and intercede before God for each of you. Thank you for having responded to my call."

December 25, 2003

"Dear children! Also today, I bless you all with my Son Jesus in my arms and I carry Him, who is the King of Peace, to you, that He grant you His peace. I am with you and I love you all, little children. Thank you for having responded to my call."

January 25, 2004

"Dear children! Also today I call you to pray. Pray, little children, in a special way for all those who have not come to know God's love. Pray that their hearts may open and draw closer to my Heart and the Heart of my Son Jesus, so that we can transform them into people of peace and love. Thank you for having responded to my call."

February 25, 2004

"Dear children! Also today, as never up to now, I call you to open your hearts to my messages. Little children, be those who draw souls to God and not those who distance them. I am with you and love you all with a special love.

This is a time of penance and conversion. From the bottom of my heart, I call you to be mine with all your heart and then you will see that your God is great, because He will give you an abundance of blessings and peace. Thank you for having responded to my call."

March 25, 2004

"Dear children! Also today, I call you to open yourselves to prayer. Especially now, in this time of grace, open your hearts, little children, and express your love to the Crucified. Only in this way, will you discover peace, and prayer will begin to flow from your heart into the world. Be an example, little children, and an incentive for the good. I am close to you and I love you all. Thank you for having responded to my call."

April 25, 2004

"Dear children! Also today, I call you to live my messages even more strongly in humility and love so that the Holy Spirit may fill you with His grace and strength. Only in this way will you be witnesses of peace and forgiveness. Thank you for having responded to my call."

May 25, 2004

"Dear children! Also today, I urge you to consecrate yourselves to my Heart and to the Heart of my Son Jesus. Only in this way will you be mine more each day and you will inspire each other all the more to holiness. In this way joy will rule your hearts and you will be carriers of peace and love. Thank you for having responded to my call."

June 25, 2004

"Dear children! Also today, joy is in my heart. I desire to

thank you for making my plan realizable. Each of you is important, therefore, little children, pray and rejoice with me for every heart that has converted and become an instrument of peace in the world. Prayer groups are powerful and through them I can see, little children, that the Holy Spirit is at work in the world. Thank you for having responded to my call."

July 25, 2004

"Dear children! I call you anew: be open to my messages. I desire, little children, to draw you all closer to my Son Jesus, therefore, you pray and fast. Especially I call you to pray for my intentions, so that I can present you to my Son Jesus, for Him to transform and open your hearts to love. When you will have love in the heart, peace will rule in you. Thank you for having responded to my call."

August 25, 2004

"Dear children! I call you all to conversion of heart. Decide, as in the first days of my coming here, for a complete change of your life. In this way, little children, you will have the strength to kneel and to open your hearts before God. God will hear your prayers and answer them. Before God, I intercede for each of you. Thank you for having responded to my call."

September 25, 2004

"Dear children! Also today, I call you to be love where there is hatred and food where there is hunger. Open your hearts, little children, and let your hands be extended and generous so that, through you, every creature may thank God the Creator. Pray, little children, and open your heart to God's love, but you cannot if you do not pray. Therefore, pray, pray, pray. Thank you for having responded to my call."

October 25, 2004

"Dear children! This is a time of grace for the family and, therefore, I call you to renew prayer. May Jesus be in the heart of your family. In prayer, learn to love everything that is holy. Imitate the lives of saints so that they may be an incentive and teachers on the way of holiness. May every family become a witness of love in this world without prayer and peace. Thank you for having responded to my call."

November 25, 2004

"Dear children! At this time, I call you all to pray for my intentions. Especially, little children, pray for those who have not yet come to know the love of God and do not seek God the Saviour. You, little children, be my extended hands and by your example draw them closer to my Heart and the Heart of my Son. God will reward you with graces and every blessing. Thank you for having responded to my call."

December 25, 2004

"Dear children! With great joy, also today I carry my Son Jesus in my arms to you; He blesses you and calls you to peace. Pray, little children, and be courageous witnesses of Good News in every situation. Only in this way will God bless you and give you everything you ask of Him in faith. I am with you as long as the Almighty permits me. I intercede for each of you with great love. Thank you for having responded to my call."

January 25, 2005

"Dear children! In this time of grace again I call you to prayer. Pray, little children, for unity of Christians, that all may be one heart. Unity will really be among you inasmuch

as you will pray and forgive. Do not forget: love will conquer only if you pray, and your heart will open. Thank you for having responded to my call."

February 25, 2005

"Dear children! Today I call you to be my extended hands in this world that puts God in the last place. You, little children, put God in the first place in your life. God will bless you and give you strength to bear witness to Him, the God of love and peace. I am with you and intercede for all of you. Little children, do not forget that I love you with a tender love. Thank you for having responded to my call."

March 25, 2005

"Dear children! Today I call you to love. Little children, love each other with God's love. At every moment, in joy and in sorrow, may love prevail and, in this way, love will begin to reign in your hearts. The risen Jesus will be with you and you will be His witnesses. I will rejoice with you and protect you with my mantle. Especially, little children, I will watch your daily conversion with love. Thank you for having responded to my call."

April 25, 2005

"Dear children! Also today, I call you to renew prayer in your families. By prayer and the reading of Sacred Scripture, may the Holy Spirit, who will renew you, enter into your families. In this way, you will become teachers of the faith in your family. By prayer and your love, the world will set out on a better way and love will begin to rule in the world. Thank you for having responded to my call."

May 25, 2005

"Dear children! Anew I call you to live my messages in humility. Especially witness them now when we are approaching the anniversary of my apparitions. Little children, be a sign to those who are far from God and His love. I am with you and bless you all with my Motherly blessing. Thank you for having responded to my call."

June 25, 2005

"Dear children! Today I thank you for every sacrifice that you have offered for my intentions. I call you, little children, to be my apostles of peace and love in your families and in the world. Pray that the Holy Spirit may enlighten and lead you on the way of holiness. I am with you and bless you all with my Motherly blessing. Thank you for having responded to my call."

July 25, 2005

"Dear children! Also today, I call you to fill your day with short and ardent prayers. When you pray, your heart is open and God loves you with a special love and gives you special graces. Therefore, make good use of this time of grace and devote it to God more than ever up to now. Do novenas of fasting and renunciation so that satan be far from you and grace be around you. I am near you and intercede before God for each of you. Thank you for having responded to my call."

August 25, 2005

"Dear children! Also today I call you to live my messages. God gave you a gift of this time as a time of grace. Therefore, little children, make good use of every moment and pray, pray, pray. I bless you all and intercede before the Most

High for each of you. Thank you for having responded to my call."

September 25, 2005

"Dear children! In love I call you: convert, even though you are far from my heart. Do not forget, I am your Mother and I feel pain for each one who is far from my heart; but I do not leave you alone. I believe you can leave the way of sin and decide for holiness. Thank you for having responded to my call."

October 25, 2005

"Little children, believe, pray and love, and God will be near you. He will give you the gift of all the graces you seek from Him. I am a gift to you, because, from day to day, God permits me to be with you and to love each of you with immeasurable love. Therefore, little children, in prayer and humility, open your hearts and be witnesses of my presence. Thank you for having responded to my call."

November 25, 2005

"Dear children! Also today I call you to pray, pray, pray until prayer becomes life for you. Little children, at this time, in a special way, I pray before God to give you the gift of faith. Only in faith will you discover the joy of the gift of life that God has given you. Your heart will be joyful thinking of eternity. I am with you and love you with a tender love. Thank you for having responded to my call."

December 25, 2005

"Dear children! Also today, in my arms I bring you little Jesus, the King of Peace, to bless you with His peace. Little children, in a special way today I call you to be my carriers of peace in this peaceless world. God will bless you. Little children, do not forget that I am your Mother. I bless you all with a special blessing, with little Jesus in my arms. Thank you for having responded to my call."

January 25, 2006

"Dear children! Also today I call you to be carriers of the Gospel in your families. Do not forget, little children, to read Sacred Scripture. Put it in a visible place and witness with your life that you believe and live the Word of God. I am close to you with my love and intercede before my Son for each of you. Thank you for having responded to my call."

February 25, 2006

"Dear children! In this Lenten time of grace, I call you to open your hearts to the gifts that God desires to give you. Do not be closed, but with prayer and renunciation say 'yes' to God and He will give to you in abundance. As in spring-time the earth opens to the seed and yields a hundredfold, so also your Heavenly Father will give to you in abundance. I am with you and love you, little children, with a tender love. Thank you for having responded to my call."

March 25, 2006

"Courage, little children! I decided to lead you on the way of holiness. Renounce sin and set out on the way of salva-tion, the way which my Son has chosen. Through each of your tribulations and sufferings God will find the way of joy for you. Therefore, little children, pray. We are close to you with our love. Thank you for having responded to my call."

April 25, 2006

"Dear children! Also today I call you to have more trust
in me and my Son. He has conquered by His death and
Resurrection and, through me, calls you to be a part of His
joy. You do not see God, little children, but if you pray you
will feel His nearness. I am with you and intercede before
God for each of you. Thank you for having responded to my
call."

May 25, 2006

"Dear children! Also today I call you to put into practice
and to live my messages that I am giving you. Decide for
holiness, little children, and think of Heaven. Only in this
way, will you have peace in your heart that no one will be
able to destroy. Peace is a gift, which God gives you in
prayer. Little children, seek and work with all your strength
for peace to win in your hearts and in the world. Thank you
for having responded to my call."

June 25, 2006

"Dear children! With great joy in my heart I thank you
for all the prayers that, in these days, you offered for my
intentions. Know, little children, that you will not regret it,
neither you nor your children. God will reward you with
great graces and you will earn eternal life. I am near you
and thank all those who, through these years, have accepted
my messages, have poured them into their life and decided
for holiness and peace. Thank you for having responded to
my call."

July 25, 2006

"Dear children! At this time, do not only think of rest for
your body but, little children, seek time also for the soul. In

silence may the Holy Spirit speak to you and permit Him
to convert and change you. I am with you and before God I
intercede for each of you. Thank you for having responded
to my call."

August 25, 2006

"Dear children! Also today I call you to pray, pray, pray.
Only in prayer will you be near to me and my Son and
you will see how short this life is. In your heart a desire for
Heaven will be born. Joy will begin to rule in your heart and
prayer will begin to flow like a river. In your words there will
only be thanksgiving to God for having created you and the
desire for holiness will become a reality for you. Thank you
for having responded to my call."

September 25, 2006

"Dear children! Also today I am with you and call all of you
to complete conversion. Decide for God, little children, and
you will find in God the peace your heart seeks. Imitate the
lives of saints and may they be an example for you; and I will
inspire you as long as the Almighty permits me to be with
you. Thank you for having responded to my call."

October 25, 2006

"Dear children! Today the Lord permitted me to tell you
again that you live in a time of grace. You are not conscious,
little children, that God is giving you a great opportunity
to convert and to live in peace and love. You are so blind
and attached to earthly things and think of earthly life. I,
little children, am not tired, although I see that your hearts
are heavy and tired for everything that is a grace and a gift.
Thank you for having responded to my call."

November 25, 2006

"Dear children! Also today I call you to pray, pray, pray.
Little children, when you pray you are close to God and He
gives you the desire for eternity. This is a time when you can
speak more about God and do more for God. Therefore,
little children, do not resist but permit Him to lead you, to
change you and to enter into your life. Do not forget that
you are travelers on the way toward eternity. Therefore,
little children, permit God to lead you as a shepherd leads
his flock. Thank you for having responded to my call."

December 25, 2006

"Dear children! Also today I bring you the newborn Jesus
in my arms. He who is the King of Heaven and earth, He
is your peace. Little children, no one can give you peace as
He who is the King of Peace. Therefore, adore Him in your
hearts, choose Him and you will have joy in Him. He will
bless you with His blessing of peace. Thank you for having
responded to my call."

January 25, 2007

"Dear children! Put Sacred Scripture in a visible place in
your family and read it. In this way, you will come to know
prayer with the heart and your thoughts will be on God. Do
not forget that you are passing like a flower in a field, which
is visible from afar but disappears in a moment. Little children, leave a sign of goodness and love wherever you pass
and God will bless you with an abundance of His blessing.
Thank you for having responded to my call."

February 25, 2007

"Dear children! Open your heart to God's mercy in this
Lenten time. The Heavenly Father desires to deliver each

of you from the slavery of sin. Therefore, little children, make good use of this time and through meeting with God in Confession, leave sin and decide for holiness. Do this out of love for Jesus, who redeemed you all with His blood, that you may be happy and in peace. Do not forget, little children: your freedom is your weakness, therefore, follow my messages with seriousness. Thank you for having responded to my call."

March 25, 2007

"Dear children! I desire to thank you from my heart for your Lenten renunciations. I desire to inspire you to continue to live fasting with an open heart. By fasting and renunciation, little children, you will be stronger in faith. In God you will find true peace through daily prayer. I am with you and I am not tired. I desire to take you all with me to Heaven, therefore, decide daily for holiness. Thank you for having responded to my call."

April 25, 2007

"Dear children! Also today I again call you to conversion. Open your hearts. This is a time of grace while I am with you, make good use of it. Say: 'This is the time for my soul.' I am with you and love you with immeasurable love. Thank you for having responded to my call."

May 25, 2007

"Dear children! Pray with me to the Holy Spirit for Him to lead you in the search of God's Will on the way of your holiness. And you, who are far from prayer, convert and, in the silence of your heart, seek salvation for your soul and nurture it with prayer. I bless you all individually with my Motherly blessing. Thank you for having responded to my call."

June 25, 2007

"**Dear children! Also today, with great joy in my heart, I call you to conversion. Little children, do not forget that you are all important in this great plan, which God leads through Medjugorje. God desires to convert the entire world and to call it to salvation and to the way towards Himself, who is the beginning and the end of every being. In a special way, little children, from the depth of my heart, I call you all to open yourselves to this great grace that God gives you through my presence here. I desire to thank each of you for the sacrifices and prayers. I am with you and I bless you all. Thank you for having responded to my call.**"

July 25, 2007

"**Dear children! Today, on the day of the Patron of your Parish, I call you to imitate the lives of the Saints. May they be, for you, an example and encouragement to a life of holiness. May prayer for you be like the air you breathe in and not a burden. Little children, God will reveal His love to you and you will experience the joy that you are my beloved. God will bless you and give you an abundance of grace. Thank you for having responded to my call.**"

August 25, 2007

"**Dear children! Also today I call you to conversion. May your life, little children, be a reflection of God's goodness and not of hatred and unfaithfulness. Pray, little children, that prayer may become life for you. In this way, in your life you will discover the peace and joy which God gives to those who have an open heart to His love. And you who are far from God's mercy, convert so that God may not become deaf to your prayers and that it may not be too late for you. Therefore, in this time of grace, convert and put God in the first place in your life. Thank you for having responded to my call.**"

September 25, 2007

"**Dear children! Also today I call all of you for your hearts to blaze with more ardent love for the Crucified, and do not forget that, out of love for you, He gave His life so that you may be saved. Little children, meditate and pray that your heart may be open to God's love. Thank you for having responded to my call.**"

October 25, 2007

"**Dear children! God sent me among you out of love that I may lead you towards the way of salvation. Many of you opened your hearts and accepted my messages, but many have become lost on this way and have never come to know the God of love with the fullness of heart. Therefore, I call you to be love and light where there is darkness and sin. I am with you and bless you all. Thank you for having responded to my call.**"

November 25, 2007

"**Dear children! Today, when you celebrate Christ, the King of all that is created, I desire for Him to be the King of your lives. Only through giving, little children, can you comprehend the gift of Jesus' sacrifice on the Cross for each of you. Little children, give time to God that He may transform you and fill you with His grace, so that you may be a grace for others. For you, little children, I am a gift of grace and love, which comes from God for this peaceless world. Thank you for having responded to my call.**"

December 25, 2007

"**Dear children! With great joy I bring you the King of Peace for Him to bless you with His blessing. Adore Him and give time to the Creator for whom your heart yearns. Do not** forget that you are passers-by on this earth and that things can give you small joys, while through my Son, eternal life is given to you. That is why I am with you, to lead you towards what your heart yearns for. Thank you for having responded to my call."

January 25, 2008

"Dear children! With the time of Lent, you are approaching a time of grace. Your heart is like ploughed soil and it is ready to receive the fruit which will grow into what is good. You, little children, are free to choose good or evil. Therefore, I call you to pray and fast. Plant joy and the fruit of joy will grow in your hearts for your good, and others will see it and receive it through your life. Renounce sin and choose eternal life. I am with you and intercede for you before my Son. Thank you for having responded to my call."

February 25, 2008

"Dear children! In this time of grace, I call you anew to prayer and renunciation. May your day be interwoven with little ardent prayers for all those who have not come to know God's love. Thank you for having responded to my call."

March 25, 2008

"Dear children! I call you to work on your personal conversion. You are still far from meeting with God in your heart. Therefore, spend all the more time in prayer and Adoration of Jesus in the Most Blessed Sacrament of the Altar, for Him to change you and to put into your hearts a living faith and a desire for eternal life. Everything is passing, little children, only God is not passing. I am with you and I encourage you with love. Thank you for having responded to my call."

April 25, 2008

"**Dear children! Also today, I call all of you to grow in God's love as a flower which feels the warm rays of spring. In this way, also you, little children, grow in God's love and carry it to all those who are far from God. Seek God's Will and do good to those whom God has put on your way, and be light and joy. Thank you for having responded to my call.**"

May 25, 2008

"**Dear children! In this time of grace, when God has permitted me to be with you, little children, I call you anew to conversion. Work on the salvation of the world in a special way while I am with you. God is merciful and gives special graces, therefore, seek them through prayer. I am with you and do not leave you alone. Thank you for having responded to my call.**"

June 25, 2008

"**Dear children! Also today, with great joy in my heart, I call you to follow me and to listen to my messages. Be joyful carriers of peace and love in this peaceless world. I am with you and I bless you all with my Son Jesus, the King of Peace. Thank you for having responded to my call.**"

July 25, 2008

"**Dear children! At this time when you are thinking of physical rest, I call you to conversion. Pray and work so that your heart yearns for God the Creator who is the true rest of your soul and your body. May He reveal His face to you and may He give you His peace. I am with you and intercede before God for each of you. Thank you for having responded to my call.**"

August 25, 2008

"Dear children! Also today, I call you to personal conversion. You be those who will convert and, with your life, will witness, love, forgive and bring the joy of the Risen One into this world, where my Son died and where people do not feel a need to seek Him and to discover Him in their lives. You adore Him, and may your hope be hope to those hearts who do not have Jesus. Thank you for having responded to my call."

September 25, 2008

"Dear children! May your life, anew, be a decision for peace. Be joyful carriers of peace and do not forget that you live in a time of grace, in which God gives you great graces through my presence. Do not close yourselves, little children, but make good use of this time and seek the gift of peace and love for your life so that you may become witnesses to others. I bless you with my Motherly blessing. Thank you for having responded to my call."

October 25, 2008

"Dear children! In a special way I call you all to pray for my intentions so that, through your prayers, you may stop satan's plan over this world, which is further from God every day, and which puts itself in the place of God and is destroying everything that is beautiful and good in the souls of each of you. Therefore, little children, arm yourselves with prayer and fasting so that you may be conscious of how much God loves you, and carry out God's Will. Thank you for having responded to my call."

November 25, 2008

"Dear children! Also today I call you, in this time of grace,

to pray for little Jesus to be born in your heart. May He, who is peace itself, give peace to the entire world through you. Therefore, little children, pray without ceasing for this turbulent world without peace, so that you may become witnesses of peace for all. May hope begin to flow through your hearts as a river of grace. Thank you for having responded to my call."

December 25, 2008

"Dear children! You are running, working, gathering - but without blessing. You are not praying! Today I call you to stop in front of the manger and to meditate on Jesus, Whom I give to you today also, to bless you and to help you to comprehend that, without Him, you have no future. Therefore, little children, surrender your lives into the hands of Jesus, for Him to lead you and protect you from every evil. Thank you for having responded to my call."

January 25, 2009

"Dear children! Also today I call you to prayer. May prayer be for you like the seed that you will put in my heart, which I will give over to my Son Jesus for you, for the salvation of your souls. I desire, little children, for each of you to fall in love with eternal life which is your future, and for all worldly things to be a help for you to draw you closer to God the Creator. I am with you for this long because you are on the wrong path. Only with my help, little children, you will open your eyes. There are many of those who, by living my messages, comprehend that they are on the way of holiness towards eternity. Thank you for having responded to my call."

February 25, 2009

"Dear children! In this time of renunciation, prayer and

penance, I call you anew: go and confess your sins so that grace may open your hearts, and permit it to change you. Convert little children, open yourselves to God and to His plan for each of you. Thank you for having responded to my call."

March 25, 2009

"Dear children! In this time of spring, when everything is awakening from the winter sleep, you also awaken your souls with prayer so that they may be ready to receive the light of the risen Jesus. Little children, may He draw you closer to His Heart so that you may become open to eternal life. I pray for you and intercede before the Most High for your sincere conversion. Thank you for having responded to my call."

April 25, 2009

"Dear children! Today I call you all to pray for peace and to witness it in your families so that peace may become the highest treasure on this peaceless earth. I am your Queen of Peace and your Mother. I desire to lead you on the way of peace, which comes only from God. Therefore, pray, pray, pray. Thank you for having responded to my call."

CHAPTER 4

THE MESSAGES
OF OUR LADY
TO THE PRAYER GROUP

(January 25, 1988 to September 12, 2008)

Marija, Ivan, and others formed a prayer group by the request of Our Lady. Our Lady asked them to assemble on Monday and Friday nights on Apparition Mountain or Cross Mountain. When Marija married and was no longer living in Medjugorje, she no longer was able to attend the prayer group. This prayer group has continued, again through Our Lady's leadership, through Ivan. They usually meet at the Blue Cross at the base of Apparition Mountain or on top of Apparition Mountain at around 9:00 p.m. They sing and pray and Our Lady usually appears to Ivan between 10:00 - 10:30 p.m. During these meetings with Our Lady in Medjugorje, tens of thousands have been drawn to attend. Attending just one prayer group meeting teaches those from around the world who attend to go back home and start the same in their families and with others.

Our Lady always says, **"Praised be Jesus,"** when She comes and, after giving Her message, prays The Lord's Prayer and one Glory Be with the group. She leaves in the sign of the light of the Cross saying, **"Go in the peace of God."**

January 25, 1988

"Thank you for this evening, you have helped me very much. Continue to pray for my intentions."

February 1, 1988

"Prepare yourself for the time of Lent by renouncing something. During Lent I will need your help for the accomplishment and fulfillment of all my plans."

February 8, 1988

"I'm asking you, yourself, to decide for the way of holiness. Dear children, I want to help you."

She went back to the sky joyfully as always.

February 15, 1988

"Be the reflection of Jesus. This way, you will be His witnesses in your lives; but you cannot be His reflection without prayer."

February 22, 1988

"Thank you for the things you have renounced during Lent. Most of all, renounce sin. Be light, to shine for others. Encourage others to prayer, fasting, and penance. Give love to others."

February 29, 1988

"Dear children, give all problems and difficulties to Jesus and pray. Pray, pray, pray! Every evening during this month, pray in front of the Crucifix in thanksgiving until the death of Jesus."

March 7, 1988

"I am your Mother and I want to warn you that satan wants to destroy everything we have started, so pray a lot."

March 14, 1988

"Dear children, in this period of Lent satan is trying by every means to destroy in you what we have started. I warn you as a Mother, let prayer be your weapon against him."

March 21, 1988

"Dear children, today again your Mother wants to warn you that satan, by every means possible, wants to ruin everything in you; but your prayers prevent him from succeeding. When you fill up all the empty spaces with prayer, you prevent satan from entering your soul. Pray, dear children, and your Mother will pray with you to defeat satan. May this time be the time in which all of us give and distribute peace to others. Therefore, please spread peace in your homes, in your families, in the streets, and everywhere."

March 28, 1988

"Pray as much as you can before Easter. Everyday pray two hours before the Crucifix."

April 4, 1988

"Give love and joy to others and pray for peace."

April 11, 1988

"Dear children, I am your Mother and I am asking you to convert. Pray now for people who curse against the Name of God."

April 18, 1988

No apparition.

May 9, 1988

"May this month be for you the month of the Rosary and reading your Bible. satan wants to disturb your plans."

May 21, 1988

Our Lady came joyfully. She prayed The Lord's Prayer and one Glory Be with the visionary as She always does.

June 6, 1988

"Dear children, it's going to be seven years soon that I have been coming to you. I ask you to renew in yourselves the messages I have given to you. These are messages of prayer, peace, fasting, and penance. Make some penance yourselves. All of the other messages come from these four basic ones, but also live the other ones. Thank you for responding to my call. I am your Mother. Open your heart to the grace."

June 13, 1988

Our Lady repeated Monday's message (June 6, 1988).

June 23, 1988

"Dear children, I am happy and so is my Son. Go to Confession to have a pure heart for the anniversary. Come to pray on the hill tomorrow between ten and midnight, but I will not appear."

June 27, 1988

"Dear children, your Mother loves you all. I'm happy to see you here, dear children. I give you love; give this love to others. Be peace workers. Help the others to change

their lives. I give you might, dear children; with this might, you can bear everything. May this might make you strong in everything. You need it; that is why I give you might."

July 4, 1988

"Dear children, I am your Mother and I warn you this time is a time of temptation. satan is trying to find emptiness in you, so he can enter and destroy you. DO NOT SURRENDER! I pray with you. Do not pray just with your lips, but pray with the heart. In this way prayer will obtain victory!"

August 1, 1988

"I ask you to pray a lot these days before Friday. I would like you to live this Friday in joy. I also ask you tonight, when you go to your houses, to pray the Glorious Mysteries in front of the Crucifix."

August 4, 1988

"My dear children, tonight my Son has sent me among you. I am happy with you. I am happy to see you in such a large number. I would like your joy to remain this whole day. Live this joy in prayer, live in joy. I give you love so you can live with love. Extend love around you. Your Mother loves you. I am happy tonight. I want your cooperation. I want to work with you. Your cooperation is necessary to me. I cannot do anything without you."

August 8, 1988

"Dear children, your Mother asks you to pray for all the young people in the world. Renew yourselves in prayer before the feast day."

August 12, 1988

"Dear children, your Mother asks you to pray as much as you can during these two days. Prepare yourselves in prayer for the feast to come. Dear children, I would like to tell you to bring peace to others during these days. Encourage others to change. You cannot, dear children, give peace if you, yourselves, are not at inner peace. Tonight I give you peace. Give peace to others! Dear children, be a light that shines. I ask you pray the Glorious Mysteries when you go back to your homes tonight. Pray them in front of the Crucifix."

August 15, 1988 (SPECIAL BLESSING)

(FEAST OF THE ASSUMPTION and the end of the Marian Year)

"Dear children, from today on I would like you to start a New Year, the Year of the Young People. During this year pray for the young people; talk with them. Young people find themselves now in a very difficult situation. Help each other. I think about you in a special way, dear children. Young people have a role to play in the Church now. Pray, dear children."

August 19, 1988

"Dear children, I would like this time to be the time of decision. Make a decision, dear children, follow me, follow me! I cannot do anything, and I want to do a lot, but I cannot do it without you. Your decisions are weak! Pray, dear children, during this time. Only through prayer can you receive this strength, this vigor. I will help you, dear children."

August 22, 1988

"My dear children, with your prayers you have helped me to fulfill the plan. Praised be Jesus, my dear children. Dear children, I would like to tell you tonight, during these days especially pray for the young. I would like to recommend to 'my' priests to create and organize groups where young people are taught and given good advice for their lives. You, dear children, who are present tonight, you, must be the messengers of the good word of peace to others, to young people especially. Your Mother wants to pray for you all tonight."

August 29, 1988

"Dear children, thank God, the Creator, even for little things. I would like you to thank God for your family, for the place where you work, and for the people God puts in your way."

September 5, 1988

"My dear children, tonight your Mother warns you that in this time satan desires you and is looking for you! A little spiritual emptiness in you is enough for satan to work in you. For this reason your Mother invites you to begin to pray. May your weapon be prayer. With prayer with the heart you will overcome satan. Your Mother invites you to pray for the young people in the whole world."

September 9, 1988

"Dear children, tonight also your Mother is warning that satan is at work. I would like you to pay special attention to the fact that satan is at work in a special way with the young. Dear children, during this period I would like you to pray in your families with your children. I would like you to

talk with your children. I would like you to exchange your experiences and help them to solve all their problems. I will pray, dear children, for the young, for all of you. Pray, dear children. Prayer is medicine that heals."

September 12, 1988

The message for tonight's encounter is:

"Our Lady calls us all to pray during this time for the hungry and poor people in the whole world. She thanks us in a special way tonight because we helped Her to fulfill the plan."

October 17, 1988

"Dear children, tonight your Mother is happy, joyful together with you. I would like to extend happiness to you. I would like to give you love, so you can bring this love and spread it to others. I would like to give you peace, so you can give this peace to others, so you can give this peace especially to families where hatred exists. I would like you, dear children, to renew the family prayer, all of you. I would like you to encourage others to renew this prayer. Your Mother will help you."

October 24, 1988

"Dear children, your Mother wants to call you to pray for the young of the whole world, for the parents of the whole world so they know how to educate their children and how to lead them in life with good advice. Pray, dear children; the situation of the young is difficult. Help them! Help parents who don't know, who give bad advice!"

October 31, 1988

"Dear children, tonight your Mother wants to encourage

you to begin to pray with the heart. This prayer is necessary to today's man for today's world. Do not pray just with
your lips. Do not pray if you don't know what you pray.
During this period too, dear children, I need your prayers,
because I have great plans. I want to collaborate with you. I
have repeated that many times in my messages. I need you.
Because of that, pray, pray with the heart!"

November 7, 1988

"Dear children, this is a time for grace. That is why I
would like you to pray as much as you can during this time.
Especially, I would like you to renew the family prayer!"

November 11, 1988 (SPECIAL BLESSING)

Our Lady appeared with five angels and gave a Special Blessing
during the 30-minute apparition to Vicka.

"Dear children, you know this time is a time of special
graces; that is why I ask you to renew in you the messages
that I give. Live those messages with the heart."

November 14, 1988

To Vicka:

"Dear children, I bless you with my Motherly blessing, and I
ask you to be the carriers of my peace and to pray for peace
in the world."

December 24, 1988

"My dear children, these are days of joy. Give me all your
problems and live in joy."

January 2, 1989

"My dear children, for this year I want to tell you, pray! Your Mother loves you. I want to collaborate with you for I need your collaboration. I want you to become, dear children, my announcers and my sons who will bring peace, love, conversion....I want you to be a sign for others. In this new year I want to give you peace; I want to give you love and harmony. Abandon all your problems and all your difficulties to me. Live my messages. Pray, pray!"

January 9, 1989

"Dear children, pray because satan is very active in this time. He wants to destroy everything you have received from me. During these days I invite you to renew the prayer in your families and to pray all the mysteries of the Rosary every evening."

February 6, 1989 (SPECIAL BLESSING)

Ivan says: *"Our Lady wants this from us during Lent."*

1.   Review and live Her messages.
2.   Read the Bible more.
3.   Pray more and offer all for the intentions of Our Lady.
4.   Make more sacrifices.

"Our Lady will be with us and will accompany us. She gave a 'SPECIAL BLESSING.'"

February 13, 1989

"Dear children, remember the four things you have to do during Lent. Tonight when you go home, I ask you to be thankful in front of the Crucifix for all that you feel you should be grateful for; thank Jesus for what you want. My Son will hear you."

February 17, 1989

"Dear children, tonight I don't ask you to do anything special. I only wish you to begin to live my messages. Dear children, I seek your action, not your words! You are all happy when I give you a beautiful message, but live the message I give! May each message be for you a new growth. Take this message into your life, in this way you will grow in life. Your Mother cannot give you other messages if you don't live the ones I already gave you. Begin tonight to live the messages."

February 24, 1989

"Tonight when you go home, pray The Lord's Prayer, the Hail Mary, and the Glory Be seven times; and then pray The Lord's Prayer, the Hail Mary, and the Glory Be five times."

February 27, 1989

"Dear children, during this time multiply your prayers and go deeper into the messages that I have given. Tonight when you go home, pray the Joyful Mysteries in front of the Crucifix."

March 3, 1989

"Dear children, I thank you because by your coming here you have helped to fulfill the plan of God. During this time pray and renew yourselves. Tonight when you come home, pray the Joyful Mysteries in front of the Crucifix."

March 17, 1989

"I ask you again to multiply your prayers to prepare yourself for Easter. Also, read the Bible, especially those passages that tell about the Passion of Jesus. Prepare yourself to look at Jesus 'eye to eye.' Tonight when you come home, pray in front of the Crucifix in thanksgiving for all the graces you receive."

March 20, 1989

"Tonight I ask you to begin from today to pray all the more. Contemplate the wounds of Jesus. Pray as much as you can in front of the Crucifix. May the cross be (just) for you in the day (of the cross.)"

March 24, 1989 (GOOD FRIDAY)

"Dear children, tonight your Mother is happy to see you in such large numbers. I wish, dear children, that you start from today to live a different life. Your Mother gives you love; give this love to others so we can be ready to live Easter. When you go back in your homes finish this day in prayer."

March 27, 1989 (EASTER MONDAY)

"Dear children, your Mother calls you to completely surrender to God. Dear children, this is a time of grace. Pray as much as you can and renew yourself through prayer. Construct yourself spiritually. This construction lasts until the end of your life. Continue to pray as much as you can and with your prayers you will help me."

May 5, 1989

"Dear children, tonight your Mother invites you to pray as much as you can during this time. This is a time of grace. Abandon yourselves to the Spirit for Him to renew you. May prayer renew your bodies, your souls, your hearts. Don't let your bodies be weak. You know that the Spirit is always willing."

May 12, 1989

"Now is a time of special graces, but satan is very active."

June 6, 1989

"Dear children, the Mother is happy to be with all of you. Dear children, you have helped me to realize the plans of God. I want to speak to you about love and give you love. In these days, prepare yourselves for the anniversary of the apparitions with love, with my messages, and with joy and the Mother will help you, dear children, and the Mother will stay with you. There is nothing more important for you but to put what I have said in first place."

June 16, 1989

"Dear children, I want more penance from you."

June 23, 1989

"Dear children, I am happy to see you in such a large number. I would like to pray for you in a special way tonight. Dear children, give me the day that comes (June 24, 1989) in prayer."

June 26, 1989

"Dear children, your Mother told you yesterday to renew the messages from now on. Your Mother asks, especially from you of the group of prayer, to live from now on the messages in prayer. If you want your Mother to give other and new messages, you first have to live those messages I have already given."

July 3, 1989

"**Dear children, your Mother asks you tonight, you, who are present** (people were present from all over the world), **when you get back into your home, renew prayer in your family. Take time for prayer, dear children. I, as your Mother, especially want to tell you that the family has to pray together. The Holy Spirit wants to be present in the families. Allow the Holy Spirit to come. The Holy Spirit comes through prayer. That is why, pray and allow the Holy Spirit to renew you, to renew today's family. Your Mother will help you.**"

July 10, 1989 or July 14, 1989

"**Dear children, you know we are living the Year of the Young People. This year ends on August 15. Your Mother wishes to dedicate one more year to the youth, but not only to the youth. May this year also be the year of the family. Dear children, in these days before the fifteenth of August, prepare yourselves, you and your family, for the new year to come so it may be the Year of the Family.**"

July 17, 1989

"**Dear children, I would like to call you to start again to live the messages. More than eight years ago your Mother told four messages: Peace, Conversion, Sacrifice, and Faith. Dear children, I would like you to live the messages through prayer. I know how much you give me promises through words, but, dear children, I want you to put that into practice. I will pray, dear children, and I will help you. Conversion is a process which goes on through your entire life.**"

July 21, 1989

"Pray for my intentions."

July 24, 1989

"Dear children, tonight your Mother is happy to see you in such large numbers. Your Mother wants to give you love tonight so you can give and share this love with others when you will come back to your homes. Live love. I want to give you peace, so you can carry it to others. You cannot give peace to others if you don't have this peace within yourselves. I need you, dear children, to cooperate with me, because there are today many plans that I cannot fulfill without you. I need your cooperation. Pray, pray, pray."

July 31, 1989

"Dear children, tonight especially I would like to invite all the parents in the world to find time for their children and family. May they offer love to their children. May this love that they offer be parental and Motherly love. Once again, dear children, I call you to family prayer. During one of the previous encounters your Mother asked you to renew the family prayer. I ask that again tonight. During this period, let us pray together for all the young people in the world."

August 7, 1989

"Tonight your Mother wants to call you to prayer. This is a time of grace. Pray, dear children, and your Mother will pray together with you. Abandon to your Mother all your problems and difficulties."

August 11, 1989

"I call you to prayer, like I have done also in the previous

encounter. I ask that during the three days to come each one of you make a sacrifice, give up something that is dear to you in life. Give up something especially during those three days."

August 14, 1989 - SPECIAL BLESSING

"My dear children, tonight your Mother is happy, happy, happy to be with you and to see you in such large numbers. I am happy for what we have done in this Year of the Youth. We have stepped a step forward. I would like to see in the future parents in the families work and pray as much as they can with their children, so they can, from day to day, strengthen their spirit. Your Mother is here to help each one of you; open yourselves to your Mother; She is waiting for you. May this moment you will live at midnight be a moment of thanksgiving for everything you received during this year."

August 18, 1989

"Dear children, tonight your Mother asks you in this period of time to pray for peace in the world."

August 21, 1989

"Tonight your Mother wants to invite you to start again to live the messages. Children, your Mother cannot give you new messages if you do not live the messages I have already given. Decide with love and joy to begin to live the messages, for your Mother to continue to guide you, for you to continue your growth in love with your Mother living the messages."

December 15, 1989

"Prepare yourselves spiritually and physically for the

Christmas Novena. In your prayers say one prayer especially for my intentions. Renounce [give up] something that you like the most."

December 18, 1989

"The prayers and sacrifices that you decide to offer in these days when I asked you were not done with love. I ask you to offer them with love as during the first days of the apparitions. What you have decided to do and to offer for my intentions during the novena was not enough. You have to choose to give more because you are able."

Our Lady prayed [in Hebrew] in Her Mother tongue.

December 21, 1989

From Marija to Father Luciano:

"Our Lady asked me to pray and offer sacrifices for priests."

December 22, 1989

Marija:

"Our Lady says this Christmas should be the most beautiful Christmas of your life."

December 22, 1989

"Dear children, tonight your Mother wants to call you to prayer, call you to prayer during those two days. Through prayer open your hearts and let us wait all together for this day which is for us the day of joy. Dear children, I wish you to decide to do something concrete during these two days."

December 25, 1989

"Dear children, here is my Son in my arms! I would like to ask you to be a light for all in the year to come. I would like to call you again to live the messages, those are messages of peace, conversion, prayer, penance, and faith. Dear children, your Mother does not ask words from you, I ask for deeds. Your Mother will help you and She will give you the strength to continue. And tonight I would like to tell you: Rejoice!"

January 1, 1990

"Dear children, tonight your Mother would like to call you, like I have done before, to renew prayer in the families. Dear children, the family needs to pray today. I wish, dear children, that you would renew [start again to live] **my messages through this prayer."**

February 2, 1990

"Pray for peace, everybody present - not just the group - pray for peace."

February 5, 1990

"Pray for peace, especially you from the group, pray for peace."

February 9, 1990

"Our Lady asks that prayer meetings would last two hours, an hour of singing, an hour of prayer."

Only this part of the message was told by Ivan, the rest is secret, just for the group.

February 12, 1990

"Dear children, your Mother is happy when She sees you in such large numbers. Dear children, you have come to me with a firm decision. Do not fear anything, I protect you and guard you. I wish, dear children, tonight again to call you to prayer because I need your help for the fulfillment of my plans. I need your cooperation [participation], dear children. Thank you for having responded to my call."

February 19, 1990

"Dear children, your Mother tonight wants to warn you that satan is active in a special way these days. Don't allow emptiness inside of you, fill this emptiness with prayer. Dear children, these days prayer is the best medicine to defend yourselves against evil. In a special way, dear children, make a decision through prayer for Lent. Tonight I am expecting from you to pray the Glorious Mysteries when you return home."

March 2, 1990

"Dear children, tonight your Mother asks and pleads: Abandon to me all your problems, all your hardships. I want to prepare you for the day that comes free from all your problems. Give me all your problems."

March 5, 1990

"Do something concrete for Easter."

March 23, 1990

"Dear children, tonight again your Mother wants to call you to prayer. Dear children, I need your prayer to fulfill the plans I have now with you and in the world also. Thank you, dear children, for listening to me. Dear children, thank you for having responded to my call."

April 13, 1990 - GOOD FRIDAY

"Dear children, I am happy to see you tonight. You know, dear children, that when my Son was dying I was alone with Him with just some other women, and so I am happy to see you here tonight in such large numbers. Tonight also when you go back home, pray a Rosary in front of the Crucifix and be thankful [to God]."

May 7, 1990

"Dear children, your Mother is so happy tonight to see you all. I want tonight to call you again to pray the Rosary, and to pray this month especially, because I am in need of your prayers."

May 11, 1990

"Dear children, tonight your Mother is happy to see you. Tonight especially, I want to ask you to give me your problems and difficulties so that you are able to pray with more freedom and more joy so that your prayer becomes a prayer with the heart. That is why I wish to ask you tonight to release yourselves from your difficulties through prayer; and I will pray for you. Dear children, I need your prayers."

May 21, 1990

"Dear children, tonight your Mother invites you to pray for peace. I need your prayers for peace these days, dear children. Pray, pray, pray."

May 25, 1990

"Dear children, tonight again your Mother wants to call you to prayer. Especially live, accept, and accomplish in prayer the message I gave tonight [May 25 Monthly Message]. **I need your prayers, dear children. This is why: pray, pray, pray!"**

June 1, 1990

"Dear children, this is a time of grace. Open yourselves to the Holy Spirit, for the Holy Spirit to make you strong. Your Mother, dear children, wants especially to call you in this time to prayer and to sacrifice."

June 8, 1990

"Dear children, your Mother is happy tonight to see you in such large numbers. Tonight also your Mother calls you to prayer. Dear children, prayer is necessary for me to fulfill many plans that I wish to accomplish. Especially tonight, I invite you to pray the Glorious Mysteries of the Rosary in front of the Crucifix when you go back to your homes. Pray these mysteries for my intentions."

June 22, 1990

"Dear children, I am happy to see you in such large numbers. Tonight again your Mother asks you to prepare yourselves through prayers during these two days for the day that comes."

June 25, 1990

"Dear children, your Mother invites you to joy. Your Mother asks you to begin to live tonight's message [the monthly message given earlier to Marija]. **Your Mother,**

again tonight, asks you to give me all your problems and all your hardships. Thank you, dear children, because we are going to continue to live in prayer everything that I say."

July 13, 1990

"Dear children, your Mother asks you, especially in this period, to pray all the more. satan wants, in this time, to be active through your weakness. This is why, dear children, your Mother invites you: pray, pray, pray. Do not allow satan to enter. Close all the entrances. Prayer is the best weapon."

July 23, 1990

"Dear children, tonight your Mother wants especially to invite you to pray in these days for peace."

July 30, 1990

"Dear children, tonight again your Mother would like to invite you in a special way to prayer. Especially you, the youngest, who will be present in large numbers during these days. I invite you to prayer. Pray, pray, pray and renew your hearts to be able to accept later everything I will tell you, all my messages. Thank you, dear children, because you will make me happy by your prayers."

August 3, 1990

"Dear children, tonight again your Mother wants to encourage you to pray all the more during this time. Join together in prayer with the young people. Especially, dear children, your Mother wants you to renew prayer in today's family."

August 10, 1990

"Dear children, your Mother tonight wants to call you in a special way to pray for peace."

August 13, 1990

"Dear children, tonight again your Mother asks in a special way for you to pray for peace, especially in this time. Pray, dear children, to help your Mother to fulfill all that She plans."

August 17, 1990

"Dear children, tonight I ask you to pray for peace in a very special way."

August 20, 1990

"I ask you to pray for peace."

The messages of August 20 and 24 were given to Ivan during his prayer group meeting. Then Our Lady prayed for peace in a different but very special way in front of Ivan.

August 24, 1990

"Pray for peace in a special way."

October 1, 1990

"Dear children, tonight your Mother asks you to pray especially for peace in this time.

October 5, 1990

"Pray for peace in this time."

For the first time during the apparitions, Ivan was heard praying The Lord's Prayer and the Glory Be three times with Our Lady. The Gospa told Ivan this prayer was for the intention of peace.

October 10, 1990

"I come here as the Queen of Peace and Reconciliation. I need your prayers and sacrifices especially in this time. Pray for peace in the world."

October 15, 1990

"Dear children, tonight I invite you to pray for peace. Dear children, I want to give you new messages. I am your Mother. I always want to teach you something new, but for this you must first live the messages that I have already given you so I can give you new messages."

October 19, 1990

"Pray for peace."

November 16, 1990

To Marija:

"Dear children, I thank you for you have come up here tonight to pray. Your Mother asks you to pray for peace in the world in this time. For that, I ask you to come up often and pray on the Apparition Hill, (Podbrdo), and Krizevac, in order to pray for peace. I also ask you to gather your family to pray together for peace and for the salvation of the world."

This was a very intense apparition. Afterwards, Marija said, *"I felt as if Our Lady wanted to take my soul."*

November 26, 1990

This message was given to Marija during the prayer group meeting on the mountain. Our Lady said She was very happy that the people had come to pray with Her.

"Dear children, I desire you to witness my presence through love."

December 21, 1990

"Dear children, tonight your Mother invites you to take this time to prepare your hearts in prayer for the day that comes, for Christmas."

December 24, 1990

Our Lady appeared with three angels.

"Dear children, tonight your Mother invites you to give Her all your problems. My dear children, REJOICE!"

December 31, 1990

"Dear children, tonight your Mother invites you to go together with me to the church in joy and in prayer. In this very specific joy, pray in church for the intention of peace."

There was a New Year's Eve Mass at 11:30 p.m.

January 7, 1991

At 10:00 p.m. Our Lady came with three angels and prayed for a very long time with Ivan for peace.

"Dear children, tonight your Mother calls you in a special way to pray for peace."

January 11, 1991

Our Lady appeared to Ivan during his prayer group meeting. Although She did not give a message, She prayed with Ivan for peace. The people who were on the mountain for the prayer meeting felt this action was a strong message from Our Lady, showing that everyone should be praying for peace as She is.

January 14, 1991

The apparition was at 9:30 p.m. (Podbrdo). Ivan said that Our Lady prayed for peace with him and thanked the people for coming up the mountain to pray. There was no message. Ivan asked that prayer for peace continue through the night and there was Adoration the whole night in the Chapel in union with 1,000 prayer groups in America. Ivan was present.

March 22, 1991

"Tonight your Mother invites you to pray more. Pray specially in your families, and by prayer prepare for the day that comes, for Easter."

March 29, 1991 (GOOD FRIDAY)

"Dear children, I want to call (invite) **you, under this cross, to take your cross as the will of God. As my Son took His cross, so you carry everything, and my Son will be glorified through your crosses. Thank you, dear children, for answering my call and carrying your cross."**

April 5, 1991

"Dear children, tonight your Mother wants to invite you, especially in this time, to pray together with me for peace."

Then Ivan prayed the Lord's Prayer and Glory Be three times with Our Lady for the intention of peace.

April 8, 1991

"I ask you to pray with me for peace."

May 3, 1991

"Dear children, today your Mother wants you to pray in a special way for peace these days. Pray, Pray, Pray. Your prayers are necessary for me."

May 10, 1991

"I invite you to pray for peace!"

May 27, 1991

"I invite you to accept and live the message I gave you on the twenty-fifth."

June 17, 1991

"I invite you to pray for peace and for conversion."

July 5, 1991

"Dear children, your Mother wants you to pray for peace in a special way with me in this time."

August 5, 1991

"Dear children, I am very happy tonight to see you in such large numbers. I want you to be happy, too; and pray, pray, pray prayers of peace in joy. I need your prayers too."

August 9, 1991

"Dear children, I invited you here in a very special way for

prayer. Dear children, pray, pray, pray in this period of time and make sacrifices."

April 16, 1992

Ivan's words regarding the Holy Thursday message which was given in a basement shelter because of the bombing:

"In that message, Our Lady invited us to persevere in prayer so that in a fervent prayer we can be able to defeat evil. In that message, She repeated something She already said in the beginning of the apparitions - that war can be stopped by fasting and praying. Therefore, it is for us a strong reason to pray, to be closer to God, so that with Him and with Mary together, we may defeat all that is imposed on us now."

June 24, 1992

"Praise be to Jesus! I am bringing you peace; bring peace to others. You are the ones who will bring peace to the world."

June 29, 1992

"Dear children, tonight in a special way I want to invite you to surrender completely to me. Give me all your problems and difficulties. I especially want from you to renew my messages in your lives. Pray, dear children, I need your prayers during this time. I thank you, dear children, that you have responded to my call."

July 10, 1992

"I ask you to pray in a special way for Pope John Paul II and for priests."

Ivan said that there will not be another open mountain apparition until the end of July.

August 3, 1992

"Dear children, I call you to persevere in prayer for peace."

August 14, 1992

"Dear children, in this time I call you to pray the Rosary in your family. Pray more and pray the Rosary. Offer this Rosary for peace."

September 4, 1992

"Dear children, today again, in a special way, I wish to invite you to pray for peace. I am in need of your prayers. Thank you, dear children, for having responded to my invitation."

September 12, 1992

"Dear children, I call you to persevere in your prayer for peace."

October 2, 1992

"Dear children, tonight also your Mother wishes to call (invite) **you in a special way to pray at this time. Dear children, satan, in this time, wishes to act through small, small things, dear children. Therefore pray! In this time, satan is strong and he desires to change your direction*; also my plan of peace, he wishes to destroy."**

* The Croatian word, skrenuti, was used which means change your direction, divert your attention toward something else.

December 14, 1992

"Tonight I invite you in a very special manner to renew

your family prayer; and during your family prayer, dear children, read especially the special passages in the Bible that concern Advent. Pray, dear children, especially during this time, and amongst your prayers prepare yourselves for the great day that is coming, that this Christmas will be different from the other Christmases, that it will be joyous, dear children. Remember, dear children, how we were happy in the stable when my Son was born! May your family be happy and all those present in the stable."

January 8, 1993

"Dear children, today your Mother calls you to pray more and more for my intentions, especially during this time....I need your prayers."

March 5, 1993

"Dear children, tonight your Mother wants to call you to pray for conversion in this time. I need your prayers to fulfill my plans."

June 17, 1994

"Our Lady appeared to Ivan at the Blue Cross. She asked us to pray for this parish."

July 11, 1994

"This evening Our Lady came joyfully. She greeted us saying **'Praised be Jesus, my dear children.'** *Then She prayed over all of us and blessed us. Ivan recommended all our needs to Her. Our Lady said to pray for the conversion of sinners. Ivan prayed one 'Our Father' and 'Glory Be' with Her. As we were praying, Our Lady left saying,* **'Go in peace, my dear children.'"**

July 15, 1994

"Ivan had his apparition at the Blue Cross - 10 p.m. Our Lady came happy and joyful. She greeted us with, **'Praised be Jesus, dear children.'** *Our Lady blessed us with Her arms extended. Ivan recommended all our intentions and Our Lady and Ivan prayed an 'Our Father' and 'Glory Be' for peace in the world. She asked us to pray for Her intentions. Our Lady disappeared in the Sign of the Cross, saying,* **'Go in peace, my dear children.'"**

July 25, 1994

Ivan's apparition was at 10 p.m. at the Blue Cross. Our Lady came happy and joyful and prayed over everyone present. Ivan prayed an 'Our Father' and 'Glory Be' as always. Our Lady continued praying and disappeared in the Sign of the Cross saying, **"Go in peace, my dear children."** Our Lady gave Ivan a private message.

July 29, 1994

"Ivan's apparition was at 10:30 p.m. on Apparition Hill. There was no special message. Our Lady came and prayed over us and blessed us with Her hands extended. Ivan recommended all of us, our intentions, our needs, and our families to Her. Our Lady prayed one 'Our Father' and one 'Glory Be' with us in an exceptional way for the sick. As She continued to pray with us, She left in an illuminated Sign of the Cross saying, **'Go in peace, my dear children.'"**

August 5, 1994

"Ivan's apparition was at 10:30 p.m. on Apparition Hill. Our Lady appeared happy and joyful. She greeted us saying, **'Praised be Jesus, my dear children.'** *She prayed over us with Her hands extended and She blessed us all. Ivan recom-*

mended all our needs and intentions and in a special way, the
sick. Our Lady gave a message":

**"Dear children, I invite you to pray in this time for the con-
version of sinners."**

"Then She prayed an 'Our Father' and 'Glory Be' with Ivan
and all present. She remained a while longer and then when
She left, She said, **'Go in the peace of God, my dear children,'** *leaving behind Her a Cross of light."*

August 6, 1994

"Ivan's apparition was at 10 p.m. at the Blue Cross. Our
Lady had a special message. Our Lady came joyful and
happy. She greeted us saying, **'Praised be Jesus, my dear**
children.' *She prayed over us and blessed us with Her hands*
extended. She said":

"Dear children, tonight in a special way, I wish to invite you
in this time, in a special way to pray more for young people
and for families. Dear children, also (your) **Mother will**
pray together with you. Pray! Pray! Pray!"

"Ivan recommended all our needs and intentions. Especially,
he recommended the needs of the sick to Our Lady. Our
Lady prayed awhile for the young people and for families
and then She prayed one 'Our Father' and one 'Glory Be'
with Ivan and all present for them. She continued praying
as She went back to Heaven and left behind a Cross of light,
saying, **'Go in peace, my dear children.'"**

August 8, 1994

"Ivan's apparition was at 10:00 p.m. at the Blue Cross.
Tonight the people prayed the full fifteen decades of the
Rosary instead of the usual singing and one mystery. Our

Lady appeared happy and joyful. She greeted us saying, **'Praised be Jesus, my dear children.'** *She prayed over us with Her hands extended and blessed us all. Ivan recommended all our intentions, our needs, and our families and in a special way, he recommended the sick to Our Lady. Our Lady prayed in a special way for peace and for the priests. After awhile, She went back to Heaven, leaving behind Her a Cross of light and saying,* **'Go in the peace of God, my dear children.'** *There was no message tonight."*

August 15, 1994

"Ivan's apparition was at 10:00 p.m. at the Blue Cross. Ivan led the group in prayer with two mysteries of the Rosary - Joyful and Glorious Mysteries instead of the usual singing and one mystery and one "Peace Chaplet." Our Lady came and was especially joyful tonight and greeted us with **'Praised be Jesus, my dear children.'** *Then with Her hands extended, She prayed over us and blessed us. Then Ivan recommended all our needs and intentions to Our Lady and especially the sick. Our Lady prayed in a very special way for peace tonight and prayed an 'Our Father' and 'Glory Be' with us. Upon leaving, She continued praying and said,* **'Go in peace, my dear children,'** *leaving behind Her a Cross of light. There was no message tonight but we must pay attention to the fact that She prayed for peace. Tonight Her presence was felt."*

August 19, 1994

"Our Lady came joyfully. She greeted us saying, **'Praised be Jesus, my dear children.'** *She prayed over us and blessed us with Her hands extended. She gave a message tonight":*

"Dear children, tonight your Mother wants to say thank you. Thank you for all your prayers. You who prayed and helped me through to this day so that I am realizing my plans. Children, don't get tired of praying. Pray fur-

ther! For yet further, I need your prayers. Thank you for responding to my call."

"Ivan recommended all our needs and intentions. Our Lady prayed with us an 'Our Father' and a 'Glory Be' for peace. As Our Lady continued praying, She left behind Her the Cross of light and said, **'Go in peace, my dear children.'"**

August 22, 1994

"Our Lady came joyfully tonight. She greeted us with the usual **'Praised be Jesus, my dear children.'** *Our Lady prayed over us with Her hands extended and She blessed us. Ivan recommended all our needs, intentions, and especially the sick. Our Lady prayed an 'Our Father' and a 'Glory Be' for peace with us. Our Lady continued praying as She left for Heaven, leaving behind a Cross of light as She said,* **'Go in peace, my dear children.'"**

There was no message tonight but Our Lady prayed for peace again. This was thought to be the last public apparition for awhile as Ivan left the next morning for Belgium and the United States afterwards for preparation of his wedding.

September 2, 1994

"Ivan returned before going to America. Our Lady came joyful tonight. She greeted us saying, **'Praised be Jesus, my dear children.'** *She extended Her hands over us and prayed for a long time and blessed us. Ivan recommended our needs and intentions to Our Lady, especially the sick. She prayed an 'Our Father' and a 'Glory Be' for peace with us. She gave a special message to the prayer group only, but Ivan said She asked during this time while the Holy Father visits this country, that we must pray for him. She also asked us to pray for Her intention (something important) until Nov. 15. "Nakana" is the word She used for Her intention! She*

*continued praying as She went back to Heaven, leaving behind Her a Cross of light. She said, '*Go in peace, my dear children.*'"*

April 25, 1995

"Our Lady came joyful and like each time has greeted us, '*Praised be Jesus Christ.*' *First She prayed over us with extended hands, and She prayed a long time with a language Vicka had not heard before (not of this earth). Vicka said, "It's not earthly language." Our Lady gave the following message":*

"Dear children, I still have many messages to give you but your hearts are closed and far away from my messages. I am in much need of your prayers."

*"Vicka then recommended all who were present and prayed for them. Our Lady then left saying, '*Go in the peace of God.*'"*

Our Lady told Vicka the next apparition would be Friday night at 11:00 p.m. on Cross Mountain.

June 23, 1995

"Tonight Our Lady came joyful. She greeted us all with '*Praised be Jesus, my dear children.*' *After that She prayed over us with Her hands extended and She blessed us all. After that, I recommended all of you and all of your intentions that you came with. After that, Our Lady said":*

"Dear children, I am happy to see you here tonight in such large number. I wish to invite you all in a special way today to pray for the conversion of sinners."

"After that, we prayed with Her for that same intention. We

prayed with Her an 'Our Father' and a 'Glory Be'. After that, Our Lady left in the sign of the light of the Cross and greeted us with **'Go in peace, my dear children.'"**

August 15, 1995 (Assumption)

Our Lady appeared on Apparition Hill at 10:30 p.m.

"Our Lady came dressed in gold and was very joyful. She also came with three angels. Ivan recommended all of us and our intentions, especially the sick. Our Lady's message":

"Dear children, in this joyful time, be tireless in prayer. Pray, pray, pray."

"She then prayed one 'Our Father' and one 'Glory Be' with Ivan. She left in the light of the Cross saying, **'Go in peace, my dear children.'"**

1995

Sr. Emmanuel reported this in her newsletter dated October 15, 1995:

"I cannot hide from you the message given to us one night on Krizevac by Our Lady which greatly saddened me. A crowd was gathered near the Cross and after 16 minutes of apparition, Vicka gave us these words":

"Dear children, I have new messages for you, but I cannot give them to you, since you are not living the messages that I already gave you. Dear children, look at these previous messages and put them into practice. Then I will be able to give you the other messages, so that you may go forward."

April 5, 1996

The following message was received through Sr. Emmanuel:

"Our Lady appeared to Ivan on the mountain the evening of Good Friday. Ivan said Our Lady was sad and sorrowful (as on every Good Friday). After blessing us, She gave this message":

"Dear children, I thank you because I know that you are united with me in sorrow. Little children, when you return to your homes this evening, pray the Sorrowful Mysteries before the Cross."

"She left saying, **'Go in the peace of God my dear children.'** *and disappeared in the sign of a luminous Cross. But this time, something exceptional happened for at the right side of this Cross, Ivan saw Jesus who was in the midst of the pain of His Passion."*

April 26, 1996

"Prayer group was very peaceful and prayerful. There were many people present. Ivan said Our Lady came and was joyful. She said, **'Praised be Jesus.'** *She then prayed with Ivan for all the young people in the world. There was no special message. She left in the light of the Cross saying,* **'Go in the peace of God, my dear children.'"**

May 21, 1996

"Our Lady came very joyful tonight. She greeted us all saying, **'Praised be Jesus, my dear children.'** *After that for a little longer time, She prayed over all of us with Her hands extended towards us and blessed us. Then Ivan recommended all of our needs and intentions and especially all of the sick. Then Our Lady said":*

"Dear children, today your Mother is calling you in a special way, that these days, in a special way, you are praying more, and through the prayer, you are to open yourselves for the Holy Spirit."

"After that Ivan prayed with Our Lady one 'Our Father' and one 'Glory Be.' Then Our Lady left praying in a sign of Cross and light, greeting us all saying, **'Go in God's peace, my dear children.'"**

June 22, 1996

"Our Lady came happy with three angels. She prayed a long time over all of us. She blessed us all. After that, Ivan recommended all and in a special way the sick. After that Our Lady said":

"Dear children, I am happy tonight when I see you in such a large number. Dear children, I wish to tell you that I carry you all in my heart and that I placed you all in my heart. I wish to invite you, especially in this time, to pray more. Dear children, I need your prayers."

"Our Lady wants, especially during these days from the group, to pray for priests, for that intention. After that, together with Our Lady, we prayed one 'Our Father' and one 'Glory Be.' After that Our Lady continued to pray. In that prayer She left in the sign of light and Cross with the greeting, **'Go in peace my dear children.'"**

July 23, 1996

"Our Lady appeared to Ivan during his prayer group meeting tonight at 10:00 p.m. at the Blue Cross. Our Lady came happy and joyful. When She came, She greeted us saying, **'Praised be Jesus, my dear children.'** *Then She prayed over us with Her hands extended, and She blessed all of us. Then*

Ivan recommended to Our Lady all our needs and intentions. Our Lady prayed in a special way for the sick. Then She gave the following message":

"Dear children, tonight I want to call you to prayer. I don't want to tell you anything else than pray. I want you to be my prayers."

"Then Our Lady prayed one 'Our Father' and one 'Glory Be' with Ivan. Then She continued to pray, leaving for Heaven, saying, **'Go in the peace of God, my dear children.'"**

June 24, 1997

"Our Lady came tonight. She was happy and joyful. She came with three angels. When She arrived, She said, **'Praised be Jesus, my dear children.'** *She prayed over the crowd and Ivan recommended all our intentions to Our Lady. She prayed for the crowd and especially the sick. She blessed everyone. Ivan prayed especially with Our Lady for peace in the world. When Our Lady left, She was very joyful, and She said,* **'Go in the peace of God, my dear children.'"**

July 22, 1997

"Our Lady appeared to Ivan tonight at 10:30 p.m. during his prayer group meeting at the Blue Cross. Our Lady appeared happy and joyful. As soon as She came, She greeted us and She said, **'Praised be Jesus, my dear children.'** *Then, with Her hands extended, She prayed over us and She blessed all of us. Ivan recommended to Our Lady all of our intentions and our needs. In a special way he recommended the sick. Our Lady gave a private message for the prayer group. Ivan prayed one 'Our Father' and one 'Glory Be' with Our Lady. Then, after awhile, Our Lady left in the sign of the Cross of light, and as She left She said,* **'Go in the peace of God, my dear children.'"**

June 9, 1998

"Tonight Our Lady appeared happy and joyful. When She came, She greeted us and She said, **'Praised be Jesus, my dear children.'** *Then She prayed over us with Her hands extended, and She blessed all of us. Ivan said She didn't give any special message, but She prayed a long time for peace. Then Ivan recommended to Our Lady our intentions, and in a special way, the sick. Our Lady prayed with Ivan one 'Our Father' and one 'Glory Be.' Then She continued to pray for peace. While praying, She left in the sign of a Cross of light, saying,* **"Go in the peace of God, my dear children."'**

June 30, 1998

"Our Lady appeared to Ivan tonight at the Blue Cross. The apparition lasted at least 10 minutes. As lightning flashed in the distance, Ivan said Our Lady came happy and joyful. She said, **'Praised be Jesus Christ, my dear children.'** *Ivan recommended everyone and our intentions to Our Lady. Our Lady prayed over all of us for an exceptionally long time with Her hands extended and She blessed us all. She prayed in a special way for the sick. She prayed one 'Our Father' and one 'Glory Be' with Ivan. Our Lady left in the light of the Cross, saying,* **'Go in the peace of God, my dear children.'"**

August 7, 1998

"Tonight Our Lady came happy and joyful, and when She came, She greeted us, **'Praised be Jesus, my dear children.'** *After that, with hands extended over us, She prayed for a long time over us and blessed all of us. Ivan recommended to Our Lady all of us, all our families, and all our needs, and in a special way, he recommended to Our Lady the sick people. Our Lady gave a message":*

"Dear children, tonight I call you in a special way, in these days, to pray for my intentions. Dear children, give me everything these days in order to be able to receive everything. Pray, dear children."

"After that, Ivan prayed with Her one "Our Father"" and one 'Glory Be.' In prayer, She left and while She was leaving, She said, **'Go in the peace of God, my dear children.'** *She went as usual in the light of the Cross".*

June 18, 1999

Our Lady appeared to Ivan at 10:00 p.m. tonight at the Blue Cross. She gave the following message:

"Dear children! I am happy, and I want you to be happy. Dear children, because of love, I am teaching you through these eighteen years. I want to lead you. And you, dear children, persevere in prayer, especially in these days. Pray for my intention. I need your prayers."

September 20, 1999

"Our Lady came very happy and joyful. She came with three angels, greeting us by saying, **'Praised be Jesus, my dear children.'** *After that She prayed over all of us, with Her hands extended, for a long time. Ivan recommended everyone present to Our Lady, especially the sick. Our Lady then gave the following message":*

"Dear children! I am happy tonight with you. Dear children, I am bringing you peace. Bring it to the others. Be happy, dear children. In these days I am inviting you in a special way to pray for conversion. Pray, dear children, especially in this period, when satan is trying to destroy your families. In a special way, dear children, pray with your children. May prayer live in your families. Be persistent. Thank you, dear children, for having answered my call."

"Ivan then prayed one 'Our Father' and one 'Glory Be' with Our Lady. As Our Lady continued to pray, She left in the light of the Cross, saying, **"Go in the peace of God, my dear children."**"

June 23, 2002

Our Lady's apparition tonight lasted around fifteen minutes. She appeared with three angels. Our Lady gave the following message:

"My children, I am calling you back to the beginning. Pray for peace, peace, peace. Peace for not only in the world but in the family. Prayer is the way to peace in the family."

June 24, 2005

"Our Lady came happy and joyful. She greeted us with Her Motherly greeting, **'Praised be Jesus.'** *She extended Her hands above us and prayed over us a long time. She blessed us all with Her Motherly blessing and She blessed all our religious objects. Ivan recommended all of us to Her and all of our intentions, our families and especially the sick people present. Our Lady's message tonight":*

"Dear children, today I invite you again, and with great joy, to accept and renew my messages. I call, in a special way, this parish which has accepted and embraced me at the beginning of the apparitions with great joy to renew my messages and to follow me. Thank you for having responded to my call."

"Then we prayed with Ivan an 'Our Father' and 'Glory Be' and Our Lady went away in the sign of the illuminated Cross and said, **'Go in the peace of God, dear children.'**"

August 12, 2005

Our Lady came happy and joyful.

> **"Dear children, in this time I call you in a special way to pray for families and for children. Pray for young people, pray for the family, pray, pray, pray. Thank you for having responded to my call."**

Our Lady left in the sign of the luminous Cross and She said:

> **"Go in the peace of God, dear children."**

June 19, 2006

Our Lady appeared to Ivan at the Blue Cross at 10:00 p.m. Ivan said that Our Lady came very joyful and happy. Our Lady prayed over everyone for a long time. The following is the message that Our Lady gave to Ivan:

> **"Dear children! Also today the Mother calls you with joy. I bring peace to you today, carry that peace to others. Be, dear children, my carriers of peace. I bring you love, dear children, carry that love to others. Also today I call you, dear children, through this time, renew my messages; live my messages. Thank you, dear children, for having responded to my call."**

June 23, 2006

Our Lady appeared to Ivan during his prayer group on top of Apparition Hill. Ivan said that Our Lady came very, very happy and joyful. The following is the message that Our Lady gave to Ivan:

> **"Dear children, also today the Mother rejoices with you. I came and introduced myself as the Queen of Peace, there-**

fore, also today I call you, dear children: pray for peace. Renew my messages and live my messages. Pray, dear children, pray. Thank you, dear children, for having responded to my call."

July 7, 2006

Our Lady appeared to Ivan during his prayer group on top of Apparition Hill. Ivan gave the following description of the apparition:

"Tonight Our Lady came very, very happy. At the beginning, She greeted us with Her Motherly greeting: **'Praised be Jesus, my dear children.'** *After Our Lady prayed for an extended time with Her hands extended over all of us. She blessed all of us with Her Motherly blessing. Afterwards, Our Lady blessed everything you brought for blessing. After I recommended all your intentions, petitions, all your families and especially the sick present".*

The following is the message that Our Lady gave to Ivan:

"Dear children, also today I call you, especially through this time, to pray in your families. Dear children, return prayer into your families; pray together with the children. Dear children, may each of your families grow in this way in holiness. Thank you, dear children, for having responded to my call."

"And after, with Our Lady, we continued to pray an 'Our Father' and 'Glory Be'. Our Lady continued to pray over us and leaving in illuminated Sign of the Cross said: **'Go in peace, my dear little children.'"**

July 14, 2006

Our Lady appeared to Ivan during his prayer group on top of

Apparition Hill. Ivan gave the following description of the apparition:

> *"Tonight Our Lady came happy. She greeted us all saying:* **'Praised be Jesus, my dear children.'** *After Our Lady continued to pray over all of us with extended hands and blessed all of us with Her Motherly blessing. She blessed all your religious articles you brought for blessing. I recommended all your intentions, families, and especially the sick present. Our Lady prayed over the sick present. Then Our Lady said":*

> **"Peace, peace, peace, dear children. Pray with your Mother for peace in the world."**

> *"And after, I prayed with Our Lady one 'Our Father' and 'Glory Be'. And after Our Lady left in prayer, saying:* **'Go in peace, my dear children.'"**

July 28, 2006

Our Lady appeared to Ivan during his prayer group on top of Apparition Hill. Ivan gave the following description of the apparition:

> *"Our Lady came happy and joyful. As always, She greeted us with Her Motherly greeting:* **'Praised be Jesus, my dear children.'** *She prayed a longer time with Her hands extended over all of us. She blessed us all with Her Motherly blessing. She blessed all your religious articles you brought for blessing and She blessed everything we brought for blessing. She prayed especially over the sick who were present. Ivan recommended all of us, our needs and families and especially the sick. Our Lady then prayed specially for the youth, all the youth who are to come here these days, and especially She called us to pray for the youth. We then prayed an 'Our Father' and 'Glory Be' with Our Lady, and then, in prayer, Our Lady left in an illuminated Sign of the Cross, saying:* **'Go in peace, my dear children.'"**

August 4, 2006

Our Lady appeared to Ivan at the Blue Cross at 9:00 p.m. Ivan gave the following description of the apparition:

"Tonight, the most important from the meeting with Our Lady was that She came joyful and happy. She greeted us with Her Motherly greeting: **'Praised be Jesus, my dear children.'** *After Our Lady prayed over us with Her arms extended and She blessed us all with Her Motherly blessing and She blessed everything you brought for blessing. Then Our Lady prayed especially over the sick who were present and I recommended all your needs, intentions, and your families; especially all the youth present and the sick. Then Our Lady said":*

"Dear children, also today the Mother with seriousness calls you: 'pray, dear children, for peace.' Peace, peace, peace, dear children, may there be peace. Dear children, the Mother intercedes before Her Son for all of you. Pray together with the Mother, at this time especially, for peace. Thank you, dear children, for having responded to my call."

"Afterwards we prayed an 'Our Father' and a 'Glory Be' with Our Lady and then Our Lady prayed over us with Her arms extended and in that prayer left in an illuminated Sign of the Cross saying, **'Go in peace, my dear children.'"**

August 11, 2006

Our Lady appeared to Ivan on top of Apparition Hill at 10:00 p.m. Ivan gave the following description of the apparition:

"Our Lady came joyful and at the beginning She greeted us all with Her Motherly greeting: **'Praised be Jesus, my dear children.'** *Then Our Lady continued to pray for a longer time, especially for peace. Then She said":*

"Dear children, also today I call you to pray for peace. Pray for peace in the world, pray for peace in your families. Thank you, dear children, for having responded to my call."

"Then She blessed us all with Her Motherly blessing. Ivan recommended all of us to Her, our intentions, and our families. Then we prayed together with Ivan and Our Lady an 'Our Father' and a 'Glory Be' and Our Lady left in an illuminated Sign of the Cross saying: **'Go in peace, my dear children.'"**

August 14, 2006

Our Lady appeared to Ivan at the Blue Cross at 10:00 p.m. Ivan gave the following description of the apparition:

"Tonight Our Lady came happy and joyful. She greeted us all with Her Motherly greeting, **'Praised be Jesus, my dear children.'** *Then with Her hands extended, She prayed a longer time over us. She then blessed us all with Her Motherly blessing and blessed all the religious objects we brought with us. She then especially prayed over all the sick people present and Ivan recommended all of us to Her and all our intentions, our families, and especially the sick people. Then Our Lady especially prayed for awhile for peace in the world. We prayed together with Our Lady an 'Our Father' and a 'Glory Be' and then Our Lady left in an illuminated Sign of the Cross saying,* **'Go in peace, my dear children.'"**

August 21, 2006

Our Lady appeared to Ivan at the Blue Cross at 10:00 p.m. Ivan gave the following description of the apparition:

"Tonight Our Lady came happy and joyful. She came with three angels. At the beginning She greeted us all with Her Motherly greeting: **'Praised be Jesus, my dear children.'**

Then She extended Her hands over us and She prayed over us. Then She blessed us all with Her Motherly blessing and also all the religious objects we brought with us. Then She prayed especially for all the sick people present here. Then Ivan recommended all of us to Her, our intentions, our families, and especially the sick people and those who specifically recommended themselves to be prayed for. Tonight Our Lady prayed specially for vocations in the Church and for priests. Then we prayed together with Our Lady and Ivan an 'Our Father' and a 'Glory Be' and then praying over us, Our Lady left in an illuminated Sign of the Cross saying, **'Go in peace my dear children.'"**

September 1, 2006

"Tonight Our Lady came joyful and happy with three angels. She greeted us all with Her Motherly greeting. She said: **'Praised be Jesus, dear children.'** *Then She extended Her hands above us and She prayed over us. Then She blessed us all with Her Motherly blessing, and also all the religious objects we brought with us. Then She prayed especially for the sick people here present. Then Ivan recommended all of us to Her, our needs, our intentions, our families, and especially the sick. Then Our Lady said":*

"Dear children, also today the Mother is calling you in a special way. Dear children, return prayer to your families. Pray, dear children, in your families so that with prayer, peace, love, and joy may return. The Mother is praying with you. Pray, dear children. Thank you fore having responded to my call."

"Then we prayed together with Our Lady an 'Our Father' and the 'Glory Be'. Then Our Lady went away in the sign of light and cross, and She said: **'Go in peace, dear children.'"**

September 8, 2006

Our Lady appeared to Ivan during his prayer group on Apparition Hill at 10:00 p.m. on Friday, September 8, 2006. The following is Ivan's description of the apparition:

"Our Lady came very very happy and joyful. She came with three angels. At the beginning, She greeted us all with Her Motherly greeting, **'Praised be Jesus, my dear children.'** *Then Our Lady prayed a longer time over us with Her hands extended. She blessed us all with Her Motherly blessing and blessed all the religious items brought for blessing. Then Ivan recommended all of us, all our needs, intentions, and families, and especially the sick. Our Lady then especially prayed for the sick present here and then said":*

"Dear children, this year how much seed I have sown. I desire that you, dear children, be my flower from that seed. Be my flower. Live my message. Pray for peace. Pray together with your Mother for peace. Thank you for having responded to my call."

"Then we prayed an 'Our Father' and a 'Glory Be' with Our Lady, and then in prayer, Our Lady left us in an illuminated Sign of the Cross with the greeting: **'Go in peace, my dear children!'"**

September 15, 2006

Our Lady appeared to Ivan during his prayer group on Apparition Hill at 10:00 p.m. on Friday, September 15, 2006. The following is Ivan's description of the apparition:

"Our Lady came happy and joyful. At the beginning, She greeted us all with Her Motherly greeting: **'Praised be Jesus, my dear children.'** *Then Our Lady prayed over us with Her hands extended. She blessed us all with Her Motherly bless-*

ing and blessed all the religious items brought for blessing. Then Ivan recommended all of us, all our needs, intentions, and families and especially the sick. Our Lady then prayed for the sick present and especially prayed for peace in the world. Then we prayed an 'Our Father' and a 'Glory Be' with Our Lady and in prayer, Our Lady left in an illuminated Sign of the Cross with the greeting: **'Go in peace, my dear children.'"**

September 18, 2006

Our Lady appeared to Ivan at the Blue Cross at 10:00 p.m. on September 18, 2006. Ivan gave the following description of the apparition:

"Our Lady came very, very happy and joyful. At the beginning She greeted us all with Her usual Motherly greeting, **'Praised be Jesus, my dear children.'** *Then Our Lady prayed a longer time over all of us here with Her hands extended. Our Lady then prayed for the sick present here. She blessed us all with Her Motherly blessing and blessed all the religious objects brought for blessing. After, Our Lady prayed especially today for the Holy Father, the bishops and priests. She prayed for firm faith for priests and for firm faith in the Church. Then we prayed an 'Our Father' and a 'Glory Be' with Our Lady and Our Lady continued to pray over us and left us in an illuminated Sign of the Cross, with the greeting,* **'Go in peace my dear children.'"**

May 28, 2007

Our Lady appeared to Ivan on top of Apparition Hill tonight at 10:00 p.m. The following is a description of the apparition:

"Our Lady came and said, **'Praised be Jesus, my dear children.'** *She prayed over us for a long time with Her hands extended. She prayed over the sick who were present, and*

then for priests. She gave us Her Motherly blessing and blessed all the religious articles that people brought with them. Ivan recommended everyone present to Our Lady, as well as their intentions, their families and especially the sick people. Our Lady continued to pray, especially for peace. We prayed with Our Lady one 'Our Father' and one 'Glory Be'. Our Lady left, praying, in the sign of the light of the Cross."

June 4, 2007

Our Lady appeared to Ivan at the Blue Cross during his prayer group. The following is a description of the apparition:

"Tonight, Our Lady came very, very happy. And at the beginning She said, **'Praised be Jesus, my little children.'** *And after, Our Lady prayed a long time with Her hands extended over us. She gave Her Motherly blessing to all of us and a blessing for all the religious articles, rosaries, everything that was brought for Her blessing. And after, Ivan recommended all of our intentions, petitions, all our families, and especially the sick people. And after, Our Lady prayed a long time, especially for the sick. And after, Ivan prayed with Our Lady one 'Our Father' and 'Glory Be', and after Our Lady, while leaving, said* **'Go in peace, my little children.'"**

June 11, 2007

Our Lady appeared to Ivan at 10:00 p.m. on top of Apparition Hill during his prayer group. The following is Ivan's description of the apparition:

"Tonight, when Our Lady came She was very, very happy. She said, **'Praised be Jesus, my little children.'** *And after, Our Lady, for a long time, prayed with Her hands extended over all of us, and blessed all of us with Her Motherly blessing. She also gave a blessing for all of your religious articles, rosaries, everything that you brought to be blessed. Then*

*Our Lady especially prayed for all the sick people present.
I recommended to Our Lady all your petitions, families,
intentions, and especially for the sick. Our Lady continued,*
'especially tonight, to pray for peace in the world.' *After
that, I prayed with Our Lady an 'Our Father' and 'Glory Be'.
And after, Our Lady while leaving, said,* **'Go in peace, my
little children.'"**

June 18, 2007

Our Lady appeared to Ivan on top of Apparition Hill at 10:00
p.m. during his prayer group. The following is Ivan's description
of the apparition:

*"Our Lady came happy and joyful. At the beginning She
greeted us with Her Motherly greeting,* **'Praised be Jesus my
dear children.'** *With great joy Our Lady prayed over us with
extended hands and then prayed over the sick people present
here. She then blessed us all with Her Motherly blessing
and blessed all the religious articles brought for blessing. I
recommended all of our intentions, us, all our families and
especially all the sick present to Our Lady. Our Lady, in a
particular way prayed for the sick. Then Our Lady said":*

**"Dear children, also today the Mother calls you with great
joy, especially in this time of grace, to renew my messages
and live my messages in your families. Pray, dear children,
pray. Thank you, dear children, for having responded to my
call."**

*"Then we prayed with Our Lady an 'Our Father' and a
'Glory Be' and then Our Lady left in the illuminated Sign of
the Cross, saying* **'Go in peace, my dear children.'"**

June 22, 2007

Our Lady appeared to Ivan on top of Apparition Hill tonight at
10:00 p.m. The following is Ivan's description:

"Tonight when Our Lady came She was very, very happy. At the beginning She greeted us with, **'Praised be Jesus my dear children.'** *And after, Our Lady, for a long time, prayed over us with Her hands extended. She then blessed us all with Her Motherly blessing. And after Our Lady prayed especially for all of you tonight who came. I then especially recommended all your intentions, petitions, all your families and especially the sick. Our Lady then prayed in a special way tonight for the conversion of sinners. I prayed with Our Lady one 'Our Father' and 'Glory Be'. Our Lady left in the illuminated Sign of the Cross saying,* **'Go in peace, my dear children.'"**

June 25, 2007

Our Lady appeared to Ivan on top of Apparition Hill tonight at 10:00 p.m. during his prayer group. The following is Ivan's description of the apparition:

"Tonight, when Our Lady came She was very, very happy. She came with three angels and greeted us by saying, **'Praised be Jesus, my dear little children.'** *Our Lady then prayed a long time with Her hands extended over all of us and blessed us all with Her Motherly blessing, and gave a blessing for all religious articles, rosaries, everything that you brought for blessing. I then recommended all your intentions, petitions, all your families, and especially for all those who are sick. Then Our Lady continued to pray a long time with Her hands extended over all of us. I then prayed an 'Our Father' and a 'Glory Be' with Our Lady. And after finishing this prayer, Our Lady spoke to me, just for me, privately. And after She finished this conversation, Our Lady left saying,* **'Go in peace, my little children.'"**

"This is tonight, important for meeting. You know Our Lady give message for all in the world through Marija. You need to live this message, this last message, Our Lady gave today."

July 9, 2007

Tonight, the evening of July 9, 2007, Our Lady appeared to Ivan during his prayer group meeting at the Blue Cross. There were several thousands of pilgrims and villagers present at the apparition tonight. Following is Ivan's description of the apparition:

> *"Today, when Our Lady came She was very, very happy, and greeted us by saying* **'Praised be Jesus, my dear children.'** *And then after, Our Lady prayed with Her hands extended over us for a long time. She especially prayed for all the sick. She blessed us all with Her Motherly blessing, as well as all of our religious articles, rosaries and everything that we brought for blessing. And then I recommended all of your intentions, petitions, all your families, especially for the sick. And then Our Lady prayed a long time for the sick present tonight. And then after Our Lady prayed a long time especially tonight for priests and vocations for the Church. And then I prayed with Our Lady an 'Our Father' and 'Glory Be'. And then Our Lady left in the illuminated Sign of the Cross saying* **'Go in peace my dear children.'** *This is important tonight."*

July 16, 2007

The apparition took place at 10:00 p.m. tonight at the Blue Cross. The following is Ivan's description of the apparition:

> *"Tonight when Our Lady came She was very, very happy. She greeted us by saying* **'Praised be Jesus my dear children.'** *Our Lady then prayed for a long time with Her hands extended over us. She then blessed us all with Her Motherly blessing. Our Lady especially prayed for all the sick present here tonight. I recommended all of your petitions, your families, and especially for the sick. Tonight, Our Lady especially prayed for vocations in the Church. I prayed with Our Lady an 'Our Father' and 'Glory Be'. And then Our Lady left saying* **'Go in peace my dear children.'"**

July 20, 2007

Our Lady appeared to Ivan at 10:00 p.m. at the Blue Cross tonight. The following is Ivan's description:

"Tonight when Our Lady came She was very, very happy. She greeted us by saying **'Praised be Jesus my dear children.'** *Our Lady then prayed for a long time with Her hands extended over us present. She then blessed us all with Her Motherly blessing. She blessed all the religious articles brought for blessing and then Our Lady prayed especially for all the sick present here tonight. Ivan recommended all of our needs, petitions, our families and especially the sick. Our Lady then said":*

"Dear children, also today, in a special way, I am calling you to return prayer into your families. Dear children, pray and grow in holiness in your families. Pray, dear children, together with your Mother for families, pray for youth. Thank you, dear children, for having responded to my call."

"After, we prayed with Our Lady an 'Our Father' and a 'Glory Be', and then Our Lady left in an illuminated Sign of the Cross saying, **'Go in peace my dear children.'"**

August 10, 2007

Ivan's prayer group met at the Blue Cross tonight. Our Lady appeared to Ivan at 10:00 p.m. Ivan's description of the apparition is below:

"Tonight when Our Lady came She was very happy. She greeted us by saying, **'Praised be Jesus my little children.'** *Our Lady then prayed for a long time with Her hands extended over us. She especially prayed for all you sick pilgrims tonight. Ivan recommended all of our needs, petitions our family and especially the sick. She then blessed us all with*

Her Motherly blessing. She blessed all the religious articles brought for blessing. Our Lady then prayed for priests for a long time. After we prayed with Our Lady an 'Our Father' and a 'Glory Be'. Our Lady left in an illuminated Sign of the Cross saying, **'Go in peace my dear children.'"**

August 17, 2007

Our Lady appeared to Ivan on top of Apparition Hill tonight. She appeared at 10:00 p.m. The following is Ivan's description of what took place during the apparition.

"Most important from the meeting tonight with Our Lady is that Our Lady came joyful and happy. She greeted us at the beginning with Her usual Motherly greeting, **'Praised be Jesus my dear children.'** *Our Lady then prayed for a long time with Her hands extended over us present. She then prayed especially over those sick present here and then blessed us all with Her Motherly blessing. She also blessed all the religious articles brought for blessing, and Ivan recommended all your needs, petitions, your families, and especially the sick present. Our Lady then said":*

"Dear children, also today the Mother, in a special way, calls you to pray at this time for all my children who have distanced themselves from my Son. Dear children, pray that they may return and may find peace, joy, and love. The Mother prays with you. Thank you, dear children, for having responded to my call."

"After, we prayed with Our Lady an 'Our Father' and a 'Glory Be' and then Our Lady left in prayer, in an illuminated Sign of the Cross saying, **'Go in peace my dear children.'"**

August 24, 2007

Ivan's prayer group met at the Blue Cross tonight. Our Lady

appeared to Ivan at 10:00 p.m. Ivan's description of the apparition is below:

> *"Today when Our Lady came She was very, very happy and said* **'Praised be Jesus my little children.'** *Our Lady extended Her hands over all of us and prayed for a long time. And She prayed tonight for all you present, especially for the sick. And afterward, Our Lady blessed all of us with Her Motherly blessing. She blessed all your articles, rosaries everything you brought for blessing. And I recommend all your intentions, petitions, all your family, and especially for sick. Our Lady continued to pray with Her hands extended over all us for a long time. And after this, I spoke with Our Lady privately, and after I finished this private conversation, I prayed with Our Lady, one 'Our Father' and one 'Glory Be'. And after finish this Our Lady left saying,* **'Go in peace my little children.'"**

> *"Today there was no message. You know tomorrow is the 25th. Every 25th of the month, Our Lady gives us a message for the world. We're expecting a message tomorrow because Our Lady gives a message tomorrow. Thank you."`*

August 31, 2007

Our Lady appeared to Ivan at 10:00 p.m. tonight on Apparition Hill. The following is Ivan's description of the apparition.

> *"Tonight when Our Lady came She was very happy and joyful. She greeted us by saying,* **'Praised be Jesus, my little children.'** *Our Lady then prayed with Her hands extended over us present. She then blessed us all with Her Motherly blessing. She blessed all of the religious articles brought for blessing and prayed especially for all the sick present here tonight. Ivan recommended all of our needs, petitions, our families and especially the sick. Our Lady spoke privately to Ivan and then we prayed with Our Lady an 'Our Father' and a 'Glory Be'. Our Lady then left in an illuminated Sign of the Cross,* **'Go in peace my dear children.'"**

September 7, 2007

Ivan's prayer group met at the Blue Cross tonight. Our Lady appeared to Ivan at 10:00 p.m. The following is the description Ivan gave of the apparition.

"Tonight the most important from the meeting with Our Lady was that Our Lady came very happy. She greeted us with a greeting, **'Praised be Jesus, my dear children.'** *Our Lady prayed especially for the sick present here tonight. Our Lady then prayed with Her hands extended over those present. She then blessed us all with Her Motherly blessing. She blessed all religious articles brought for blessing. As always, I recommended all of you, your needs, petitions, your families, and especially the sick. Our Lady continued to pray especially for peace in the world. We then prayed an 'Our Father' and a 'Glory Be' with Our Lady. Our Lady spoke with me and I with Her privately. Then Our Lady left in the illuminated Sign of the Cross saying,* **'Go in peace my dear children.'** *This is what is important from tonight."*

May 19, 2008

Ivan's prayer group met at the Blue Cross tonight. The apparition began at 10:00 p.m. and lasted about 6 minutes. The following is Ivan's description of the apparition:

"This evening Our Lady came – She was very, very happy. After saying, **'Praised be Jesus, my little children,'** *Our Lady prayed especially tonight for all the sick present. She prayed for their intentions. Afterwards She prayed for all of us for a long time, and blessed all of us with Her Motherly blessing. I then recommended all of your intentions, all your families, and especially the sick to Her. Our Lady, tonight, especially prayed for peace in the world. I prayed with Our Lady an 'Our Father' and a 'Glory Be'. Our Lady then left, saying* **'Go in peace, my little children.'"***

May 26, 2008

"Tonight when Our Lady came She was very, very happy. She greeted us by saying **'Praised be Jesus my dear children.'** *Our Lady then prayed for a long time with Her hands extended over us present. She then blessed us all with Her Motherly blessing. She blessed all the religious articles brought for blessing. Ivan recommended all of our needs, our families and especially all of the sick. Tonight Our Lady prayed especially for vocations in the Church. After we prayed with Our Lady an 'Our Father' and a 'Glory Be' and then Our Lady left in an illuminated Sign of the Cross saying,* **'Go in peace my dear children.'"**

May 30, 2008

"Tonight, most important from the meeting with Our Lady was that Our Lady came joyful and happy. At the beginning, as always, She greeted us by saying **'Praised be Jesus my dear children.'** *Our Lady then prayed for a long time with Her hands extended over us present. She then blessed us all with Her Motherly blessing. She blessed all the religious articles brought for blessing. As always, so today, I recommended all of you, your needs, your intentions, your families and in a special way the sick to Our Lady. Then Our Lady prayed especially for all the sick present here tonight. Our Lady then said":*

"Dear children, also today, the Mother calls you, pray for my children who have distanced themselves from my Son. Pray. Pray that they may return to my Son and find peace in Him. The Mother prays with you. Thank you for having responded to my call."

"After we prayed with Our Lady an 'Our Father' and a 'Glory Be' and then Our Lady left in an illuminated Sign of the Cross saying, **'Go in peace my dear children.'"**

June 9, 2008

Our Lady appeared to Ivan at 10:00 p.m. and stayed for several minutes. The following is Ivan's description of the apparition:

"Tonight Our Lady came joyful and happy. At the beginning, as always, She greeted us with Her Motherly greeting, **'Praised be Jesus, my dear children.'** *Then with Her arms extended, She prayed over us for a time and blessed us with Her Motherly blessing. She blessed all the religious articles brought for blessing. Our Lady prayed especially for all the sick present. Then Ivan recommended all of us and our intentions and especially the sick to Our Lady. Our Lady then said":*

"Dear children, also today the Mother calls you: renew my messages, live my messages. Dear children, I am with you and I intercede before my Son for all of you. Pray. Pray, my dear children. Thank you for having responded to my call."

"After, we prayed with Our Lady an 'Our Father' and a 'Glory Be' and then Our Lady left in an illuminated Sign of the Cross saying, **'Go in peace, my dear children.'"**

June 20, 2008

Our Lady appeared to Ivan at 10:00 p.m. at the Blue Cross. The apparition lasted several minutes. There were several thousand pilgrims present tonight for the apparition. The following is Ivan's description of the apparition:

"Tonight Our Lady came very happy. She greeted us with Her Motherly greeting, **'Praised be Jesus, my dear children.'** *Our Lady prayed a long time for all of us, for our intentions. She blessed all of us with Her Motherly blessing. She blessed all the religious articles brought for blessing. Our Lady prayed a long time with Her hands extended. Our Lady prayed espe-*

*cially for all the sick present. Then Ivan recommended all of us, our intentions, our families, and especially the sick to Our Lady. After that, Our Lady continued to pray for all of us with Her hands extended. After that She left saying, '***Go in peace, my dear children.'***"

June 27, 2008

Our Lady appeared to Ivan during his prayer group on top of Apparition Hill at 10:00 p.m. The apparition lasted several minutes. The following is Ivan's description of the apparition.

*"Tonight when Our Lady came She was very, very happy. She greeted us by saying, '***Praised be Jesus, my dear children.***' Our Lady then prayed for a long time with Her hands extended over us present. She then blessed us all with Her Motherly blessing. She blessed all the religious articles everyone brought for Her blessing. Ivan recommended all of our needs, our families and especially all of the sick. Tonight Our Lady prayed for peace in the world. After we prayed with Our Lady an 'Our Father' and a 'Glory Be' and then Our Lady left in an illuminated Sign of the Cross saying, '***Go in peace, my dear children.'***"

August 15, 2008

Our Lady appeared to Ivan during his prayer group on top of Apparition Hill at 10:00 p.m. The apparition lasted about eight minutes. The following is Ivan's description of the apparition.

*"Tonight Our Lady came exceptionally joyful and happy. When She came She greeted all of us with Her Motherly greeting saying, '***Praised be Jesus, my dear children, my dear little children.***' She then prayed over all of us with Her hands extended for a longer time. In a special way She prayed over those who are sick, present on the hill. She then blessed us with Her Motherly blessing. She blessed all of the religious*

articles that have been brought for blessing. Ivan recommended all of the sick. With Her hands extended, Our Lady continued to pray over all of us. And then She said":

"Dear children, also today I call you with responsibility to accept my messages. Live, dear children, my messages. Today, in a special way, I call you, renew family prayer. Dear children, only by the renewal of the family prayer can today's world be renewed spiritually. Spiritual renewal, dear children, is necessary for today's world. Dear children, know that the Mother prays with you. The Mother intercedes with Her Son for all of you. The Mother loves all of you. Dear children, thank you for having responded to my call."

"Afterwards, Ivan prayed together with Our Lady an 'Our Father' and 'Glory Be'. There was a brief conversation between them. And then Our Lady left in an illuminated Sign of the Cross, with the greeting, **'Go in peace, my dear children.'"**

August 29, 2008

Our Lady appeared to Ivan during his prayer group at the Blue Cross at 10:00 p.m. The apparition lasted almost eight minutes. The following is Ivan's description of the apparition.

"The most important from tonight's meeting with Our Lady is that Our Lady came joyful and happy. As always, at the beginning, She greeted us with Her Motherly greeting: **'Praised be Jesus my dear children.'** *Our Lady then prayed for a long time specially for the conversion of sinners. Our Lady then prayed specially over all of you sick who were present, and then for a time, She prayed over all of us present with Her hands extended. She then blessed us all with Her Motherly blessing, and She blessed all that you brought for blessing. I then recommended all of your needs, your intentions, your families, and especially all of the sick. A brief conversation*

*between us followed. I spoke to Her and She spoke to me.
And then I prayed with Our Lady an 'Our Father' and a 'Glory Be'. Our Lady then, in prayer in a Sign of the Cross left,
saying,* **'Go in peace my dear little children.'"**

September 5, 2008

Our Lady appeared to Ivan during his prayer group on top of
Apparition Hill at 10:00 p.m. The apparition lasted about ten
minutes. The following is Ivan's description of the apparition:

*"Most important from tonight's meeting with Our Lady is that
Our Lady came joyful and, at the beginning, greeted us all with
Her Motherly greeting:* **'Praised be Jesus, my children.'** *Our
Lady then prayed for a longer time for unity of the Church and
for priests. She then blessed us all with Her Motherly blessing
and blessed all that you brought for blessing. With Her hands
extended over us, She then prayed over us for a while and She
prayed over the sick. Then we conversed, I spoke with Her
and She with me, which remains only between us. Then I recommended all of you, all of your needs, your intentions, your
families, and especially all of the sick. I then prayed an 'Our
Father' and 'Glory Be' with Our Lady and afterwards, as She
prayed over us, She left in prayer, in an illuminated Sign of the
Cross, with a greeting,* **'Go in peace, my dear children.'** *This
would be the most important from tonight's meeting described
in the words that I have.*

September 12, 2008

Our Lady appeared to Ivan during his prayer group at the Blue
Cross at 10:00 p.m. The apparition lasted about six minutes. The
following is Ivan's description of the apparition:

*"Tonight, the most important from the meeting with Our Lady
is that Our Lady came happy and joyful and at the beginning,
as always, greeted us all with Her Motherly greeting:* **'Praised**

be Jesus, my dear children.' *Our Lady tonight prayed for a longer time with Her arms extended over all of you here, and especially She prayed over those of you present here who are sick. She then blessed us all with Her Motherly blessing and She blessed everything that you brought for blessing. I recommended all of you, all of your needs, your intentions, your families and especially the sick. Then Our Lady, with Her arms extended, continued to pray over all of us here. I then prayed one 'Our Father' and 'Glory Be' with Her and Our Lady then left in an illuminated Sign of the Cross, saying:* **'Go in peace my dear children.'"**

CHAPTER 5

THE MESSAGES
OF OUR LADY
WHILE MARIJA WAS IN AMERICA

(November 19, 1988 to February 18, 2009)

"...I AM HERE TO HELP YOU!..." (November 24, 1988, Thanksgiving Day)

Marija, her brother, and two friends traveled to America where Marija underwent surgery to donate one of her kidneys to her brother, Andrija. They arrived on November 18, 1988. Our Lady did many beautiful things. A human issue caused Mary and Joseph to travel to Bethlehem. The census was the means God used to get them to Bethlehem, and therefore, God's words, *"And you, O Bethlehem, in the land of Judah, are by no means least among the rulers of Judah; for from you shall come a Ruler who will govern my people Israel,"* was fulfilled. Likewise, the kidney transplant was the means and human issue to get Marija to Birmingham, Alabama, thereby initiating Our Lady's plans She foretold in the October 6, 1986 message (page 184).

Marija stayed almost three months. Other than their homes, never had a visionary stayed in one place for such a long time. Over time, Our Lady began to unfold a beautiful love story, establishing a way of life.

Whenever Caritas Community members are at an apparition, detailed information is gathered of the entire events leading up to the apparition, the apparition itself, as well as what occurs after the apparitions. It would be too lengthy to provide this information here in this chapter, so an appendix has been provided at the end of the book with the detailed descriptions of some of the different apparitions.

November 19, 1988, 10:40 a.m.

Our Lady came and was very happy. She blessed everyone. Marija recommended everyone present to Our Lady and Our Lady prayed The Lord's Prayer and one Glory Be. Our Lady said She would appear at 10:30 p.m., Sunday night.

The apparition took place in the *bedroom* of the couple whom Marija was living with. The location of the apparitions surprised the couple. Day by day, through the weeks and into the months, it became clear why Our Lady wanted these apparitions in the Bedroom. The apparitions began there when Marija was shown around to familiarize her with the house. The last place she was shown was the couple's bedroom. Upon standing at the foot of the bed, Marija firmly and even authoritatively said, *"The apparitions will take place here."* The couple, standing on either side of her, looked at each other shocked.

In time, it became clear as to how the Bedroom was chosen, not by Marija, but chosen by Our Lady, Herself. The impact Medjugorje had made in the life of the founder* was profound. After his first pilgrimages to Medjugorje, he began to pray that God would show him how to become holy, especially in living out his vocation as a husband and father. This became a very focused prayer, and, for several years, he prayed this every day. When Our Lady came and began to appear in the Bedroom, Marija would kneel at the foot of the Bed while the husband,

---

* The host of the home where Marija stayed and the founder of the Community of Caritas are the same man. He later became known as "A Friend of Medjugorje" through his writings of the messages of Medjugorje.

wife and children would gather on their knees around it. Our Lady would then appear upon the Bed.

Hanging over the Bed was a special crucifix that Fr. Slavko had given the founder in Medjugorje. It had hung in the apparition room in Medjugorje and had been blessed by Our Lady on hundreds of occasions, through Our Lady's apparitions over it as the visionaries daily gathered before it to pray. Before leaving Medjugorje, the founder brought the Crucifix to Marija and asked her to say a prayer over it, and that she would particularly seek the grace from Our Lady that this Crucifix would become a great tool of conversion for the United States. Marija went into a deep prayer while holding it and then bent to kiss it with great reverence. Seeing Marija's attitude towards the Crucifix deepened the founder's own reverence and awe of it. The couple spent months praying for inspiration in where to hang the Crucifix in their home.

On one particular night, with a fire in the heart of the wife, it became clear to her that it was to go above their bed in their bedroom. Through the whole night, her heart burned to hang this Crucifix over the bed, though she did not particularly want to. The flame was quenched only when she hung it just before dawn. The Bedroom quickly became known as a pilgrimage site once Our Lady appeared in this room.

Because of the actions of Our Lady to bless the Field for the first time on Thanksgiving Day, November 24, 1988, the Field became known as a pilgrimage site dedicated to the conversion of our Nation. However, though Our Lady was present for more than two and a half months, only one time did She instruct everyone to go out to the Field. All other apparitions took place in the home. What began to be understood through Our Lady's actions is that before healing can come to the nation, it must first come through the family. As spiritually healthy individuals are raised in good families, good families make good nations, thereby, it is the path to heal nations. As both sites have been blessed and consecrated to the Virgin Mary by Her very presence in the apparitions, these sites are not mere symbols but actual places of grace, healing and renewal for the family and for our Nation.

November 20, 1988, 10:30 p.m.

Our Lady came and was very happy. She blessed individually everyone in the room. Marija recommended all present to Our Lady and She prayed The Lord's Prayer and the Glory Be. Our Lady's message:

"May your life be prayer. May your work be offered as a prayer and may everything that you do bring you toward me. Let everything that you do and everybody that you meet be an encounter with God."

She made the Sign of the Cross over everyone and left saying, **"Go in peace."**

November 21, 1988, 10:40 a.m. (SPECIAL BLESSING)

Our Lady appeared with three angels and was very happy. She looked around at everybody, even the people outside. A Catholic school, St. Rose Academy, closed today so that children could come to the apparition and many were present. Our Lady prayed in Hebrew over the whole crowd. She gave all a SPECIAL BLESSING. Our Lady said:

"Live the messages that I give."

November 22, 1988, 10:40 a.m.

Our Lady came and was very happy. She looked around the crowd of about 400 people, inside and outside the home where Marija was staying. Our Lady blessed everyone. Marija recommended everyone present to Our Lady and She prayed The Lord's Prayer and the Glory Be. Our Lady's message:

"Live in humility all the messages that I give. I want you to be carriers of peace."

Our Lady gave a blessing of peace and left.

November 23, 1988, 10:30 p.m.

Our Lady came and was very happy. She blessed everyone. Marija recommended everyone present to Our Lady and She prayed The Lord's Prayer and the Glory Be. Our Lady's message:

"I invite you to pray and give your life completely to God. I will give you strength and I will help you in all of your needs. You can ask for everything that you need to help you. I will intercede for you in front of God."

The Blessed Mother said She would appear the next morning in a field near a large pine tree and Our Lady extended an invitation for all to come.

November 24, 1988, 10:40 a.m. (THANKSGIVING DAY)

The apparition took place near a large tree in a field near the home where Marija was staying. Our Lady came and was very happy. She looked at all who had gathered there. She blessed everyone. Marija recommended every person present to Our Lady and She prayed The Lord's Prayer and the Glory Be. Our Lady's message:

"I invite you to live my messages. I am here to help you! I will intercede for you to God for all your intentions."

Several hundred people were present. When She left, Our Lady said: **"Go in peace."**

November 25, 1988, 10:40 a.m.

The next three monthly messages for the world were given to Marija while she was in Birmingham.

"Dear children, I call you to prayer for you to have an encounter with God in prayer. God gives Himself to you, but He wants you to answer in your own freedom to His invitation. That is why, little children, during the day find yourselves a special time when you can pray in peace and humility and have this meeting with God, the Creator. I am with you and I intercede for you in front of God. Watch in vigil so that every encounter in prayer be the joy of your contact with God. Thank you for having responded to my call."

November 26, 1988, 10:40 a.m.

Our Lady came and was very happy. With Her hands extended, She prayed over everyone and blessed them. Marija recommended all those present, especially the sick, to Our Lady, and She prayed The Lord's Prayer and the Glory Be. Our Lady's message:

"I ask you once again to pray. Especially pray for my intentions. If you pray for my intentions, I will be glorified through you. All your prayers are going to help you through my hands."

November 27, 1988, 10:30 p.m.

Our Lady came and was very happy. She blessed the people and all their religious objects with the Sign of the Cross. Marija recommended everyone present, especially the sick, to Our Lady, and She prayed The Lord's Prayer and the Glory Be. Our Lady's message:

"I want you to be in prayer. I want to protect you under my mantle. Pray. Pray. Pray."

November 28, 1988, 10:30 p.m.

Our Lady came and was very happy. She prayed over everybody. Marija recommended every person present to Our Lady, and She prayed The Lord's Prayer and the Glory Be. Our Lady blessed everyone and went to Heaven. Our Lady gave no words, but Her presence and being very happy were Her message.

November 29, 1988, 10:30 p.m. (SPECIAL BLESSING)

Our Lady came and was very happy. She blessed and prayed over everyone. Marija recommended all those present, especially the sick, to Our Lady. Our Lady prayed The Lord's Prayer and the Glory Be. Our Lady extended Her arms above all who gathered there and for a certain time prayed in that manner. Tonight Our Lady gave the SPECIAL BLESSING. Our Lady's message:

"Bless [with the Special Blessing] **even those who don't believe. You can give them this Blessing from the heart to help them in their conversion. Bless everyone you meet. I give you a special grace. I desire you to give this grace to others."**

Our Lady left saying, **"Go in peace."**

The November 29th SPECIAL BLESSING was given on a day which was not a feast day or a special occasion. Our Lady spoke specifically about what She desired with this SPECIAL BLESSING. This was rare, and it was interpreted as Our Lady's desire to spread this important gift. Those gathered in the Field were surprised and elated because no one expected this gift.

Marija has said:

1. This is a blessing which has the power to convert and to help people.

2. It may be used on believers and non-believers to help them convert or to help them progress in their conversion process.

3. Once Our Lady gives it to you, it lasts your whole life.

4. You do not have to be in the presence of the one you are blessing.

5. You can only give it individually from you to the individual, whereas a priest can bless a crowd. Our Lady's blessing is from one person to the next.

6. If you receive this blessing from Our Lady and in turn bless another with it, that person has it to the same degree you first received it from Our Lady. This second person may then give it to a third, and the third to a fourth, etc. All will receive this gift to bless others just as if Our Lady gave it directly. This blessing will last your entire lifetime.

7. You must be at the site of the apparition to receive it directly from Our Lady.

8. To bless someone, a spontaneous prayer is fine. You can say, *"I extend to you the blessing of Our Lady."* If you choose to say more, it is acceptable. When giving this Special Blessing to a non-believer, a family member, friend, or non-acquaintance, you may do so silently, in his presence or from a distance. You may extend this blessing every day, even several times a day, to help this person to convert.

N.B. The blessing from a priest is Christ's blessing. This Special Blessing is Our Lady's blessing. You should not think of yourself as a priest, blessing as a priest does. Use this blessing in a humble way and extend it to even those you pass individually on the street. The Blessed Mother has given us a great gift, and She desires us to use it.*

November 30, 1988, 10:30 p.m.

Our Lady came and was very happy. She blessed and prayed over everyone. Marija recommended all those present to Our Lady, and She prayed The Lord's Prayer and the Glory Be. Our Lady extended Her arms and prayed in Hebrew over everyone. Her message:

"I wish that all your life be love, only love. Everything that you do, do it with love. In every little thing, see Jesus and His example. You also do as Jesus did. He died out of love for you. You also offer all you do with love to God, even the smallest little things of everyday life."

Then Our Lady made the Sign of the Cross and left saying, **"Go in peace."** All gathered in the Bedroom were awed over hearing this message, and it has become for some their favorite message of all the messages over the course of Our Lady of Medjugorje's apparitions.

December 1, 1988, 10:30 a.m.

Our Lady came and was very happy. With Her hands extended, She prayed over everyone and blessed them. All present, especially the sick, were recommended to Our Lady by Marija, and Our Lady prayed The Lord's Prayer and the Glory Be. Our Lady also blessed the religious objects which were brought to the site. She made the Sign of the Cross and as She returned to

_____

* For more information on Our Lady's Special Blessing, write for the booklet *"A Blessing to Help Save the World"* from Caritas of Birmingham, 100 Our Lady Queen of Peace Drive, Sterrett, Alabama 35147 USA, or call 205-672-2000, ext. 315 24 hrs. This special writing follows the first time Our Lady gave the Special Blessing and includes more details of what Our Lady has said on this extraordinary blessing. You can also order online or download free at mej.com. Do a search for *"A Blessing to Help Save the World."*

Heaven, Our Lady said, **"Go in peace."** No words. Today Our Lady wanted Her presence to be the message.

December 2, 1988, 10:30 p.m.

Our Lady came and was very happy. She prayed over everyone. She smiled and prayed "one by one" over each person present in the room. Marija recommended all those present to Our Lady. She prayed The Lord's Prayer and the Glory Be. The message:

"I invite you to pray and to abandon yourself totally to God."

Our Lady then made the Sign of the Cross and went away saying, **"Go in peace."**

December 3, 1988, 10:30 p.m.

Our Lady came and was very happy. Marija recommended all those present to Our Lady. Marija asked Our Lady if She would pray over each individual as She had done yesterday. Very pleased, Our Lady smiled. She looked at everyone and began to pray over each one individually with Her hands over them. Our Lady prayed The Lord's Prayer and the Glory Be. The message:

"Dear children, I give you my love, so you give it to others."

Marija asked if Our Lady would appear tomorrow in the morning. Our Lady smiled and said:

"Yes, at 10:40 as in Medjugorje."

(The time, 10:40 a.m. Central Time, corresponds to the same moment of the apparition in Medjugorje.)

Then Our Lady made the Sign of the Cross saying, **"Go in peace,"** and She left. Marija's voice was beautiful, gentle, full of love and intensity when she talked about the apparition just after Our Lady left. All felt Our Lady's presence and sensed that She was happy in a special way. Those gathered really felt Our Lady gave them Her love. One witness said he felt as though love permeated even the walls of the Bedroom.

December 4, 1988, 10:40 a.m.

Our Lady came, and She was very happy. Marija recommended all those present to Our Lady, especially the sick. Our Lady prayed over everyone, and She blessed them all. She prayed The Lord's Prayer and the Glory Be. The message:

"I invite you to live the profoundness of the messages that I give."

Our Lady also blessed the objects, and from the Bedroom blessed those gathered at the Tree. She made the Sign of the Cross while leaving saying, **"Go in peace."**

December 5, 1988, 10:40 a.m.

Our Lady came, and She was very happy. Marija recommended all the people present to Her. Our Lady extended Her hands and prayed over everyone and said The Lord's Prayer and the Glory Be. She left saying, **"Go in peace."** No special message.

Marija left to go back to Medjugorje for one week to inform her family and priest about the operation. She returned to the host's home near Sterrett, Alabama on December 12, 1988.

December 13, 1988

When Our Lady appeared, She conveyed to Marija Her desire to start a Community at the site. Marija turned to the host in whose house she was living and said to him immediately after the apparition, *"Our Lady wants to start a Community here."* The husband and wife were deeply struck by these words.

Father Robert Faricy, a Jesuit who wrote several books on Medjugorje, was present during the apparitions on December 13 and 14, 1988. He was amazed and said:

"I visited Marija in Birmingham and prayed with her and the others when Our Lady came to her in the bedroom. Not even in Medjugorje did I feel so strongly Mary's presence as I did during Her apparition to Marija in Birmingham."

December 14, 1988, 10:40 a.m.

"I would like you to pray for my intentions."

She left saying, **"Go in peace."**

December 15, 1988, 10:40 a.m.

"Dear children, I love you and I wish you to pray for my intentions with the love you have for me, so that every plan of God about each one of you may be fulfilled."

This message only intensified in the hearts of those who were present that Our Lady had come to implement a special plan.

Referring to Marija's operation, Our Lady said:

"I will be with you tomorrow."

December 16, 1988

Today Marija underwent surgery after test results showed that she could donate her kidney to her brother, Andrija. During the operation, with Rosary in her hand and while under anesthesia,

Our Lady appeared over Marija while she lay on the operating table. Marija later said Our Lady stayed with her and smiled for what seemed to her about two hours. For the next month, except for Christmas Eve, Our Lady did not speak to Marija. She appeared to her each day at Mass during Communion. Suddenly, on January 15, 1989, Our Lady told Marija that the next day She would again give messages. There was great joy in everyone's hearts.

December 24, 1988, (near midnight) (SPECIAL BLESSING) (The monthly message):

The December 25, 1988 monthly message was actually given on December 24, 1988, near midnight, and extended into Christmas Day. The message:

> **"Dear children, I call you to peace. Live it in your heart and all around you so that all will know peace - peace which does not come from you but from God. Little children, today is a great day! Rejoice with me! Glorify the Nativity of Jesus through the peace that I give. It is for this peace that I have come as your Mother, Queen of Peace. Today I give you my Special Blessing. Bring it to all creation, so that all creation will know peace. Thank you for having responded to my call."**

December 25, 1988, 6:00 p.m.

Our Lady appeared again on Christmas Day during Mass in the loft of the home where Marija was staying. Marija said that Our Lady was robed in gold, holding a living, moving Baby Jesus in Her arms. The same little Jesus who laid in a manger 2000 years ago!!

January 15, 1989

Our Lady appeared to Marija during Communion while Marija

was in the loft attending Mass, which was being celebrated downstairs in the home where she was staying. Our Lady said to Marija:

"Tomorrow, again, I will appear in the Bedroom and give messages."

January 16, 1989

Today Our Lady began to give messages to Marija again. During this apparition Our Lady, with a wonderful smile on Her face, blessed a newborn baby* making a Sign of the Cross in his direction. The message:

"I call every one of you to live the messages I give and to witness by your lives."

January 17, 1989, 5:40 p.m.

"Pray for my intentions. With this prayer, I would like to help each one of you."

January 18, 1989, 5:40 p.m.

"Pray for my intentions."

January 19, 1989, 5:45 p.m.

"I ask you to pray and demand, asking boldly for the graces from me. I will intercede in front of God for you."

---

* In the middle of thousands of people coming to the apparitions, the host's wife where Marija was living gave birth. The sacrifice and trials of daily hosting hundreds of strangers who came into the house was through the last three months of her pregnancy. The period of stopping of the messages was seen as Our Lady's sensitivity to help settle the demands in the house. The mother gave birth to their 4th child two weeks late on the Feast of the Holy Family, December 31, 1988.

January 20, 1989, 5:40 p.m.

No public message; however, Our Lady did give a special private message for someone in the room.

January 21, 1989, 5:40 p.m.

"I am calling you to prayer; only through prayer can you come close to God. I am calling you to pray every day and to dedicate a special time in your day only for prayer."

January 22, 1989, 5:40 p.m.

"I wish you to pray for my intentions. Only in this way can you come closer to God. I will guide you to Him. Pray, dear children, I am with you."

January 23, 1989, 5:40 p.m.

"I would like you to pray for my intentions."

Again, Our Lady gave a private message for the same individual She gave a message to on January 20th.

January 24, 1989

Today Marija was late for the apparition and couldn't get to the home at the appointed time. A local television station had made many requests to set up in the Bedroom. Today they were allowed. As soon as Marija came in the house and saw the television camera, she said, *"This is why Our Lady did not wait until I got home for the apparition."* Our Lady came to her just before arriving at the house, but gave no special message; however, Our Lady did say that She extended Her blessing and received all the intentions of the several thousand people who were present near the tree.

January 25, 1989, 10:40 a.m. (The Monthly Message)

"Dear children, today I am calling you to the way of holiness. Pray that you may comprehend the beauty and the greatness of this way, where God reveals Himself to you in a special way. Pray that you may be open to everything that God does through you so that in your life you may be enabled to give thanks to God and to rejoice over everything that He does through each individual. I give you my blessing. Thank you for your response to my call."

January 26, 1989, 10:40 a.m. - Apparition in the Bedroom

This day ended Our Lady's apparitions for the period of November 1988 through January 1989. The apparition was very intense and emotional. The family that Marija lived with gave everything of themselves for this period and could hardly recite the Rosary, knowing that Our Lady was leaving. Our Lady told them:

"Dear children, I desire that your lives become prayer."

Our Lady ended the apparition with the same message She began them with. November 20, 1988 - Her first words, **"May your life be prayer..."** It was clear, through the 3 months of Her presence, that Our Lady desired something to unfold that She was initiating.

Marija said that Our Lady was always very happy. Marija flew to Italy and convalesced for another two months before returning to Medjugorje.

The Apparitions of February 1 - 3, 1994

February 1, 1994

It was five years before Marija, now with her husband Paolo, came back to the Birmingham area for a private visit with the original host family for a few days in the beginning of February, 1994. There were three apparitions during their visit. The first two were in the bedroom where She appeared most of the time when Marija was here from November, 1988 to January, 1989. The third apparition took place in the Field. On February 1, 1994, Our Lady appeared at 10:45 a.m. Marija, Paolo, and the host family were the only ones present during this apparition. When Our Lady appeared She was very joyful and immediately smiled. She said:

"I am happy to be here."

Those words were of great consolation to the host family. They had undergone serious persecution for the last five years, and Our Lady giving those six words, was a message that made everything worth the trials they suffered for Her plans.

February 2, 1994

Our Lady appeared to Marija at 10:45 a.m. in the Bedroom. She gave no special message. The whole Community was present.

February 3, 1994

Marija came out to the Field to pray the Rosary in preparation for Our Lady's apparition. She knelt in the same spot where Our Lady appeared to her five years before, on November 24, 1988. This was the second apparition out in the Field. Our Lady appeared to Marija at 10:45 a.m. Marija said that Our Lady prayed over everyone and blessed them in a special way. Marija then said Our Lady extended Her arms outward and prayed for a long time. She then extended a second blessing while looking out from over the people. Marija was asked what this second blessing meant. She said that she did not know. She was asked if this is something Our Lady does, and Marija answered, *"Two blessings in one apparition? No! – Rarely!"* Those present felt peace fill the whole valley. Our Lady gave the following message:

"Do not forget that I am your Mother and that I love you. Go in Peace."

The apparition lasted 10 minutes and it was felt Our Lady did something there in the Field and valley, though not completely understood and somewhat of a mystery. It would manifest later in Our Lady using the Bedroom and Field as Her special places for tens of thousands of conversions. It is presently believed Our Lady has placed some kind of seal over the valley and the mission.

The Apparitions of May 1998

Four years passed before Marija returned to Caritas. She came with her family for a private visit, with one public apparition at the end of the week.

May 17, 1998

The founder and his family gathered with Marija's family in the Bedroom at 11:00 a.m. for the apparition. The founder had asked Marija to ask Our Lady to return this evening in the Field when the Community would be coming together for a prayer group meeting. Our Lady nodded "yes". Marija said she had not had two apparitions in one day in many years. It was also a great joy for her.

It was a beautiful spring evening. The Community laid out

blankets around Our Lady's statue as music played and laughing children ran barefoot through the grassy field. They ran to greet Marija and Paolo and their children as they joined the Community in the Field that evening for the apparition. Everyone was excited knowing Our Lady would soon be present. That evening in the Field, the Rosary was prayed and when Our Lady appeared in the apparition, She prayed over everyone and blessed them and then said:

"Do not forget that I am your Mother and that I love you. Go in peace." [see appendix, page 575.]

May 18-19, 1998

On May 18 and 19, Our Lady appeared in the Field at approximately 11:40 a.m. Our Lady prayed over everyone and blessed them. On May 19, the Community had prayed the Patriotic Rosary. It was the first time Marija had heard this prayed. [see appendix, page 575.]

May 20, 1998

Marija, Paolo, the founder and his wife had been on a horseback ride in the mountains above Caritas. They were making their way through the Field towards the statue of Our Lady where the Community members waited to begin praying the Rosary for the apparition. Suddenly the horse Marija was riding was kicked by another horse beside her. Marija received the full force of the kick to her leg. It was a serious injury, and she had to be taken to the emergency room at the hospital, accompanied by her husband and the founder and his wife. As they were driving to the hospital, at 11:40 a.m., Our Lady appeared to Marija in the moving vehicle. Our founder watched Marija's face in the rearview mirror and saw that at the moment of apparition, Marija's face that had been contracted in pain, immediately relaxed and there was no sign that she was feeling any pain during Our Lady's visit. But as soon as Our Lady left, Marija noticeably winced as the sensation of pain returned. The apparition was short. Our Lady prayed over and blessed not only them, but also all the Community in the Field.

May 21, 1998

Miraculously, Marija's leg was not broken, but the injury was still serious, and for the next few days she had to stay off it, which brought the apparitions back to the house. The apparition on this day was in the living room of the house in which only the family was present. Marija sat in a chair with her leg elevated, facing a beautiful picture of Our Lady hanging on the fireplace. It was here that Our Lady appeared. The founder asked Marija to ask Our Lady a question. It was a question that he had asked when Our Lady was present in 1988. At that time, ten years ago, Our Lady responded by saying on January 20, 1989:

"I will inform later."

The founder had not questioned Our Lady concerning this since he first asked Her about it, but felt during this visit, to present the question again. When Our Lady appeared, the apparition was only a few minutes long. Our Lady came, prayed over everyone and blessed them. Our Lady indicated in regard to the question that:

"The time has not yet come."

May 22, 1998

All the wives and mothers of the Community were invited to attend the apparition today. They gathered in the living room where the apparition would again take place. Marija sat in the same chair, everyone faced the fireplace where the picture of Our Lady hung, and prayed the Rosary. At around 11:45 a.m., Our Lady appeared. Marija said that She hesitated for a moment before She prayed over everyone and blessed them. [see appendix, page 575.]

May 23, 1998

Our Lady returned to the Bedroom today. All the husbands and fathers of the Community, as well as the heads of the Single Consecrated men's and women's houses were present. The founder asked Marija to ask Our Lady to pray over everyone individually in the apparition. When Our Lady appeared, She granted the request and placed Her hands over each person individually in prayer. Our Lady gave a message. She said:

"Do not forget that I am your Mother and that I love you."
[see appendix, page 575.]

May 24, 1998

This would be the last apparition of Marija's visit and the only public one. There were 300-400 people present. The apparition took place in the Field. When Our Lady appeared, though She gave no message, Marija said She lovingly looked at each face present in the Field that day. Marija said that Our Lady makes this gesture only rarely, and the look of love on Our Lady's face as She does this always touches Marija deeply. [see appendix, page 575.]

The Apparitions of December 8-13, 1999

Marija Lunetti, one of the six visionaries of Medjugorje, came to be with the Community of Caritas during their annual Five Days of Prayer for the Reconciling of Ourselves, Our Families, and Our Nation Back to God. Our Lady appeared to her every day. Approximately forty to fifty thousand pilgrims moved through and came to all or part of these special five days of prayer. Our Lady did many beautiful things while She was here with them. The following is a description of the apparitions and Our Lady's messages given during these days.

December 8, 1999 Feast of the Immaculate Conception - Two Apparitions the Same Day

Close to five thousand people were present during this apparition which took place in the Field. At the moment of the apparition, Marija separated herself from the crowd and knelt in front of Our Lady's statue. Our Lady appeared to Marija at 10:45 a.m. The following are Marija's own words in describing the apparition:

"When Our Lady appeared, She came all dressed in gold. I recommended each of you and every intention of your hearts. Our Lady extended Her hands over all of us and prayed over us for a long time. I asked Our Lady to bless each and every one of us and to bless all the religious objects that you brought. Our Lady then smiled at all of us and prayed a moment and then She raised Her arm and blessed us with the Sign of the Cross. I then asked Our Lady if She had something that She wanted to tell us. Our Lady then looked at me and smiled and said:

'Do not forget that I am your Mother and that I love you.'

"Our Lady then raised Her hand again (a second time) and blessed us and then left."

During the apparition, Marija had asked Our Lady what time She would appear the following day. Marija told the Community later that Our Lady changed the time of the apparition from the morning to 5:40 p.m. in the evening. This was a sign for them that Our Lady was "running the events there," that She had come with special plans of Her own and had Her own schedule She wished them to follow. Unknown to the Community, Marija had also asked if Our Lady would appear again that evening for a private apparition for the Community. Our Lady said, **"yes, in the home, at a twenty 'til six."** Our Lady appeared to Marija at 5:40 p.m. Our Lady stayed with them for several minutes, a longer apparition than normal. Marija said that Our Lady looked at each of the Community members individually, smiled, blessed them all and then told them the words She had spoken earlier in the day:

"Do not forget that I am your Mother and I love you." [see appendix, page 575.]

December 9, 1999

The Rosary began at 4:30 p.m. out in the Field. There were close to eight thousand people present. The following is Marija's description of the apparition:

*"I would like to describe how Our Lady arrived tonight. She arrived tonight on a cloud like She usually does in Her gray dress, covered with a white veil. Her head was crowned with twelve stars. Tonight Our Lady was happy. She looked at each of us present, and I recommended each and every one of you and all of your intentions. In a very special way, I recommended all of the sick. Then Our Lady extended Her arms and began to pray over us. I asked Our Lady to bless all of us, to bless all of the things we ask to be blessed, and to bless our petitions. Our Lady blessed all of the things, and then She said, '*__Go in peace.__*' At the end, I asked Her, 'What time are you coming tomorrow?' And Our Lady said, '*__At the same time as tonight and in the same place.__*' Then She smiled and left. That is everything."*

December 10, 1999

Our Lady appeared to Marija around 5:40 p.m. tonight out in the Field. The following is Marija's description of the apparition.

"When Our Lady appeared, I recommended everyone and their intentions to Our Lady. She responded by extending

*Her arms and prayed over us for a very long time. Then Our
Lady looked at each of us present. I then asked Our Lady if
She had anything to tell us. Smiling, Our Lady said:*

'Do not forget that I love you.'

*"Then Our Lady blessed us with the Sign of the Cross and
left. Our Lady said that tomorrow's apparition would be at:*

'The same time, same place.'"

December 11, 1999

The fourth day of the five days of prayer was a special Christmas
celebration. Our Lady had told Marija She would be appearing
in the middle of this special event. Every pilgrim was asked to
bring a flower to present before the crib of Jesus to show their
love and commitment to Him. Twelve thousand people came
that night carrying their flowers and their hearts in their hands
to Our Lady. The following is Marija's explanation of Our
Lady's apparition that night in the Field:

*"At the moment when Our Lady arrived tonight, She looked
at each and every one of us. She remained in silence, and I
understood that I was being permitted to be able to recommend all of us. As I began to recommend everyone and all
the intentions that we have in our hearts, Our Lady remained
in silence. Then I began to recommend all of the sick that are
here. And Our Lady remained in silence and watched all of
us still! I kept looking at Our Lady, and I smiled and said,
'Well, I recommend all the little ones and the big ones.' And
Our Lady gave me a big smile in return. Then Our Lady
began to pray over us. After She prayed over us, I felt in my
heart that maybe Our Lady wanted to say something to us.
And so I said, 'Well, do you have something to tell us?' And
Our Lady said:*

'Thank you with all my heart.'"

*"But the thing that I wanted to leave as a surprise for the end
was that Our Lady wasn't alone. She came with three angels.
Our Lady gave us a surprise even though it wasn't Christmas.
She celebrated with us by bringing angels."* [see appendix,
page 575.]

December 12, 1999

Our Lady appeared to Marija around 5:40 p.m. in the Field
among thousands of pilgrims. The following is Marija's description of this apparition.

*"At the moment of the apparition, when Our Lady appeared,
She immediately began praying over us, and She prayed for
a long time. Then I recommended to Our Lady each and
every one of you and all your intentions and in a special way
the sick and all our loved ones who aren't here with us. I
asked Our Lady to bless us and all the objects we carry with
us. Our Lady made the Sign of the Cross and She blessed
all of us."*

Our Lady told Marija that She would appear to her the following morning at 8:00 a.m. for a private apparition with the
Community.

December 13, 1999

The Community gathered in the Bedroom around 7:00 a.m. to
begin praying in preparation for the apparition. As Our Lady
appeared, they could tell by Marija's face this apparition was
special. Marija, throughout this apparition, had a smile on her
face. In ecstasy, Marija's face is always serious. As the apparition ended, Marija's eyes followed Our Lady back to Heaven
for several moments. Marija then broke her constant routine
of always saying the Magnificat and said in English, *"Our Lady*

came with five angels!" She began then to pray the Magnificat as she and all of the Community wept. Following is Marija's description of the apparition:

> *"Our Lady came with **five angels** today! Our Lady prayed over us and blessed us. She looked at each and every one of us."*

After the apparition, the Community asked Marija to describe the angels. She said they were small, like the size of a two-year-old. Two had black hair, two had brown hair, and one had blonde hair. Two were on each side of Our Lady and the blonde haired angel fluttered above Her head. Marija said that they were gazing at Our Lady, never taking their eyes off of Her. Marija also said that never, in all her apparitions, has she seen the angels look away from Our Lady even for a second. [see appendix, page 575.]

The Apparitions of December 10 - 15, 2001

Our Lady again came back with Her apparitions to Marija, visionary of Medjugorje. Marija came to be with the founder and his family at Caritas during their annual Five Days of Prayer for the Reconciling of Ourselves, Our Families, and Our Nation back to God. All those who participated had beautiful days with Our Lady. Marija described Our Lady as being very happy and joyful during Her apparitions. The following is a description of the apparitions of Our Lady and Our Lady's messages given during these days.

December 10, 2001

Marija arrived on Monday evening, December 10th. She had already had her regular apparition on the plane flying over from Italy, but she surprised the founder by saying Our Lady would appear a second time that evening for an apparition in the Bedroom. His family and the Community were delighted and overjoyed knowing Our Lady would appear a second time in the same day. They gathered in the Bedroom and began to pray. Suddenly, at 8:00 p.m., Our Lady appeared to Marija. She came happy and joyful. Marija recommended each one present and all their intentions to Our Lady. Our Lady began to pray over all, continuing to do so for a long time. Marija said that Our Lady lovingly looked at each and every face in the room. She blessed them and then ascended back up into Heaven. Our Lady told Marija that She would appear the next day at 5:40 p.m.

December 11, 2001

The following is Marija's description of what took place during the apparition on December 11, 2001, at 5:40 p.m.:

"At the moment of the apparition, when Our Lady appeared, I recommended each and every one of you, and all the intentions you have carried in your heart. In a special way I recommended all the sick. And Our Lady, when She came, She put Her arms out, extended them over the crowd, and prayed for a long time over all of us. And then Marija asked Our Lady to bless all the objects that we brought with us to be blessed. And Our Lady again extended Her hand and made the Sign of the Cross above us all and above our objects. And then She said, 'Go in peace.' And in this way She left."

During the apparition, Marija asked Our Lady to bless 50,000 containers of salt in the print shop of the *Tabernacle of Our Lady's Messages*. This was a special project the Founder had worked on for several months. Marija relayed that during the apparition, Our Lady extended, for a second time, a blessing especially for this. When Marija was asked before the group if Our Lady blessed the salt, she said emphatically, *"There can be no question."*

December 12, 2001

The following is Marija's description of the apparition of December 12, 2001, in the Field:

"When Our Lady came tonight, I recommended all those present here and all of our intentions that we have in our hearts. And Our Lady began to pray over us, but She didn't pray a long time. Today is the Feast Day of Our Lady of Guadalupe. I don't know why Our Lady only stayed for a short time, maybe She had to get back to the feast in Mexico or maybe because it is raining. Anyway, Our Lady blessed us tonight. And She looked at each and every one of us and was happy. And She said:

'Go in peace. We will see each other tomorrow, at the same time, at the same place.'"

December 13, 2001

The following is Marija's explanation of what took place during her apparition on December 13, 2001, during the Christmas in the Field celebration:

"At the moment of apparition, when Our Lady appeared, I recommended each and every one of us and all of our intentions. And Our Lady extended Her hands over us, and She prayed over us for a long time. Then I asked Our Lady to bless us and all the objects that we brought with us. Our Lady blessed us and blessed the objects. And then Our Lady remained a little time with us, and I asked Her if She had something to say to us. And after I asked Her this question, Our Lady smiled and She said:

'Do not forget that I am your Mother, and I love you.'

"Then Our Lady made the Sign of the Cross and left."

December 14, 2001

The following is Marija's description of the apparition of December 14, 2001 in the Field:

"When Our Lady appeared today, I prayed for each of you and asked Our Lady to bless us and to hear our intentions. In a special way, I prayed for all the sick. Our Lady extended Her hands over the crowds, and She prayed a long time over us. Then I asked Our Lady if She had something to tell us. Our Lady smiled and said:

'Live my messages.'

"And then She blessed us, and She left saying, **'Go in peace.'** *And She left with a smile on Her lips."*

December 15, 2001

Marija left on this day to go back to Italy to her family. The founder of Caritas asked Our Lady through Marija during her apparition on December 14th, if She would appear early on Saturday so that the Community could be present for one more apparition and receive Her blessing once more. Our Lady said, **"Yes."** The Community began to gather in the Bedroom at 6:30 a.m. Our Lady appeared to Marija at precisely 8:00 a.m. The following is Marija's description of this apparition on Saturday, December 15, 2001:

"When Our Lady came, I recommended each of us and all our intentions in our hearts. Our Lady prayed over us for a long time. I presented a private question to Our Lady. Immediately upon asking the question, Our Lady smiled and gave a private answer. Our Lady looked at each of us and then blessed us. She ascended back to Heaven, saying, **'Go in peace.'** *Our Lady was very happy and joyful during this apparition."*

The private question from the founder was related to something that Our Lady had spoken to him about fourteen years before through Marija. Through the years he had asked Our Lady on several occasions, never receiving an affirmative message. He, along with the Community, was very happy that in this apparition Our Lady gave light of an affirmation to him. [see appendix, page 575.]

The Apparitions of August 8 - 25, 2003

Paolo, Marija and their four boys returned to Caritas for a personal visit and a time of rest and vacation. They arrived on August 7 to Birmingham, Our Lady appeared at Caritas on August 8, and then a week at a secluded Florida beach was planned with the Community from August 9-15. The following week they returned to Caritas.

August 8, 2003

The first apparition of Marija's visit took place in the Bedroom at 11:44 a.m. Our founder, who was present with his family and Marija's family, asked Marija to ask Our Lady two questions. The first, if She would come again this evening in the Field, so that the Community could be present (who were all gathered in the Field during this apparition) and secondly, if She would appear in the evenings, as She does in Medjugorje, rather than in the mornings.

After the apparition, Marija said that on both occasions when Our Lady was asked these questions, She smiled and agreed, by giving a nod "yes," both times. She agreed to return again this evening in the Field, and She agreed to have Her apparitions in the evenings. Marija said Our Lady was happy throughout the apparition.

In the evening, Our Lady appeared in the Field, at 6:40 p.m., in the presence of all the Caritas Community. Marija said:

"Our Lady came. She pray over us and She blessed us."

August 9, 2003

Early this morning the Community with Paolo and Marija's family, left for Florida. Realizing that they would not make the beach house in time for the apparition, they pulled off on the side of the road, climbed over a rock barrier, knelt down in the sand as they took in their first site of the ocean, and began to pray the Rosary. Just before Marija went into ecstasy, the founder leaned over to ask Marija to ask Our Lady exactly what time the apparition would be each day. When Marija asked Our Lady this question, Our Lady smiled and gave the following message:

"Because it is your vacation, I will come whenever you pray."

Everyone was stunned by this message. Being given the ability to have the apparition at their choosing made for a beautiful week in which each apparition was prepared for in a special way so that their hearts were fully prepared to receive Our Lady each time.

August 10, 2003

The Community worked the next day setting up an altar for Our Lady. They had brought a large statue of Our Lady with them and set it upon a table that overlooked the ocean. The apparition on this day took place at 3:35 p.m. Our Lady prayed over everyone and blessed them. Our Lady continued to appear each day in the house at the time the Community prepared for the apparition in prayer. [see appendix, page 575.]

August 11, 2003

The apparition did not take place until after dinner. Even though it was late, the Rosary was peaceful, and the prayer was felt deeply. The apparition was longer than normal. Marija said afterwards that Our Lady had prayed a long time over everyone, praying the whole time, until She ended the apparition with Her blessing. [see appendix, page 575.]

August 12, 2003

This was another late night apparition. The Rosary began around 9:35 p.m. It was, again, peaceful and prayer was deep. There has been a strong feeling of the presence of Our Lady each evening. In the apparition tonight, Our Lady prayed over everyone and blessed them. [see appendix, page 575.]

August 13, 2003

As the altar was being prepared today, the founder suggested everyone write out petitions to Our Lady. He then asked Marija if they could present their petitions to Our Lady "during" the apparition. Marija agreed. When Marija went into ecstasy that evening, one by one, each person carried their petition up to Our Lady and dropped it into a small sailboat canister. It took several minutes for all of them to do so. All during this time, Marija gazed silently at Our Lady. When Marija came out of ecstasy she told us what had happened:

> *"The moment of apparition, I recommend all of us and our intentions and Our Lady pray over us and I recommend our special letters and Our Lady smiled and She said:*

> **'I wish to give you graces. Ask for them.'"**

Having just spent nearly an hour writing down all their petitions, they were in awe of Our Lady's word. [see appendix, page 575.]

August 14, 2003

The apparition took place later in the afternoon. The Community gathered around 4:00 p.m. to pray the Rosary. When Our Lady came, Marija particularly recommended a couple on their wedding anniversary to Our Lady. Marija said Our Lady prayed over everyone and blessed them. [see appendix, page 575.]

August 15, 2003

Today was the Feast of Our Lady's Assumption into Heaven. It was also the last day of the Community's stay in Florida. Tomorrow they would return to Caritas. Still very moved by Our Lady's message two days ago, the founder suggested that they again write out their petitions and with Marija's approval, present them to Our Lady during the apparition. Our Lady continued to stay until the last petition was placed at Her feet. When Marija came out of ecstasy, she let out a happy sigh, then after pausing slightly, she said:

"Our Lady came with angels...thousands of angels."

Marija went on to describe what she had seen. She initially said hundreds of angels, but later with her husband translating, she qualified that it was countless, thousands of angels. The angels were all baby angels. They were wearing something like roman tunics all in pastel colors. They were all behind Our Lady, not far in distance. When Marija was asked what the angels were looking at, Marija replied, *"At us."* This surprised the Community because Marija said the angels, when appearing with Our Lady, always stare only at Our Lady (refer to the December 13, 1999 message on page 445). The apparition was shorter today, two and a half minutes, but Marija said that always on feast days the apparitions are shorter. Marija thinks it's because Our Lady must get back to Heaven for the celebration. The Community ended their "vacation" with much to ponder and be thankful for. When they returned home, on August 16, Our Lady imme-

diately returned to Her normal apparition time. The apparitions
returned to the Bedroom. Our Lady continued to appear each
day, praying over all those gathered and giving them Her blessing.

August 18, 2003

Today's apparition was longer than usual. The Community gathered at 6:00 p.m. in the Bedroom. Our Lady appeared around
the normal time of 6:40 p.m. Marija said of the apparition:

> *"Our Lady pray over us, and She blessed us. She pray long
> time over us."*

Marija was then asked if the apparition was long for her today
because it was long for those gathered. She said:

> *"All the time She pray over us."*

August 19, 2003

The founder of Caritas arranged to have several tractor-trailer
rigs of salt delivered to the *Tabernacle of Our Lady's Messages*,
with the hope that Our Lady would bless the salt as She had
done in the apparitions at Caritas in December of 2001, with
the first loads of salt. This would be the first apparition in the
Tabernacle of Our Lady's Messages, and though the salt was on
the first floor, where the print shop is located, the Community
desired to have the apparition in the writing office of their
founder, where all the writings concerning Our Lady's messages
take place. The Community met at 6:00 p.m. to begin the Rosary,
with Marija and Paolo joining them. Marija said:

> *"Our Lady blessed us, and She prayed over us."*

Marija asked Our Lady to bless the salt during the apparition.
Marija said:

*"Our Lady bless also, I ask for all salt, on first floor...She
bless, She make sign of cross...I recommend all of our intentions and what we have in our hearts, and I ask to bless all salt
together. She make little prayer over us, and after She bless."*
[see appendix, page 575.]

August 21, 2003

This was the only public apparition during Marija's visit. It was
a very hot, humid evening, with record-breaking heat. The air
was still, the heat suffocating. As the third Rosary began, a large
storm cloud covered the sun. At the same time, a strong, cool
wind began to blow, and continued all through the Rosary up
to apparition time refreshing everyone. Marija described what
happened in the apparition:

*"The moment of apparition, I recommend all of our inten-
tions, all that we have in our hearts. And Our Lady pray over
us. And I ask also that She bless all objects that we have here.
And Our Lady after praying, She blessed all objects with the
Sign of the Cross, and I recommend in a special way all these
people who are here and in a special way all sick people and
Our Lady one other time, She open Her hands and She begin
to pray, and She pray five minute, I don't know (a long time).
And after She give blessing like Sign of the Cross, and She say
'Go in peace,' and She leave. Today Our Lady is tranquil,
and She watch all of us."*

When Our Lady "watches all of us," She actually scans the
crowd, looking at each face. Marija says it is a very endearing
grace as it shows that each face is dear to Her. [see appendix,
page 575.]

August 25, 2003

Paolo, Marija and their children would be returning to Italy
today. The apparition took place in Atlanta, from where they

would be leaving. Today, also, Our Lady would give the monthly message to the world before their flight home. The founder and his family were present for the apparition.

The Community back home was made aware of when the apparition would be. They went to the Field early to pray in preparation for Our Lady's words. When Marija knelt down, she said, *"Let's ask for a beautiful message today."* The apparition lasted 4 ½ minutes. The message:

August 25, 2003 — Monthly Message to the World

"Dear children! Also today I call you to give thanks to God in your heart for all the graces which He gives you, also through the signs and colors that are in nature. God wants to draw you closer to Himself and moves you to give Him glory and thanks. Therefore, little children, I call you anew to pray, pray, pray and do not forget that I am with you. I intercede before God for each of you until your joy in Him is complete. Thank you for having responded to my call." [see appendix, page 575.]

The Apparitions of April 30 to May 6, 2004

April 30, 2004

Marija had arrived, with her youngest son, Giovanni, for five days with Our Lady held at Caritas in which thousands of pilgrims were expected, May 1-5, 2004. This evening, the Community gathered in the Bedroom to greet and welcome Our Lady in the apparition. Marija said:

"Today when Our Lady came She prayed over all of us and blessed us all. I asked Her about tomorrow and Our Lady answered:

'Tomorrow morning, here, and the day after in the after-noon in the Field by the Tree.'

"She blessed us all and left." [see appendix, page 575.]

May 1, 2004

Our Lady had said that today's apparition would be in the Bedroom this morning, so as the pilgrims gathered in the Field, many of the Community members were gathered in the Bedroom. Our Lady appeared around 11:40 a.m. Marija told them that Our Lady prayed over everyone and blessed them. She said that she recommended everyone's intentions and all that they have in their hearts. She also asked Our Lady to bless all the pilgrims in the Field. Our Lady responded to that request by blessing them with the Sign of the Cross.

May 2, 2004

The apparition was in the evening in the Field just as Our Lady requested. The apparition took place around 6:40 p.m. The following is Marija's description of the apparition:

"Everybody sit down. I wanted to greet each and every one of you that are here tonight and have come to be with us. Tonight, when Our Lady came, She was very happy and probably because She saw all of you here. And when you prayed, Our Lady listened to you. I recommended each one of you and everything that you held in your heart. Our Lady prayed over us and She gave us Her blessing. In a special way I asked Our Lady to pray for those who are sick here. And Our Lady gave us a second blessing. And then I asked Our Lady to bless everything that you brought with you, your rosaries, your medals and anything else that you wanted blessed, and Our Lady, again, blessed everything. And then at the end, Our Lady spoke, and She said:

'My dear children, do not forget that I am your Mother, and that I love you, and that I bless you.'

"And then She went back to Heaven...unfortunately. It would be a real joy for us to always remain with Our Lady."

For tomorrow, Our Lady said the apparition would be in the Bedroom in the morning. [see appendix, page 575.]

May 3, 2004

Today there were several priests present for the apparition in the Bedroom, along with a few pilgrims and the Community. Marija's description follows:

"Our Lady blessed us and prayed over us. And I recommend all our intentions and Our Lady blessed one other time. I ask Our Lady to bless us and all those in the Field. She pray over us a long time."

Marija said that Our Lady, once again, requested the apparition to be in the Bedroom tomorrow, **"Same time. Same place."**

May 4, 2004

In yesterday's apparition, Our Lady said the apparition would be in the Bedroom again, in the morning. Today there were other pilgrims along with several priests with the Community who were present for the apparition. Marija's description of the apparition:

"The moment of the apparition Our Lady came. I recommend all our intention. And Our Lady pray over us and She bless us all. She bless also all objects for blessing. Also Our Lady pray and bless also people who is in Field. She blessed two times. One for religious objects, one for people present. Our Lady said:

'Same time. Same place.'" [see appendix, page 575.]

May 5, 2004

Most of the Community was in the Field praying the Patriotic Rosary with the pilgrims. Concerning the apparition, Marija said:

> *"Our Lady blessed us all. She prayed over us. She blessed all those in the Field. I ask in special way bless also those in Field and all the objects. Two blessings."* (objects and people). [see appendix, page 575.]

May 6, 2004

Marija had asked Our Lady to come early this morning, as she had to immediately leave for the airport after the apparition. Our Lady agreed. The Community gathered at 7:00 a.m. to begin praying the Rosary to prepare for the apparition at 8:00 a.m. The founder had a special request to make of Our Lady. As the Community and mission were experiencing heavy persecution, he asked Marija to ask Our Lady for words that would help them to endure any attack that would come, especially in light of all the conversions that had just taken place through the apparitions these last five days. Marija's description of the apparition:

> *"Our Lady came and I recommended all of us, and She prayed over all of us who were present. She blessed all religious articles with a Sign of the Cross and in the end She gave a message* (in regards to the question asked):

'I give you my love. You give it to others.'

> *"And She left with a smile on Her face."* [see appendix, page 575.]

The Apparitions of July 20 - August 8, 2005

Marija and her family returned to Caritas to spend a week of rest before the five days of prayer, August 1-5, in which thousands of pilgrims would return not only to be with Our Lady, but for the added joy of celebrating Our Lady's birthday with Her, on August 5th. Marija arrived on July 19th with her four boys, Michele, Francesco, Marco and Giovanni. Marija's husband, Paolo, would be arriving the following week.

July 20, 2005

The first apparition of Marija's visit was with the founder's family while they were out of town. Marija said:

"Our Lady blessed us and prayed over us with hands extended. Our Lady said apparition tomorrow would be the same time."

Our Lady didn't say where the apparition would be because no plans had been made yet for the next day. As it turned out, the apparition would be in the Bedroom with the Caritas Community gathered together to welcome Our Lady back.

July 21, 2005

Our Lady gave the Community a very special grace upon Her return to their home. When Marija and her boys arrived, the Community had just enough time to say hello, when it was time to prepare for the apparition. Our Lady came at about 6:40 p.m. Marija said:

"I said to Our Lady, welcome here. Our Lady is smiling and She pray over us and give to us Her Special Blessing. She pray before, and after She give Special Blessing. She smiling."

Our Lady's smile and the gift of Her Special Blessing caused all those gathered to be happy and in smiles too. [see appendix, page 575.]

July 22-24, 2005

Each evening the apparition was in the Bedroom. Our Lady continued to bless and pray over everyone gathered.

July 25, 2005

Today Our Lady gave Her monthly message to the world, a big joy for the Community to receive that grace here, in the Bedroom. Also the message was a consolation as they had just before finished a nine day bread and water fasting novena.

> **"Dear children! Also today, I call you to fill your day with short and ardent prayers. When you pray, your heart is open and God loves you with a special love and gives you special graces. Therefore, make good use of this time of grace and devote it to God more than ever up to now. Do novenas of fasting and renunciation so that satan be far from you and grace be around you. I am near you and intercede before God for each of you. Thank you for having responded to my call."**

July 26-30, 2005

The apparitions continued to be in the Bedroom, and Our Lady prayed over and blessed everyone each day.

July 31, 2005

The apparition this evening was in the living room of the founder's home. This would be the last private apparition before the apparitions would be opened up to the public for five days of prayer in preparation for Our Lady's birthday, August 5th.

After praying the Rosary, Marija went into ecstasy, as normal, but half way through everyone in the room knew something special was taking place. Marija, still in ecstasy, began to pray out loud, the Our Father and Glory Be. We knew she was praying with Our Lady in the apparition. The apparition lasted almost six minutes—a very long time for an apparition. By the time the apparition ended, everyone was excited to hear what had taken place. Marija, herself was excited, and began to describe the apparition:

"One special gift today when Our Lady come. She pray over all, one by one. I don't know how long apparition was today? Very Long! Our Lady said to pray Our Father and Glory Be for Her intentions. I ask also for all those in Field. Our Lady said apparition, **'will be in the Field tomorrow, same time.'"**
[see appendix, page 575.]

August 1-5, 2005 Apparitions
In Preparation of Our Lady's Birthday

August 1, 2005 - Monday

Today was the first day of the five days of prayer with Our Lady. Pilgrims joined the Community in praying three Hail Mary's on the top of each hour, offering a nine-hour novena each day for Our Lady's intentions for Her birthday. The apparition was in the evening in the presence of thousands in the Field. Marija described what took place in the apparition:

"The moment Our Lady came, I recommend all our intentions, all what we have in our hearts. Our Lady prayed over us and She blessed us all. And I ask also for blessing of letters (petitions) that we have here, intentions, and objects for blessing and Our Lady smiling while She blessed and She said, **'Go in peace.'"**

When Marija asked about the apparition tomorrow, August 2nd, Our Lady said:

"Same time. Same place." [see appendix, page 575.]

August 2, 2005 - Tuesday

The apparition was in the Field, in the evening. Our Lady appeared at 6:45 p.m. Marija said:

"In the moment of the apparition, when Our Lady came, I recommended all of you, all your intentions. And Our Lady prayed over us, and She blessed us all."

When Marija asked about the apparition for tomorrow, August 3rd, Our Lady said:

"Same time. Same place."

August 3, 2005 - Wednesday

Just as on the previous two days, the nine-hour novena continued to be prayed by the Community and pilgrims for Our Lady's intentions for Her birthday. The apparition was in the Field, in the evening. Our Lady appeared at 6:41 p.m. Marija said:

"At the moment when Our Lady came, like always, I recommend to Our Lady all our intentions, all what we have in our hearts. Our Lady extended Her hands and prayed over us. I then asked Her to bless all objects with Her blessing. And Our Lady blessed. And I asked Our Lady for tomorrow, and Our Lady said:

'Same time. Same place.'"

August 4, 2005 - Thursday - Mary's Eve

This night was the eve of Our Lady's birthday. Our Lady appeared at 6:46 p.m. The apparition was in the Field. Marija said:

> *"In the moment of apparition, when Our Lady came, I recommend to Our Lady all our intentions. Our Lady prayed over us for a long time. After, I asked Our Lady to bless us and to bless all objects that we have with us. And Our Lady, with the Sign of the Cross, blessed all of us and our objects. And I asked about (tomorrow's) apparition, and Our Lady said,*

> **'Same time, same place.'**

> *"And Our Lady always says,* **'Go in peace.'"**

After the apparition, the pilgrims were asked to leave the Field. A very special event was planned for the evening. A special house had been built to represent the house of St. Joachim and St. Anne, Mary's parents, and brought to the Field. Two thousand twenty-one candles, one for every year of Our Lady existence were lit inside. On a back wall of the house was an enlarged antique picture depicting Mary's birth, lit up with the candles. That night, pilgrims knelt before the image of Our Lady as a tiny baby, enraptured by the re-creation of that moment of Her creation.

A special Rosary had been written for this night, called the Mysteries of Mary. The 3rd Mystery of Mary spoke of a tremendous storm that suddenly descended just moments before She was born.

Though it was August, it felt like Christmas. Those present sensed they were partaking in something mystical. Indeed, it was the first public celebration of the Eve of Mary ever held on August 4, in the history of the world. Our Lady, for the past four days was strangely silent, only saying **"Same time. Same place."**

But after the birthday apparition the next day, August 5, 2005, it became plainly evident that Our Lady was creating a craving, an anticipation in their hearts for Her words or action, that on Her birthday She would more than satisfy them. [see appendix, page 575.]

August 5, 2005 - Friday - Mary's Birthday

Great anticipation was felt as pilgrims entered the Field that evening. The sky was partly cloudy, but also blue patches were scattered and the sun was shining. There was no rain. All those in the Field gathered around Our Lady's Nativity to begin praying the Rosary.

Rapidly, after beginning the Rosary with clear skies, the weather began changing. The wind picked up, gray clouds began to roll in, and thunder could be heard in the far distance. As each decade was prayed, the thunder became louder, lightning began appearing and rain could be heard and seen in the distance, but heading toward the crowd in the Field. The nearer to apparition time, the more severe the weather became. As Marija and her husband made their way up to Our Lady's little house for the apparition, the storm suddenly broke out in full fury. Thunder so loud it shook the ground, lightning cracking down all around, torrential rain and wind pouring down so hard that umbrellas were useless, and then, amazingly, hail began pounding down on people in the open Field, where a lone pine tree reached up in the sky, where lightning bolts were everywhere.

Yet the reaction of all those who were present was of wonder, awe and yes, joy...because there was a realization that God was allowing a recreation of Our Lady's birth in the storm that we were experiencing, just as we heard the night before in the 3rd Marian Mystery, when Our Lady was born. As the word "hail" was said, beginning the 'Hail Holy Queen', hail began falling upon the people! No one left the Field. Many were laughing out loud with pure joy, even while being pelted with hail. The prayers had to be shouted to be heard above the storm, and then just at the exact moment Marija went into ecstasy, a lightning bolt struck, coming out of the sky exactly down to the point where Our Lady appeared, just over the little house, so loud and so bright, yet without causing any harm. Our Lady appeared at 6:48 p.m. The apparition lasted nearly four minutes. Marija's description of the apparition follows:

"When Our Lady came I recommended all of us and all our intentions. Our Lady prayed over us for a long time, and She blessed us with Her Special Motherly blessing. Our Lady came with a gold dress, and there were three angels around Her. Then She said:

'Dear children! Do not forget that I am your Mother and I love you.'"

Marija relayed Our Lady then said:

"I thank you for your novenas."

Then Our Lady gave the final blessing and said:

"Go in peace." [see appendix, page 575.]

August 6, 2005 - Saturday

The apparition was in the Bedroom this evening. Marija said it was a short apparition today,

"She come, She pray over us, and She go. Tomorrow:

'Same time, same place.'"

August 7, 2005 - Sunday

A surprise awaited all the Community who gathered in the Bedroom for the apparition this evening. One of the young couples of the Community became engaged. A big deep joy filled the room as the Rosary began. Marija asked Our Lady to bless the couple, which Our Lady did by making the Sign of the Cross. Marija said,

"I recommend all our intentions. Our Lady begin to pray over everyone. I make special recommendation of these two. Our Lady make sign of cross. She was tranquil today. Apparition tomorrow at 8:00 a.m."

August 8, 2005 - Monday

Caritas had chartered a plane to fly to Medjugorje with 200 pilgrims leaving today. The pilgrimage was titled "Birth to Assumption Pilgrimage" and invited people to come to Caritas to celebrate Our Lady's birthday, and then to pilgrimage to Medjugorje to celebrate Our Lady's Assumption. For this reason, Our Lady appeared early this morning. The Community gathered at 7:00 a.m. to begin the Rosary. Marija said:

"Our Lady blessed us and prayed over us. And I asked Our Lady to bless those in the Field. Our Lady make sign of cross (in response to Marija's request).*"*

The Apparitions of November 24 - 25, 2005

November 24, 2005 - Thursday, Thanksgiving Day

Marija returned to Caritas for a very short visit in November 2005. Thanksgiving Day is a feast day celebrated in the Community, not only because of what that day is for our Nation, but because it marks the very first time Our Lady appeared and blessed the people in the Field. It was Our Lady who chose November 24, 1988, Thanksgiving Day, to be Her first apparition in the Field. In this year of 2005, Thanksgiving Day fell on the exact date of this apparition, 17 years ago.

The Community had much to reflect upon in this Rosary, and much to be thankful for, especially this day when Our Lady was with them to celebrate. The apparition took place at the normal time of 10:40 a.m. Marija said:

"Our Lady prayed over us, and She blessed us."

Our Lady was strong in the wind today. [see appendix, page 575.]

November 25, 2005 - Friday

Another big grace awaited the Community during Marija's short visit. They were in the presence of Our Lady when She gave the November monthly message to the world through Marija. The apparition took place in the Bedroom. The apparition lasted 4 minutes, 28 seconds. These were the words Our Lady gave on this day:

"Dear children! Also today I call you to pray, pray, pray until prayer becomes life for you. Little children, at this time, in a special way, I pray before God to give you the gift of faith. Only in faith will you discover the joy of the gift of life that God has given you. Your heart will be joyful thinking of eternity. I am with you and love you with a tender love. Thank you for having responded to my call." [see appendix, page 575.]

The Apparitions of July 1-21, 2008

Marija arrived in the United States on Saturday, June 28, 2008. The Five Days of Prayer, July 1-5, with visionary Marija Lunetti, was a solemn event in which thousands of pilgrims from all 50 states came together to be with Our Lady. The purpose of the gathering was to formally make a solemn act of consecration of the United States of America on July 4th, the birthday of our Nation, to the Hearts of Jesus and Mary.

June 29, 2008

Our Lady appeared to Marija in the Bedroom at 11:40 a.m. The Community of Caritas was present. After the apparition, Marija told the Community that Our Lady did something special. She started on one side of the room and slowly looked at every face present before Her, scanning the entire room of faces, finishing at the other side of the Bedroom. As if She was marking each face in the Community, Marija said Our Lady moved Her head to peer around those who were blocked by other Community members as if to show or emphasize how each one is important to Her. In response to Marija's question about the apparition the next day, Monday June 30th, Our Lady responded that the apparition would be **"Same time, same place."**

June 30, 2008

The apparition today was in the Bedroom at 11:40 a.m. There were already many pilgrims who had arrived for the July 1-5 events and were praying in the Field during the time of the apparition. Marija asked Our Lady to bless them. At this request, Our Lady turned towards the Field and extended Her hand in a blessing. Marija asked Our Lady about the apparition tomorrow, and Our Lady responded again, **"Same time, same place."**

July 1, 2008 - Day of Repentance and Seeking Forgiveness

More than 35 pilgrims were randomly chosen to attend today's apparition in the Bedroom, while the Community joined all the other pilgrims in the Field. Marija asked everyone to kneel down and pray in preparation for the apparition. She said to pray for all those who are not here, for those who are in the Field, as well as those we recommend in our prayers and in our hearts. In a special way, she prayed for all sick people. The following is Marija's description of today's apparition:

"In moment of apparition, when Our Lady came, I recommended to Our Lady our intentions. Our Lady prayed over

us, and She blessed us all. I recommended also all religious objects to be blessed. Also, people who are in the Field. And Our Lady blessed also all the people there."

Marija asked Our Lady where and when the apparition would be the following day on July 2. Our Lady responded, **"Same time, same place."** [see appendix, page 575.]

July 2, 2008 - Day of Individual Consecrations

Today's apparition was in the Bedroom at 11:40 a.m. It was on this day that all those present made an individual consecration to the Hearts of Jesus and Mary.

In the midst of about 50 people, kneeling tightly in the Bedroom, Our Lady appeared to Marija over the Bed. The apparition lasted almost three minutes. The following is Marija's description of the apparition:

"In the moment of the apparition, when Our Lady came, I recommended, like always, all of your intentions. Our Lady prayed over all of us, and She blessed us all. I recommended all the sick people, and in a special way I asked also to bless all religious objects, and all the people who are there in the Field. Our Lady then prayed over everyone for a short time, and She made the Sign of the Cross in a blessing. And I asked Our Lady for tomorrow. I said tomorrow is a special day, the Vigil for the 4th, and Our Lady smiling, said that the apparition would be at 10:00 at night in the Field." (Immediately upon hearing this, several in the room wanted Marija to repeat what she had just said as they were shocked to hear Our Lady's choice for a vigil apparition in anticipation of honoring God for the birth of our Nation on the 4th of July.) *"She said, not here, but in the Field, tomorrow night, 10:00 p.m. Our Lady said* [the apparition is] *for everybody. These days Our Lady appears always here (in the Bedroom), saying* **'Same time, same place.'** *And I think all other people are a little bit jealous of us. So thank God. So not two times will*

*there be an apparition, but only tomorrow night, in the Field
for everybody. You go out now and tell everyone this beautiful news. And God bless you all."* [see appendix, page 575.]

July 3, 2008 - Day for Consecration of Our Families

Prayer for tonight's vigil began around 8:00 p.m. When Our
Lady appeared, Marija's face was intense during the long apparition that lasted more than eight minutes. Afterwards, Marija
surprised the thousands gathered in the Field by saying for the
July 4th apparition, Our Lady again said She would appear in the
Field at 10:00 p.m. Knowing that this was something out of the
ordinary, and feeling that Our Lady was giving everyone another
day to spend in prayer for our Nation's conversion, joy swept
through the crowd. Marija then asked the pilgrims, *"Would you
rather sleep or would you rather pray?"* and then she said, *"I
think we must pray very much in these next 24 hours for your
nation."* Marija stayed in the Field until well after midnight with
everyone who wanted to stay, praying the Our Father, Hail Mary
and Glory Be over and over again, with songs sung intermittently. [see appendix, page 575.]

July 4, 2008 - Consecration of Our Nation

Prayer in preparation for the apparition began around 8:00 p.m.
Just moments before Our Lady's apparition, everyone together
prayed the Solemn Consecration of Our Nation to Our Lady.
Marija then began to pray the seven Our Father's, Hail Mary's,
and Glory Be's and suddenly Our Lady appeared. Marija's face
was serious throughout the apparition that lasted for five minutes. At the end of the apparition, Marija said that Our Lady had
come with three angels tonight. She prayed over everyone present, blessed them and blessed all their religious articles. Marija
recommended all those present and in a special way all the sick.
Our Lady gave the following message:

**"Thank you for all your prayers, be my extended hands in
this peaceless world."**

Our Lady said, **"Tomorrow's apparition will be in the Bedroom at 11:40 a.m."** And Our Lady finished, saying, **"Go in peace."** [see appendix, page 575.]

July 5, 2008 - A Day of Thanksgiving

The apparition was in the Bedroom today with just the Community of Caritas present. There were several thousand pilgrims gathered in the Field, praying the Rosary in unison with the Community present in the Bedroom. Before the apparition began, the founder asked Marija to ask Our Lady if it would be possible for Her to give Her Motherly Special Blessing to all those gathered in the Field. Our Lady appeared in the Bedroom of the Apparitions at 11:48 a.m. The apparition lasted three minutes. The following is Marija's description of the apparition:

"Our Lady blessed us all. Our Lady prayed over us, and She blessed us. She also blessed all those gathered in the Field. She also blessed all of our religious articles. I recommended all of our intentions, especially I recommended all the sick people. And afterwards I said, 'Terry asked me about the Special Blessing.' Our Lady smiled and said:

'Today I give you my Motherly blessing, take it to your homes, to your families.'"

Everyone was thrilled, in awe and moved that Our Lady gave Her Special Blessing.

July 6, 2008

The apparition took place in the Bedroom. It was a special apparition for the Community as beforehand, it was announced that one of the young couples in the Community had just become engaged to be married, just moments before the Rosary. The following is Marija's description of the apparition:

"When Our Lady appeared, I recommended everyone to Our Lady and their intentions. In a special way, I recommended this young couple. Before giving Her blessing, Our Lady looked at the couple and smiled and then blessed everyone in the Bedroom. Our Lady also blessed all the pilgrims in the Field."

When Marija asked Our Lady where and when the apparition would be the following day, Our Lady said it would be in the Bedroom at 10:00 p.m. Everyone was surprised at Her actions of appearing July 7th, also at 10:00 p.m. [see appendix, page 575.]

July 7, 2008

The Rosary began at 9:00 p.m. Just before 10:00 p.m., Our Lady appeared to Marija in the Bedroom. Our Lady prayed over everyone and blessed them. Our Lady also blessed everyone in the Field. When Marija asked about tomorrow's apparition, Our Lady said, **"Same time, same place,"** in the Bedroom at 10:00 p.m. [see appendix, page 575.]

July 8, 2008

It was a beautiful, star-filled night for the crowd who had gathered for Our Lady's apparition. Light from the half-moon flooded the Field, giving enough light to see the surrounding pilgrims that circled Our Lady's statue. When the Rosary began at 9:00 p.m., everyone knelt and faced the house where Our Lady would appear. Just before 10:00 p.m., Our Lady appeared to Marija in the Bedroom. Our Lady prayed over everyone and blessed them. Our Lady also blessed everyone in the Field. When Marija asked about tomorrow's apparition, Our Lady said, **"Same time, same place,"** in the Bedroom at 10:00 p.m.

July 9, 2008

The following is Marija's description of the apparition that took place in the Bedroom at 10:00 p.m.:

"When Our Lady appeared, She prayed over and blessed all of us and also everyone in the Field."

Our Lady told Marija that the apparition would be **"the same time tomorrow, at 10:00 p.m.,"** but did not say a location. Marija would be leaving for a week of family retreat with the founder's family, so this was the last apparition until she returns to Caritas. [see appendix, page 575.]

July 10 to July 17, 2008

Marija was on family retreat this week. During this time, Our Lady still continued to appear to her at 10:00 p.m.

July 18, 2008

Upon Marija's return, the apparitions continued in the Bedroom. The Rosary began at 9:00 p.m., and the apparition took place at 10:00 p.m. Following is Marija's description of the apparition:

"Tonight when Our Lady came, I recommended all our intentions, in a special way those present here (in the Bedroom) and Our Lady prayed over us and She blessed us all. I asked also blessing for those in the Field and Our Lady blessed also those in the Field, and Our Lady blessed them and all objects brought for blessing."

Marija said that Our Lady told her the apparition would be at the **"Same time, same place,"** tomorrow night.

July 19, 2008

Tonight, the Bedroom was filled with roses, numbering 4,000, all of which represented those souls from across the nation who wanted to be represented during Our Lady's apparitions. Marija took some of the roses and formed them into a heart on the Bed with the Community girls helping. When it was finished, the whole room was breathtaking. The following is Marija's description of the apparition:

> *"In the moment of the apparition, when Our Lady came, I recommended to Our Lady all of our intentions, and in a special way I asked Our Lady to bless all people who is present here and in the Field. And I also offered Our Lady the soul of little Sebastian (a little boy who had died early this morning) and asked help for his mother and father. I asked Our Lady to give Sebastian peace and to carry him in Her heart. She immediately begin to pray. I ask also to Our Lady to bless all candles and all the roses present from all people across the United States. And Our Lady, She stood with Her hands extended and prayed over all of us. She pray over also all these people (who gave the candles and roses). And after She give blessing. She go. And tomorrow:* **'Same time, same place.'"** [see appendix, page 575.]

July 20, 2008

Sunday, July 20, was the last public apparition of Marija's visit to the United States for the July 1-5, 2008 consecrations. The apparition was at 10:00 p.m. in the Bedroom. It lasted over 4 minutes. The following is Marija's description of the apparition:

> *"In the moment of the apparition when Our Lady came, I recommended all your intentions, and Our Lady prayed over us and blessed us. She prayed over us a long time with Her hands extended. She also blessed the people in the Field."*

Marija said that Our Lady had chosen the time for tomorrow's apparition, Monday, July 21, and that it would be in the morning before Marija's departure.

July 21, 2008

Today's apparition was a private apparition for the Community in the Bedroom. The Rosary began at 8:00 a.m. Our Lady appeared to Marija around 9:00 a.m., and the apparition lasted over four minutes. The following is Marija's description of the apparition:

> *"In the moment of the apparition, when Our Lady came, She immediately began to pray, and She prayed a long time over us with Her hands extended. She prayed the whole time* [of the apparition] *and in the end, I just have time to recommend all your petitions, and She gave blessing and left."*

Marija explained this with joy and said, *"Our Lady does this, but not often."* Our Lady's words before the Father in this last apparition cannot be more than what is best, so we were left with this joy and contentment.

The Unexpected Apparitions of February 11 - 18, 2009
(Compiled by the Community of Caritas)

On February 13, 2009, one of the young couples in the Community was married. In the midst of all the wedding preparations, two days before the wedding, one of the married women of the Community gave birth to a beautiful baby girl. Just three weeks earlier, a baby boy was born to another Community mother. It has been a month of beautiful new beginnings in the Community. In preparation, as we do with all the marriages here, the Community began a 54-day Rosary novena for the couple being married that would end the evening before the wedding day. However, the last night the Community would be able to say it all together would be two days before the wedding, on February 11, 2009.

February 11, 2009

The Community gathered in the Bedroom at 5:00 p.m. The founder, having to be out of town that day, came late for the Rosary, but he stopped the prayer and asked everyone to close their eyes and think about the joys the Community was experiencing these days until their hearts were filled with thanksgiving for all the gifts God had been giving to them. He then told them to open their eyes. Gasps and cries of surprise and joy were heard throughout the room. They were shocked. While their eyes had been closed, the visionary Marija had slipped in at the foot of the Bed. It was almost like having an apparition themselves. Not only Marija, but her husband Paolo and their six year old son, Giovanni had also "appeared." Several in the Community said it was "shock and awe."

The Community learned that Marija and Paolo had come to attend the wedding, but it was kept a secret in order to add to the joy of the week. As if that surprise wasn't enough, Our Lady had not appeared to Marija at her normal apparition time, but had waited so that the Community could be present in the apparition. Everyone was stunned with joy. The Community prayed the Rosary novena for the wedding couple and then Our Lady appeared about 5:55 p.m. The following is a description given by one of the Community members of the apparition:

At the moment of the apparition, Marija recommended to Our Lady the Community and Our Lady immediately smiled. After the apparition, Marija, with joy but struggling for words, said "I think Our Lady was surprised too." Our founder, wondering why Marija said that, asked, "Did Our Lady look surprised?" And Marija tried to find better words to describe and relay Our Lady's expression, because it wasn't exactly surprise, but that Our Lady was reacting to our surprise in some way. It was an emotional expression we had never heard used to describe Our Lady before. Our founder then asked, "Was it like She was amused?" And while Marija happily nodded yes, she said it was like joy but different. After discussing Our Lady's reaction, it was more like an emotion of joy, sharing of the surprise and amusement. Marija said Our Lady then blessed us.

The founder, knowing tomorrow would be a difficult day to get everyone together because of the wedding preparations, asked Marija to have Our Lady choose the time for tomorrow's apparition. Our Lady would know what would be best when all the Community could attend Her apparition. Marija asked, and Our Lady astounded them all when She said:

"I will come when you pray." [see appendix, page 575.]

February 12, 2009

Tonight the apparition was around 10:00 p.m. The wedding couple knelt beside the Bed where they had become engaged, also in the presence of Our Lady, seven months earlier. The apparition lasted approximately five minutes. The following is Marija's description of the apparition:

"At the moment Our Lady come, I recommend all our intentions. In a special way, I pray for this young couple getting married and for little Victoria, the little baby that was born on the 11th. After, I recommend every one of us and Our Lady beginning to smile and She pray for everyone. She watch us all. She looked at each of us. She watch us, and after She pray all together and She give blessing. And in beginning when Our Lady just come, She stay...and She...like She have time, so I recommend many people in a special way."

Marija asked Our Lady about the apparition for tomorrow and Our Lady said:

"I will come whenever you pray."

February 13, 2009

Today was the wedding of the young couple in the Community. Our Lady's apparition would be after Holy Communion when the couple would consecrate their marriage to Our Lady at the foot of Her statue in the church. While they knelt at the foot of Our Lady's statue, the Ave Maria was sung. Marija then came up and knelt between the couple. They were also joined by four priests and a deacon who had concelebrated the wedding Mass. The apparition lasted two minutes and 40 seconds. The following is Marija's description:

"In the moment of apparition when Our Lady come, Our Lady pray over bride and after Our Lady pray over groom and after She bless them together. After She bless all us and all that we have in our hearts, and Our Lady smiling. She make Sign of the Cross over everyone. Our Lady then said:

'Tomorrow's apparition will be in the Bedroom at 10:40 a.m.'"

February 14, 2009

The apparition today was in the Bedroom. The Community with many friends of the mission were present. The apparition lasted two minutes. The following is Marija's description of the apparition:

"In moment of apparition, when Our Lady come, I have just time to recommend all us. Our Lady stay little bit. I said, today is St. Valentine's Day, and I ask Our Lady in special way for all us, who is married and who is not married to have with Our Lady's blessing, a good companion, is possible to say. And Our Lady smiling. After I recommend, we have little Victoria, she is first time for apparition and so I recommend also Victoria to Our Lady. Our Lady smiling, beginning to pray. She pray all time and after I say also people who is in Field. When Our Lady pray I also I recommend and ask blessing for all people in Field and Our Lady continue to pray. And after She bless us, and She go. In reality, Our Lady gave three blessings. Our Lady smiled whole time, and She watched us."

Our Lady said concerning the apparition tomorrow: **"Same time. Same place."**

February 15, 2009

The apparition was in the Bedroom at 10:40 a.m. It lasted one minute and 20 seconds. The following is Marija's description of the apparition:

> *"In moment of apparition when Our Lady come, I recommend all our intentions, and Our Lady pray over us and She blessed us. Our Lady said tomorrow's apparition would be:* **'Same time. Same place.'"**

February 16, 2009

The apparition took place in the Bedroom today. In addition to the Community and all the Community children, there were several families present for the apparition today with many children. Marija presented all the children to Our Lady in the apparition today and Our Lady immediately smiled. The apparition lasted 4 minutes and 17 seconds. The following is Marija's description of the apparition:

> *"In moment of apparition, when Our Lady come, I recommend to Our Lady all of us, in special way all kids. And Our Lady beginning to smile. She pray for long time over us and after She give blessing and She said,* **'Go in peace.'** *And She leave. Our Lady said for tomorrow's apparition:* **'Same time. Same place.'"**

February 17, 2009

Our founder and Marija's husband were out of town early yesterday morning before apparition time. They were scheduled to be back Tuesday morning, but our founder knew it would be impossible to make it back for the apparition, especially since Our Lady said in yesterday's apparition, **"Same time. Same place."**

The Community met in the Bedroom and began the Rosary at 10:00 a.m., with the anticipation that Our Lady would appear at around 10:40 a.m. However, in today's apparition, Our Lady refrained from appearing at this normal time. They had prayed two full Rosaries and had started a third and still Our Lady had not appeared. As time passed without Our Lady appearing, some in the room began to wonder if Our Lady was purposely waiting to give the founder an opportunity to make it back for the apparition. Finally, almost 30 minutes past the normal apparition time, Our Lady appeared. For those who had been hoping the founder would make it, there was a little feeling of disappointment, knowing that it had been so close. But then, in the silence of the apparition, they suddenly heard the kitchen screen door open and shut, and the founder came running in. He knelt beside Marija, and as the apparition was long, lasting four minutes, the apparition was only just half over. It was a big joy for everyone to see this unfold. The following is Marija's description of the apparition:

"In the moment of the apparition, I recommended all of us. In a special way I recommend this couple today on their wedding anniversary and I said and all families of the Community. And Our Lady beginning to smile. And I then recommended all families of all present and Our Lady beginning to pray, and She pray long time. I recommend all people who is in Field, and I pray. Our Lady give blessing and She go."

When Marija asked Our Lady about tomorrow's apparition, Our Lady said, **"I will come whenever you pray."** [see appendix, page 575.]

February 18, 2009

Today was the last apparition, as Paolo and Marija would be leaving. Rosary was scheduled for 10:00 a.m. The Community began arriving around 9:30 a.m. and began writing petitions to Our Lady. Our founder told Marija that if, today, Our Lady gives time to ask a question in the apparition, he would like her to ask Our Lady to give some sweet words to end Her visit with the Community. The following is Marija's description of the apparition:

> *"In moment of apparition, when Our Lady come, I recommend like always all us in special way, everyone present today. I ask Our Lady if She has some words to say to us. And Our Lady beginning to smile, said:*

> **'I give my love to you, you give it to others.'**

> *"And after She beginning to pray over us and after She make blessing and She go."*

The surprise visit ended as quickly as it had begun, but with so many joys in-between, and a beautiful message in which Our Lady gave to us Her love. [see appendix, page 575.]

CHAPTER 6

THE MESSAGES OF OUR LADY ON
THE SECOND OF THE MONTH TO
MIRJANA FOR NON-BELIEVERS

(February 2, 1990 - May 2, 2009)

Mirjana, one of the six visionaries of Medjugorje and the first to stop seeing Our Lady on a daily basis, began having interior locutions of Our Lady in 1987 to pray for non-believers. Most people didn't know this was taking place until 1989. Mirjana says that non-believers are those who do not know God's love. She said that Our Lady has told her that there are times when even Her most faithful children are non-believers, that there are moments during the day that even the most faithful among us do not believe.

Mirjana now has apparitions on the second of each month. In 1997, Our Lady opened up the apparitions so that all those who want to attend may be present. The following are several of the messages that Our Lady has given to Mirjana throughout the years during her apparitions on the second of the month.

February 2, 1990

Mirjana received this apparition in Portland, Oregon in the United States of America while visiting Father Milan Mekulich who presided at her marriage. Mirjana had been receiving interior locutions on the second day of each month but on this occasion she was graced by an apparition and a message for the world.

483

"I have been with you nine years. For nine years I wanted to tell you that God, your Father, is the only way, truth and life. I wish to show you the way to Eternal Life. I wish to be your tie, your connection to the profound faith. LISTEN TO ME!

"Take your Rosary and get your children, your families with you. This is the way to come to salvation. Give your good example to your children: give a good example to those who do not believe. You will not have happiness on this earth, neither will you come to Heaven if you are not with pure and humble hearts, and do not fulfill the law of God. I am asking for your help to join me to pray for those who do not believe. You are helping me very little. You have little charity or love for your neighbor and God gave you the love and showed you how you should forgive and love others. For that reason, reconcile and purify your soul. TAKE YOUR ROSARY AND PRAY IT. All your sufferings take patiently. You should remember that Jesus was patiently suffering for you.

"Let me be your Mother and your tie to God, to the Eternal Life. Do not impose your faith on the unbelievers. Show it to them by your example and pray for them. MY CHILDREN, PRAY!"

Mirjana told Fr. Milan that Our Lady was referring to the Sacrament of Reconciliation, for Catholics, when She said, "...reconcile and purify your soul."

Through the years, Our Lady has given several bold and strong messages when the visionaries have had their apparitions in America, as this message given to Mirjana in America shows. Marija's apparitions in America have been profound, Our Lady being boldly forward in messages given in Alabama about Her Special Blessing and to spread it, which the mentality in Medjugorje has oppressed. Jakov had his last apparition in

America. It is viewed by some that Our Lady has done this because the mentality in America is more apt to release what Our Lady says and get the information out.

February 2, 1997

Mirjana continued to see Our Lady monthly for the next seven years. There was no emphasis on making people aware of these important second of the month apparitions until Our Lady finally broke it open. Many have been waiting for this for years. The following is Mirjana's account of Our Lady's visit with her on February 2, 1997:

> *"Please tell everyone that Our Lady's apparition to me on the 2nd of the month will now be like the regular apparitions to Vicka, Ivan, Jakov, and Marija. Our Lady said that whoever wants to be present at that apparition can come. Our Lady said that much prayer is needed for those who have not yet come to know the love of God. This is all."*

March 2, 1997

On March 2, 1997, Mirjana received her apparition at the Blue Cross for about four minutes, surrounded by several hundred people. She was serious and stated that Our Lady wept from beginning to end. Our Lady gave the following message:

> **"Dear children, pray for your brothers who haven't experienced the love of the Father, for those whose only importance is life on earth. Open your hearts towards them and see in them my Son, who loves them. Be my light and illuminate all souls where darkness reigns. Thank you for having responded to my call."**

January 2, 2000

Mirjana had her monthly apparition of Our Lady. A large

crowd gathered. Our Lady gave the following message:

"Never as much as today, my heart is begging for your help! I, your Mother, am begging my children that they help me to realize what the Father has sent me for. He has sent me among you because His love is great. At this great and holy time in which you have entered, pray in a special way for those that have not experienced yet the love of God. Pray and wait!"

October 2, 2002

When Our Lady came, Mirjana described Her as being in deep sadness. She gave the following message:

"Dear children, pray, pray, pray for those who don't feel the love of God."

January 2, 2003

Mirjana received the following message from Our Lady for instructions to help non-believers:

"Dear children, as a mother invites her children, I invited you and you responded to me. Allow me to fill your heart with love, so that it becomes a heart of love that you will be giving to others without reserve. In that way, you will best help me in my mission of converting those of my children who have not yet experienced the love of God and the love of my Son. Thank you!"

October 2, 2003

"Dear children, give me your hearts completely. Allow me to take you to my Son, Who is the true peace and happiness. Do not allow the false brightness that is surrounding you and being offered to you to deceive you. Do not allow

satan to reign over you with the false peace and happiness. Come to me, I am with you."

December 2, 2004

Instructions to help non-believers:

"Dear children, I need you. I am calling you and seek your help. Reconcile with yourself, with God, and with your neighbors. Then help me. Convert unbelievers. Dry the tears from my eyes."

January 2, 2005

There was an apparition, but no words from Our Lady.

February 2, 2005

"Dear children, my Motherly heart prays to you to accept prayer because it is your salvation. Pray, pray, pray, my children."

March 2, 2005

"Dear children, do as I do. Come, extend love, and with your example give my Son to everyone."

April 2, 2005

The following is Mirjana's description of her April 2, 2005 apparition of Our Lady. The apparition lasted from 9:17 a.m. to 9:22 a.m. Mirjana said the following:

Our Lady blessed us all and all the items brought for blessing with Her Motherly blessing, but again She stressed that the most important blessing is from a priest. Our Lady said:

"At this moment, I ask you to renew the Church."

Mirjana asked, *"Can I do this, can we do this?"* Our Lady answered:

"My children, but I will be with you! My apostles, I will be with you and will help you! First renew yourselves and your families, and then everything will be easier."

Then Mirjana said, *"Only you be with us, Mother."*

May 2, 2005

The following is the message that Our Lady gave to Mirjana during her May 2, 2005 apparition.

"Dear children, I am with you to take you all to my Son. I wish to bring you all to salvation. Follow me, because only in this way will you be able to find true peace and happiness. My little children, come with me."

The apparition lasted about 5 minutes, from 9:15 a.m. until 9:20 a.m.

July 2, 2005

The following is the message that Our Lady gave to Mirjana during her July 2, 2005 apparition.

"Dear children, as a Mother I rejoice with you, for as a Mother I invite you. I am bringing my Son to you. My Son, your God. Cleanse your hearts and bow your head before your only God. Let my Motherly heart leap with joy. Thank you."

The apparition lasted 5 minutes, from 9:07 a.m. until 9:12 a.m.

August 2, 2005

"Dear children, I have come to you with open arms, to take you all into my embrace, under my mantle. I cannot do this while your heart is filled with false glitters and false idols. Cleanse your heart and allow my angels to begin to sing in it! Then I will take you under my mantle and give you my Son, the true peace and happiness. Do not wait my children. Thank you."

September 2, 2005

"Dear children, I, as a Mother, am coming to you and showing you how much God, your Father, loves you. And you? Where are you, children of mine? What is in your heart in the first place? What is not permitting you to put my Son in the first place? My children, permit God's blessing to fall upon you. May God's peace permeate you, the peace that my Son, and He alone, gives."

The apparition lasted from 9:06 a.m. until 9:10 a.m.

October 2, 2005

"Dear children, I come to you as a Mother. I am bringing you my Son; peace and love. Purify your hearts and take my Son with you. Give true peace and joy to others."

The apparition lasted from 9:16 a.m. until 9:20 a.m.

November 2, 2005

Mirjana said, *"The Gospa gave no message. She was sad and sorrowful. She told me things that I cannot say. I prayed that She may enter our hearts. I asked Her, 'How can we help you?' The Gospa gave no answer."*

December 2, 2005

**"Dear children, in this holy time, permit the love and grace
of my Son to descend upon you. Only hearts that are pure,
filled with prayer and merciful, can sense the love of my Son.
Pray for those who do not have the grace to sense the love
of my Son. My children, help me! Thank you."**

The apparition lasted 5 minutes, from 9:08 a.m. until 9:12 a.m.

January 2, 2006

**"Dear children, my Son is born. Your Savior is here with
you. What prevents your hearts from receiving Him? What
all is false within them? Purify them by fasting and prayer.
Recognize and receive my Son. He alone gives you true
peace and true love. The way to eternal life is He - my Son!
Thank you."**

March 2, 2006

Our Lady did not give any message, but Mirjana shared the following:

"Our Lady was very sad. Sadly She said":

"Praised be Jesus!"

*"She blessed all the religious articles and all of the people
present during the apparition. Our Lady was talking about
the situation in the world with special attention on those who
have not yet come to know God's love. She said":*

"God is love! God is love! God is love!"

Mirjana says that she was asking some questions about the sick
people and she got answers from Our Lady, but she can not
share with us anything else.

April 2, 2006

The following is the message Our Lady gave to Mirjana during her apparition on April 2, 2006:

"Dear children, I am coming to you, because, with my own example, I wish to show you the importance of prayer for those who have not come to know the love of God. You ask yourself if you are following me? My children, do you not recognize the signs of the times? Do you not speak of them? Come follow me. As a mother I call you. Thank you for having responded."

May 2, 2006

The following is the message Our Lady gave to Mirjana during her apparition on May 2, 2006:

"Dear children, I am coming to you as a mother. I am coming with an open heart full of love for you, my children. Cleanse your hearts from everything that prevents you from receiving me; from recognizing the love of my Son. Through you, my heart desires to win – desires to triumph. Open your hearts; I will lead you to this. Thank you."

June 2, 2006

Our Lady appeared to Mirjana on the 2nd of June. After the apparition, Mirjana shared with us the following:

"Our Lady did not give message. Our Lady blessed all of us who were present and all the religious articles that we brought with us for blessing. With serious expression on Her face, Our Lady emphasized again the priestly blessing. With pain and love at the same time, Our Lady said":

"Remember, children of mine, that is my Son blessing you. Do not accept it so lightly."

"After that Our Lady was telling me about some things that are supposed to happen and She said":

"There is no way without my Son. Do not think that you will have peace and joy if you do not have Him in the first place."

Mirjana said: *"I cannot say that Our Lady was sad or joyful, She was more like concerned (preoccupied) with the care on Her face."*

July 2, 2006

"Dear children, God created you with free will to comprehend and to choose life or death. I as a Mother, with Motherly love, desire to help you to comprehend and to choose life. My children, do not deceive yourselves with false peace and false joy. Permit me, my children, to show you the true way, the way that leads to life – to my Son. Thank you."

August 2, 2006

"Dear children, in these peaceless times, I am coming to you to show you the way to peace. I love you with an immeasurable love and I desire for you to love each other and to see in everyone my Son – the immeasurable Love. The way to peace leads solely and only through love. Give your hand to me, your Mother, and permit me to lead you. I am the Queen of Peace. Thank you.

Mirjana added:

"Again, after a long time, I saw the sky opening and then a sign of a Cross, a heart and the sun."

September 2, 2006

Our Lady did not give the usual messages but started with the following words:

> " You know that we have been gathering for me to help you to come to know the love of God."

She then spoke about the future and said:

> "I am gathering you under my Motherly mantle to help you to come to know God's love and His greatness. My children, God is great. Great are His works. Do not deceive yourselves that you can do anything without Him, not even to take a single step. My children, instead set out and witness His love. I am with you. Thank you."

Our Lady also spoke of the blessing from priests, that it is the greatest blessing we can get on earth, as it is a blessing from Jesus, Her Son.

October 2, 2006

> "Dear children! I am coming to you in this your time, to direct the call to eternity to you. This is the call of love. I call you to love, because only through love will you come to know the love of God. Many think that they have faith in God and that they know His laws. They try to live according to them, but they do not do what is the most important; they do not love Him. My children, pray and fast. This is the way which will help you to open yourselves and to love. Only through the love of God is eternity gained. I am with you. I will lead you with the Motherly love. Thank you for having responded."

Our Lady added:

"My children, priests' hands are blessed hands of my Son, respect them."

November 2, 2006

"Dear children! My coming to you, my children, is God's love. God is sending me to warn you and to show you the right way. Do not shut your eyes before the truth, my children. Your time is a short time. Do not permit delusions to begin to rule over you. The way on which I desire to lead you is the way of peace and love. This is the way which leads to my Son, your God. Give me your hearts that I may put my Son in them and make my apostles of you – apostles of peace and love. Thank you!"

Afterwards, in conclusion, Our Lady said for us not to forget our shepherds in our prayers.

December 2, 2006

"Dear children, in this joyful time of expectation of my Son, I desire that all the days of your earthly life may be a joyful expectation of my Son. I am calling you to holiness. I call you to be my apostles of holiness so that, through you, the Good News may illuminate all those whom you will meet. Fast and pray, and I will be with you. Thank you!"

Our Lady blessed everyone present and all the religious items present for blessing. She again accentuated the importance of priestly blessing.

January 2, 2007

"Dear children, in this holy time full of God's graces, and His love which sends me to you, I implore you not to be with a heart of stone. May fasting and prayer be your weapon for drawing closer to and coming to know Jesus, my Son. Follow

me and my luminous example. I will help you. I am with you. Thank you."

Mirjana stated the following about the apparition:

"The expression on Our Lady's face during the entire time was one of pain and sorrowful. She spoke to me of things that I cannot yet speak of. She blessed both us and the religious articles. The expression on Our Lady's face was especially serious when She was emphasizing the priestly blessing and was asking for prayer and fasting for them."

February 2, 2007

There was no open apparition on February 2, 2007.

March 2, 2007

Mirjana said that Our Lady was resolute. She said:

"Today I will speak to you about what you have forgotten:

"Dear children, My name is Love. That I am among you for so much of your time is love, because the Great Love sends me. I am asking the same of you. I am asking for love in your families. I am asking that you recognize love in your brother. Only in this way, through love, will you see the face of the Greatest Love. May fasting and prayer be your guiding star. Open your hearts to love, namely, salvation. Thank you."

April 2, 2007

Pilgrims were gathered well before 6:00 a.m. There were several thousand present both inside and outside the building where the apparition was. All the children present were allowed to gather around the altar where Mirjana would pray. Our Lady appeared to Mirjana at 9:09 a.m. The apparition lasted until 9:14 a.m. The following is Our Lady's message:

"Dear children, do not be of a hard heart towards the mercy of God, which has been pouring out upon you for so much of your time. In this special time of prayer, permit me to transform your hearts that you may help me to have my Son resurrect in all hearts, and that my heart may triumph. Thank you."

Our Lady added:

"Your shepherds need your prayers."

Our Lady blessed all those present and all religious articles, emphasizing that Her's is a Motherly blessing and that the greatest blessing is that of a priest.

May 2, 2007

"Dear children! Today I come to you with a Motherly desire for you to give me your hearts. My children, do this with complete trust and without fear. In your hearts, I will put my Son and His mercy. Then, my children, you will look at the world around you with different eyes. You will see your neighbor. You will feel his pain and suffering. You will not turn your head away from those who suffer, because my Son turns His head away from those who do so. Children, do not hesitate."

Our Lady blessed everyone and all the religious articles.

June 2, 2007

"Dear children, in this difficult time, God's love sends Me to you. My children, do not be afraid. With complete trust give me your hearts that I may help you to recognize the signs of the time in which you live. I will help you to come to know the love of My Son. Through you I will triumph. Thank you."

"Our Lady blessed all of us and the religious articles brought for blessing. Again, She reminded us to pray for priests and that a priest's blessing is a blessing from Her Son Jesus."

July 2, 2007

"Dear children! In the great love of God, I come to you today to lead you on the way of humility and meekness. The first station on that way, my children, is Confession. Reject your arrogance and kneel down before my Son. Comprehend, my children, that you have nothing and you can do nothing. The only thing that is yours and what you possess is sin. Be cleansed and accept meekness and humility. My Son could have won with strength, but He chose meekness, humility and love. Follow my Son and give me your hand so that, together, we may climb the mountain and win. Thank you!"

"Again Our Lady spoke about the importance of priests and their blessing."

The apparition took place around 9:00 a.m., and lasted several minutes.

August 2, 2007

Crowds of people had already arrived before 4:00 a.m., though the gates did not open for another hour. Once the gates opened, pilgrims streamed in and didn't stop for the next four hours, even right up to the moment of the apparition at 9:00 a.m. The apparition lasted about 5 minutes.

"Dear children! Today I look in your hearts and looking at them my Heart seizes with pain. My children! I ask of you unconditional, pure love for God. You will know that you are on the right path when you will be on earth with your body and with your soul always with God. Through this unconditional and pure love, you will see My Son in every person.

You will feel oneness in God. As a Mother, I will be happy because I will have your holy and united hearts. My children, I will have your salvation. Thank you."

At the beginning of the apparition, Our Lady showed Mirjana what is waiting for us if there is not the holiness in our hearts and our brotherly union in Christ. Mirjana said, *"It was not nice at all."* She asked us to pray for our shepherds because She said that without them there is no unity.

September 2, 2007

"Dear children, in this time of God's signs, do not be afraid because I am with you. The great love of God sends me to lead you to salvation. Give me your simple hearts purified by fasting and prayer. Only in the simplicity of your hearts is your salvation. I will be with you and lead you. Thank you."

Our Lady blessed every one and all of the religious articles.

October 2, 2007

Mirjana arrived about 8:50 a.m. Many more family, friends, and pilgrims pressed tightly close to her. As Mirjana was in her last moments before Our Lady would appear to her, she was in silent prayer, softly crying. Our Lady appeared to Mirjana a little after 9:00 a.m. and stayed for about 5 minutes. The following is the message that Our Lady gave to Mirjana:

"Dear children, I call you to accompany me in my mission of God with an open heart and complete trust. The way on which I lead you, through God, is difficult but persevering and in the end we will all rejoice through God. Therefore, my children, do not stop praying for the gift of faith. Only through faith will the Word of God be light in this darkness which desires to envelop us. Do not be afraid, I am with you. Thank you."

Mirjana also stated that Our Lady blessed all of our religious articles.

November 2, 2007

Our Lady appeared to her at 9:09 a.m. The apparition lasted a little over 6 minutes. The following is Our Lady's November 2, 2007 message to Mirjana given on the day dedicated for non-believers.

> **"Dear children! Today I call you to open your heart to the Holy Spirit and to permit Him to transform you. My children, God is the immeasurable good and therefore, as a Mother, I implore you to pray, pray, pray, fast and hope that it is possible to attain that good, because love is born of that good. The Holy Spirit will reinforce that 'good' in you and you will be able to call God your Father. Through this exalted love, you will sincerely come to love all people and, through God, consider them brothers and sisters. Thank you."**

While Our Lady was blessing, She said, **"On the way on which I lead you to my Son, those who represent Him walk beside me."**

December 2, 2007

The following is the message Our Lady gave to Mirjana during her apparition on December 2, 2007. Mirjana said that Our Lady was very sad. Her eyes were filled with tears throughout the whole time.

> **"Dear children! Today, while I am looking at your hearts, my heart is filled with pain and shudder. My children, stop for a moment and look into your hearts. Is my Son – your God truly in the first place? Are His Commandments truly the measure of your life? I am warning you again. Without faith there is no God's nearness. God's Word which is the light of salvation and the light of common sense."**

Mirjana added: "*I asked Our Lady painfully not to leave us and not to give up on us. Our Lady painfully smiled to my request and left. This time She did not finish Her message with the words, "Thank you." Our Lady blessed all of us and all the religious articles we had with us.*"

January 2, 2008

> **"Dear children! With all the strength of my heart I love you and give myself to you. As a mother fights for her children, I pray for you and fight for you. I ask you not to be afraid to open yourselves, so as to be able to love with the heart and give yourselves to others. The more that you do this with the heart, the more you will receive and the better you will understand my Son and His gift to you. May everyone recognize you through the love of my Son and through Me. Thank you!"**

Our Lady blessed everyone present and all the religious articles. And She asked for prayer and fasting for our shepherds.

February 2, 2008

> **"Dear children! I am with you. As a mother, I am gathering you, because I desire to erase from your hearts what I see now. Accept the love of my Son and erase fear, pain, suffering and disappointment from your heart. I have chosen you in a special way to be a light of the love of my Son. Thank you."**

March 2, 2008

> **"Dear children! I implore you, especially at this Lenten time, to respond to God's goodness because He chose you and sent me among you. Be purified of sins and in Jesus, my Son, recognize the sacrifice of atonement for the sins of the entire world. May He be the meaning of your life. May your**

life become service to the Divine Love of my Son. Thank you my children."

Mirjana added that Our Lady blessed all those present and all religious articles brought for blessing. And She called us anew to pray for our shepherds.

April 2, 2008

The apparition began at 9:00 a.m. and lasted 5 minutes. The following is the message Our Lady gave to Mirjana:

"Dear children, also today as I am with you in the great love of God I desire to ask you: 'are you also with me?' Is your heart open for me? Do you permit me to purify and prepare it for my Son? My children you are chosen because, in your time, the great grace of God descended on earth. Do not hesitate to accept it. Thank you."

"Our Lady blessed everyone present and all religious articles. As She was leaving, behind Her in the blueness was a most beautiful warm light."

May 2, 2008

The apparition started at 9:07 a.m. and lasted 5 minutes. The following is the message Our Lady gave to Mirjana:

"Dear children! By God's Will I am here with you in this place. I desire for you to open your hearts to me and to accept me as a mother. With my love I will teach you simplicity of life and richness of mercy and I will lead you to my Son. The way to Him can be difficult and painful but do not be afraid, I will be with you. My hands will hold you to the very end, to the eternal joy; therefore do not be afraid to open yourselves to me. Thank you."

"Pray for priests. My Son gave them to you as a gift."

June 2, 2008

"Dear children, I am with you by the grace of God to make you great, great in faith and love, all of you. You, whose heart has been made hard as a stone by sin and guilt*...,

* As Our Lady spoke this, She was looking at those present to whom this refers to, with a painful expression and tears in Her eyes.

"...but you devout souls, I desire to illuminate with a new light. Pray that my prayer may meet open hearts, that I may be able to illuminate them with the strength of faith and open the ways of love and hope. Be persevering. I will be with you."

"Our Lady blessed all those present and all religious articles brought for blessing."

July 2, 2008

"Dear children! With Motherly love I desire to encourage you to love your neighbor. May my Son be the source of that love. He, who could have done everything by force, chose love and gave an example to you. Also today, through Me, God expresses immeasurable goodness to you and, you children, are obliged to respond to it. With equal goodness and generosity behave towards the souls whom you meet. May your love convert them. In that way my Son and His love will resurrect in you. Thank you."

Our Lady added: **"Your shepherds should be in your hearts and your prayers."**

August 2, 2008

"Dear children; in my coming to you, here among you, the greatness of God is reflected and the way with God to eter-

nal joy is opening. Do not feel weak, alone or abandoned. Along with faith, prayer and love climb to the hill of salvation. May the Mass, the most exalted and most powerful act of your prayer, be the center of your spiritual life. Believe and love, my children. Those whom my Son chose and called will help you in this as well. To you and to them especially, I give my Motherly blessing. Thank you."

"Our Lady blessed all those present and all the religious articles brought for blessing."

September 2, 2008

"Dear children, today, with my Motherly heart, I call you gathered around me to love your neighbor. My children, stop. Look in the eyes of your brother and see Jesus, my Son. If you see joy, rejoice with him. If there is pain in the eyes of your brother, with your tenderness and goodness, cast it away, because without love you are lost. Only love is effective; it works miracles. Love will give you unity in my Son and the victory of my heart. Therefore, my children, love."

"Our Lady blessed all those who were present and all the religious articles. Once again She called us to pray for our shepherds."

October 2, 2008

"Dear children, again I call you to faith. My Motherly heart desires for your heart to be open, so that it could say to your heart: believe. My children, only faith will give you strength in life's trials. It will renew your souls and open the ways of hope. I am with you. I gather you around me because I desire to help you, so that you can help your neighbors to discover faith, which is the only joy and happiness of life. Thank you."

"Our Lady blessed all those present and all religious articles. Once again She called us to pray for priests, especially at this time."

November 2, 2008

"Dear children, today I call you to a complete union with God. Your body is on earth, but I ask you for your soul to be all the more often in God's nearness. You will achieve this through prayer, pray with an open heart. In that way you will thank God for the immeasurable goodness which He gives to you through Me and, with a sincere heart, you will receive the obligation to treat the souls whom you meet with equal goodness. Thank you, my children."

Our Lady added:

"With the heart I pray to God to give strength and love to your shepherds to help you in this and to lead you."

December 2, 2008

"Dear children! In this holy time of joyful expectation, God has chosen you, the little ones, to realize His great intentions. My children, be humble. Through your humility, with His wisdom, God will make of your souls a chosen home. You will illuminate it with good works and thus, with an open heart, you will welcome the birth of my Son in all of His generous love. Thank you dear children"

January 2, 2009

"Dear children! While great Heavenly grace is being lavished upon you, your hearts remain hard and without response. My children, why do you not give me your hearts completely? I only desire to put in them peace and salvation – my Son. With my Son your soul will be directed to noble

goals and you will never get lost. Even in greatest darkness you will find the way. My children, decide for a new life with the name of my Son on your lips. Thank you."

February 2, 2009

"Dear children! With a Motherly Heart, today I desire to remind you of, mainly to draw your attention to, God's immeasurable love and the patience which ensues from it. Your Father is sending me and is waiting. He is waiting for your open hearts to be ready for His works. He is waiting for your hearts to be united in Christian love and mercy in the spirit of my Son. Do not lose time, children, because you are not its masters. Thank you."

March 2, 2009

"Dear children! I am here among you. I am looking into your wounded and restless hearts. You have become lost, my children. Your wounds from sin are becoming greater and greater and are distancing you all the more from the real truth. You are seeking hope and consolation in the wrong places, while I am offering you sincere devotion which is nurtured by love, sacrifice and truth. I am giving you my Son."

April 2, 2009

"Dear children, God's love is in my words. My children, that is the love which desires to turn you to justice and truth. That is the love which desires to save you from delusion. And what about you, my children? Your hearts remain closed; they are hard and do not respond to my calls. They are insincere…With a motherly love I am praying for you, because I desire for you to resurrect in my Son. Thank you."

"In the translation after the sentence, '…They are insincere…', Mirjana relayed that at this point she begged Our

*Lady to stay longer and it was then Our Lady began, '...**With a motherly love...**'"*

May 2, 2009

"Our Lady was very sad. She only gave a message and blessed us."

"Dear children! Already for a long time I am giving you my Motherly heart and offering my Son to you. You are rejecting me. You are permitting sin to overcome you more and more. You are permitting it to master you and to take away your power of discernment. My poor children, look around you and look at the signs of the times. Do you think that you can do without God's blessing? Do not permit darkness to envelop you. From the depth of your heart cry out for my Son. His Name disperses even the greatest darkness. I will be with you, you just call me: 'Here we are Mother, lead us.' Thank you."

CHAPTER 7

THE INTERIOR LOCUTION
FROM OUR LADY
TO JELENA AND MARIJANA

(February, 1982 to March 3, 1990)

Jelena Vasilj and Marijana Vasilj are two young girls (not related) who, after the apparitions occurred to the six visionaries, would pray to Our Lady while others their age would be out playing. One day they heard the voice of Our Lady and saw Her in an interior way. These interior apparitions have continued since that time. While they are different from the apparitions of the six visionaries whose messages are more general in nature, these messages are stronger in detail and of great value.

Jelena hears and sees Our Lady with the heart. She sees Our Lady as if in a movie, in two dimensions. Our Lady appears to her and to Marijana wearing a white dress. Marijana sees and hears Our Lady in the same manner.

The following messages have been given to Jelena unless otherwise stated.

The End of February-Beginning of March, 1982

To Jelena:

"Dear children, if you knew how much I love you, your heart would cry."

"If there is someone there who asks you for something, give it to him."

"I also stand in front of many hearts, and they do not open up. Pray so that the world may welcome my love."

"Dear children, I would like for the whole world to be my child, but it does not want it. I wish to give everything for the world. For that, Pray!"

April 4, 1982 - April 10, 1982

Jelena asked Our Lady about the meaning of her vision. She saw Jesus being held by the hand by Mary. There were many words written on the arm and palm of Jesus' hand. Jelena could read the inscription, "Glory," on the palm of Jesus' hand.

"These are the names of all those who have been inscribed in the heart of Jesus."

December 29, 1982

Jelena asks if the ten secrets may be revealed to her:

"I do not appear to you as to the other six because my plan is different. To them I entrusted messages and secrets. Forgive me if I cannot tell you the secrets which I have entrusted to them. This is a grace which is for them, but not for you. I appeared to you for the purpose of helping you to progress in spiritual life and through your intermediary I want to lead people to holiness."

Beginning of 1983

Jelena asked Our Lady about the authenticity of the apparitions received by the six visionaries and about the date of the sign which She promised to send:

"Pardon me, but you cannot know it; it is a special gift for them. You will have to believe it like all the others. In the meantime, everything that they say corresponds to truth."

March 1, 1983

"Transcribe all the lessons which I give you for the spiritual life; later you will deliver them to the authorities of the Church."

April 4, 1983

Jelena delivers a message to Father Tomislav Vlasic regarding problems in his parish which she was not aware of. Jelena says: *"Do not have recourse to anyone. When you have a problem, you must remain smiling and praying. When God begins a work, no one will stop it."*

Our Lady said:

"Pray, fast, and allow God to act."

"Do not pity anyone. If the police cause you some anxiety, continue on your way joyful and calm. Pray for them. When God begins His work, no one can stop it."

According to Father Vlasic, these internal locutions were received by Jelena after December 15, 1982:

"Hurry to be converted. Do not wait for the great sign. For the unbelievers, it will then be too late to be converted. For you who have the faith, this time constitutes a great opportunity for you to be converted, and to deepen your faith. Fast on bread and water before every feast, and prepare yourselves through prayer.

"Fast once a week on bread and water in honor of the Holy Spirit outside of Friday.

"Have the largest possible number of persons pray and fast during the Novena of the Holy Spirit, so that it may spread over the Church. Fast and pray for the Bishop."

April 20, 1983

In tears Our Lady said to Jelena:

> **"I give all the graces to those who commit grave sins, but they do not convert. Pray! Pray for them! Do not wait for Friday. Pray now. Today your prayers and your penance are necessary to me."**

April 25, 1983

> **"Be converted! It will be too late when the sign comes. Beforehand, several warnings will be given to the world. Hurry to be converted. I need your prayers and your penance.**
>
> **"My heart is burning with love for you. For you it is enough to be converted. To ask questions is unimportant. Be converted. Hurry to proclaim it. Tell everyone that it is my wish, and that I do not cease repeating it. Be converted, be converted. It is not difficult for me to suffer for you. I beg you, be converted.**
>
> **"I will pray to my Son to spare you the punishment. Be converted without delay. You do not know the plans of God; you will not be able to know them. You will not know what God will send, nor what He will do. I ask you only to be converted. That is what I wish. Be converted! Be ready for everything, but be converted. That is part of conversion. Goodbye, and may peace be with you."**

April 29, 1983

Jelena asks Our Lady why both Marijana (aged 11) and she see Our Lady but Marijana does not hear Her words (at this stage, Marijana was not able to hear Our Lady, but later on she too was able to hear Her):

"I do not want to separate you."

(Does this suggest that Our Lady is saying that these two girls complete each other?)   Also, Our Lady respects their friendship.

May 25, 1983

> **"Assemble about twenty young people who are ready to follow Jesus without reservation. Bring them together within a month's notice. I will initiate them into the spiritual life. There can even be more than twenty. Even some adults and children can participate, all those who will accept the rule.**
>
> **"I will ask these people to do penance for certain intentions. They will fast and pray for the Bishop. They will give up what they cherish the most: drink, coffee, pleasures, television. It is necessary to have persons who wish to consecrate themselves to religious life.   Others have to be ready to consecrate themselves specially to prayer and fasting. I will give them rules to follow.**
>
> **"The persons who will follow these rules, will be consecrated whatever their state in life may be."**

May 28, 1983

> **"It is very beautiful to remain Thursdays for the adoration of my Son in the Blessed Sacrament of the Altar. It is likewise beautiful to venerate the Crucifix each Friday. I wish that every Saturday, which is the day that the Church had dedicated to me, you will consecrate to me at least a quarter of an hour. Meditate during this time, on my life, my messages, and pray."**

June 10, 1983

After an argument, two of the three involved, Jelena and Marijana, reconcile and enter the church. When the third girl, Anita, enters the church she suddenly extends her hand to the others who become filled with joy. Our Lady says:

"I had been waiting for quite a while for your success. Continue in this manner."

June 16, 1983

Our Lady dictates the rules for the prayer group to Jelena which will be totally abandoned to Jesus:

1. **"Renounce all passions and all inordinate desires. Avoid television, particularly evil programs, excessive sports, the unreasonable enjoyment of food and drink, alcohol, tobacco, etc.**

2. **"Abandon yourselves to God without any restrictions.**

3. **"Definitely eliminate all anguish. Whoever abandons himself to God does not have room in his heart for anguish. Difficulties will persist, but they will serve for spiritual growth and will render glory to God.**

4. **"Love your enemies. Banish from your heart hatred, bitterness, preconceived judgments. Pray for your enemies and call the Divine Blessing over them.**

5. **"Fast twice a week on bread and water. Join the group at least once a week.**

6. **"Devote at least three hours to prayer daily, of which at least is half an hour in the morning and half an hour in the evening. Holy Mass and the prayer of the Rosary are included in this time of prayer. Set**

aside moments of prayer in the course of the day,
and each time that circumstances permit it, receive
Holy Communion. Pray with great meditation. Do
not look at your watch all the time, but allow yourself to be lead by the grace of God. Do not concern
yourself too much with the things of this world, but
entrust all that in prayer to Our Heavenly Father.
If one is very preoccupied, he will not be able to pray
well because internal serenity is lacking. God will con-
tribute to lead to a successful end the things of here
below if one strives to work for God's things.

"Those who attend school or go to work must pray
half an hour in the morning and in the evening, and, if
possible, participate in the Eucharist. It is necessary
to extend the spirit of prayer to daily work, that is to
say, to accompany work with prayer.

7.   "Be prudent because the devil tempts all those who
have made a resolution to consecrate themselves to
God, most particularly, those people. He will suggest to them that they are praying too much, they are
fasting too much, that they must be like other
young people and go in search of pleasures. Have
them not listen to him, nor obey him. It is to the voice
of the Blessed Virgin that they should pay attention.
When they will be strengthened in their faith, the devil
will no longer be able to seduce them.

8.   "Pray very much for the Bishop and for those who
hold positions in the Church. No less than half of their
prayers and sacrifices must be devoted to this intention."

Our Lady tells Jelena:

"I have come to tell the world that God is truth; He exists.

True happiness and the fullness of life are in Him. I have come here as Queen of Peace to tell the world that peace is necessary for the salvation of the world. In God, one finds true joy from which true peace is derived."

The Spring of 1983

Regarding Anita to whom Our Lady appeared but who is rarely able to join Jelena and Marijana because of her duties, Our Lady said to Jelena:

"If she cannot come because of her obligations, have her pray for a quarter of an hour at least, and I will appear to her and bless her."

June 22, 1983

"Love your enemies and bless them!"

June 28, 1983

"Pray for three hours a day. You don't pray enough. Pray at least a half hour in the morning and in the evening."

July 2, 1983

"Devote five minutes to the Sacred Heart. Each family is an image of it."

July 4, 1983

"You have begun to pray three hours a day, but you look at your watch, preoccupied with your work. Be preoccupied with only the essential. Let yourself be guided by the Holy Spirit in depth, then your work will go well. Do not hurry. Let yourself be guided and you will see that everything will be accomplished well."

July 26, 1983

> **"Be on your guard. This period is dangerous for you. The devil is trying to lead you astray from the way. Those who give themselves to God will be the object of attacks."**

August 2, 1983

> **"Consecrate yourself to the Immaculate Heart. Abandon yourselves completely. I will protect you. I will pray to the Holy Spirit. Pray to Him also."**

August 15, 1983

> **"See how I am happy here! There are many who honor me. In the meanwhile, do not forget that in other places there are still more persons who hurt me and offend me."**

> **"Do not be in anxiety. May peace unite your hearts. Every disorder comes from satan."**

Regarding the youth who are going back to school:

> **"Be careful not to diminish the spirit of prayer."**

> **"satan is enraged against those who fast and those who are converted."**

September 16, 1983

This message was given to Jelena for the Pope:

> **"Pray, pray, pray! Do not be discouraged. Be in peace because God gives you the grace to defeat satan."**

> **"In my messages, I recommend to everyone, and to the Holy Father in particular, to spread the message which I**

have received from my Son here at Medjugorje. I wish
to entrust to the Pope the word with which I came here:
'MIR'(peace), which he must spread everywhere. Here is a
message which is especially for him: that he bring together
the Christian people through his word and his preaching;
that he spread, particularly among the young people, the
messages which he has received from the Father in his
prayer, when God inspires him."

September 29, 1983

"I desire for a great peace and a great love to grow in you.
Consequently, pray!"

Regarding three priests from Liverpool:

"Preach my messages. Speak about the events at Medjugorje.
Continue to increase your prayers."

Autumn, 1983

"Dear children, one lives not only from work. One lives
also from prayer."* [See endnote, page 574.]

October 20, 1983

To Jelena for the prayer group:

"I ask you for a commitment of four years. It is not yet the
time to choose your vocation. The important thing is, first
of all, to enter into prayer. Later, you will make the right
choice."

To Jelena for the parish:

"May all the families consecrate themselves to the Sacred
Heart each day. I am very happy when the entire family
meets to pray each morning for half an hour."

October 24, 1983

For the prayer group:

> **"If you pray, a source of life will flow from your hearts. If you pray with strength, if you pray with faith, you will receive graces from this source, and your group will be strengthened."**

October 25, 1983

> **"Pray! Pray! Prayer will give you everything. It is with prayer that you can obtain everything."**

October 26, 1983

> **"I pour out my blessing over you, and my heart wishes to be with you."**

October 27, 1983

> **"Pray, pray, pray. You will get nothing from chatter, but only from prayer. If someone asks you about me, and about what I say, answer: 'It is no use to explain. It is in praying that we will understand better.'"**

October 28, 1983

> **"I see that you are tired. I wish to support you in your effort, to take you in my arms so that you may be close to me. To all those who wish to ask me questions, I will answer: 'There is only one response, prayer, a strong faith, and intense prayer, and fasting.'"**

October 29, 1983

> **"I give you my heart; accept it! I would not want to distress**

you, nor to stop talking to you, but I cannot stay always with you. You have to get used to it. In the meantime, I wish to be constantly with you, with the heart. It is necessary to pray much, not to say: 'If today we have not prayed, it is nothing serious.'

"You must strive to pray. Prayer is the only road which leads to peace. If you pray and fast, you will obtain everything that you ask for."

October 30, 1983

"Why do you not put your trust in me? I know that you have been praying for a long time but really surrender yourself. Abandon your concerns to Jesus. Listen to what He says in the Gospel: 'And who among you, through his anxiety, is able to add a single cubit to the length of his life?' (Mt. 6:27).

"Pray also, in the evening when you have finished your day. Sit down in your room, and say to Jesus: 'Thank you.'

"If in the evening you fall asleep in peace and in prayer, in the morning you will wake up thinking of Jesus. You will then be able to pray for peace; but if you fall asleep in distraction, the day after will be misty, and you will forget even to pray that day."

October 31, 1983

"I know that you prayed today, and that you did all your work while praying. Still, I have a particular intention for which I am asking you to say each day the Lord's Prayer seven times, seven Hail Mary's, and the Creed."

November 4, 1983

"I wish that you tell them that tomorrow is a day of fasting in order to sanctify yourselves in the Holy Spirit. And pray! Let this message be conveyed to the group."

November 5, 1983

"I know, my children, that you have worked and prayed today. But, I beseech you, be generous, persevere, continue to pray."

November 6, 1983

"Where are the prayers which you used to address to me? My clothes were sparkling. Behold them soaked with tears. Oh, if you would know how the world today is plunged into sin. It seems to you that the world sins no longer, because here, you live in a peaceful world where there is neither confusion nor perversity.

"If you knew how lukewarm they are in their faith, how many do not listen to Jesus, oh, if you knew how much I suffer, you would sin no more. Oh, how I need your prayers. Pray!"

November 7, 1983

"Do not go to Confession through habit, to remain the same after it. No, it is not good. Confession should give an impulse to your faith. It should stimulate you and bring you closer to Jesus. If Confession does not mean anything for you, really, you will be converted with great difficulty."

November 8, 1983

"Pray and fast! All that you can do for me is to pray and fast."

November 9, 1983

"Pray! I have such a great need for your prayers. Give me your hearts."

November 10, 1983

"I ask you to pray. That is all that I expect of you. Do not forget to pray to the Lord, morning and evening. Pray, pray."

November 11, 1983

"Pray! You can do everything; yes, you can do it through prayer. Place an image of the hearts of Jesus and Mary in your homes."

November 12, 1983

"Give me your hearts, open them to me."

In response to the question, *"How?"* Our Lady says:

"You must redouble your efforts. Day after day, increase your fervor."

November 13, 1983

"Pray, and do it with fervor. Include the whole world in your prayer. Pray, because prayer makes one live."

When asked a question, Our Lady said:

"Pray and you will understand that some day."

November 14, 1983

"**Pray, because prayer is life. Through it and in it, you live in prayer.**"

November 15, 1983

"**Pray and fast!**"

Regarding an intention of the group:

"**I have often reproached you. Pray with me. Begin right now.**"

November 16, 1983

"**Pray and fast. May all the members of your group come on Tuesday if they can. Speak to them about fasting. Fast three days a week for the Bishop. If that cannot be done by everyone the same day, have each one do it whenever he is able.**"

November 17, 1983

"**Pray! If I always ask you to pray, do not think that your prayers are not good. But I invite you to prolong your personal prayer, to pray more intensely for the others.**"

November 18, 1983

"**In Medjugorje, many have begun well, but they have turned toward material goods, and they forget the only good.**"

November 19, 1983

"**My children, pray only!**"

November 20, 1983

"My children, do not believe everything that people tell you. One must not, because it weakens one's faith."

November 21, 1983

"Tuesday, that is tomorrow, the whole group will find peace in prayer. All its members will be invigorated in prayer, as it is the wish of Jesus. He entrusts something to each one, and wishes something from each one. It is necessary to make them come back to their promises, which were made at the beginning, and to pray."

November 22, 1983

"Pray, pray, pray....Pray, my children. Pray, because only prayer can save you."

November 23, 1983

"Oh my sweet children, pray! I ask you only to pray. You yourselves can see that only prayer can save."

November 24, 1983

"Pray and fast!"

November 25, 1983

"Pray and fast."

November 26, 1983

"Prayer and fasting."

November 27, 1983

"My children, pray and keep your soul pure. I wish to be constantly with you."

November 28, 1983

"Pray, pray! Have the parish pray each day to the hearts of Jesus and Mary during the Novena of the Immaculate Conception."

The following prayers were given on this same day:

CONSECRATION TO THE HEART OF JESUS

**O Jesus, we know that You are merciful (Mt. 11:29),
and that You gave Your Heart for us,
that was crowned with thorns by our sins;
We know that even today You are still pleading
with us so that we will not be lost.
Jesus, remember us when we are in sin.
By means of Your Sacred Heart,
grant us, that all men love one another;
Cause hatred to disappear among men.
Show us Your love,
for we all love You,
and want You to protect us
with your Shepherd's Heart
and free us from all sin.
Jesus, enter into each heart.
Knock on the door of our hearts.
Be patient and unwearied with us.
We are still closed, since we still have not
yet understood Your love for us.
Knock persistently and grant, O good Jesus,
that we open our hearts to You,
at least when we will have remembered the passion
You suffered for us. Amen.**

CONSECRATION TO THE
IMMACULATE HEART OF MARY

O Immaculate Heart of Mary, overflowing
with goodness, Show us Your love for us.
May the flame of Your heart, O Mary,
Descend upon all mankind.
We love You so.
Impress true love in our hearts
that we may have a continuous desire for You.
O Mary, meek and humble of heart,
Remember us when we are in sin.
You know that all men sin.
Grant to us by means of Your Immaculate Heart,
to be healed from every spiritual illness.
In doing so, we then will be able to gaze
upon the goodness of Your Maternal Heart,
And thus be converted through
the flame of Your Heart. Amen.

November 29, 1983

   "Pray!"

For the group's intentions:

"I am your Mother full of goodness, and Jesus is your great
friend. Do not fear anything in His presence. Give Him
your heart. From the bottom of your heart tell Him your
sufferings, thus you will be invigorated in prayer, with a free
heart, in a peace without fear."

November 30, 1983

   "Pray, pray, pray!"

November, 1983

The Blessed Virgin tells Jelena that the Mass should always be accompanied by prayers to the Holy Spirit:

"Before Mass it is necessary to pray to the Holy Spirit."

December 1, 1983

"Thanks to all of you who have come here, so numerous during this year, in spite of snow, ice and bad weather, to pray to Jesus. Continue, hold on in your suffering. You know well that when a friend asks you for something, you give it to him. It is thus with Jesus. When you pray without ceasing, and you come in spite of your tiredness, He will give you all that you ask from Him. For that, pray."

December 2, 1983

"Thank you, thanks to everyone!"

Regarding the cold evening:

"Be kind to come to Mass without looking for an excuse. Show me that you have a generous heart."

December 4, 1983

"Pray, pray, pray only. Prayer should be for you not only a habit but also a source of happiness. You should live by prayer."

December 6, 1983

"Pray, pray! If you pray, I will keep you and I will be with you."

December 7, 1983   (VIGIL OF THE IMMACULATE
CONCEPTION)

> "Tomorrow will really be a blessed day for you, if every
> moment is consecrated to my Immaculate Heart. Abandon
> yourselves to me. Strive to make your joy grow, to live in
> the faith, to change your hearts."

December 8, 1983

> "Thank you my children for coming in such large numbers.
> Thank you. Continue your efforts and be persevering and
> tenacious. Pray without ceasing."

December 11, 1983

> "Pray and fast! I wish that prayer be renewed in your heart
> every day. Pray more, yes, more each day."

December 12, 1983

> "Pray, pray, thus I will protect you. Pray and abandon your
> hearts to me, because I wish to be with you."

December 13, 1983

> "Pray and fast! I do not wish to say anything else to you."

December 14, 1983

> "Pray and fast! I am asking you for prayer."

December 15, 1983

> "Fast on Thursday and Friday for the Bishop."

Regarding catastrophic predictions:

"That comes from false prophets. They say: 'Such a day, on such a date, there will be a catastrophe.' I have always said that misfortune will come if the world does not convert itself. Call the world to conversion. Everything depends on your conversion."

December 16, 1983

"Pray and fast only!"

December 17, 1983

"Pray and fast!"

December 18, 1983

"In this novena for Christmas, pray as much as you can. I ask you."

December 19, 1983

"Pray!"

December 20, 1983

"Pray!"

For the group's intention

"Fast on Wednesday, Thursday, and Friday."

December 21, 1983

"My children, I say to you again, pray and fast."

December 22, 1983

"Pray! What is most important for your body is prayer."

December 23, 1983

"Pray, pray, especially tomorrow. I desire your prayers."

December 24, 1983

"Pray, pray my children. I wish that this night be spent in prayer."

December 25, 1983

"My children, pray! I cannot tell you anything else than pray. Know that in your life, there is nothing more important than prayer."

December 26, 1983

"My children, pray. Pray again. Do not say: 'Our Lady only repeats, pray.' I cannot tell you anything else than to pray. You needed to live this Christmas in prayer. You have rejoiced very much this Christmas, but your hearts have not attained and lived what you have desired. No one withdrew to his room to thank Jesus."

December 27, 1983

"My children, pray, pray, pray. Remember that the most important thing in our lives is prayer."

December 28, 1983

"My children, understand that the most important thing in our lives is prayer."

December 29, 1983

"I wish that one love, one peace, flourish in you. Therefore, pray."

December 30, 1983

"My children, pray and fast. I wish to strengthen you, but prayer alone is your strength."

December 31, 1983

"For you, I only wish that this new year will really be a holy one. On this day, go then to Confession and purify yourself in this new year."

Prayers for the Bishop were requested of the group.

1983

"When others cause you some difficulty, do not defend it, rather, pray."

1983

"I desire that you be a flower, which blossoms for Jesus at Christmas, a flower which does not cease to bloom when Christmas has passed. I wish that you have a shepherd's heart for Jesus."

"Dear children, when someone comes to you and asks you a favor, answer by giving. I find myself before so many hearts which do not open themselves to me. Pray, so that the world willingly wants to accept my love."

1983

"Take me seriously. When God comes among men, he does not come to joke but to say serious things.

"It is better to stay in church and pray with faith than to gather together with onlookers near the seers during an apparition."* [See endnote, page 574.]

January 1, 1984

"My children, pray! I say again, pray, because prayer is indispensable to life."

January 2, 1984

Jelena's prayer group thought they could stop saying the prayer to the Holy Spirit, thinking Our Lady only wanted it said until Christmas.

"Why have you stopped saying the prayer to the Holy Spirit? I have asked you to pray always and at all times so that the Holy Spirit may descend over all of you. Begin again to pray for that."

January 3, 1984

"My children, pray; I say it again, pray! Know that in your life the most important thing is prayer."

January 4, 1984

"Before all, pray; I say it again, pray! Know that in your life the most important thing is prayer."

January 8, 1984

"**My children, pray! I say it again, pray! I will say it to you again. Do not think that Jesus is going to manifest Himself again in the manger; friends, He is born again in your hearts.**"

January 15, 1984

"**I know that I speak to you very often about prayer; but know that there are many people in the world who do not pray, who do not even know what to say in prayer.**"

January 17, 1984

"**Pray and fast! I wish that in your hearts prayer and fasting flourish.**"

January 18, 1984

"**I wish to engrave in every heart the sign of love. If you love all mankind, then there is peace in you. If you are at peace with all men, it is the kingdom of love.**"

"**Pray and fast!**"

For the group's intention:

"**Have everyone get up early, some to go to school, others to go to work, still others to help the poor like themselves, also those who need help.**"

January 19, 1984

"**Pray and fast, because without prayer you cannot do anything.**"

January 21, 1984

"Pray and fast. Do not give up on meditation. At home meditate at least half an hour."

January 22, 1984

"Pray and fast. I permit all those who want to make a sacrifice to fast, at the most, three times a week. May they not prolong it."

January 23, 1984

"Pray and fast. You have not understood well, what it means to pray. May you understand that; I desire it very much."

January 24, 1984

"Pray much. I desire to permeate [saturate] you with prayer."

January 25, 1984

"Pray and fast. You need vigor (or strength) in your prayer. May you pray in recollection for a long time and fervently."

January 26, 1984

"Thank you for adoring my Son in the Sacred Host. That touches me very much. As for you, pray! I desire to see you happy."

January 27, 1984

"Pray and fast. I wish that you always deepen your life in

prayer. **Every morning say the Prayer of Consecration to the Heart of Mary. Do it in family. Recite each morning the Angelus** (once), **The Lord's Prayer, the Hail Mary, and the Glory Be five times in honor of the Holy Passion, and a sixth time for our Holy Father, the Pope. Then say the Creed and the Prayer to the Holy Spirit; and, if it is possible, it would be well to pray one part of the Rosary."**

January 28, 1984

"I wish that all of you pray, and that my heart extends to the whole world. I wish to be with you."

January 29, 1984

"Pray and fast! I wish for you to purify your hearts. Purify them and open them to me."

January 30, 1984

"Pray! I desire to purify your hearts. Pray. It is indispensable, because God gives you the greatest graces when you pray."

January 31, 1984

"Pray! Do not think of anything, pray. Do not think of anything else except of those for whom you pray. Then prayer will be better and you will be faithful to it."

For the group:

"Continue to help the poor, the sick, and to pray for the dead. You should not feel any fear. Let all free themselves completely and let them abandon their hearts to me so that I can be with them. Have them listen to me and discover me in the poor, and in every man."

February 1, 1984

"It is raining at this time, and you say: 'It is not reasonable to go to church in this slush. Why is it raining so much?' Do not ever speak like that. You have not ceased to pray so that God may send you rain which makes the earth rich. Then do not turn against the blessing from God. Above all, thank Him through prayer and fasting."

February 2, 1984

"Pray, because I need more prayers. Be reconciled, because I desire reconciliation among you and more love for each other, like brothers. I wish that prayer, peace, and love bloom in you."

February 3, 1984

Regarding questions to Our Lady about the diary of Vicka which arrived from the Bishop on January 13, 1984:

"It is up to you to pray and I will take care of the rest. You cannot even imagine how powerful God is. That is why, pray! Pray because He wants to be with you and wants to cleanse you from all sin."

February 4, 1984

"Pray, because prayer is very necessary to you. With prayer, your body and soul will find peace. There are some young people who have consecrated themselves to me. But there are in the parish some persons who are not entirely consecrated. As soon as Mass has ended, they are in a hurry to leave the church. That is not good. That way they will never be able to give themselves completely. It is not good for them to linger about the church. One must be pious and set a good example for others, in order to awaken in them the faith. It is necessary to pray as much as possible while offering your heart. One has to consecrate himself if he wants to be truly better."

February 5, 1984

"Pray and fast. I desire to live in your hearts."

Especially for the Prayer Group:

"Some of them still have a week of rest. They do not fast...others have come here and fast on Wednesday, Thursday, and Friday. Others help the poor and the sick. Others love everybody and want to discover Jesus in each one. Some are not convinced, others are. Those are mine. See how they honor me. Lead them to me so that I may bless them."

February 6, 1984

"Pray, pray, I ask of you."

February 8, 1984

"From you, I expect only prayer. Thus, pray."

February 9, 1984

"Pray, pray! How many persons have followed other beliefs or sects and have abandoned Jesus Christ! They create their own gods; they adore idols. How that hurts me! If they could be converted! How unbelievers are in large numbers! That will change only if you help me with your prayers."

February 10, 1984

> **"Pray and fast! I desire humility from you; but you can become humble only through prayer and fasting."**

February 11, 1984

> **"Open your hearts to me, I desire to bless them fully."**

February 12, 1984

> **"I ask of you to pray and fast! Pray for the peace and humility of your hearts."**

February 13, 1984

> **"Fast and pray! Give me your hearts. I desire to change them completely. I desire for them to be pure."**

February 14, 1984

> **"Pray and fast! I desire you to purify your hearts completely. I wish to make you happy."**

February 15, 1984

Regarding a very strong, icy wind blowing which everyone noticed on the way to church:

> **"The wind is my sign. I will come in the wind. When the wind blows, know that I am with you. You have learned that the cross represents Christ; it is a sign of Him. It is the same for the Crucifix you have in your home. For me, it is not the same. When it is cold, you come to church; you want to offer everything to God. I am, then, with you. I am with you in the wind. Do not be afraid."**

February 17, 1984

"My children, pray! The world has been drawn into a great whirlpool. It does not know what it is doing. It does not realize in what sin it is sinking. It needs your prayers so that I can pull it out of this danger."

February 20, 1984

"Pray and fast! I desire to purify you and to save you. For that, help me with your prayers."

February 21, 1984

"Pray and fast! I expect generosity and prayer from your hearts."

February 23, 1984

"I hold all of you in my arms. You are mine. I need your prayers so that you may be all mine. I desire to be all yours and for you to be all mine. I receive all your prayers. I receive them with joy."

February 24, 1984

"Pray and fast! I desire to be with you always. I desire to stay in your hearts always and for you to stay in mine."

February 25, 1984

"Know that I love all of you. Know that you are all mine. To no one do I desire to give more than to you. Come to me all of you. Stay with me. I want to be your Mother. Come, I desire all of you."

February 26, 1984

> **"Pray and fast! Know that I love you. I hold all of you on my knees."**

February 27, 1984

> **"Do not be tired. I desire to be with you."**

February 28, 1984

> **"Pray and fast! Love everyone on earth, just as you love yourselves."**

For the intention of the prayer group:

> **"Have each one decide alone. In the meantime it would be good that this week they fast on Thursday. Have them read the Bible and meditate on it."**

February 29, 1984

> **"Pray! It may seem strange to you that I always speak of prayer, and yet I say: pray! Why do you hesitate? In Holy Scripture you have heard it said, 'Do not worry about tomorrow, each day will have its own worries.' Then do not worry about the other days. Be content with prayer. I, your Mother, will take care of the rest."**

March 1, 1984

To Marijana:

> **"Pray and fast. When I tell you to pray, do not think that you have to pray more, but pray. Let prayer and faith awaken in your hearts."**

To Jelena:

> "Each Thursday, read again the passage of Matthew 6:24-34, before the Most Blessed Sacrament, or if it is not possible to come to church, do it with your family."

March 5, 1984

> "Pray and fast! Ask the Holy Spirit to renew your souls, to renew the entire world."

March 17, 1984

In preparation for the feast of the Annunciation:

> "Pray and fast, so that during this novena, God will fill you with His Power."

March 21, 1984

> "Today I rejoice with all my angels. The first part of my program has been achieved."

Crying:

> "There are so many men who live in sin. Here there are likewise among you some people who have offended my heart. Pray and fast for them."

March 22, 1984

> "Yesterday evening I said that the first wish of my plan was realized."

March 27, 1984

> "In the group, some have given themselves up to God so

that He may guide them. **Allow the Will of God to be realized in you."**

March 30, 1984

**"My children, I wish that the Holy Mass be for you the
gift of the day. Attend it, wish for it to begin. Jesus gives
Himself to you during the Mass. Thus, look forward to that
moment when you are cleansed. Pray very much so that the
Holy Spirit will renew your parish. If people attend Mass
with lukewarmness, they will return to their homes cold,
and with an empty heart."**

April 3, 1984

**"I ask for you to pray for the conversion of all men. For
that, I need your prayers."**

April 14, 1984

**"How can you not be happy? Jesus gives Himself to you. I
wish to inundate souls. If I am sad this evening, the reason
is that many have not prepared themselves for Easter. They
do not permit Jesus on that day to unite Himself to their
souls."**

April 15, 1984 - April 22, 1984 (HOLY WEEK)

**"Raise your hands and open your hearts. Now, at the time
of the Resurrection, Jesus wishes to give you a special gift.
This gift of my Son is my gift. Here it is. You will be sub-
jected to trials and you will endure them with great ease.
We will be ready to show you how to escape from them if
you accept us. Do not say that the Holy Year has ended and
that there is no need to pray. On the contrary, double your
prayers because the Holy Year is just another step ahead."**

The Risen Jesus, with rays of light coming forth from His wounds, appeared and said:

"Receive my graces and tell the whole world that there is no happiness except through Me."

April 19, 1984: Our Lady dictated this prayer to Jelena:

HOW TO GIVE ONESELF TO MARY
MOTHER OF GOODNESS, OF LOVE AND OF MERCY

Oh my Mother!
Mother of goodness, love and mercy!
I love you immensely, and I offer myself to you.
Through your goodness, your love,
And your mercy, save me!
I wish to be yours.
I love you immensely
And I wish that you protect me.
In my heart, oh Mother of goodness,
Give me your goodness,
So that I go to Heaven.
I ask you for your immense love
That you may give me the grace
That I will be able to love each one
Just like you loved Jesus Christ.
I ask you in grace
That I be able to be merciful to you.
I offer myself completely to you
And I wish that you will be with me at each step,
Because you are full of grace.
I wish never to forget your grace,
And if I should lose it,
I will ask, make me find it again. Amen.

Jelena asked Our Lady this question for Father Vlasic: *"How could Jesus pray all night? With what method?"* Our Lady said:

"He had a great longing for God and for the salvation of souls."

April 20, 1984

"You should be filled with joy. Today Jesus died for your salvation. He descends into Hell and opens the gates of Paradise. Let joy reign in your hearts!

"When you pray, pray more. Prayer is a conversation with God. To pray means to listen to the Lord. Prayer is for me a service, because after it, all things become clear. Prayer leads to knowing happiness."

April 21, 1984

"Raise your hands, yearn for Jesus because in His Resurrection, He wants to fill you with graces. Be enthusiastic about the Resurrection. All of us in Heaven are happy, but we seek the joy of your hearts. My Son's gift and mine, at this moment is this: you will be comforted in your trials, they will be easier for you because we will be close to you. If you listen to us, we will show you how to overcome them.

"Pray much tomorrow. May Jesus truly rise in your families. Where there is war, may peace come. I wish that a new man would be born in your hearts. My children, I thank you. Continue to bring about the Resurrection of Jesus in all men. The Holy Year has ended, but it represents only a step in our life. Continue to pray."

April 24, 1984

"Many times, confronting justice and confronting your sins, many times I returned from your home in tears. I could not say a single word. I am your Mother and I do not want to

oppose you. But what I shall do in you is up to you.

"We must rejoice in Jesus, to make Him happy."

May 19, 1984

"Dear children, at this time it is especially necessary for you to consecrate yourselves to me and to my heart. Love, pray, and fast."

May 21, 1984

"O dear children, how I wish that you would turn to me. See, my little children, it is the end of the school year and you have not even reached halfway. That is why now you must become a little more serious."

May 23, 1984

"I wish that the parish prepare itself through a novena, to receive the sacrament of Confirmation on the day of the feast of the Ascension."

May 25, 1984

"I truly wish that you would be pure on the day of Pentecost. Pray, pray that your spirit be changed on that day."

May 26, 1984

"Dear children, thank you for every prayer. Try to pray continuously, and do not forget that I love you and wish that all of you would love one another."

Regarding questions Jelena was requested to ask:

"For all of these questions, there is an answer: pray to the

Holy Spirit so that He may enlighten you, and you will come to know all that you wish."

May 28, 1984

"Love is a gift from God. Therefore, pray that God may give you the gift to love."

May 30, 1984

"The priests should visit families, more particularly those who do not practice anymore, and who have forgotten God. Priests should carry the Gospel of Jesus to the people, and teach them how to pray. And the priests themselves should pray more and also fast. They should give to the poor what they don't need."

May, 1984

Regarding the celebration of Our Lady's two thousandth birthday:

"Throughout the centuries, I have given myself completely to you. Is it too much to give me, three days? Do not work on those days. Take your rosaries and pray. Fasting has been forgotten during the last quarter of the century within the Catholic Church."

Jelena tells Our Lady that if she tells the people to pray four hours a day they will back out.

"Don't you understand, that it is only one-sixth of the day?"

June 1, 1984

"May the love of God be always in you, because without

it, you cannot be fully converted. Let the Rosary in your hands make you think of Jesus.

"Dear children, strive to penetrate into the Mass, just as you should."

June 2, 1984

"Thank you for every prayer. Continue to pray, but pray with the heart. Dear children, again it is necessary for you to pray to the Holy Spirit and it would be good for you to pray The Lord's Prayer seven times in the church, as one does it for Pentecost."

During the Pentecost Novena, before each Our Father, the priest asks for one of the seven gifts of the Holy Spirit.

June 4, 1984

"Dear children, I am happy that you have begun to pray as I requested of you. Continue."

June 8, 1984

"Dear children, you need love. I have said it to you many times, and I remind you. Continue only to pray and be happy because I am with you."

June 11, 1984

"I wish that you continue to pray and to fast."

To the group:

"I wish that you would become like a flower in the spring. The love which I give you is great, but sometimes you reject it, and thus, it becomes less. Always accept immediately the

gifts which I give you so that you can profit from them."

Mid-June, 1984

"Prepare yourselves through prayer for the third anniversary of the beginning of the apparitions. June 25th should be celebrated as the Feast of Mary, 'Queen of Peace.'"

June 21, 1984

"If you knew how much I love you, you would cry with joy. When anyone is before you and asks you something, you will give it to him. I am before so many hearts, but they remain closed. Pray so that the world receives my love."

"Each member of the group is like a flower; and if someone tries to crush you, you will grow and will try to grow even more. If someone crushes you a little, you will recover. And if someone pulls a petal, continue to grow as though you were complete."

To Marijana:

"My only wish is that you become as joyful and enthusiastic as you were during the first days of my apparitions."

June 23, 1984

"Dear children, I am very happy that there are so many people here this evening. Thank God alone."

August 2, 1984

"Dear children, today I am joyful and I thank you for your prayers. Pray still more these days for the conversion of sinners. Thank you for having responded to my call."

After Easter, Our Lady speaks to Jelena or Marijana on Tuesdays, Wednesdays, Saturdays, and Sundays rather than everyday.

The Beginning of August, 1984

"This message is dedicated to the Pope and to all Christians. Prepare the second millennium of my birth which will take place August 5, 1984. Throughout the centuries, I consecrated my entire life to you. Is it too much for you to consecrate three days for me? Do not work on that day, but take up the Rosary and pray."

August 2, 1984

"I am happy for your participation at Mass. Continue as you did this evening. Thank you for having resisted the temptation of satan."

August, 1984

"Christians make a mistake in considering the future because they think of wars and of evil. For a Christian, there is only one attitude toward the future. It is hope of salvation."* [See endnote, page 574.]

"Your responsibility is to accept Divine peace, to live it, and to spread it, not through words, but through your life."* [See endnote, page 574.]

August, 1984

"The only attitude of the Christian toward the future is hope of salvation. Those who think only of wars, evils, punishment do not do well.

"If you think of evil, punishment, wars, you are on the road

to meeting them. Your responsibility is to accept Divine peace, live it, and spread it."* [See endnote, page 574.]

September 10, 1984

"Dear children, you must understand that one has to pray. Prayer is no joke, prayer is a conversation with God. In every prayer you must listen to the voice of God. Without prayer one cannot live. Prayer is life."

October 5, 1984

"I love you. Love me, love one another."

November 17, 1984

"Pray. Do not ask yourself about the reason why I constantly invite you to prayer. Intensify your personal prayer so that it will become a channel for the others."

December 21, 1984

"Dear children! I would like each of you to be like a flower which is going to open at Christmas for Jesus, a flower which does not cease to bloom after Christmas. Be the good shepherds of Jesus."

December 29, 1984

The anniversary of Jelena's first anniversary:

"Today is the feast of the Mother of goodness, of mercy, and of love."

Our Lady blessed the group for the first time and they were strongly changed because of it.

"Up until now I have given it to no one."

The group was motivated to receive Our Lady's blessing.

"Receive it, do not neglect it as before. I can give you my blessing, but I cannot give it to you if you do not want it."

To Jelena:

"I wish that a great love, a great peace would flourish in you. Thus, pray."

1984

The following were given by Fr. Tomislav Vlasic during a homily given on Easter Sunday, 1984.

"If you want to be very happy, live a simple, humble life, pray a great deal, do not delve into your problems, but let yourselves be guided by God." * [See endnote, page 574.]

"Do not complicate matters. Yes, you can walk on a deeper spiritual way but you will have difficulties. Take the simple way, do not delve into your problems, but let yourselves be guided by Jesus Christ." * [See endnote, page 574.]

February 20, 1985

"I give you advice; I would like you to try to conquer some fault each day. If your fault is to get angry at everything, try each day to get angry less. If your fault is not to be able to study, try to study. If your fault is not to be able to obey, or if you cannot stand those who do not please you, try on a given day to speak with them. If your fault is not to be able to stand an arrogant person, you should try to approach that person. If you desire that person to be humble, be humble yourselves. Show that humility is worth more than pride.

"Thus, each day, try to go beyond, and to reject every vice from your heart. Find out which are the vices that you most need to reject. During this Lent, you should try and truly desire to spend it in love. Strive as much as possible."

February 25, 1985

"Know that I love you. Know that you are mine. I do not wish to do anything more for anyone, that I do not wish to do for you. Come all of you to me. Remain with me and I will be your Mother always. Come, because I wish to have all of you."

Lent, 1985

"Fast on bread and water during the first week of the Passion and on Holy Wednesday, Holy Thursday, and Good Friday."

March 25, 1985

Jelena asks why Our Lady is so beautiful:

"I am beautiful because I love. If you want to be beautiful, love. There is no one in the world who does not desire beauty."

May 3, 1985

"Sometimes prayers said in a loud voice keep Jesus at a distance, because when men want to conquer with their own strength there is no place for God. Prayers said out loud are good when they come from the heart."

May 19, 1985

"Dear children, at this time I ask you particularly to consecrate yourselves to me and to my Immaculate Heart. Love, pray, and fast."

June 1, 1985

"Always have the love of God in you, because without this love, you are not able to convert yourselves completely. Let the Rosary be in your hands in memory of Jesus. Dear children, strive to go deep into the Mass as you should."

Mid-June, 1985

Our Lady gave Jelena this explanation after she saw a beautiful pearl divide itself. Each section glittered and then faded.

"Jelena, man's heart is like this splendid pearl. When he belongs completely to the Lord, he shines even in the darkness. But when he is divided, a little to satan, a little to sin, a little to everything, he fades and is no longer worth anything."* [See endnote, page 574.]

June 22, 1985

Our Lady inspired Jelena to write down this prayer and to say it in her prayer group:

PETITION TO GOD

Oh God, our hearts are in deep obscurity,
in spite of our link to Your Heart.
Our hearts are between You and satan;
do not permit it to be like that!
Every time our hearts are divided
between good and evil,
let them be enlightened by Your light
and let them be unified.

Never permit,
for there to be able to exist in us two loves,
that there can never co-exist in us two faiths,
and that there can never co-exist in us:
lying and sincerity,
love and hatred,
honesty and dishonesty,
humility and pride.

Help us, on the contrary,
so that our hearts may be elevated toward You
just like that of a child.
May our hearts be rebuilt and captivated with peace and continue to always have
the longing for peace.

May Your Holy Will and Your Love
dwell in us, that at least
sometimes we would really wish to be Your
children and when, Oh Lord,
we will desire to be Your children,
remember our past desires
and help us to receive You again.

We open our hearts to you
so that Your Holy Love will remain in us.
We open our souls to you,
so that they may be touched by Your Holy Mercy
which will help us to see clearly all our sins,
and will make us realize
that which makes us impure is sin.

God, we want to be Your children,
humble and devout,
to the point of becoming your cherished and sincere children,
such as only the Father
would be able to desire that we be.

Help us, Jesus, our Brother,
to obtain the goodness of the Father in our regard,
and to be good to Him.
Help us, Jesus,
to understand well what God gives us,
although sometimes we fail to perform a good act,
as though it were for us an evil.

This prayer was inspired by Our Lady and She said it was the most beautiful prayer that could be said for a sick person:

PRAYER FOR A SICK PERSON

O my God,
behold this sick person before You.
He has come to ask You
what he wishes
and what he considers as the most important thing for him.
You, O my God,
make these words enter into his heart:
"What is important, is the health of his soul."

Lord, may Your Will in everything
take place in his regard, if You want him to be cured,
let health be given to him;
but if Your will is something else,
let him continue to bear his cross.

I also pray to You for us,
who intercede for him;
purify our hearts,
to make us worthy to convey
Your Holy Mercy.

Protect him and relieve his pain.
that Your Holy Will be done in him,
that Your Holy Name be revealed through him.
Help him to bear his cross with courage.

Recite the Glory Be three times before this prayer and the preceding one.

June 25, 1985

"A heart which belongs to the Lord is splendid, even if it is flooded with difficulties and trials. But if the heart engaged in difficulties strays away from God, it loses its splendor."

June, 1985

"Dear children, if there is someone and he asks you for something, give it to him. I, too, ask before many hearts, and they do not open up. Pray so that the world may receive my love."

July, 1985

To Jelena's group:

"I cannot speak to you. Your hearts are closed.

"You have not done what I told you; I cannot speak to you. I cannot give you graces as long as you remain closed." * [See endnote, page 574.]

To Jelena's group:

"Each of you has a special gift which is your own and can alone understand it interiorly." * [See endnote, page 574.]

To Jelena's prayer group:

"It seems when you carry my messages, be on your guard that they are not lost. Carry my messages with humility, in such a way that on seeing happiness in you, persons will desire to be like you. Do not carry my messages to simply throw them to others." * [See endnote, page 574.]

July 28, 1985 - August 4, 1985

> **"During these days, I wish that you consider this idea: After so long and so much time, I have not met Jesus, my friend. After so long and so much time, I have not encountered my Mother, Mary. In these days, I want to encounter them."*** [See endnote, page 574.]

August, 1985

> **"Do not be afraid of satan. That isn't worth the trouble, because with a humble prayer and an ardent love, one can disarm him."*** [See endnote, page 574.]

September, 1985

A prayer given by Our Lady for Jelena's prayer group to say:

> **"My soul is full of love like the sea. My heart is full of peace like the river. I am not a saint, but I am invited to be one."*** [See endnote, page 574.]

October, 1985

On three successive evenings, Jelena was given these:

> **"If you wanted to accept my love, you would never sin."*** [See endnote, page 574.]

On the fourth evening in response to Jelena's question about Her repeating the same message, Our Lady says:

> **"But I don't have anything else to say to you."*** [See endnote, page 574.]

Crying, Our Lady adds:

"There are many who finish their prayers, even without entering into them."* [See endnote, page 574.]

October, 1985

In response to a question asked by a group of pilgrims from Milan asking when Our Lady would go there:

"When you open your hearts to me."* [See endnote, page 574.]

December 7, 1985

"I have only one wish for tomorrow's feast. I ask of you to find at least a quarter of an hour for you to come before me and entrust your problems to me. No one will understand you as I do."

December 31, 1985

"Next year is the year of peace; not because men have named it so, but because God has programmed it. You will not have peace through the presidents but through prayer."

To another of the little seers:

"When you hear the bells at midnight, you will fall on your knees, bow your head to the ground so that the King of Peace will come. This year I will offer my peace to the world. But afterwards, I will ask you where you were when I offered you my peace."

December, 1985

"If you have not listened to my messages, the day of joy will become, for me, a day of sadness."* [See endnote, page 574.]

January 21, 1986

During the second day of the prayer group retreat:

"This evening, rest."

January 22, 1986

To the same prayer group:

"I know that you are tired, but I cannot tell you rest. Today, I tell you, pray, and do not go to bed before having prayed at least a quarter of an hour for the group. Tomorrow will be a better day."

January 27, 1986

To Jelena's prayer group:

"Every second of prayer is like a drop of dew in the morning which refreshes fully each flower, each blade of grass and the earth. In the same way prayer refreshes man. When man is tired, he gets rest. When he is troubled, he finds peace again. Man renews himself and can, once again, listen to the words of God.

"How the scenery is beautiful when we look at nature in the morning in all its freshness! But more beautiful, much more, is it when we look at a man who brings to others peace, love, and happiness. Children, if you could know what prayer brings to man! Especially personal prayer. Man can thus become a really fresh flower for God. You see how drops of dew stay long on flowers until the first rays of sun come."

Follow up to the January 27, 1986 Message

> "Nature, in this way, is renewed and refreshed. For the
> beauty of nature, a daily renewal and refreshment is neces-
> sary. Prayer refreshes man in the same way, to renew him
> and give him strength. Temptations, which come on him
> again and again, make him weak and man needs to get from
> prayer always a new power for love and freshness. This is
> why [you should] pray and rejoice for the freshness God
> gives you."

February 22, 1986

Before the blessing at the end of the prayer group meeting:

> "Dear children, you will be able to receive Divine love only
> in proportion to when you understand that, on the cross,
> God offers you His immense love."

February, 1986

To Jelena and Marijana:

> "Understand that you are nothing, incapable, really noth-
> ing. It is the Father who will do everything."* [See endnote,
> page 574.]

August 11, 1986

> "Dear children, open your hearts and let Jesus guide you.
> For many people it seems to be hard, but it is so easy! You
> don't have to be afraid because you know that Jesus will
> never leave you, and you know that he leads you to salva-
> tion."

1986

To Jelena's prayer group after fasting and prayer:

"I have listened to your prayer and yet you will not receive what you have wished. You will receive other things because it is not up to you to glorify yourself, but to Me to glorify Myself in you."* [See endnote, page 574.]

"Do not be afraid. Confide yourself to the Father. Pray until you are sure that He guides everything.

"In difficulties, when you carry the cross, sing, be full of joy."* [See endnote, page 574.]

1986

"When people ask you to speak about the apparition, say: 'Let us pray together to understand the apparitions of the Gospa.'"* [See endnote, page 574.]

1986

For Jelena's group:

"I beg you, destroy your house made of cardboard which you have built on desires. Thus, I will be able to act for you."* [See endnote, page 574.]

1986

For Jelena's group:

"I wish only that you would be happy, that you would be filled with joy, that you would be filled with peace and announce this joy."

To the prayer group:

"If you would abandon yourselves to me, you will not even feel the passage from this life to the next life. You will begin to live the life of Heaven on earth."* [See endnote, page 574.]

September, 1986

"Today it is not words nor deeds which are important. The important thing is only to pray, to remain in God."* [See endnote, page 574.]

October, 1986

This message is from Jesus to Jelena:

"I am joyful, but my joy is not complete until you are filled with joy. You are not yet filled with joy because you are not yet at the stage of understanding my immense love."* [See endnote, page 574.]

Undated

Regarding the similarity of the third secret of Fatima and the signs announced at Medjugorje:

"Do not fear anything. You must forget what is behind you in your life. I only want that from now on you be new people. Do not fear anything when I am near you. I love you."

Regarding a discussion with Father Petar Ljubicic and Father Bonifacio:

"It does not suffice to pray. You must change your life, your heart. Love the others, have love for others. Love

what you do and always think about Jesus and you will
understand what is good and what is bad."

Undated

"I pray for you because I love you. If you want to love, pray
for your brothers and sisters. Today many people need lots
of prayers. Pray and be a model to others because through
you I want to lead people towards the light."

March 1, 1987

"Dear children, sometimes you oppress your hearts with
certain things, and this is not necessary. Sometimes you
are afraid by this and that. Why do you need that? Who is
with Jesus need not fear. Do not worry with anxiety about
what will happen tomorrow or in a few years from now.
Abandon yourselves to Jesus and only in that way will you
be the sheep that follow their shepherd."

April 12, 1987

"If you love from the bottom of your heart, you receive a
lot. If you hate, you lose a lot. Dear children, love makes
great things. The more you have love inside of you, the
more you can love people around you. That is why, pray
unceasingly to Jesus for Him to fill your hearts with love."

May 16, 1987

"O children! Remember: the only way for you to be always
with me and to know the will of the Father is to pray. That
is why I call you today again; don't let my calls be without
effect. Continue to pray in spite of everything and you will
understand the will of the Father and His love.

"Dear children, when God calls men, it is really a great

thing. Think about how it would be sad to let pass those opportunities that God allows without taking them. So do not wait for tomorrow or the day after tomorrow. Say 'yes!' to Jesus now! And may this 'yes!' be forever."

June 16, 1987

"Dear children, my heart is full of grace and love. My heart is the gift I give you. Be united! Pray together! Love together!"

July 11, 1987

"O children! I want you to live each new day with love and peace. I want you to be the carriers of peace and love. People need so much those graces of peace and love, but they have lost them because they don't pray! Create in your hearts a permanent prayer, because only thus will you be able to be prepared vessels. Through prayer your Father will build you into the vessels He wants. For this abandon yourselves completely to Him."

July 30, 1987

"Dear children, today I invite you in a special way to pray for the plans of God to be fulfilled: first of all with you, then with this parish which God Himself has chosen. Dear children, to be chosen by God is really something great, but it is also a responsibility for you to pray more, for you, the chosen ones, to encourage others so you can be a light for people in darkness.

"Children, darkness reigns over the whole world. People are attracted by many things and they forget about the more important.

"Light won't reign in the world until people accept Jesus, until they live His words, which is the Word of the Gospel.

"Dear children, this is the reason for my presence among you for such a long time: to lead you on the path of Jesus. I want to save you and, through you, to save the whole world. Many people now live without faith; some don't even want to hear about Jesus, but they still want peace and satisfaction! Children, here is the reason why I need your prayer: prayer is the only way to save the human race."

Date Unknown

The Lord's Prayer and commentary was dictated by Our Lady to Jelena:

"OUR - This is your Father. Why are you afraid of Him? Hold out your hands to Him. [Make a short pause.] OUR FATHER means that He has given Himself to you as Father. He has given you everything. You know that your earthly fathers do everything for you, so much more does your Heavenly Father. OUR FATHER means: I give you everything my child."

"FATHER - Who is this Father? Whose is this Father? Where is this Father?

"WHO ARE IN HEAVEN - [Make a short pause.] This means: your earthly father loves you, but your Heavenly Father loves you even more. Your father can get angry: He does not; He offers you only His love.

"HALLOWED BE THY NAME - In exchange you must respect Him, because He has given you everything and because He is your Father and you must love Him. You must glorify and praise His name. You must say to sinners: He is the Father; yes, He is my Father and I wish to serve Him and to glorify only His name. This is the meaning of 'Hallowed Be Thy Name.'

"**THY KINGDOM COME** - This is how we thank Jesus and mean to tell Him: Jesus, we know nothing; without Your Kingdom, we are weak if You are not present together with us. Our kingdom passes whilst Yours does not pass away. Re-establish it!

"**THY WILL BE DONE** - O Lord, make our kingdom collapse. Let Your Kingdom be the only true one, and make us realize that our kingdom is destined to end and that at once, NOW, we allow Thy will to be done.

"**ON EARTH AS IT IS IN HEAVEN** - Here, Lord, it is said how the angels obey you, how they respect you; let us be like them, too; let our hearts open, too, and may they respect You like the angels do now. And make it possible for everything on earth to be Holy as it is in Heaven.

"**GIVE US THIS DAY OUR DAILY BREAD** - Give us, Lord, bread and food for our soul; give it to us now, give it to us today, give it to us always; that this bread may become food for our soul, may nourish us, may that bread sanctify You, may that bread become eternal. O Lord, we pray to you for our bread. O Lord, let us receive it. O Lord, help us to understand what we must do. Let us realize that our daily bread cannot be given to us without prayer.

"**AND FORGIVE US OUR TRESPASSES** - Forgive us Lord our trespasses. Forgive us them because we are not good and we are not faithful.

"**AS WE FORGIVE THOSE WHO TRESPASS AGAINST US** - Forgive us them so that we, too, may forgive those we were not capable of forgiving until now. O Jesus, forgive us our trespasses, we beseech You. You [meaning us] pray that your sins may be forgiven you in the same measure as you forgive those who trespass against you, without realizing that if your sins were really forgiven as you forgive those of others, it would be a very miserable thing. **This is what your Heavenly Father is telling you with these words.**

"AND LEAD US NOT INTO TEMPTATION - Lord, deliver us from hard trials. Lord, we are weak. Do not let our trials, O Lord, lead us to ruin.

"BUT DELIVER US FROM EVIL - Lord, deliver us from evil. May we succeed in finding something worthwhile in our trials, a step forward in our life.

"AMEN - So be it, Lord, Thy will be done."

March 3, 1990

To Marijana for the group:

"Dear children, this evening I call you in a special way to pray for all unborn children. Pray especially for the mothers who consciously kill their children. Dear children, I am sad because many children are being killed. Pray that there will be as few as possible of these mothers, and as few as possible of these cases in the world."

PART V

CONCLUSION:
HOW IMPORTANT IS
MEDJUGORJE
IN THE HISTORY
OF THE WORLD?

CONCLUSION

HOW IMPORTANT IS MEDJUGORJE IN THE HISTORY OF THE WORLD?

After reading these messages, you might think that Our Lady's messages are simplistic, that they are not that important, or that they are repetitive. After only one reading, this is understandable; however, Our Lady indicates there are mysteries to be discovered in Her messages.

October 23, 1986

> **"...Without your prayers, dear children, I cannot help you to fulfill the messages which the Lord has given me to give to you."**

Indeed, there is mystery in these messages and the clue to discovering the mysteries is prayer.

Throughout the Sixties and Seventies, the saying, *"If it feels good, do it,"* was popular. It seemed the devil roamed with freedom. Then astoundingly in 1981, Our Lady indicated that A GREAT WAR IS GOING TO TAKE PLACE. Our Lady announces to the earth . . . A DECLARATION OF WAR.

August 2, 1981

> **"...A great struggle is about to unfold. A struggle between my Son and satan. Human souls are at stake."**

As with many of Our Lady's messages, this message, read with prayer and contemplation, is so full of information that after thinking about it, we should realize that we all are underestimating the magnitude of Medjugorje. In World War II, countries fought for domination. Few complained about being drafted; indeed, many volunteered freely from this country (U.S.A.). They left their jobs, their businesses, their homes to fight. There was no price too high to pay. The volunteerism was so strong it was as if martial law had been declared. Factories changed over to producing arms and the whole country geared up for war without reservations.

Now . . . in 1981, Our Lady states that a full-fledged war is about to start between Heaven and hell - not for countries, but for the souls of the earth caught in the middle. A WAR OF THE WORLDS.

As with World War I and II, there is a battle plan with this war also. For three years Our Lady spoke of . . . **"The plan"**; **"Pray for the plan"**; **"Pray that satan does not thwart my plan"**; **"Pray for the plan My Son and I have"**; **"Pray that God's plan may be realized."** Then, after three years of speaking of this mysterious plan, She reveals it.

January 25, 1987

> **"Dear children, behold, also today I want to call you to start living a new life as of today. Dear children, I want you to comprehend that God has chosen each one of you, in order to use you in a great plan for the salvation of mankind. You are not able to comprehend how great your role is in God's design. Therefore, dear children, pray so that in prayer you may be able to comprehend what God's plan is in your regard. I am with you in order that you may be able to bring it about in all its fullness..."**

When we refer to a "battle plan" in this context, we do not mean aggressiveness. We define "battle plan" as the sense of mobilization that one needs in his struggle with the devil.

We have to step in combat against satan, and we have to be ready for sacrifice in this spiritual war. In a message given to the Medjugorje Prayer Group through Jelena, who receives interior locutions, Our Lady says:

July 30, 1987

"...darkness reigns over the whole world..."

We ought to be conscious of this tragic situation of the world today, then we should step in against satan. How? Our Lady tells us:

August 8, 1985

"Dear children, today I call you especially now to advance against satan by means of prayer. satan wants to work still more now that you know he is at work. Dear children, put on the armor for battle and with the Rosary in your hand defeat him!..."

Our Lady uses words "armor" and "battle" on purpose so we may realize that the activity of satan is like the invasion of a country by a foreign army. He takes strongholds and destroys. His only purpose is to use us for his own end. His main purpose is destruction. Our Lady gives us five weapons against satan:

1. Prayer (purification of the spirit)
2. Fasting (purification of the body)
3. Reading of the Bible (purification of the intelligence)
4. Confession (to make God's love grow in us)
5. Holy Communion (to make God's love grow in us)

Our Lady's plan for the salvation of mankind on earth is to defeat satan using these five weapons. We have to understand that the Medjugorje plan is a plan for the entire planet, that this war is a war of love against destruction, and that Our Lady's goal in this struggle is the reign of love. The Blessed Mother tells us:

November 20, 1986

To Marija:

> **"...You know that I love you and that I burn out of love for you. Therefore, dear children, you also decide for love so that you will burn out of love and daily experience God's love. Dear children, decide for love so that love prevails in all of you, but not human love, rather God's love..."**

We have to know that love is our first weapon against satan because love is the thing he hates and fears the most. Our armor is the fatal weapon of love, and this love encompasses the five weapons against the Ruler of Darkness!

November 25, 1987

Our Lady says that we have to pray,

> **"...that satan does not entice us with his pride and deceptive strength..."**

satan's weapon is also passivity or indifference "that destroy peace and prayer." That means that the devil is creating a certain inactivity and laziness that attacks the root of conversion; we have to be mobilized always. The victory happens through love and living in holiness.

July 10, 1986

> **"...today I am calling you to holiness. Without holiness you cannot live. Therefore, with love overcome every sin and with love overcome all the difficulties which are coming to you. Dear children, I beseech you to live love within yourselves..."**

In this battle of the "worlds" against satan, Our Lady puts a weapon in our hands, the only instrument against the powers of darkness, love!

July 31, 1986

"...Let your only instrument always be love. By love turn everything into good which satan desires to destroy and possess. Only that way will you be completely mine and I shall be able to help you..."

God is seeking soldiers to draft - Privates, Captains, Generals. Our Lady tells us our role is "great." One cannot give enough to this plan. We cannot do enough to live the messages. We should be willing to give everything and abandon ourselves completely because in today's WAR OF THE WORLDS, our homes, our money, and our businesses are not important. Only that we love.

All this does not mean to leave your state in life. If you've been given riches, give richly to the plan. If you are talented, use your talents abundantly for this plan. If you are a housewife, give Our Lady the ammunition She needs by praying at your kitchen sink. Everyone has a great role. Remember, Our Lady did more for the Kingdom of God by being a Mother than all the angels, prophets, and mankind together.

Our Lady wants each of us to have a special peace within us. This peace is reflected through our countenance and it will identify whose side we are on. Heaven will win if we write the messages of Our Lady on our hearts and live them.

Once you understand the plans God and Our Lady have for the world today, you cannot overemphasize, over stress, or exaggerate them. We are in the midst of something of such magnitude that there are few other times in human history to which it can be compared.

* ENDNOTE

Not all, but some of these messages are through a third party, usually a parish Franciscan. Some of these messages have been mentioned in various talks and may have been reworded from the exact way Our Lady gave them, perhaps for the sake of clarity, for a generalization of the message, or for making a point about a certain subject. The substance of these messages is correct; however, some of these dates may be approximated.

** ENDNOTE 2

If you would like to read more about Mirjana and the sign she received when her watch turned backwards, order the booklet, *Mirjana, A Mystery is Revealed* by writing: Caritas of Birmingham, 100 Our Lady Queen of Peace Drive, Sterrett, Alabama 35147 USA or call (205) 672-2000, ext. 315, 24 hours.

Messages of Our Lady
American Messages

In order to stay with the short description format of <u>Words From Heaven</u>, some descriptions of Our Lady's apparitions were shortened. The full descriptions follows:

The Apparitions of May 1998

Four years passed before Marija returned to Caritas. She came this time with her husband, Paolo, and her three young sons, all under the age of four. In those four years, not only had her own family grown, but the Caritas Community as well. The founder invited Marija and Paolo to come and see the life of the Community as Our Lady was inspiring it through Her messages. For this reason it was to be a private visit, and a week of rest and peace for Marija and her family. It was only after they arrived that the founder asked if Marija would consent to one public apparition. She agreed, and it was arranged for the final day of their visit, May 24. The first apparition took place Sunday morning, May 17, in the Bedroom of the founder's home.

May 17, 1998

The founder and his family gathered with Marija's family in the Bedroom at 11:00 a.m. for the apparition. The Caritas Community members met in the Field, and knelt facing the home, knowing Our Lady would be appearing there. After the apparition, the oldest son of our founder ran out to the Field and called the Community to meet at the lake down by the house. Coming down from the house to meet them, the founder then told them that he asked Marija to ask Our Lady to return this evening in the Field when the Community would be coming together for a prayer group meeting. Everyone was overjoyed when they learned Our Lady would have a second apparition. Marija said she had not had two apparitions in one day in many years. It was also a great joy for her.

It was a beautiful spring evening. The Community laid out blankets around Our Lady's statue as music played and laughing children ran barefoot through the grassy field. They ran to greet Marija and Paolo and their children as they joined the Community in the Field that evening for the apparition. Everyone was excited knowing Our Lady would soon be present. The Rosary began and when Our Lady appeared, She prayed over everyone and blessed them and then said:

"Do not forget that I am your Mother and that I love you. Go in peace."

These were the words Our Lady had left with them when last in the Field in Her visit in 1994. The Community was happy to receive Her words again, and the joy of Our Lady's presence stayed with them the rest of the evening as they sang and visited while all the children ran and played around them. And so began a beautiful week with Our Lady and Marija's family.

May 18-19, 1998

Each day of Marija and Paolo's visit was dedicated to sharing with them different aspects of the life and mission Our Lady had actively inspired through the Community's prayer inspired by Her messages. From the high-tech print shop in *The Tabernacle of Our Lady's Messages*, to their agrarian life, a week didn't seem long enough to show them what had transpired in just four short years. Each morning, the Community gathered in the Field at the normal time of day for their Rosary. On May 18 and 19, Our Lady appeared in the Field at approximately 11:40 a.m. Our

Lady prayed over everyone and blessed them. On May 19, the Community had prayed the Patriotic Rosary. It was the first time Marija had heard this prayed.

May 22, 1998

All the wives and mothers of the Community were invited to attend the apparition today. They gathered in the living room where the apparition would again take place. Marija sat in the same chair, everyone faced the fireplace where the picture of Our Lady hung, and prayed the Rosary. At around 11:45 a.m., Our Lady appeared. Marija said that She hesitated for a moment before She prayed over everyone and blessed them. The founder had wanted to ask Our Lady, through Marija, if She would individually pray over each of the women present, but he hesitated in being so bold. Yet, he felt that when Our Lady had hesitated in the apparition, it was a sign to him that he should have followed the inspiration and asked Marija to present this request to Our Lady.

May 23, 1998

Our Lady returned to the Bedroom today. Marija still had to sit in a chair with her leg up, but they arranged for her to do so in the Bedroom. All the husbands and fathers of the Community, as well as the heads of the Single Consecrated men's and women's houses. The founder asked Marija to ask Our Lady to pray over everyone individually in the apparition. When Our Lady appeared and heard this request, She responded by immediately placing Her hands over each person individually in prayer. Though Our Lady had given no message over the past five days, today She broke Her silence and again said the words:

"Do not forget that I am your Mother and that I love you."

May 24, 1998

This would be the last apparition of Marija's visit. Upon Marija's arrival at the beginning of the week, she had agreed to have one public apparition before she and her family returned to Italy. For the past several days, Community members manned the phones, calling everyone they could from across the United States to invite them to the apparition. Though they had only 3-4 days to decide, there were some people who immediately booked flights to fly in just for the apparition. The apparition took place in the Field. When Our Lady appeared, though She gave no message, Marija said She lovingly looked at each face present in the Field that day. Marija said that Our Lady makes this gesture only rarely, and the look of love on Our Lady's face as She does this always touches Marija deeply.

One final note concerning this visit of Our Lady. The founder had written a special novena to Jesus that the Community prayed before Marija and her family arrived. The Community had spent weeks planting flowers around the grounds of Caritas, and Cosmos seeds had been sown along the walking path through the Field, leading to Our Lady's statue and the Pine Tree. In the novena, the Community consecrated all the flowers to Jesus and asked, as a surprise to Our Lady, that each flower could represent 1,000 souls that would be saved through the Caritas mission, and that Jesus would keep this a secret from Our Lady until She arrived and saw them in full bloom. At the beginning of the week, though there were many buds on the Cosmos plants, not many flowers had bloomed out yet. This was the situation day by day, but towards the end of the week, the buds began popping open. On the final day, with Our Lady appearing in the Field, the Cosmos had come out in their full glory. They were dazzling to behold. Over 300 people had come in response to the invitation to be present. It was in the midst of this beautiful scene, when Our Lady had appeared and lovingly looked at each face present.

The Apparitions of December 8-13, 1999

Marija Lunetti, one of the six visionaries of Medjugorje, came back with Our Lady to be with the Community of Caritas during their annual Five Days of Prayer for the Reconciling of Ourselves, Our Families, and Our Nation Back to God. Approximately forty to fifty thousand pilgrims participated during these special five days of prayer. Our Lady did many beautiful things while She was here with them. The following is a description of the apparitions and Our Lady's messages given during these days.

December 8, 1999 Feast of the Immaculate Conception - Two Apparitions the Same Day

Close to five thousand people were present during this apparition which took place in the Field. At the moment of the apparition, Marija separated herself from the crowd and knelt in front of Our Lady's statue. Our Lady appeared to Marija at 10:45 a.m. The following are Marija's own words in describing the apparition:

"When Our Lady appeared, She came all dressed in gold. I recommended each of you and every intention of your hearts. Our Lady extended Her hands over all of us and prayed over us for a long time. I asked Our Lady to bless each and every one of us and to bless all the religious objects that you brought. Our Lady then smiled at all of us and prayed a moment and then She raised Her arm and blessed us with the Sign of the Cross. I then asked Our Lady if She had something that She wanted to tell us. Our Lady then looked at me and smiled and said:

'Do not forget that I am your Mother and that I love you.'

"Our Lady then raised Her hand again (a second time) and blessed us and then left."

After the apparition, Marija spoke to the crowd gathered and
said she had brought miraculous medals that Our Lady had
blessed. She wanted to personally hand out the medals to as
many pilgrims as possible. She gave out more than twelve thousand medals that day in the Field to pilgrims. During the apparition, Marija had asked Our Lady what time She would appear
the following day. Marija told the Community later that Our
Lady changed the time of the apparition from the morning to
5:40 p.m. in the evening. This was a sign for them that Our Lady
was "running the events there," that She had come with special
plans of Her own and had Her own schedule She wished them
to follow. Unknown to the Community, Marija had also asked if
Our Lady would appear again that evening, for a private apparition for the Community. Our Lady said, **"yes, in the home, at
a twenty 'til six."** They knew clearly that "in the home" meant
the "Bedroom" where Our Lady had appeared so many times
before to Marija on previous visits. Later that evening, one by
one, the Community gathered and found a small spot to kneel in
the Bedroom to pray the Rosary. Our Lady appeared to Marija
at 5:40 p.m. Our Lady stayed with them for several minutes,
a longer apparition than normal. Marija said that Our Lady
looked at each of the Community members individually, smiled,
blessed them all and then told them the words She had spoken
earlier in the day:

"Do not forget that I am your Mother and I love you."

December 11, 1999

The fourth day of the five days of prayer was a special Christmas
celebration, and the day that everyone looked forward to with
so much anticipation. The Field was surrounded by luminaries.
There were three bonfires on the edge of the circle of the Field.
And right by Our Lady's statue was a beautiful lit up Nativity.
Our Lady had told Marija She would be appearing right in the
middle of this special event. Every pilgrim was asked to bring
a flower to present before the crib of Jesus to show their love

and commitment to Him. Twelve thousand people came that night carrying their flowers and their hearts in their hands to Our Lady. The following is Marija's explanation of Our Lady's apparition that night in the Field:

"At the moment when Our Lady arrived tonight, She looked at each and every one of us. She remained in silence, and I understood that I was being permitted to be able to recommend all of us. As I began to recommend everyone and all the intentions that we have in our hearts, Our Lady remained in silence. Then I began to recommend all of the sick that are here. And Our Lady remained in silence and watched all of us still! I kept looking at Our Lady, and I smiled and said, 'Well, I recommend all the little ones and the big ones.' And Our Lady gave me a big smile in return. Then Our Lady began to pray over us. After She prayed over us, I felt in my heart that maybe Our Lady wanted to say something to us. And so I said, 'Well, do you have something to tell us?' And Our Lady said:

'Thank you with all my heart.'

"But the thing that I wanted to leave as a surprise for the end was that Our Lady wasn't alone. She came with three angels. Our Lady gave us a surprise even though it wasn't Christmas. She celebrated with us by bringing angels."

December 13, 1999

The Community gathered in the Bedroom around 7:00 a.m. to begin praying in preparation for the apparition. Marija and the Community prayed the Joyful mysteries of the Rosary, singing Christmas carols between each decade. The founder of the Community of Caritas had asked the Community to write out petitions and place them on the bed, from the oldest to the youngest. Of this apparition, all prayed in thanksgiving for such a beautiful five days and for this unexpected seventh apparition. For Our Lady to change the time of the apparition because of

Marija's flying out this day and come early was a great grace. As Our Lady appeared, they could tell by Marija's face this apparition was special. They didn't know why, but Marija throughout this apparition had a smile on her face. In ecstasy, Marija's face is always serious. As the apparition ended, Marija's eyes followed Our Lady back to Heaven for several moments. Marija then broke her constant routine of always saying the Magnificat and said in English, *"Our Lady came with five angels!"* She began then to pray the Magnificat as she and all of the Community wept. Following is Marija's description of the apparition:

> *"Our Lady came with **five angels** today! Our Lady prayed over us and blessed us. She looked at each and every one of us."*

After the apparition, the Community asked Marija to describe the angels. She said they were small, like the size of a two-year-old. Two had black hair, two had brown hair, and one had blonde hair. Two were on each side of Our Lady and the blonde haired angel fluttered above Her head. Marija said that they were gazing at Our Lady, never taking their eyes off of Her. Marija also said that never, in all her apparitions, has she seen the angels look away from Our Lady even for a second.

The Apparitions of December 10 - 15, 2001

December 15, 2001

Marija left on this day to go back to Italy to her family. The founder of Caritas asked Our Lady through Marija during her apparition on December 14th, if She would appear early on Saturday so that the Community could be present for one more apparition and receive Her blessing once more. Our Lady said, **"Yes."** The Community began to gather in the Bedroom at 6:30 a.m. They all wrote out their personal intentions and placed them on the Bed. They prayed the Sorrowful and Glorious Mysteries of the Rosary in preparation for Our Lady's apparition. Our Lady appeared to Marija at precisely 8:00 a.m. The following is Marija's description of this apparition on Saturday, December 15, 2001:

"When Our Lady came, I recommended each of us and all our intentions in our hearts. Our Lady prayed over us for a long time. I presented a private question to Our Lady. Immediately upon asking the question, Our Lady smiled and gave a private answer. Our Lady looked at each of us and then blessed us. She ascended back to Heaven, saying, **'Go in peace.'** *Our Lady was very happy and joyful during this apparition."*

The private question from the Founder was related to something that Our Lady had spoken to him about fourteen years before through Marija. Through the years he had asked Our Lady on several occasions, never receiving an affirmative message. He, along with the Community, was very happy that in this apparition Our Lady gave light of an affirmation to him.

In the development of the event of December 10th-15th, Our Lady had made a full circle, giving more than could be deserved. For months, the Community had worked around the clock, literally, and Our Lady spoke in many more ways than just words. For She gave a sign that She too is with them around the clock. Our Lady's first apparition here for the December 8th-14th event was private and took place at **8:00 p.m.** in the Bedroom; night-time. Marija was not told beforehand what time the apparition would be. Upon arriving at the house, they immediately began praying the Rosary in preparation for Our Lady's apparition, so the 8:00 p.m. apparition coincided precisely with the finishing of the Rosary. The December 15th apparition, the last apparition of the event, was at **8:00 a.m.** in the Bedroom; morning time. Our Lady chose the time on both of these occasions, six days apart from each other. Our Lady, in these six days, made a full circle, a completion, which yet again speaks to all **"through men, nature, and so many things..."**(Her words on March 25, 1990). Her gestures are signs, their purpose to speak to all in order to lead all more deeply into conversion. Our Lady's coming at **8:00 p.m.** and finishing Her stay here, six days later at **8:00 a.m.,** shows how She wants to bring all from night into the day, from darkness to light, from the haze to a new morning - for Christianity...to the springtime. What made the Founder ponder this in the first place was Marija's insistence immediately upon her arrival at his home, *"that we must pray the Rosary now,"* although Marija was not given a time. With more than 85 apparitions in the Community of Caritas, mostly in the Bedroom, over the years, Our Lady has never come at 8:00 a.m. nor 8:00 p.m. in the evening. Generally, the times She has chosen have been 10:40 a.m., 5:40 p.m., 10:30 p.m. These two apparitions that took place on December 10th and December 15th were spontaneous apparitions, uncommon. They were not planned and were at the discretion of Our Lady Herself. She chose the time and the place both times, and from Her actions, came forth the understanding of what She wished all to understand through them. The Community of Caritas is called to witness to others. Our Lady's 8:00 p.m. to 8:00 a.m. gesture speaks of Her bringing all to a **"new dawn."**

The Apparitions of August 8 - 25, 2003

August 10, 2003

The Community worked the next day setting up an altar for Our Lady. They had brought a large statue of Our Lady with them and set it upon a table that overlooked the ocean. They wandered through the house looking for decorations for the altar. Soon starfish began to be collected and arranged at Our Lady's feet. When the last starfish was found in the house and placed by the others, all were touched to count a total of 12 starfish, 12 stars, for Our Lady's crown. The apparition on this day took place at 3:35 p.m. Our Lady prayed over everyone and blessed them. Just after the apparition, a few of the children spotted dolphins swimming by. It took several moments for everyone to focus on them, as the dolphins were quite a distance away, but suddenly everyone began to realize that hundreds of dolphins were swimming by. It was a sight to see, really amazing. Everyone felt it was a special grace given by Our Lady. After yesterday's apparition about being on vacation, finding the 12 "star"fish for Our Lady's altar, and now the dolphins, there was a special sense of Our Lady's presence felt by all. Our Lady continued to appear each day in the house at the time the Community prepared for the apparition in prayer.

August 11, 2003

Today, some left for the day to go fishing and didn't return until late evening. It was decided, therefore, that the apparition would not take place until after dinner. Even though it was late, the Rosary was peaceful and the prayer was felt deeply. The apparition was very beautiful and peaceful. It was also a longer apparition. Marija said afterwards that Our Lady had prayed a long time over everyone, praying the whole time, until She ended the apparition with Her blessing.

August 12, 2003

This was another late night apparition. The Rosary began around 9:35 p.m. The rest of the Community from Caritas was driving to meet everyone in Florida. They had hoped that they could make it for the apparition, but were too late. The Rosary again was peaceful and prayer was deep. There had been a strong feeling of the presence of Our Lady each evening. In the apparition tonight, Our Lady prayed over everyone and blessed them.

August 13, 2003

A few Community members had stayed behind at Caritas but now joined everyone in Florida. They came with bunches of beautiful flowers to prepare Our Lady's altar for the feast of Her Assumption that would take place in a few days. There was a special joy in the room having the whole Community together. As the altar was being prepared today, the founder suggested everyone write out petitions to Our Lady, he then asked Marija if they could present their petitions to Our Lady "during" the apparition. Marija agreed. When Marija went into ecstasy that evening, one by one, each person carried their petition up to Our Lady and dropped it into a small sailboat canister. It took several minutes for all of them to do so. All during this time, Marija gazed silently at Our Lady. When Marija came out of ecstasy she told us what had happened:

"The moment of apparition, I recommend all of us and our intentions and Our Lady pray over us and I recommend our special letters and Our Lady smiled and She said:

'I wish to give you graces. Ask for them.'"

Having just spent nearly an hour writing down all their petitions, they were in awe of Our Lady's words and realized that it makes Our Lady happy when people come to Her with all their problems and needs, their hopes and dreams.

August 14, 2003

The apparition took place later in the afternoon. The Community gathered around 4:00 p.m. to pray the Rosary. Immediately after the apparition the Community would leave for Holy Mass to celebrate the Vigil of Our Lady's Assumption. It was the wedding anniversary of one of the couples in the Community, so they were placed up front with Marija, along with their children. The beauty of this time of day, with the sun positioning itself to begin setting, the rays on the water, the blue of Our Lady's statue, the colors of the flowers, the open and bright room, the freshness of the air by the ocean, the little girls in their sweet summer dresses, and the pleasure of the coolness of the air after being in the hot sun all day, created a near perfect setting for Our Lady's apparition. It was a little piece of Heaven. The Rosary was beautiful. When Our Lady came, Marija particularly recommended the couple on their wedding anniversary to Our Lady. Marija said Our Lady prayed over everyone and blessed them.

August 19, 2003

The founder of Caritas arranged to have several tractor-trailer rigs of salt delivered to the *Tabernacle of Our Lady's Messages*, with the hope that Our Lady would bless the salt as She had done in the apparitions at Caritas in December of 2001, with the first loads of salt. The Blessed Salt has been used by thousands of people as a sacramental for protection and to call down God's blessing. This would be the first apparition in The *Tabernacle of Our Lady's Messages*, and though the salt was on the first floor, where the print shop is located, the Community desired to have the apparition in the writing office of their founder, where all the writings concerning Our Lady's messages take place. Everyone was of one mind to the decision. The Community met at 6:00 p.m. to begin the Rosary, with Marija and Paolo joining them. Marija said:

"Our Lady blessed us, and She prayed over us."

Marija asked Our Lady to bless the salt during the apparition. Marija said:

"Our Lady bless also, I ask for all salt, on first floor...She bless, She make Sign of Cross...I recommend all of our intentions, and what we have in our hearts, and I ask to bless all salt together. She make little prayer over us, and after She bless."

August 21, 2003

This was the only public apparition during Marija's visit. The apparition took place in the Field, with the cosmos flowers in full bloom, lining the path to the inner circle of the Field. Marija commented that the number of angels in the apparition on August 15th numbered like the Cosmos in the Field. They (flowers) added beauty and grace to the surroundings as pilgrims began gathering in at 5:30 p.m. to prepare for Our Lady's coming. It was a very hot, humid evening, with record-breaking heat. Three Rosaries were prayed before the apparition. The air was still, the heat suffocating. As the third Rosary began, a large storm cloud covered the sun. At the same time, a strong, cool wind began to blow, and continued all through the Rosary up to apparition time refreshing everyone. It was beautiful to watch the expressions on people's faces. There was not one person in the Field who did not recognize Our Lady's presence in the wind. Marija described what happened in the apparition:

"The moment of apparition, I recommend all of our intentions, all that we have in our hearts. And Our Lady pray over us. And I ask also that She bless all objects that we have here. And Our Lady after praying, She blessed all objects with the Sign of the Cross, and I recommend in a special way all these people who are here and in a special way all sick people and Our Lady one other time, She open Her hands and She begin to pray, and She pray five minute, I don't know (a long time). And after She give blessing like Sign of the Cross, and She say **'Go in peace,'** *and She leave. Today Our Lady is tranquil, and She watch all of us."*

When Our Lady "watches all of us," She actually scans the crowd, looking at each face. Marija says it is a very endearing grace as it shows that each face is dear to Her.

August 25, 2003

Paolo, Marija and their children would be returning to Italy today. The apparition took place in Atlanta, from where they would be leaving. Today, also, Our Lady would give the monthly message to the world before their flight home. The founder and his family were present for the apparition. Not having much to make an altar for Our Lady, a very colorful quilt that had been in the car was used as a covering for a makeshift altar for the apparition. Though some thought it might be "too colorful" the founder said, "Our Lady likes color," and so it stayed.

The Community back home was made aware of when the apparition would be. They went to the Field early to pray in preparation for Our Lady's words. The apparition lasted 4 ½ minutes. The message Our Lady gave this day will always be a reminder to the Community of the special "vacation" they spent with Our Lady. When Marija knelt down, she said, *"Let's ask for a beautiful message today."* The message:

August 25, 2003—Monthly Message to the World

> **"Dear children! Also today I call you to give thanks to God in your heart for all the graces which He gives you, also through the signs and colors that are in nature. God wants to draw you closer to Himself and moves you to give Him glory and thanks. Therefore, little children, I call you anew to pray, pray, pray and do not forget that I am with you. I intercede before God for each of you until your joy in Him is complete. Thank you for having responded to my call."**

For those in the room who were involved in using the quilt on the altar, it made them think that Our Lady had "heard" their conversation about the color of the quilt. But also, there were so many beautiful memories from the past two and a half weeks, being with Our Lady in nature—the sea, the altar in the beach house, the 12 starfish, the beautiful flowers that surrounded Our Lady's statue, the cosmos blooming in the Field, the cool wind the night of the 21st of August's apparition…their whole time with Our Lady signs were given to draw them closer to Her heart and to the heart of God.

The Apparitions of April 30 to May 6, 2004

April 30, 2004

Marija had arrived, with her youngest son, Giovanni, for five days with Our Lady held at Caritas in which thousands of pilgrims were expected, May 1-5, 2004. This evening, the Community gathered in the Bedroom to greet and welcome Our Lady in the apparition. Marija said:

"Today when Our Lady came She prayed over all of us and blessed us all. I asked Her about tomorrow and Our Lady answered:

'Tomorrow morning, here, and the day after in the afternoon in the Field by the Tree.'

"She blessed us all and left."

The Community was excited for two reasons. First, that Our Lady was letting us know Her preference for when and where the apparitions would be each day. And secondly, because She referred to both the Bedroom and the Field, adding the words **"by the Tree"** in Her message, showing them that She recognized these special places of prayer with Her words.

May 2, 2004

The apparition was in the evening in the Field just as Our Lady requested. The apparition took place around 6:40 p.m. Our Lady was crowned with a wreath of flowers the evening before, but a storm during the night had blown the crown off the statue. When Marija came out to the Field, she immediately noticed Our Lady had no crown and said we must make another crown. A new one was put together so that they were able to crown Our Lady just before Her apparition. It was beautiful. The following is Marija's description of the apparition:

"Everybody sit down. I wanted to greet each and every one of you that are here tonight and have come to be with us. Tonight, when Our Lady came, She was very happy and probably because She saw all of you here. And when you prayed, Our Lady listened to you. I recommended each one of you and everything that you held in your heart. Our Lady prayed over us and She gave us Her blessing. In a special way I asked Our Lady to pray for those who are sick here. And Our Lady gave us a second blessing. And then I asked Our Lady to bless everything that you brought with you, your rosaries, your medals and anything else that you wanted blessed, and Our Lady, again, blessed everything. And then at the end, Our Lady spoke, and She said:

'My dear children, do not forget that I am your Mother, and that I love you, and that I bless you.'

"And then She went back to Heaven...unfortunately. It would be a real joy for us to always remain with Our Lady."

There was a large gathering in the Field. Many profound conversions took place in the midst of these apparitions. For tomorrow, Our Lady said the apparition would be in the Bedroom in the morning. The Community was again in awe to see Our Lady directing the events of these days.

May 4, 2004

In yesterday's apparition, Our Lady said the apparition would be in the Bedroom again, in the morning. Today there were other pilgrims along with several priests with the Community who were present for the apparition. Marija's description of the apparition:

"The moment of the apparition Our Lady came. I recommend all our intention. And Our Lady pray over us and She bless us all. She bless also all objects for blessing. Also Our

*Lady pray and bless also people who is in Field. She blessed
two times. One for religious objects, one for people present.
Our Lady said:*

'Same time. Same place.'"

Tomorrow is the last day of the apparitions for the pilgrims, and
most everyone expected Our Lady to say the apparition would
be in the Field, but they were surprised to hear Marija say that
Our Lady wanted the apparition in the Bedroom once again. For
the Community, we believed Our Lady's actions were reconfirm-
ing the foundation of the Community and mission of Caritas by
emphasizing the Bedroom. She was bringing the Community
back to its roots.

May 5, 2004

Most of the Community was in the Field praying the Patriotic
Rosary with the pilgrims. From the Bedroom, the patriotic songs
could be heard sung over the loud speaker. Concerning the
apparition, Marija said:

*"Our Lady blessed us all. She prayed over us. She blessed
all those in the Field. I ask in special way bless also those
in Field and all the objects. Two blessings."* (objects and
people).

The five days of prayer went quickly, but the grace was abound-
ing to all those present. One priest said that his entire priest-
hood was renewed during his time at Caritas. Each priest who
attended heard several hundred confessions during the week,
and was amazed at how many hadn't been to the sacrament for
many, many years. It was quite a testimony to them of the grace
that accompanies Our Lady. She won the hearts of many souls.

May 6, 2004

Marija had asked Our Lady to come early this morning, as she had to immediately leave for the airport after the apparition. Our Lady agreed. The Community gathered at 7:00 a.m. to begin praying the Rosary to prepare for the apparition at 8:00 a.m. The founder had a special request to make of Our Lady. As the Community and mission were experiencing heavy persecution, he asked Marija to ask Our Lady for words that would help them to endure any attack that would come, especially in light of all the conversions that had just taken place through the apparitions these last five days. Marija's description of the apparition:

"Our Lady came and I recommended all of us, and She prayed over all of us who were present. She blessed all religious articles with a Sign of the Cross and in the end She gave a message (in regards to the question asked):

'I give you my love. You give it to others.'

"And She left with a smile on Her face."

Marija was visibly excited, and her voice was filled with joy when she told us Our Lady had given a message. Marija then went into the private bathroom adjacent to the Bedroom to write down the message. For several minutes, all those in the Bedroom knelt in silence, many in tears. When Marija came out, it was time for good-byes, but it was a sweet ending to a beautiful week with Our Lady.

The Apparitions of July 20 - August 8, 2005

July 21, 2005

Months of work were finally coming to an end as the Community

neared the time of the five days of prayer, though there was still
another week filled with many things that still needed to be
completed. Perhaps because of all the work and very long hours,
Our Lady gave the Community a very special grace upon Her
return to their home. When Marija and her boys arrived, the
Community had just enough time to say hello, when it was time
to prepare for the apparition. Our Lady came at about 6:40 p.m.
Marija said:

> *"I said to Our Lady, welcome here. Our Lady is smiling and
> She pray over us and give to us Her Special Blessing. She
> pray before, and after She give Special Blessing. She smil-
> ing."*

Our Lady's smile and the gift of Her Special Blessing caused all
those gathered to be happy and in smiles too.

July 31, 2005

The apparition this evening was in the living room of the founder's home. This would be the last private apparition before the
apparitions would be opened up to the public for five days of
prayer in preparation for Our Lady's birthday, August 5th.

After praying the Rosary, Marija went into ecstasy, as normal,
but half way through everyone in the room knew something special was taking place. Marija, still in ecstasy, began to pray out
loud, the Our Father and Glory Be. We knew she was praying
with Our Lady in the apparition. The apparition lasted almost
six minutes—a very long time for an apparition. By the time the
apparition ended, everyone was excited to hear what had taken
place. Marija, herself was excited, and began to describe the
apparition:

> *"One special gift today when Our Lady come. She pray over
> all, one by one. I don't know how long apparition was today?
> Very Long! Our Lady said to pray Our Father and Glory Be*

for Her intentions. I ask also for all those in Field. Our Lady
said apparition, **'will be in the Field tomorrow, same time.'***"*

Marija began searching for words to describe what else had happened. She said that when Our Lady was praying over each one
of the Community, She was also blessing each person. Marija
said as She went to each person in the room, that Our Lady was
pressing up against Marija—Marija felt like she was something
like a fence or a barrier to Our Lady who was trying to reach
past Marija to reach each one of the Community and Marija's
own family. Marija felt like she should move out of Our Lady's
way. This had never happened to Marija in an apparition. It was
moving to her and to all those in the room as she explained in
more detail, her feeling. Marija said she did not see the individual when Our Lady was praying over each one. Our Lady
prayed in silence. To Marija, the apparition felt like at least an
hour and that Our Lady prayed something like five minutes a
piece over each of the Community members in the room. When
Our Lady first appeared, She came joyful, then She became serious when praying over each person.

In more detail, Marija said that it felt to her that Our Lady
was *too* close, that she needed to move back. One Community
member who was kneeling close to Marija, saw her eyes going
back and forth throughout the apparition. Marija said it was
something like the first days of the apparitions in Medjugorje
when Our Lady said people could touch Her, and came up to
approach Her.

August 1-5, 2005 Apparitions
In Preparation of Our Lady's Birthday

August 1, 2005 - Monday

Today was the first day of the five days of prayer with Our
Lady. All the pilgrims were joining the Community in praying

three Hail Mary's on the top of each hour, offering a nine-hour novena each day for Our Lady's intentions for Her birthday. This prayer was in response to Our Lady's July 25, 2005 monthly message, given in the Bedroom a few days before, in which Our Lady asked for novenas **"so that satan be far from you and grace be around you."** The apparition was in the evening in the presence of thousands in the Field. Marija described what took place in the apparition:

> *"The moment Our Lady came, I recommend all our intentions, all what we have in our hearts. Our Lady prayed over us and She blessed us all. And I ask also for blessing of letters (petitions) that we have here, intentions, and objects for blessing and Our Lady smiling while She blessed and She said,* **'Go in peace.'"**

When Marija asked about the apparition tomorrow, August 2nd, Our Lady said:

"Same time. Same place."

August 4, 2005 - Thursday - Mary's Eve

This night was the eve of Our Lady's birthday. Our Lady appeared at 6:46 p.m. The apparition was in the Field. Marija said:

> *"In the moment of apparition, when Our Lady came, I recommend to Our Lady all our intentions. Our Lady prayed over us for a long time. After, I asked Our Lady to bless us and to bless all objects that we have with us. And Our Lady, with the Sign of the Cross, blessed all of us and our objects. And I asked about (tomorrow's) apparition, and Our Lady said,*

'Same time, same place.'

> *"And Our Lady always says,* **'Go in peace.'"**

After the apparition, the pilgrims were asked to leave the Field. A very special event was planned for the evening, one that the Community had been excited to experience ever since they learned Marija would come for Our Lady's birthday this year. The Community jumped into action. They had built a sweet little life size house to represent the house of St. Joachim and St. Anne, Mary's parents. While tractors were busy moving the house in place, everyone in the Community began lighting the 2,021 candles for every year Our Lady had existed. On a back wall of the house was an enlarged antique picture depicting Mary's birth. The picture was soon lit up with all the candles that filled the entire house. That night, pilgrims were allowed to re-enter the Field, they knelt before the image of Our Lady as a tiny baby, enraptured by the re-creation of that moment of Her creation.

A special Rosary had been written for this night, called the Mysteries of Mary and in between each decade a meditation was offered to bring the hearts of all those gathered back to the moment when the infant Mary was born. The 3rd Mystery of Mary spoke of a tremendous storm, according to several mystics who had visions of Mary's birth, that suddenly descended just moments before She was born. Lightening, thunder, torrential rain and even hail rained down as if a huge battle was being waged in the Heavens over this tiny baby who would one day bring the world its Savior.

Our Lady's Nativity had never been celebrated on August 4th like this before. It was profoundly beautiful, and many people remained in the Field the entire night, along side the Community, under a star-filled sky so that this moment of grace would not pass too quickly. Though it was August, it felt like Christmas. Those present sensed they were partaking in something mystical. Indeed, the first public celebration of the Eve of Mary ever held on August 4, in the history of the world. Our Lady, for the past four days was strangely silent, only saying **"Same time. Same place."** But after the birthday apparition the next day, August

5, 2005, it became plainly evident that Our Lady was creating a craving, an anticipation in their hearts for Her words or action, that on Her birthday She would more than satisfy them.

August 5, 2005 - Friday - Mary's Birthday

Birthday cake and milk from the Community of Caritas dairy cows were in abundance for the Birthday party the Community gave Our Lady joined by thousands of pilgrims in the Field in the morning. But the party they gave Our Lady was nothing compared to the party She gave that afternoon in the Field for Her apparition. Great anticipation was felt as pilgrims entered the Field that evening. The sky was partly cloudy, but also blue patches were scattered and the sun was shining. There was no rain and many left their umbrellas behind as there wasn't a forecast for bad weather. All those in the Field gathered around Our Lady's Nativity to begin praying the Rosary.

Rapidly, after beginning the Rosary with clear skies, the weather began changing. The wind picked up, gray clouds began to roll in, and thunder could be heard in the far distance. As each decade was prayed, the thunder became louder, lightning began appearing and rain could be heard and seen in the distance, but heading toward the crowd in the Field. The nearer to apparition time, the more severe the weather became. As Marija and her husband made their way up to Our Lady's little house for the apparition, the storm suddenly broke out in full fury. Thunder so loud it shook the ground, lightning cracking down all around, torrential rain and wind pouring down so hard that umbrellas were useless, and then, amazingly, hail began pounding down on people in the open Field, where a lone pine tree reached up in the sky, where lightning bolts were everywhere.

Yet the reaction of all those who were present was of wonder, awe and yes, joy...because there was a realization that God was allowing a recreation of Our Lady's birth in the storm that we were experiencing, just as we heard the night before in the 3rd

Marian Mystery, when Our Lady was born. As the word "hail" was said, beginning the 'Hail Holy Queen', hail began falling upon the people! No one left the Field. Many were laughing out loud with pure joy, even while being pelted with hail. The prayers had to be shouted to be heard above the storm, and then just at the exact moment Marija went into ecstasy, a lightning bolt struck, coming out of the sky exactly down to the point where Our Lady appeared, just over the little house, so loud and so bright, yet without causing any harm. Our Lady appeared at 6:48 p.m. The apparition lasted nearly four minutes. Marija's description of the apparition follows:

"When Our Lady came I recommended all of us and all our intentions. Our Lady prayed over us for a long time, and She blessed us with Her Special Motherly blessing. Our Lady came with a gold dress, and there were three angels around Her. Then She said:

'Dear children! Do not forget that I am your Mother and I love you.'"

Marija relayed Our Lady then said:

"I thank you for your novenas."

Then Our Lady gave the final blessing and said:

"Go in peace."

The joy of the storm, hail, lightning and then for Our Lady to thank the group for the 9-hour daily novenas for Her birthday was such tangible evidence that Our Lady was attentive in watching everything we did. This left the crowd in awe. Marija said that she thinks the sacrifice of being here, under the rain was just the candle on the cake. The 15-minute ride back to the hotels ended up taking 2-3 hours. Traffic lights and power lines were down from the rapidly moving storm that came from nowhere. Without power, people stayed outside their hotels late into the night, talking of this wonder. Many people relayed it as a Fatima miracle experience. The storm came directly out of the east, which no one in the valley had ever seen happen before, as storms always come out of the west and south. A neighbor three miles down the road said that he saw the biggest bolt of lightning he'd ever seen in his life over the Caritas area, though he's not a believer in the Field. Eerily, the sun was setting in the west, causing it to cast its rays under the storm clouds; a phenomenon also never witnessed, as the storm came from the east.

August 6, 2005 - Saturday

The apparition was in the Bedroom this evening. Marija said it was a short apparition today,

> *"She come, She pray over us, and She go. Tomorrow:*
>
> **'Same time, same place.'"**

<u>The Apparitions of November 24 - 25, 2005</u>

November 24, 2005 - Thursday, Thanksgiving Day

Marija returned to Caritas for a very short visit in November 2005. Though it was a short visit, it was during a very beautiful and significant time in the Community. Thanksgiving Day is a feast day celebrated in the Community, not only because of what that day is for our Nation, but because it marks the very first time Our Lady appeared and blessed the Field. It was Our Lady who chose November 24, 1988, Thanksgiving Day, to be Her first apparition in the Field. She told Marija that She invited "everyone" to come to the apparition, and She gave a message that day inviting us to live Her messages and that She would intercede for everyone who came to pray here. Through reflecting on Our Lady's actions through prayer, the founder of Caritas realized that Our Lady chose to appear in the Field for the purpose of calling the United States of America back to its religious and historical roots. This site had been consecrated to Our Lady's Immaculate Heart for the intention of our Nation's conversion. As She owned the Field, through this consecration, She decided to make use of it for our Nation's future. In this year of 2005, Thanksgiving Day fell on the exact date of this apparition, 17 years ago.

Pumpkins, flowers, corn stalks and hay bales decorated Our Lady's statue in the Field, along with messages of Our Lady and words from the pilgrims who first made their way to this continent. The Community had much to reflect upon in this Rosary, and much to be thankful for, especially this day when Our Lady was with them to celebrate. The apparition took place at the normal time of 10:40 a.m. Our Lady came on the 3rd set of 7,7,7 — on the 3rd Hail Mary. Marija said:

"Our Lady prayed over us, and She blessed us."

Our Lady was strong in the wind today.

November 25, 2005 - Friday

Another big grace awaited the Community during Marija's short visit. They were in the presence of Our Lady when She gave the November monthly message to the world through Marija. The apparition took place in the Bedroom. The apparition lasted 4 minutes, 28 seconds. Marija immediately left the room after the apparition to write down the message. After relaying the message to the parish in Medjugorje, she came back to translate the message for the Community. These were the words Our Lady gave on this day:

"Dear children! Also today I call you to pray, pray, pray until prayer becomes life for you. Little children, at this time, in a special way, I pray before God to give you the gift of faith. Only in faith will you discover the joy of the gift of life that God has given you. Your heart will be joyful think-

ing of eternity. I am with you and love you with a tender love. Thank you for having responded to my call."

The Apparitions of July 1-21, 2008

July 1, 2008 - Day of Repentance and Seeking Forgiveness

More than 35 pilgrims were randomly chosen to attend today's apparition in the Bedroom, while the Community joined all the other pilgrims in the Field. Marija asked everyone to kneel down and pray in preparation for the apparition. She said to pray for all those who are not here, for those who are in the Field, as well as those we recommend in our prayers and in our hearts. In a special way, she prayed for all sick people, because, as Marija said, what is impossible for man is possible for God. We ask Our Lady, who is here present, for the grace of healing. Our Lady appeared during the fifth Our Father, Hail Mary and Glory Be. The apparition was three minutes and forty-five seconds long. The following is Marija's description of today's apparition:

"In moment of apparition, when Our Lady came, I recommended to Our Lady our intentions. Our Lady prayed over us and She blessed us all. I recommended also all religious objects to be blessed. Also, people who are in the Field. And Our Lady blessed also all the people there."

Marija asked Our Lady where and when the apparition would be the following day on July 2. Our Lady responded, **"Same time, same place."**

July 2, 2008 - Day of Individual Consecrations

Today's apparition was in the Bedroom at 11:40 a.m. It was on this day that all those present made an individual consecration to the Hearts of Jesus and Mary. The crowds had grown since the day before, filling the inner circle of the Field as well as the outer edges of the Field where people were finding a bit of shade from the trees. There was a deep prayerfulness among those who were gathered.

In the midst of about 50 people, kneeling tightly in the Bedroom, Our Lady appeared to Marija over the Bed. The apparition lasted almost three minutes. The following is Marija's description of the apparition:

"In the moment of the apparition, when Our Lady came, I recommended, like always, all of your intentions. Our Lady prayed over all of us and She blessed us all. I recommended all the sick people, and in a special way I asked also to bless all religious objects, and all the people who are there in the Field. Our Lady then prayed over everyone for a short time and She made the Sign of the Cross in a blessing. And I asked Our Lady for tomorrow. I said tomorrow is a special day, the Vigil for the 4th, and Our Lady smiling, said that the apparition would be at 10:00 at night in the Field." (Immediately upon hearing this, several in the room wanted Marija to repeat what she had just said as they were shocked to hear Our Lady's choice for a vigil apparition in anticipation of honoring God for the birth of our Nation on the 4th of July.) *"She said, not here, but in the Field, tomorrow night, 10:00 p.m. Our Lady said* [the apparition is] *for everybody. These days Our Lady appears always here (in the Bedroom), saying* **'Same time, same place.'** *And I think all other people are a little bit jealous of us. So thank God. So not two times will there be an apparition, but only tomorrow night, in the Field for everybody. You go out now and tell everyone this beautiful news. And God bless you all."*

July 3, 2008 - Day for Consecration of Our Families

Prayer for tonight's vigil began around 8:00 p.m. Not since the apparitions in 1988 had Our Lady appeared in a night time apparition. Everyone was moved by this uncommon gesture of Our Lady. As pilgrims gathered in the Field, the scene that greeted them was stunning, as a special platform had been built around Our Lady's statue with thousands of red, white, and blue candles lit to light up Our Lady's image. That night Marija's face was intense during the long apparition that lasted more than eight minutes. Afterwards, Marija surprised the thousands gathered in the Field by saying for the July 4th apparition, Our Lady again said She would appear in the Field at 10:00 p.m. Knowing that this was something out of the ordinary, and feeling that Our Lady was giving everyone another day to spend in prayer for our Nation's conversion, joy swept through the crowd. Marija then asked the pilgrims, *"Would you rather sleep or would you rather pray?"* and then she said, *"I think we must pray very much in these next 24 hours for your Nation."* Marija stayed in the Field until well after midnight with everyone who wanted to stay, praying the Our Father, Hail Mary and Glory Be over and over again, with songs sung intermittently.

July 4, 2008 - Consecration of Our Nation

Prayer in preparation for the apparition began around 8:00 p.m. Just moments before Our Lady's apparition, everyone together prayed the Solemn Consecration of Our Nation to Our Lady. Small lights lit up the entire Field from flashlights of people turning their eyes to this prayer, but though the light was from flashlights, the effect was more like candlelight. Everyone then, in one voice, prayed this beautiful prayer to Our Lady. You could hear the words echoing through the Field. Everyone was intense in their prayer. It was the most beautiful scene, as the love for our country could be seen on every face, and heard in every voice. Marija then began to pray the seven Our Father's, Hail Mary's, and Glory Be's, and suddenly Our Lady appeared. Marija's face was serious throughout the apparition that lasted for five minutes. At the end of the apparition, Marija said that Our Lady had come with three angels tonight. She prayed over everyone present, blessed them and blessed all their religious articles. Marija recommended all those present and in a special way all the sick. Our Lady gave the following message:

"Thank you for all your prayers, be my extended hands in this peaceless world."

Our Lady said, **"Tomorrow's apparition will be in the Bedroom at 11:40 a.m."** And Our Lady finished, saying, **"Go in peace."**

July 7, 2008

The apparition took place in the Bedroom. It was a special apparition for the Community as beforehand, it was announced that one of the young couples in the Community had just become engaged to be married, just moments before the Rosary. The following is Marija's description of the apparition:

"When Our Lady appeared, I recommended everyone to Our Lady and their intentions. In a special way, I recommended this young couple. Before giving Her blessing, Our Lady looked at the couple and smiled and then blessed everyone in the Bedroom. Our Lady also blessed all the pilgrims in the Field."

When Marija asked Our Lady where and when the apparition would be the following day, Our Lady said it would be in the Bedroom at 10:00 p.m. Our Lady had chosen to appear at 10:00 p.m. on two different nights during the Five Days of Prayer, July 3rd and 4th, but the next three days (July 5, 6, & 7), the apparitions were in the Bedroom at 11:40 a.m. Not since the first apparitions in 1988-89, twenty years ago, has Our Lady chosen to appear at 10:00 p.m. in the evening. Everyone was surprised at Her actions of appearing July 8th, also at 10:00 p.m.

July 8, 2008

It was a beautiful, star-filled night for the crowd who had gathered for Our Lady's apparition. Light from the half-moon flooded the Field, giving enough light to see the surrounding pilgrims that circled Our Lady's statue. When the Rosary began at 9:00 p.m., everyone knelt and faced the house where Our Lady would appear. Just before 10:00 p.m., Our Lady appeared to Marija in the Bedroom. Our Lady prayed over everyone and blessed them. Our Lady also blessed everyone in the Field. When Marija asked about tomorrow's apparition, Our Lady said, **"Same time, same place,"** in the Bedroom at 10:00 p.m.

July 9, 2008

Though the five days of prayer were over, several pilgrims, knowing Marija was still here, traveled long distances to be here tonight. Several of them were randomly selected from the Field to be present in the Bedroom for the apparition. The following is Marija's description of the apparition that took place in the Bedroom at 10:00 p.m.:

> *"When Our Lady appeared, She prayed over and blessed all of us and also everyone in the Field."*

Our Lady told Marija that the apparition would be **"the same time tomorrow, at 10:00 p.m.,"** but did not say a location. Marija would be leaving for a week of family retreat with the founder's family, so this was the last apparition until she returns to Caritas.

July 19, 2008

Tonight the apparition in the Bedroom was indescribably beautiful. The Bedroom was filled with roses, numbering 4,000, all of which represented those souls from across the Nation who wanted to be represented during Our Lady's apparitions. For two days several girls worked to arrange the flowers in vases. While several of the Community women were discussing where all the vases would go, Marija took some of the roses and formed them into a heart on the Bed, with the Community girls help-ing. What developed was too beautiful for words. What flowers couldn't fit on the bed, were left in vases and arranged around the Bed. Nearly 100 small tea-light candles were added in and amongst the flowers on the Bed. When it was finished, the whole room was breathtaking. Added to the setting of the flowers, the simple adoration music from Medjugorje was played during the beginning of the Rosary and between each decade. The candles were lit on the Bed and Bed stand, filling the Bedroom with a soft glow. Different pilgrims praying in the Field were randomly selected to come to the Bedroom for the apparition. As they entered the room, they could not help but be visibly moved. The following is Marija's description of the apparition:

"In the moment of the apparition, when Our Lady came, I recommended to Our Lady all of our intentions, and in a special way I asked Our Lady to bless all people who is pres-ent here and in the Field. And I also offered Our Lady the soul of little Sebastian (a little boy who had died early this morning) and asked help for his mother and father. I asked Our Lady to give Sebastian peace and to carry him in Her heart. She immediately begin to pray. I ask also to Our Lady to bless all candles and all the roses present from all people across the United States. And Our Lady, She stood with Her hands extended and prayed over all of us. She pray over also all these people (who gave the candles and roses). And after She give blessing. She go. And tomorrow: **'Same time, same place.'"**

The Unexpected Apparitions of February 11 - 18, 2009
(Compiled by the Community of Caritas)

February 11, 2009

All members of the Community, from the youngest to the oldest meet every Wednesday and Friday evenings for prayer group.

We gather at various places. This Wednesday night prayer group on February 11th took place amidst the busyness of preparing for the wedding on Friday. Our founder was gone half of the day but specifically had given instructions to have prayer group in the Bedroom at 5:00 p.m. He had said if he was not back, to not delay but go ahead and begin the Rosary. He had stressed, though we were very busy preparing for the wedding, we would not be Martha, but rather her sister, Mary Magdalene, who took the better part and was with Jesus; that our prayer group would not neglect our time in prayer with Our Lady. After the first decade, he finally arrived and stopped us. He told everyone that he wanted us to momentarily get our thoughts away from the wedding preparations and everything that still needed to be done, and to enter into prayer with all our thoughts on Our Lady. He asked us to close our eyes and to meditate on the gift of these new babies born into the Community as well as the wedding taking place in the next days. He said it was almost like we were experiencing Christmas all over again this week with so many special gifts and celebrations.

Before he left, earlier that day, he had prearranged to have a Christmas song played in the Bedroom during the prayer group. He relayed it was to help us realize we are gifted with the presence of Our Lady in our midst when we pray. He told us to close our eyes and meditate on all the gifts we received through Our Lady. After a while, he told us, "Open your eyes." Gasps and cries of surprise and joy were heard throughout the room. We were shocked. While eyes were closed meditatively, without notice, the visionary Marija had slipped in at the foot of the Bed. The founder, while the song was still playing, said, "Open your eyes." Marija Lunetti and her husband Paolo came into view before us. Our founder had picked them up at the airport and they stayed in the kitchen while the founder came on into the Bedroom. Their cue to come in was when they heard the music. When they came in, Marija then tiptoed in through the Community members and knelt in her normal place at the foot of the Bed when she is there for the apparitions, and several

Community members commented that it was almost like having an apparition themselves. They closed their eyes - they were not there. They opened their eyes - and Marija, Paolo and Giovanni, their six-year-old son, suddenly had appeared before them. Seeing Marija as if from nowhere, kneeling, where she has had one hundred eleven apparitions over the last 21 years, brought forth many emotions amongst the Community. To say it was a very joyful reunion cannot describe what everyone felt. Several in the Community said it was "shock and awe."

Amidst the joy and hugs, we learned that they had come to attend the wedding, but it was kept a secret from everyone in order to add to the joy of this week. As if that surprise and that joy wasn't enough, the Community learned that Our Lady had not appeared to Marija at her normal apparition time, but had waited so that the Community could be present in the apparition. The Community was stunned with joy. There are not many words that can describe such a moment when on an ordinary day, a day with no hint of anything coming, there suddenly comes the news, and within 30 minutes of Marija arriving, you are bowed before the Queen of all creation. Before Our Lady appeared, She allowed us to pray the entire Rosary novena which included two long prayers for the wedding couple, and it was when we had finished these prayers that Our Lady came. She appeared about 5:55 p.m. The following is a description given by one of the Community members of the apparition:

> *"At the moment of the apparition, Marija recommended to Our Lady the Community and Our Lady immediately smiled. After the apparition, Marija, with joy but struggling for words, said "I think Our Lady was surprised too." Our founder, wondering why Marija said that, asked, "Did Our Lady look surprised?" And Marija tried to find better words to describe and relay Our Lady's expression, because it wasn't exactly surprise, but that Our Lady was reacting to our surprise in some way. It was an emotional expression we had never heard used to describe Our Lady before. Our founder*

then asked, "Was it like She was amused?" And while Marija
happily nodded yes, she said it was like joy but different. After
discussing Our Lady's reaction, it was more like an emotion
of joy, sharing of the surprise and amusement. Marija said
Our Lady then blessed us."

Our founder knew tomorrow would be a difficult day to get
everyone together because some would be cleaning and decorat-
ing the church for the wedding, others would be preparing food
and decorations for the reception, the wedding party rehearsal
was to take place, etc. So he asked Marija to have Our Lady
choose the time for the apparition the next day. Our Lady would
know what would be best when all the Community could attend
Her apparition. Marija asked, and Our Lady astounded us all
when She said:

"I will come when you pray."

Knowing how hectic the day would be with wedding preparations, the wedding rehearsal and dinner, and everything in-between, She allowed the founder to find the time of the day that
would be best for everyone, when we would all be together, so
no one would miss the apparition.

February 17, 2009

Our founder and Marija's husband, Paolo, were out of town early
yesterday morning before apparition time. It was a sacrifice to
be gone from his home with Our Lady here still appearing. They
were scheduled to be back Tuesday morning, but it would be
impossible to make it back for the apparition. Their flight was
scheduled to arrive in Birmingham at 10:15 a.m. It is normally a
55 minute drive from the airport to Caritas but can be much longer if traffic is bad, and late morning the roads are usually filled
with cars. Our founder had told his wife, in a tongue-in-cheek
sort of way, to pray for a long apparition, because it would have
to be a "really" long apparition if he had even a slight change of

making it, especially since Our Lady said in yesterday's apparition, **"Same time. Same place."** Though we knew Our Lady could do anything, it was thought to be wishful thinking of any chance of getting back for Our Lady's apparition today.

Rosary began in the Bedroom at 10:00 a.m. with mostly Community members and some pilgrims present. As the time approached 10:40 a.m., Marija got up from kneeling just outside the doorway, entered into the Bedroom, and knelt at the foot of the Bed. The Rosary continued, with different people praying each decade. We were surprised. It had almost reached ten minutes past apparition time (10:50 a.m.) when we began to notice that Marija gave no sign that apparition time was approaching.

At this point, some in the room began to wonder if Our Lady meant to wait until our founder arrived. Two full Rosary's were prayed, and Our Lady had not appeared! A third Rosary was started while we waited for Marija to go into ecstasy. Some of us began to take notice, began to wonder, questioning ourselves. The daughter of our founder decided to try and call Paolo to see where her dad was. When she reached him, our founder was shocked to find out that Our Lady had not yet appeared. It was 10:55 a.m. He was approximately 15 minutes from home. The third Rosary, remarkably, continued up until the fourth Glorious mystery, when Marija began to pray the Hail Holy Queen. Suddenly Marija interiorly felt Our Lady was coming and that it was time for the apparition. Some of the Community were praying silently that Our Lady would wait, but as Marija began praying the 7-7-7, they knew that after one or two sets Our Lady would come as it was way past the normal time of the apparition, and after all, She had said the day before, **"Same time. Same place."** Still they hoped for many sets to be prayed. Their hearts grew hopeful again when still after 3, 4, and 5 more sets, Our Lady hadn't come. But then suddenly, Marija's voice disappeared. Our Lady was present. One to two minutes went by and then in the silence of the apparition, everyone heard the kitchen screen door open and slam shut and unbelievably, our founder came running in. He was motioned to come forward. He stopped outside of the Bedroom to kneel down, but was motioned to go into the Bedroom where an empty spot waited for him beside Marija. Our Lady was still appearing and continued to appear for the second half of the apparition. Our Lady waited for 30 minutes after Her normal apparition time, which allowed our founder to be present. He, as the rest of the Community, were all very moved. The apparition lasted 4 minutes. The following is Marija's description of the apparition:

> *"In the moment of the apparition, I recommended all of us. In a special way I recommend this couple today on their wedding anniversary and I said and all families of the Community. And Our Lady beginning to smile. And I then recommended all families of all present and Our Lady beginning to pray, and She pray long time. I recommend all people who is in Field, and I pray. Our Lady give blessing, and She go."*

When Marija asked Our Lady about tomorrow's apparition, Our Lady said, **"I will come whenever you pray."**

February 18, 2009

Today was the last apparition, as Paolo and Marija would be leaving. Rosary was scheduled for 10:00 a.m. The Community began arriving around 9:30 a.m. and began writing petitions to Our Lady. Our founder told Marija that if, today, Our Lady gives time to ask a question in the apparition, he would like her to ask Our Lady to give some sweet words to end Her visit with the Community. The following is Marija's description of the apparition:

> *"In moment of apparition, when Our Lady come, I recommend like always all us in special way, everyone present today. I ask Our Lady if She has some words to say to us. And Our Lady beginning to smile, said:*

'I give my love to you, you give it to others.'

"And after She beginning to pray over us and after She make blessing and She go."

The surprise visit ended as quickly as it had begun, but with so many joys in-between, and a beautiful message in which Our Lady gave to us Her love. Marija, Paolo and son Giovanni, after saying their good-byes to everyone left for the airport to return to Italy. The Community remained in the Bedroom to say some final prayers in thanksgiving for Our Lady's goodness to us through Her surprise visit.

Appendix

INDEXES

The words and dates in these indexes are from Part IV—the Messages and Responses of Our Lady.

An extensive Index is provided to help you in your research and study. Sometimes the messages of Our Lady can only be remembered through one word. The Word Index is designed with this need in mind. Following the Word Index is a Phrase Index. Also included in this edition is a Chronological Index of Dates for those who remember a message by its date or want to see if a message was given on a particular date. (See Chronological Index for more information.)

644 Index

PHRASE INDEX

694   <u>Index</u>

WORDS FROM HEAVEN

CHRONOLOGICAL INDEX (C)

This system of chronologically indexing Our Lady's messages was designed to facilitate the checking of dates to learn what Our Lady was saying during certain events or periods in our lives or in history. For example: If we check dates 7/25/90 - 10/25/90, we can see that Our Lady gave a prophetic message and then continued giving simple messages which had great meaning. During this time, Iraq invaded Kuwait and few realized the global consequences. Looking back on Our Lady's messages, we find them to be simple yet profound. Our Lady did something that has not been done since the beginning of the apparitions. Week after week, Our Lady told Ivan to pray for peace during this time.* This showed that Our Lady knew the danger to the world; however, during this same period, most of us did not understand the extent and depth of the situation as it actually was. You will also find that Our Lady sometimes gave more than one message on the same day. Check the Chronological Index - 12/24/88, Ivan received a message in Medjugorje while Marija received a messages in Alabama, in America. During Marija's apparition, Our Lady gave a Special Blessing.

Studying Our Lady's messages can tell us many things. We pray this Chronological Index will help all of us in our desire to understand Our Lady's messages.

* It is reasonable to assume that these messages are mainly about the Middle East crisis; however, one must understand that these are living messages. They have been purposely given by Our Lady with simplicity so that ten years from now this message of peace would speak to us not about the Middle East crisis but about some personal crisis in our lives, our country, the world, etc...

FROM THE AUTHOR

It is felt that the making of this book was the work of the Holy Spirit working through many people. Many messages would not have been preserved had it not been for certain individuals, such as Father Vlasic. We thank those individuals for their many contributions and, in particular, Father Faricy, for his spiritual direction and help regarding Medjugorje.

–ORDER FORM–

Shipping & Handling		
Order Sub-total	U.S. Mail *(Standard)*	UPS *(Faster)*
$0-$10.00	$5.00	$9.00
$10.01-$20.00	$7.50	$11.50
$20.01-$50.00	$10.00	$14.00
$50.01-$100.00	$15.00	$19.00
Over $100.00	15% of total	18% of total

For overnight delivery, call for pricing.
***International (Surface):
Double above shipping Cost.
Call for faster International delivery.

Words From Heaven®11th Ed.
Priced for bulk distribution

(Check One)	Suggested Donation	
☐ 1	$12.00	
☐ 5	$11.00 EA	($55.00)
☐ 10	$10.00 EA	($100.00)

TOTAL+S&H: $_____

or call in your order and donation 24 hours a day! 205-672-2000 USA ext. 315

The Federal Tax Exempt I.D. # for Caritas of Birmingham is 63-0945243.

☎ Ph: **205-672-2000 ext. 315 USA 24 hrs.**

📠 Fax: **205-672-9667 USA 24 hrs.**

✉ Mail: **Caritas of Birmingham
100 Our Lady Queen of Peace Drive
Sterrett, AL 35147-9987 USA**

☐Payment Enclosed

☐Bill My Credit Card ☐ *VISA* ☐ MasterCard ☐ Discover

Credit Card Number

☐☐☐☐ ☐☐☐☐ ☐☐☐☐ ☐☐☐☐

Expiration date: ☐☐-☐☐ e-mail Address: _____

Telephone: ( ) -

Signature:_____

Ship to (Please Print):
Name:_____

I.D. #_____ Tel. ( ) -_____

Address:_____

_____

City:_____ State:_____

Zip:_____ Country:_____

Don't Miss a Visit to the Caritas Mission House

Apparition Hill, Cross Mountain, the Visionaries, St. James Church, and Caritas Mission House, these are the five "**must do's**" to have a complete Medjugorje pilgrimage. Throughout the years, pilgrims from every nation have made the Caritas of Birmingham Mission House in Medjugorje a part of their pilgrimage. Countless numbers have relayed to us it is there, in the Mission House, where they came to understand more fully Our Lady's messages and plans for the world. It is why people, who have returned home from their pilgrimages, have told others going to Medjugorje to go to the Caritas Mission House, stating that the Caritas Mission House was a high point of their pilgrimage and a "**must do**" to make a pilgrimage to Medjugorje a complete and more profound experience.

"After coming in the Caritas Mission House, I decided not to leave my husband and seek to bring prayer and healing into my family."
    Pilgrim
    Ireland

Medjugorje©

Cross Mountain (Križevac)

Apparition Hill (Podbrdo)

Apparition Trail

Caritas Mission House

Park

St. James Church

School

"I found peace and love in the Mission House."
    Pilgrim
    South Africa

"The Mission House was the only meeting place in Medjugorje to learn more about and discuss the Messages."
    Pilgrim
    England

"Following Caritas' mission for several years and observing their work in spreading Our Lady of Medjugorje's messages, it's no wonder to me as to how they became the largest Medjugorje Center in the world."
    Pilgrim
    Scotland

Community of Caritas

Look for the St. Michael statue.
Caritas of Birmingham Mission House is operated by the Community of Caritas.
The Mother house is located at: 100 Our Lady Queen of Peace Drive • Sterrett, Alabama 35147 USA

www.mej.com   *Extensive up-to-date information on Medjugorje as it happens.*